Teaching Grade R

SECOND EDITION

Editors: Lorayne Excell
&
Vivien Linington

Teaching Grade R

First published 2015
Second edition 2023

Juta and Company (Pty) Ltd
PO Box 14373, Lansdowne, 7779, Cape Town, South Africa

© 2023 Juta and Company (Pty) Ltd

ISBN 978 1 48513 143 4
WebPDF 978 1 48513 144 1

All rights reserved. No part of this publication may be reproduced or transmitted in any form or by any means, electronic or mechanical, including photocopying, recording, or any information storage or retrieval system, without prior permission in writing from the publisher. Subject to any applicable licensing terms and conditions in the case of electronically supplied publications, a person may engage in fair dealing with a copy of this publication for his or her personal or private use, or his or her research or private study. See Section 12(1)(a) of the Copyright Act 98 of 1978.

Production specialist: Mmakasa Ramoshaba
Editor: Wendy Priilaid
Proofreader: Language Mechanics
Illustrator: Leon Brits
Cover designer: Genevieve Simpson
Typesetter: Thea Brits
Indexer: Kobie Ferreira

Acknowledgement:
Figure on page 360 – Edumedia
With thanks to Elizabeth Walton for her text on inclusion in the current South African educational context on page 105.

Typeset in Bembo Std 11.5pt on 13.5pt

Printed in South Africa by

The author and the publisher believe on the strength of due diligence exercised that this work does not contain any material that is the subject of copyright held by another person. In the alternative, they believe that any protected pre-existing material that may be comprised in it has been used with appropriate authority or has been used in circumstances that make such use permissible under the law.

Contents

About the authors xiii
Preface xv

CHAPTER 1: What is Grade R? 1
Introduction: Grade R unpacked 1
The purpose and importance of the Grade R year 2
The challenges of successfully implementing the Grade R year 7
    Location of the Grade R classroom 7
    The age of the Grade R child 9
    Class size 9
    Language 9
    Grade R teachers' qualifications 10
    Effective implementation of the Grade R year 10
Case study 11
Summary 13
Bibliography 14
Glossary 16

CHAPTER 2: Perspectives on early childhood education 18
Introduction: Grade R – A theoretical entry into a world of diversity and complexity 18
Developmental and learning theories 21
    What are growth, development and learning? 22
    Holistic development 22
    A concept of whole-child development 22
Specific theories 23
    Maslow's hierarchy of needs 23
    Bronfenbrenner's bioecological systems perspective 24
    Maturational theory: Gesell 27
    Theory of behaviourism and learning 29
Cognitive development 30
    Piaget: cognitive development 30
    Vygotsky: a social constructivist theory 32
Affective development 34
    Erikson's theory of psychosocial development 34
    Gardner's theory of multiple intelligences (MI) 35
Case study 36

Early childhood and neuroscience	37
Implications for teaching and learning	38
A critique of developmental theories	39
The sociology of childhood: the sociological child	39
Sociocultural context	40
The child as an active participant	41
African perspective	42
Early education: an African perspective	43
Summary	44
Bibliography	44
Glossary	47
CHAPTER 3: Guiding principles of the Grade R curriculum, teaching and learning	48
Introduction: the Grade R curriculum and the principles that guide it	48
Principle 1: Emphasise holistic development	49
What does this principle entail?	49
How is this principle manifested in the classroom?	51
Principle 2: A thematic and integrated curriculum	53
What does this principle entail?	53
How is this principle manifested in the classroom?	53
Principle 3: Language as a tool for learning and thinking in a structured and stimulating learning environment	54
What does this principle entail?	54
How is this principle manifested in the classroom?	55
Principle 4: Learning through play	56
What does this principle entail?	56
How is this principle manifested in the classroom?	56
Principle 5: Child-centred approach	57
What does this principle entail?	57
How is this principle manifested in the classroom?	58
Principle 6: Diversity, equity and culturally responsive pedagogy	58
What does this principle entail?	58
How is this principle manifested in the classroom?	58
Case study	60
Summary	61
Bibliography	61
Glossary	62

CHAPTER 4: Knowing the Grade R child ... 63
Introduction: Who is the Grade R child? ... 63
A developmental and sociological perspective ... 63
Welcoming the child into Grade R ... 64
Advice to parents to help their child adjust to Grade R ... 65
First day in Grade R: suggestions for the teacher ... 66
Ideas for the teacher to keep in mind ... 66
Guidelines for teachers' practice ... 67
Milestones for the Grade R child ... 68
Physical development ... 68
Social and emotional development ... 69
Cognitive development ... 69
Perceptual-motor development and the Grade R child ... 72
Perceptual-motor behaviours ... 73
Spatial awareness and orientation behaviours ... 75
Balance ... 75
Body image and postural control ... 75
Spatial orientation/position in space ... 76
Lateral midline/vertical midline ... 77
Laterality ... 77
Dominance ... 78
Temporal awareness behaviours (an understanding of time) ... 78
Fine motor development ... 79
Eye–hand coordination ... 79
Eye movement ... 80
Eye–foot coordination ... 80
Eye–hand–foot coordination ... 81
Sensory perceptual-motor development ... 81
Visual perception ... 81
Auditory perception ... 85
Tactile and kinaesthetic perception ... 87
Olfactory perception ... 88
Gustatory perception ... 88
Transition into Grade 1 ... 89
The late developer ... 89
The gifted child ... 89
Questions for reflection and discussion ... 90
Summary ... 90

Bibliography 90
Glossary 91

CHAPTER 5: Who is the Grade R teacher? 94
Introduction: Who is the Grade R teacher? 94
    The personal lens 95
Personal beliefs and values 97
The professional lens 98
    The roles of the Grade R teacher 98
    Teachers as deliverers 100
    Teachers as adaptors 100
    Teachers as creators 101
Qualification pathways for the Grade R teacher 102
Ethical considerations in a South African context 103
Further teaching requirements in South Africa 104
Summary 104
A final consideration 105
    Inclusive education 105
Bibliography 106
Glossary 106

CHAPTER 6: A transdisciplinary approach: an enhancement of positive community engagement 107
Introduction 107
The child in community 108
What is a community? 108
Establishing community partnerships 109
    A rights-based and inclusive school 111
    An effective school 111
    A safe, protective and supportive school 112
    A health-promoting and health-seeking school 113
    An equity- and equality-promoting and gender-sensitive school 114
    A community partnership-building school 114
Case study 114
Establishing partnerships 115
    How to establish partnerships 115
The teacher–parent/caregiver partnership 117
Sustaining partnerships 119

Summary 119
Bibliography 120
Glossary 120

CHAPTER 7: An optimal learning environment 122
Introduction: the Grade R learning environment 122
The purpose of the curriculum 122
The temporal environment: getting it right, planning for the day 124
    The daily programme 125
    Daily programme/timetable – Grade R 126
The physical learning environment: the place 127
Case study 129
The indoor learning environment 130
    Planning the indoor learning environment 130
    Setting out the different indoor play areas 132
The outdoor learning environment 140
    Outdoor equipment 140
    Value of sand and water play 146
Role of the teacher 147
    Taking responsibility: making the checklist work 148
Summary 153
Bibliography 153
Glossary 154

CHAPTER 8: Teaching and learning 155
Introduction 155
How does a young child learn? 155
    A young child learns through participation 156
Case study 1 157
    Understanding the degrees of participation and their influence on learning 158
    Children do not learn in the same way 159
How do we teach for optimal learning in Grade R? 160
    Teaching for participatory learning 160
    Teaching with teacher-initiated support 164
Case study 2 164
    Teaching techniques for child-initiated support 165
    Teaching according to the developmental level and needs of the child 168

A time to reflect 169
The teacher's view of the child 170
What do we teach in Grade R? 171
    Curriculum realisation 174
    General aims of a curriculum in a South African context 175
    The role of the Grade R teacher in curriculum implementation 176
    Planning for learning 178
    The sequence of planning teaching–learning and assessment
    activities in Grade R 179
    Phases in the lesson/activity presentation (ring planning) 183
    Child support 183
    Learning and teaching support material (LTSM) 183
Summary 187
Bibliography 187
Glossary 189
Appendix 1: Themes/topics from CAPS: Life Skills 192
Appendix 2: Time allocation per subject for the Foundation Phase ... 192
Appendix 3: Yearly planning Grade R 192
Appendix 4: Weekly planning Grade R 194
Appendix 5: Lesson plans for Grade R 194
Appendix 6: Some resources for stories 196

CHAPTER 9: Assessment 198
Introduction 198
Assessment as part of teaching and learning 199
The aim of assessment 201
Case study 1 202
Types of assessment 203
    Formative assessment 203
    Summative assessment 204
Appropriate assessment practice in Grade R 204
Planning assessment 205
Assessment strategies 206
    Some useful assessment strategies 207
    Observation 208
Assessment context 210
Case study 2 210
Assessment process 211

Role players in assessment 212
Recording and reporting 212
Culture and language fairness in assessment 213
Assessment and curriculum 214
    Self-assessment by the teacher 215
Summary 217
Bibliography 218
Glossary 219
Appendix 1: CAPS Assessment 220
Appendix 2: Grade R Mathematics – assessment sheets 221
Appendix 3: Comprehensive checklist/holistic rubric 223

CHAPTER 10: Learning and teaching through play 227
Introduction 227
    What does the word 'play' mean? 228
Play from a theoretical perspective 228
The value of play 230
Play classified according to age-related stages 232
Case study 1 234
Different types of play from a practical perspective 234
    Functional play 234
    Constructive play 234
    Manipulative play 235
    Fantasy play (socio-dramatic play) 235
    Games with rules 235
The role of the teacher 235
    Interest and understanding 236
    Setting the stage for play: structuring the environment and
    encouraging play 237
A critique of play: Is play always beneficial? 238
Case study 2 239
A further interpretation of play: playful pedagogies 239
Summary 246
Bibliography 246
Glossary 248

CHAPTER 11: Pathway to literacy 249
What is literacy? 249
    Language- and literacy-related activities and strategies that can
    be integrated in the Grade R daily programme 249
    Different ways of reading a book 250
    Dramatising stories 253
    Making the story real 254
    Listening activities to promote language 255
    Writing development: emergent writing 256
    Strengthening hand and finger muscles 256
    Linking fine motor development with emergent writing activities 258
    Creating an environment that encourages print awareness and
    language development 258
    The reading corner/area 259
Summary 259
Bibliography 260
Glossary 261

**CHAPTER 12: Language diversity: teaching a second language
in Grade R** 262
Introduction 262
Setting the South African context 264
What do we mean by linguistic and cultural diversity? 265
    Implications and interventions for effective early childhood
    education 265
The impact of theories on the development of an FAL 267
Distinguishing between language skills and language components 268
    Phonology and language development 268
    Morphology and language development 269
    Semantics 270
    Syntax 270
Teaching–learning activities 271
    Themes 272
    Songs and rhymes 273
    Examples of South African-authored storybooks 274
    Making the book 'talk' 275
Parent involvement 276
Case study 1 277
Case study 2 278

Case study 3 278
Case study 4 279
Summary 279
Bibliography 280
Glossary 281
Appendix 1: Suggestions for a daily programme that specifically acknowledges diversity 282
    Arrival 282
    First teacher-guided activity 283
    Free play and art activities 283
    Second teacher-guided activity 283
    Routines 283
    Outside play 284
    Story time 284
Appendix 2: Rhymes and songs 284

CHAPTER 13: Early concept development in mathematics/ numeracy 287
Introduction: Why Mathematics in Grade R? 287
How children learn Mathematics 288
What do we teach in Grade R? 291
    Exploring the foundational concepts and skills 293
    Vertical and horizontal matching 295
Basic mathematical concepts and mathematical content areas 300
    Content area: Numbers, operations and relationships 300
    Content area: Patterns and functions 302
    Content area: Space and shape (geometry) 303
    Content area: Measurement 308
    Content area: Data handling and analysis of data 312
What is the Grade R teacher's role? 313
    Maximising the physical environment to stimulate effective learning of mathematics 314
Case study 1 317
Case study 2 320
    To summarise 322
Providing appropriate resources for effective teaching and learning of mathematics 322
    Some additional concrete resources 323
Summary 327

Bibliography 327
Glossary 327

CHAPTER 14: Life Skills 330
Life Skills in a South African context 330
    What is the subject of Life Skills? 330
    Why is Life Skills an important subject? 330
    The role of the teacher in the mediation of life skills 332
Beginning knowledge 333
    Social sciences concepts 333
    Strategies for developing environmental awareness 335
    Natural sciences 336
    Suitable activities for Grade R 344
    Technology 347
Personal and social well-being 350
    Health and wellness: promotion of health 351
The creative arts 353
    The main aims of creative arts education 353
    The visual arts 355
    Music 365
    Drama 371
    Dance 372
Physical education 372
Enhancing creativity within the Creative Arts and Physical Education domain 374
    How to recognise creativity 375
    Enabling a quality Grade R environment to promote creative behaviour 375
Development and assessment of creative arts in Grade R 379
    Science, technology, engineering, art and mathematics (STEAM) 380
Summary 381
Bibliography 382
Glossary 384

Index 385

About the authors

Lorayne Excell, now retired, has an appointment as a Visiting Researcher at the Wits School of Education. Her specialisation and research interests are still in early childhood education with a specific focus on the Grade R year. Lorayne has worked extensively with Vivien Linington over the last 20 years training Grade R practitioners, researching the early childhood education field and actively promoting a pedagogy of play as a way to enhance quality Grade R teaching and learning.

Vivien Linington is still involved with the Wits School of Education and actively involved her two fields of interest, early childhood education and educational theory. Together with Lorayne Excell, she has researched and published in areas such as social justice, professional teacher development, and the importance of quality early childhood education as well as the central role of play.

Hasina Banu Ebrahim is Full Professor at UNISA and the UNESCO Co-chair in Early Education, Care and Development. Her Teaching responsibilities have included Early Childhood Development, Grade R Teaching and Curriculum in the Early Years. She is the co-editor of *Curriculum, Pedagogy and Assessment: A Handbook for Early Childhood Education*. She researches policy, practice and teacher education in the early years.

Dr Susan Greyling is the Academic Manager for the Faculty of Education at the Unit for Open Distance Learning (UODL) at North-West University (NWU). She was an Early Childhood Education lecturer in the Faculty of Education at NWU (Potchefstroom Campus). She was the Programme Leader for the Diploma in Grade R Teaching and coordinated the design and delivery of modules in the teacher education programmes for distance learning. She coordinated the community-service project at UODL, and her research interests include early childhood education as well as educational management.

Corné Kruger is a lecturer in the Faculty of Education Sciences of the North-West University (Potchefstroom Campus). She is mainly responsible for the design and delivery of the Mathematics modules in the teacher education programmes for distance learning. Her research interests include the development of a reflective practice by Mathematics teachers and the mediation of meaningful learning of Mathematics in the Foundation Phase (Grades R–3).

Dr Annemarie Loubser was a senior lecturer specialising in early childhood teacher education at the North-West University (Potchefstroom Campus). She was Programme Leader for the BEd Foundation Phase degree and was responsible for the design and presentation of modules in the Grade R programmes for distance learning. Her field of research is early childhood education and she focuses on the perceptual motor development of the Foundation Phase learner.

Nkidi Phatudi is a Professor and Acting School Director: Teacher Education at the College of Education, University of South Africa. She taught literacy in the early years for first and second language pedagogy in the postgraduate and undergraduate programme. She led the mother tongue learning group research team funded by EU–DHET. She has supervised doctoral and master's students in language teaching and learning. She edited a book on EFAL, published articles and contributed book chapters on a range of topics in ECD, including language teaching and learning in the early years. Her research focus includes the transition of children from home and preschool into Grade 1, transitions from mother tongue instruction to English as medium of instruction (Grade 3 to Grade 4), and second language teaching. She introduced the Teaching Reading module in seven African languages in a BEd programme at Unisa.

Dr Linda Rutgers, now retired, is a former lecturer in Teacher Education in the Department of Curriculum Studies in the Faculty of Education at the University of Stellenbosch. Her portfolio includes facilitating and teaching the modules on early literacy education, theory and practice in early childhood education, literacy education and leadership to both undergraduate and postgraduate students who are prospective Early Childhood Development (Grades R–3) teachers. Her areas of research are emergent and early literacy, teacher leadership development, literacy leadership development and coaching as a personal and professional development strategy. Currently serving as an independent early learning consultant and coach.

Dr Mantsose Jane Sethusha (DEd, University of South Africa) is a senior lecturer in the College of Education in the Department of Early Childhood Education at the University of South Africa. Her research areas are in the fields of early childhood education, teacher education and classroom assessment. She teaches BEd and PGCE programme modules such as Early Childhood and Foundation Phase Teaching and Assessment, and is also responsible for teaching practice supervision for students.

Dr Naseema Shaik is a Senior lecturer and Coordinator of the Diploma in Grade R in the Faculty of Education at the Cape Peninsula University of Technology. She teaches in the Foundation Phase with a particular specialisation in Grade R. She holds a PhD and her research interests include child participation, participatory pedagogies in the early years and professional teacher development. She is passionate about developing quality teaching and research in the field of early childhood education.

Dr Elsabé Wessels taught a multilingual class for learners aged 5–6 from 1983 until 2011. From 2001 she also specialised in teaching reading and learner support. Since January 2012, she is involved at the North-West University (Mafikeng Campus) where she lectures in pre-primary studies and English (Home Language) for the Foundation Phase. Her areas of research include teaching-learning in Grade R, reading and the professional development of teachers.

Preface

While traditional child development theories on early childhood education are important for early childhood education, they may not be sufficient for the young child in today's world. This book explores 'playful pedagogy', a participatory and child-centred approach to teaching and learning.

This is a central theme throughout this book as we look at playful ways of learning language, mathematics and all the elements that comprise life skills. These elements include basic scientific concepts, the creative arts (visual art, music, dance and drama) as well as movement. Playful and practical ways to promote the acquisition of dispositions or characteristics, for example perseverance, which are central to success in formal learning are considered throughout the book.

An approach to teaching and learning that foregrounds a playful pedagogy places the teacher in a particular position. It calls for knowledge and insight, and a constant awareness of contextual appropriateness and cultural sensitivity. However, the teacher is not seen as the holder of all knowledge, but rather as a co-constructor with the child of a world that is constantly changing.

The view of the child foregrounded in this book is one that acknowledges the child in his/her own right. Children are not simply little people becoming adults. They are already competent and capable beings whose voices should be heard in decisions that affect their lives.

In this book, children are regarded as the centre of a partnership involving themselves, their parents/caregivers, the school and the community. The necessity of networking between the school and the other stakeholders is emphasised.

This book is based in South Africa on South Africa. It considers our context and the different challenges that emerge from this. It explores the current Grade R realities, and the tensions and possibilities that this year offers. It does not view Grade R as a watered-down Grade 1, but considers instead the unique features of this last year before formal schooling. It aligns with current educational policy in South Africa, but suggests practical and playful ways to meet the educational needs of young children within this policy framework.

This book aims to light the flame of inquiry for both teachers and the children they are teaching and, in addition, provide practical ways and insights through which this flame can be fanned.

Lorayne Excell
Vivien Linington
2021

Chapter 1

What is Grade R?

**Lorayne Excell, Vivien Linington,
Jane Sethusha**

In this chapter we consider

- what the Grade R year is
- the purpose of Grade R within the South African context
- the contested nature of this year
- the challenges of this year within the South African context
- the different contexts for Grade R provisioning.

INTRODUCTION: GRADE R UNPACKED

Grade R stands for the reception year. It is the year before the child starts formal schooling in Grade 1, hence Grade R is the final year of the preschool phase. Grade R is therefore not a formal learning year as it is accepted that in this year learning takes place predominantly through play.

The idea of quality early childhood education is not new. The importance of education in the early years was mentioned by the ancient Greeks and also throughout the centuries by various educationists such as Pestalozzi, Froebel, Rousseau, Locke, Montessori and Isaacs. They all recognised the importance of preschool education, and promoted some form of early childhood education. Today, there is plenty of evidence to show that quality preschool education including the Grade R year will make a difference to a child's overall development and learning capabilities.

In South Africa, preschool education started in the 1930s. However, the rollout was irregular, and preschool services were not readily available for the majority of children. In fact, most of South Africa's children had no access to any type of preschool services and only a few had access to quality preschool education. One of the exciting visions of the new democratic government when it came into power in 1994 was for all South Africa's children to have access to some form of preschool education, and so one preschool year, Grade R, was introduced.

Initially the hope was for Grade R to become a compulsory preschool year for all children in South Africa by 2010. However, this was not to be. It was envisaged that by 2014 all public schools would offer at least one Grade R class, which by 2019 would become a compulsory preschool year. In other words, it was the intention that all children would have access to at least one year of preschool before starting formal schooling. In the current National Development Plan Vision 2030, mention is also made of a possible pre-Grade R year, which would imply two years of state-legislated preschool education prior to Grade 1. At the start of 2021 neither compulsory Grade R nor the introduction of a pre-Grade R year became a reality. The implementation of a pre-Grade R year is still, however, under discussion.

With the introduction of a diploma in Grade R Teaching (SAQA, 2012) un- and under-qualified Grade R teachers are now being supported in professional development. The diploma is geared towards developing teachers who can demonstrate general educational principles as well as focused knowledge and skills for Grade R teaching. The qualification requires a depth of specialisation of knowledge, together with practical skills and experience in a Grade R classroom teaching context.

THE PURPOSE AND IMPORTANCE OF THE GRADE R YEAR

Within the South African context, Grade R was initially introduced as a bridging year. Because of past inequities, many of South Africa's children had had little, if any, preschool education, and many children were failing Grade 1. Although the failure rate could not, of course, be solely attributed to the lack of preschooling, it is acknowledged that this was a contributory factor. Seemingly simple things like turn taking, active listening and fine motor skills such as cutting along a line might not have been sufficiently developed in the home environment. It was hoped that one year of preschool education would help children to cope more successfully in Grade 1. Development and learning begin before birth – in fact at the time of conception – and are processes that unfold over many years. Though Grade R is undoubtedly important, it cannot be seen as the solution to all schooling difficulties. However, if Grade R is to make even a small difference in the lives and learning capabilities of children, we have to offer them a quality year of schooling.

Grade R children in South Africa learn in the context of the Curriculum and Assessment Policy Statement (CAPS) (DBE, 2011). This policy prescribes what all learners should know and be able to do, as well as a minimum level, depth and breadth of what should be learned in each of the three prescribed subjects: Home Language, Mathematics and Life Skills. Broadly speaking, CAPS defines skills and abilities that children should achieve. The curriculum outlines suggested topics, but teachers are encouraged to adapt them to suit their different contexts. The forms of adaptation chosen will be informed by each teacher's understanding of the purpose of the Grade R year.

There are, of course, different ideas about the purpose of the Grade R year. What do you think?

Try this out
Why do you think Grade R is important for a child? Write down your reasons in, or around, the **Y** shape, and then read the next paragraph.

Find out more
Different people have different ideas about the purpose and importance of Grade R. A common and narrow interpretation is that Grade R is merely a preparation for Grade 1, and the focus is purely on early literacy and numeracy. In the broadest sense, Grade R is the year in which various aspects of development and learning are refined (see chapters 2 and 4). Children as people and learners in their own right are ready for the next phase in the cycle of life. The Grade R year not only prepares children for Grade 1, but it also reinforces the idea of holistic, culturally responsive development, and the importance of children becoming lifelong learners. This includes the acquisition and enhancement of important life skills.

The years before formal schooling (that is, before children start Grade 1) are among the most important in children's lives. Experiences during this time affect all areas of development. The skills, attitudes, values and concepts that will enable children to become successful learners are developed during the early or formative years. Furthermore, the Constitution of the Republic of South Africa (RSA, 1996a) and various education policy documents such as the South African Schools Act (RSA, 1996b) and *White Paper 5 on Early Childhood Education* (DoE, 2001a) support the idea of democratic citizenship and lifelong learning. The successful attainment of these ideals is largely dependent upon a rich and stimulating early childhood.

Learning experiences in the early years are also responsible for shaping how children see themselves as learners and for the attitudes (dispositions) that children develop towards later learning, for example, responsibility. We also know if children have positive attitudes towards themselves and towards learning, they are much more likely to succeed in formal schooling and to become lifelong learners.

Try this out
What kind of attitudes towards learning (learning dispositions) do you think children should develop towards school and learning? Jot down four or five that you think will enable children to succeed at school.

Find out more

Carr (in Bruce, 2004) has identified **five learning dispositions** (attitudes towards learning) that should be developed in preschool children.

These are courage, trust, perseverance, responsibility and self-confidence.

Something to consider

WHAT do you think each of these dispositions or attitudes refer to, and WHY do you think each one is important?

1. **Courage** is a form of bravery that involves acting on our beliefs and values. It promotes self-esteem and independence, and often involves taking a risk. For example, not being sure about the answer to a question but willing to give it a try requires courage.
2. **Trust** is having faith in others and ourselves, and the decisions we make. Being open to new experiences stems from trusting the people around us and the environment in which we learn. For example, one way that children learn is through exploration. Children need to trust that the adults will look after them and that the equipment offered is safe to explore if they are to have meaningful learning opportunities.
3. **Perseverance** is to keep on trying, often in the face of difficulty, such as with a puzzle. If a child makes a mistake, he/she should be prepared to try again. Error should be viewed as part of the learning process.
4. **Responsibility** means being accountable for our actions. Responsibility is closely linked to respect for ourselves, for others, for our belongings and ultimately for our own learning.
5. **Self-confidence** refers to having a belief in ourselves, our actions and decisions, and the fact that we are someone of value. A child who lacks self-confidence might be unwilling to engage with new challenges that are presented in school.

Can you think of other learning dispositions that you would like to develop in your Grade R children?

Something to consider

Living in the 21st century requires an openness to change and new ways of thinking. This is relevant for both teachers and children as well as the world in general. Figure 1.1 has drawn on research on what is called the 6Cs. Researchers Fullan and Scott (2014), and Golnikoff and Hirsch-Pasek (2016) agree on the following four competences, namely communication, critical thinking, creativity and collaboration.

»

The other two competences are viewed slightly differently by different researchers, who tend to add two of their own and include confidence, content, connectivity, citizenship and character. Golnikoff and Hirsch-Pasek (2016) have chosen confidence and content from this second group. We agree with this choice as we think they have particular relevance for the young child and the Grade R teacher.

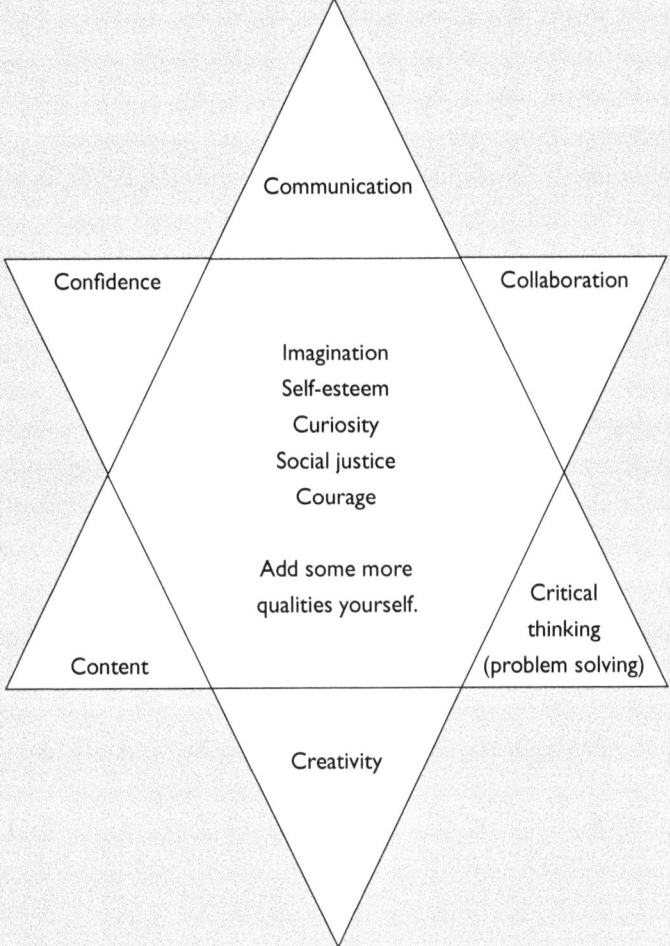

Figure 1.1 A holistic view of knowledge, skills, attitudes and values for the 21st century
Source: Adapted from Golnikoff & Hirsch-Pasek (2016); Fullan & Scott (2014)

What follows is some elaboration on the meaning of these competences. You may wish to add further meaning for yourself as it relates to your specific context. Each of the six competences is interrelated and they build on one another. Hopefully, the refinement of these competences will continue throughout a person's life. We will now unpack the meaning of each competence.

1. **Collaboration:** the ability to work with other children and negotiate difficulty.
2. **Communication:** using verbal and body language to convey a message effectively. To communicate effectively a child needs to use active listening, and develop good vocabulary and emergent literacy skills (see Chapter 11)
3. **Critical thinking:** involves problem solving and offering a thoughtful opinion backed by reason.
4. **Creativity:** the ability to use one's imagination in one's own innovative and probably different way.
5. **Confidence:** realistic belief in oneself and one's abilities to try things out.
6. **Content:** displaying an interest in acquiring new information in subject areas and, where appropriate, inquiring further.

In the centre of Figure 1.1 are some ideas of the qualities teachers should nurture and areas that they can explore with Grade R children. These qualities and areas of inquiry form a basis for the foundation of the 6Cs.

Try this out

Do you agree with the 6Cs we have chosen, or would you choose different ones? Give reasons for your answer. Could you add further qualities and areas to the ones mentioned in the centre of Figure 1.1?

Promotion of the 6Cs in the early years is pivotal to creating successful and democratic citizens for the 21st century. Building successful competences naturally involves the promotion of positive attitudes. One of the main purposes of Grade R is to foster these two areas of development and learning.

Find out more

Promoting positive attitudes towards learning is seen as an important purpose of the Grade R year. If we support this purpose, we will realise that the aim of Grade R is deeper than the common acceptance that Grade R is merely preparing children for Grade 1 where the focus is predominantly on literacy and numeracy. Encouraging good attitudes toward learning implies that children will be given the tools to engage in successful lifelong learning. This does not exclude the importance of developing emergent literacy and numeracy skills in young children, nor does it imply that aspects of holistic development are not important. Rather, what is being implied is that in order to succeed in formal schooling situations, children should have a range of different learning experiences. If they do, they acquire certain competences which promote preparedness for formal schooling.

Research (Queensland State Authority, 2006: 3) has shown that the following six factors are important indicators of preparedness for formal schooling:
1. Social and emotional competence with a focus on social learning and independence

2. Health and physical well-being, particularly in being able to make healthy choices and gross (large) muscle and fine (small) muscle development
3. Language development and communication, particularly oral language (talking) as part of early literacy
4. Early mathematical understanding with an emphasis on early numeracy
5. Thinking and problem-solving skills, investigating, reasoning, imagining and responding
6. Positive learning dispositions (characteristics that enable the child to learn).

These factors include a wide range of developmental aspects as well as taking contextual factors into consideration. A good or quality Grade R year involves much more than just being prepared for Grade 1. As Heckman (2000) notes, the social, educational and economic benefits of quality preschool education, including Grade R, are all apparent in later years. This is especially so for children who come from more disadvantaged contexts (Richter et al, 2012).

THE CHALLENGES OF SUCCESSFULLY IMPLEMENTING THE GRADE R YEAR

Teaching in a Grade R context is a complex, interactive process between the teacher, the learning environment and the children. Grade R teaching requires teachers who are passionate about teaching young children. A skilful teacher will have a wide range of appropriate knowledge and teaching strategies and tools to maximise (make the most of) children's learning (see Chapter 5). Development does not, of course, exist in isolation and therefore the teacher must consider all aspects of the child's context or background (see Chapter 4). The parents, caregivers and community play an important role in early education (see Chapter 6). Many other factors such as the historical, political, economic, social, cultural and religious contexts as well as individual learning styles and interests may also present challenges to learn and teach successfully. In the following sections, some of the additional challenges within the South African context are described.

Location of the Grade R classroom

This is an important challenge. There are various kinds of early childhood development (ECD) contexts in South Africa. An ECD centre or site can be anything from a shack in an informal settlement in which an adult looks after the children of neighbours who go to work, to a well-equipped day-care centre in a township or the suburbs. There are rural, urban and informal settlements, all of which may provide Grade R classes. In each of these contexts there are varying levels of organisation, availability of resources, policy interpretation, health and safety precautions, and quality of care and teaching. However, the majority of Grade R classrooms are now part of a primary school.

Grade R attached to public primary schools

According to policy documents, 85% of Grade R classrooms are located in public primary schools, with the other 15% in the community, in ECD sites or in independent schools. Many primary schools still lack the necessary infrastructure to accommodate a quality Grade R year, which inevitably results in a number of challenges relating to overcrowding and a lack of physical, financial and human resources.

In some instances, existing classrooms are not necessarily ideal for Grade R children. For example, these classrooms may be situated far from toilets or in the middle of the Foundation Phase block where child-initiated or free play becomes difficult because of high noise levels affecting other grades. Furthermore, the existing infrastructure is often unsuitable for the type of experiential learning through meaningful play where more space is required. In some schools, there is no separate outside play area specifically for children.

In addition, many principals and Foundation Phase heads of department (HoDs) know little about the unique nature of this year, thus it becomes easy to blur the Grade R and Grade 1 years together and view them as one unit with a more formal approach. This is not the case, however. Grade R is a very specialised year, and not a mini Grade 1. The Grade R child's developmental and learning needs differ, and these differences can be attributed to the stage of development and age of the Grade R child, which should be reflected in the physical environment.

Community-based sites

Some school communities in South Africa build their own structures in a quest to accommodate Grade R children. The vast majority of these are privately or community run, and there is a significant variation in terms of access and quality levels. Although registration is a statutory requirement, many sites are not yet registered. Greater attention is now being given to registration issues, and plans are in place to provide greater support for this process. Some of the classrooms are open-plan structures that accommodate 50 or more children. In this kind of setting, it is often a challenge to have good lighting and to make room for the different learning areas in the classroom as stipulated in the curriculum (DoE, 2011) (see Chapter 7). As a result, the quality of teaching and learning is often compromised, and teachers may spend much of their time babysitting children and protecting them from potential dangers.

It is extremely important that community-based services meet the needs of young children and include attention to water and environmental sanitation, health, nutrition, physical development and curriculum. This approach promotes and protects the rights of the young to survival, growth and development, and is in line with the idea of a child-friendly school (see Chapter 6).

Rural challenges

Villages and rural communities are often difficult to reach, the physical conditions in schools are frequently inadequate, and children's achievements in comparison to other schools are often weak. Although there have been significant infrastructural improvements since 1994, according to the National Education Infrastructure Management System: National Assessment Report (Department of Education, 2007 & Department of Basic Education 2011b), some rural schools still lack clean running water, electricity, proper toilet facilities, fencing and security, libraries, appropriate sports facilities as well as computers. These are not easy conditions in which to provide a sound education for young people.

The age of the Grade R child

Age becomes a further complicating factor. According to the South African Schools Act (1996), children must start Grade 1 the year they turn seven. However, changes to the school admission policy have resulted in children being able to start Grade 1 in the year they turn six if this happens before 30 June. Consequently, children entering Grade R can be anywhere between four and six years of age, therefore from a developmental and teaching and learning perspective, many of these children are definitely preschool children. However, from a curriculum perspective, the Grade R year is the first year of the Foundation Phase and must therefore follow a set curriculum as outlined in CAPs. The necessity to align the needs of a preschool child and the requirements of a formal curriculum can cause major difficulties and tension unless handled with insight.

Class size

The teacher–child ratio is set at 1:30. However, across all provinces a number of schools are overcrowded, especially in rural areas. Furthermore, where children speak many different home languages and come from differing contexts, it can become a challenge for the teacher to meet each child's learning needs. Overcrowding deepens this challenge. One way of coping with this is through the use of class assistants, who are available in some provinces.

Language

Challenges related to language differ from province to province. In Gauteng it is particularly complex as one class may have children whose home language is any one of South Africa's 11 official languages or a language from across the border, for example Portuguese from Mozambique or French from Zaire. Language can be a barrier or a carrier to understanding. If children do not understand the language of learning and teaching (LoLT), they are immediately at a disadvantage. In addition, language carries cultural perspectives and histories that shape how people think and understand the world. The current language-in-education policy aims to maintain the home language (also referred to as the mother tongue) while providing access to the effective use of at least one additional language and a conversational language (see Chapter 12). This does not apply, however, to Grade R.

Grade R teachers' qualifications

Since 2015 the Department of Higher Education and Training has introduced new formal qualifications for Grade R teachers (DHET, 2015). As a result, many un- and under-qualified Grade R teachers are now upgrading their qualifications to a Grade R Diploma, which provides a pathway to the BEd Foundation Phase degree. These qualifications are offered through universities, NGOs and other further-education sectors. They meet the key objective within the DBE to improve the qualifications of Grade R teachers in line with the Higher Education Qualifications Framework, the Teacher Education Plan and the Department of Higher Education and Training (SAIDE, 2013; DHET, 2015). Quality teaching in Grade R is of the utmost importance. This upgrading endeavour provides effective and continuous support for teachers to develop a career pathway and to gain qualifications that ensure quality teaching. According to Excell and Linington (2011), Grade R teachers should be able to do the following:

- Demonstrate an in-depth understanding of the many theoretical perspectives that inform early childhood education (ECE), including how children learn.
- Create an appropriate early-learning environment.
- Be sensitive to contextual and other factors.
- Implement an appropriate and purposeful play-based Grade R programme where play is used to enhance learning and teaching.
- Use teacher-guided activities to generate inquiry and the co-construction of knowledge.
- Align developmental milestones with professional practice that is age and stage appropriate, and does not privilege some learners while marginalising others.
- Implement appropriate assessment strategies.
- Focus on issues relating to diversity and social justice.
- Mediate learning and reflect on their own practice.

Effective implementation of the Grade R year

The biggest challenge is related to the correct implementation of this year. Given the children's differing contexts and their ages and stages of development, a more play-based, informal approach to teaching and learning is preferable. However, because many of the Grade R classes are situated in primary schools and because Grade R is the first year of the Foundation Phase, a more formal approach is frequently adopted. This more formal approach remains a subject of debate. An important question to ask is: Can most Grade R children cope with and benefit from the demands of a more formal approach to Grade R which is often implemented in the primary schools? Usually, the answer is a resounding NO! The answer lies in a skilful interpretation of the CAPS curriculum, which is the focus of this book.

> **What if ...**
> Your Grade R class is situated in the primary school, and the Foundation Phase (FP) HoD tells you your children need more experience with worksheets to strengthen their understanding of left and right. What more appropriate ways could you suggest to reinforce this understanding in children? (See Chapter 4 for possible ideas.)

CASE STUDY

Two Grade R teachers, Mrs Dlamini and Mrs Sowazi, are planning their Grade R programme for the next week. Mrs Dlamini suggests that they use a maths worksheet where children have to identify the number 5 among a whole range of numbers and then circle all of them. Mrs Sowazi, who has recently attended a course on early numeracy, shakes her head. 'Isn't there a way the children can experience the "fiveness" of five?' she asks. Mrs Dlamini says, 'But we have always used worksheets, why should we change now?' Mrs Sowazi replies, 'Because I was told that children learn better through movement involving their own bodies. And they need to handle actual objects if they are to really understand what five means'. 'Really!' exclaims Mrs Dlamini. 'I hadn't thought about that. Perhaps we could start our activity with a song that involves actions.' The two teachers start discussing activities that involve movement, song and actual objects that could be used to explore the number five (see chapters 13 and 14 for a more in-depth explanation).

This case study illustrates different possible ways you could approach teaching and learning in the Grade R year. Which approach do you think is better and why? Think about your own particular context.

> **Something to consider**
>
> Given the fact that most Grade R classes are in the primary school, some teachers argue for an approach which amounts to little more than a watered-down Grade 1 or a worksheet-bound school readiness programme. The reason they give is that they must prepare the children for Grade 1. But what is preparedness? This is a question you must ask yourself as your answer will guide your daily practice.
>
> If your understanding of school readiness is broader than a Grade 1 preparation package, then you might ask what else Grade R teachers can do. Could a different approach be adopted in the Grade R classroom located in a primary school? We would argue that it can.

There are teachers who push for an approach steeped in ECD methodology which addresses contextually relevant holistic development and the necessity of play, and others who support the notion of lifelong learning and the foundations that need to be put in place to ensure a child's preparedness in every sense of the word. This would include the promotion of a love of learning and the acquisition of the competences required to further it. (Reread the earlier section on the purpose of Grade R.)

But this view of Grade R, through a broader lens, places the teacher and the school in a specific role and requires a particular kind of management of the Grade R classroom. It means that Grade R teachers need a deep understanding of what should be happening in a quality Grade R classroom and a specialised knowledge and understanding about:

- children and their particular contexts (socio-economic, cultural, etc) and how these can impact learning
- what young children ought to know and learn
- how best they learn
- how they should be taught.

In other words, excellent teaching based on theory and ongoing action research should underpin the Grade R year.

> **Something to consider**
>
> **Teaching and excellence**
> MacNaughton and Williams (2004) correctly argue that all children deserve excellent teaching. They state that 'teaching is a process through which ... [teachers] ... assist and encourage children's learning' (2004: 4). Teaching aims to optimise (make the most of) children's learning.
>
> You, as a Grade R teacher, should therefore reflect on (think about) children's responses and act on them in a way that you believe will most assist their learning. We call this action research. Teaching is a highly value-based process, and you need to be constantly aware of this fact. To teach effectively you have to think and make decisions about:
> - what you need to prepare
> - what you are going to do
> - what you are going to say
> - whether you need to do or say anything
> - how you plan the environment
> - why you have chosen a particular approach.
>
> Your decisions will be based on your knowledge and understanding of:
> - child development
> - individual children's characteristics (see Chapter 4) and special needs
> - important contextual factors including the cultural values of the children's families
>
> »

- parental/caregiver desires for their children's learning
- what children at this age know and can do, and what they need to be able to do, to know and to learn about – in other words, what knowledge, skills, attitudes and values they need to function effectively in a specific society (part of this can be found in the current CAPS documents)
- what is ethical; in other words, what is the right thing to do.

This is what we will be covering throughout the rest of the book. Each chapter deals with a specific aspect of what constitutes quality teaching and learning in the Grade R year.

Questions for reflection and discussion

What is your view? Briefly reflect on your own understanding of the purpose, importance and challenges of implementing a quality Grade R year. Has your own opinion changed in any way after reading this chapter?

SUMMARY

In this chapter, we clarified that Grade R stands for the reception year and is the year before the child starts formal schooling. It is also the first year of the Foundation Phase. We have discussed the meaning of the Grade R year and explored some of the different reasons for offering this year. Grade R children need what all preschool children need – a safe, hygienic and stimulating environment with warm, caring and appropriately qualified teachers who deliver an interactive, play-based programme which is aimed at the holistic development of each child (social, emotional, physical, intellectual, aesthetic, moral and spiritual). Grade R should deepen the foundation blocks essential for optimal learning in formal school. It should enhance the acquisition of skills and concepts required for future learning such as those that form part of emergent literacy and numeracy, and those that are particularly important in the 21st century. Through meaningful play opportunities, children develop positive dispositions towards learning such as concentration, perseverance and self-discipline. Play promotes a sense of curiosity and wonder about the world. Through play, essential gross, fine-motor and perceptual-motor skills including coordination are refined, and children are encouraged to cooperate, solve problems and explore their own creativity. All this promotes their confidence and encourages independence. In addition to play, Grade R children need to be exposed to a variety of subjects such as art, music, drama, language and mathematics. They need to be active participants in their own learning. We noted that many South African children arrive in Grade R with their developmental and learning potential significantly compromised. This places a specific responsibility on the Grade R teacher who has to support these children, often under difficult conditions including under-resourced educational settings.

Finally, we have shown how this year can easily become a more formal, watered-down Grade 1 year, which is not an ideal scenario. We have suggested that this more formal approach should be avoided, and argued that, through excellent teaching, an appropriate Grade R year can be implemented, almost irrespective of the context. It depends to a large extent on the knowledge, skills and commitment of the teacher.

The remainder of this book will give you ideas on how to implement a contextually, culturally and developmentally appropriate Grade R programme to maximise the learning opportunities for all children in your Grade R classroom.

BIBLIOGRAPHY

Biersteker, L. 2010. *Scaling up Early Childhood Development in South Africa: Introducing the Reception year (Grade R) for children aged 5 years and the 1st year of schooling*. Brookings: Wolfensohn Center for Development.

Biersteker, L, Ngaruiya, S, Sebatane, E & Gudyanga, S. 2008. 'Introducing pre-primary classes in Africa: Opportunities and challenges', in *Africa's future, Africa's challenge* edited by M Garcia, A Pence & J Evans. Washington: The International Bank for Reconstruction and Development/World Bank: 227–248.

Bloch, G. 2007. *The persistence of inequality in education: Policy and implementation priorities*. Paper presented for the EASA conference, 8–11 January, Club Mykonos.

Bloch, G. 2009. *The toxic mix: What's wrong with South African schools and how to fix it*. Cape Town: Tafelberg.

Braun, SJ & Edwards, EP. 1972. *History and theory of early childhood education*. Belmont, CA: Wadsworth Publishing Company.

Bruce, T. 2004. *Developing learning in early childhood*. London: Paul Chapman Publishing.

Carr, M. 2001. *Assessment in early childhood settings: Learning stories*. London: Paul Chapman.

Christie, P. 2008. *Opening the doors of learning*. Johannesburg: Heinemann.

Department of Basic Education. 2011a. *National Curriculum Statement (NCS). Curriculum and Assessment Policy Statement (CAPS), English Home Language, Intermediate Phase, Grades 4–6*. Pretoria, South Africa.

Department of Basic Education. 2011b. National Protocol for Assessment Grades R–12, Government Notices No 722 and No 723, *Government Gazette* No 34600 of 12 September 2011 and amended as Government Notice No 1115 and No 1116, *Government Gazette* No 36042 of 28 December 2012. Pretoria.

Department of Basic Education. 2012. *Draft Curriculum and Assessment Policy Statements document*. Pretoria: DBE.

Department of Education. 1996. *Interim policy for Early Childhood Development*. Pretoria: DoE.

Department of Education. 1997. *Illustrative learning programme for Grade R (reception) year.* Pretoria: DoE.

Department of Education. 2001a. *Education White Paper 5 on Early Childhood Development. Meeting the challenges of early childhood education.* Pretoria: DoE.

Department of Education. 2001b. *The National Early Childhood Education Pilot Project.* Pretoria: DoE.

Department of Education. 2001c. *The Nationwide Audit of ECD Provisioning in South Africa.* Pretoria: DoE.

Department of Education. 2007. National Policy on Assessment and Qualifications for Schools in the General Education and Training Band. *Government Gazette,* 500 (29626). Pretoria.

Department of Higher Education and Training (DHET). 2015. *Minimum requirements for teacher educator qualifications.* Pretoria: DHET.

Excell, L & Linington, V. 2011. 'Taking the debate into action: Does the current Grade R practice in South Africa meet quality requirements?' *SA-eDUC Journal* 8(2): 3–12.

Excell, L, Linington, V & Helsby, M. 2010. *Grade R practitioner's course.* University of the Witwatersrand: Johannesburg.

Fullan, M & Scott, G. 2014. *New pedagogies for deep learning.* White Paper. Collaborative Impact SPC, Seattle, Washington. https://michaelfullan.ca/education-plus/ (Accessed 7 January 2021).

Gauteng Department of Education (GDE). 2005. *Implementing of Grade R in Gauteng.* Gauteng Circular 28/2005. Johannesburg: GDE.

Gestwicki, C. 2007. *Developmentally appropriate practice: Curriculum and development in early education.* New York: Delmar Thomson Learning.

Golinkoff, RM & Hirsh-Pasek, K. 2016. *Becoming brilliant: What science tells us about raising successful children.* American Psychological Association. https://doi.org/10.1037/14917-000 (Accessed 7 January 2021).

Heckman, JJ. 2000. Policies to foster human capital. *Research in Economics* 54(1): 3–56, March. http://www.sciencedirect.com/science (Accessed 3 June 2008)

Hyslop, J. 1999. *The classroom struggle. Policy and resistance in South Africa 1940–1990.* Pietermaritzburg: University of Natal Press.

Jackman, HL. 2005. *Early childhood curriculum: A child's connection to the world.* 3rd ed. New York: Thomson Delmar Learning.

Johansson, E & Pramling Samuelsson, I. 2006. 'Play and learning – inseparable dimensions in preschool practice'. *Early Child Development and Care* 176(1): 47–65. http://www.ipkl.gu.se/english/contact/staff/Ingrid_Pramling/nsionsinpreschoolpractice (Accessed 12 December 2010).

Kagan, D. 1992. 'Implications of research on teacher belief'. *Educational Psychologist* 27(1): 69–90.

MacNaughton, G. 2003. *Shaping early childhood.* Berkshire: Open University Press.

MacNaughton, G & Williams, G. 2004. *Teaching young children. Choices in theory and practice.* Berkshire: Open University Press.

Porteus, K. 2004. 'The state of play in early childhood development', in *Changing class. Education and social change in post-apartheid South Africa,* edited by L Chisholm. Cape Town: HSRC: 339–366.

Prochner, L & Kabiru, M. 2008. 'ECD in Africa: A historical perspective', in *Africa's future, Africa's challenge,* edited by M Garcia, A Pence & J Evans. Washington: The International Bank for Reconstruction and Development/World Bank: 117–134.

Queensland State Authority, 2006. *Early Years Curriculum Guidelines.* Brisbane: QSA.

Republic of South Africa. 1996a. *The Constitution of the Republic of South Africa.* Pretoria: Government Printer.

Republic of South Africa. 1996b. The South African Schools Act (Act 84 of 1996). Pretoria: Government Printer.

Richter, L, Biersteker, L, Burns, J, Desmond, C, Feza, N, Harrison D, Martin, P, Saloojee, H & Slemming, W. 2012. *Diagnostic review of Early Childhood Development.* Pretoria: Human Science Research Council (HSRC).

Riley, J. 2003. *Learning in the early years.* London: Paul Chapman.

Schweinhart, LJ & Weikart, DP. 1993. 'Success by empowerment: The High/Scope Perry preschool study through age 27'. *Young Children* 49(1): 54–58, November.

South African Government Information Online: Update on progress and achievements for 2012/13.

South African Institute for Distance Education (SAIDE). 2010. *Grade R Research Project.* Braamfontein, South Africa.

South African Qualifications Authority (SAQA). 2012. Registered qualification.

Taylor, N. 1989. *Falling at the first hurdle. Research report no. 1.* Johannesburg: University of the Witwatersrand.

The SACMEQ III Project in South Africa. *A study of the conditions of schooling and the quality of education in South Africa.* Country report.

Webber, VK. 1978. *An outline of the development of pre-school education in South Africa 1930 to 1977.* Johannesburg: The South African Association for Early Childhood Education.

GLOSSARY

Action research – a cyclical approach to researching practice, based on identifying a problem, planning and carrying out an intervention, and then reflecting on the outcomes of that intervention. Further cycles of plan, do and reflect will follow if necessary

Aesthetic – having to do with feelings, ideas and perceptions about beauty

Compulsory – enforced by law, obligatory

Conception – the beginning of a new life; when the sperm fertilises the egg (ovum)

Context – background, circumstances, which can be differing social, economic, political, historical and physical situations

Cultural perspective – a particular way of looking at things which have been influenced by culture

Curriculum – a plan for learning and teaching, covering the why, what, how and who of teaching and learning

Developmentally appropriate practice – teaching practices that consider children's current abilities and individual differences, and learning experiences that are both appropriate and respectful of children's different social and cultural backgrounds

Formal schooling – compulsory, structured schooling controlled by a formal curriculum and assessment approach

Holistic development – a viewpoint that considers the interrelationship of the various aspects of a child's development: physical, social, emotional, cognitive, language, perceptual-motor, creative and moral/spiritual. It also includes a child's history, present status and relationships with others

Lifelong learner – a person whose mind is open to new knowledge and ways of seeing things from all perspectives throughout life

School readiness – the ability to adjust to the demands of formal schooling

Universal – the term which replaced the statement that Grade is compulsory. In this context it means that a Grade R space is available to every child of appropriate age

Chapter 2

Perspectives on early childhood education

Lorayne Excell, Vivien Linington, Naseema Schaik

In this chapter we consider

- how beliefs influence our understanding of children
- how children grow, develop and learn
- a range of different developmental and learning theories and how these impact Grade R practice, namely:
  - Maslow's hierarchy of needs
  - Bronfenbrenner's bioecological systems perspective
  - Arnold Gesell's maturational perspective
  - Skinner and behaviourism
  - Bandura and social learning theory
  - Piaget and constructivism
  - Vygotsky and social constructivism
  - Erikson's theory of psychosocial development
  - Gardner and multiple intelligences
  - Neuroscience
- the sociology of childhood
  - the sociological child
  - an African perspective on childhood.

INTRODUCTION: GRADE R – A THEORETICAL ENTRY INTO A WORLD OF DIVERSITY AND COMPLEXITY

Teaching in a Grade R context is a complex, interactive process between the teacher and the children. A skilful teacher will have a wide range of teaching strategies and tools to maximise (make the most of) children's learning. In the reception year the focus is on the development of the whole or total child – that is, we focus on culturally responsive holistic development and learning, acknowledging the children's specific contexts.

Often, how and what we teach are determined by our own beliefs, attitudes and value systems. These influence what we think young children should learn and also how we think they learn. Our beliefs, attitudes and values can also have a strong influence on our classroom practice, even though we might not be aware of this influence.

> Beliefs are part of our individual value system. They are what we think is important. They do not have to be based on fact. Beliefs help to form our attitudes. Together our beliefs and attitudes help to form our value systems – what we think is right or wrong, or good or bad, our judgement of what is valuable or important in life, for example respect.

Try this out
Spend about five minutes thinking through your beliefs about children and how they learn. Jot them down on a piece of paper. Remember that you are not looking for the right answer, but rather a reflection on your current understanding.

Something to consider

Facts about children
- Children begin developing and learning before they are born, and continue to develop and learn throughout their childhood and into adulthood.
- They learn most in their first seven years of life; this is when the foundations are laid for later learning.
- They usually want to learn, but require appropriate learning opportunities if this is to be successful.
- They are unique, and learn and develop at their own pace.
- They are curious and adventurous, and learn through exploration and discovery.
- They are born into a particular social and cultural context – 'a way of being in the world' – and this influences what and how they think.
- They are affected in many different ways by the context (circumstances) in which they develop.
- They are involved in a process of learning and development, which are closely intertwined.
- They are capable and competent beings – young citizens whose voice should be taken into consideration in decisions that affect them.

How children learn
- They learn through exploration and discovery.
- They learn through their senses: sight, hearing, touch, taste and smell.
- They are sensorimotor, hands-on learners. (Sensorimotor means they learn about their environment through their senses and motor (muscle movement) actions.) In other words, they are active, kinaesthetic learners.

»

- They learn by doing and through interacting with concrete (actual) materials. They therefore need many opportunities to interact (to become involved) with a variety of different teaching and learning materials.
- They learn through social experiences, and interactions with peers and adults help shape their learning.

In addition
- Language is important for learning as it is central to thinking.
- Children do not learn by sitting still for a long time and listening to a teacher talk.
- They learn though imitation (copying others), especially adults, so adults should role model appropriate behaviours for children.
- Children are human beings in their own right and should be given opportunities to make appropriate choices and the teacher should guide these choices.
- Children's development and learning are influenced by factors both within themselves and within their environment. However, whatever their personal and environmental contexts, all children have the right to receive excellent teaching.

Try this out

What do you think these ideas about how children develop and learn mean for the Grade R teacher? How will they inform your practice?

Did you mention some of the following points?
a. Find out what the children know and can do, and then use this as your starting point. Move **from the known to the unknown**.
b. **Listen** to the children you teach.
c. Have a **broad general knowledge and relevant content knowledge** so that you can support and extend the children's learning.
d. Offer a **stimulating and varied learning environment** that will encourage children to become involved with the learning process and make appropriate choices.
e. Encourage children to talk, listen to each other and so **develop their language competence**.
f. Give children plenty of **opportunities to explore** their environment using all their senses.
g. Encourage children to participate in all activities so that **total development** can be promoted.
h. Understand the **importance of play** in children's learning and know how to mediate and facilitate play. (We will discuss play in detail in Chapter 10.)
i. Establish a **warm, caring and respectful relationship** with each child.
j. Identify each child's **specific needs and interests** and try to ensure they are met.

k. Promote positive acceptance of and respect for **diversity** (difference). You should challenge discrimination when it occurs and help children to be active in creating a fair and just world. This will begin to ensure an excellent education for all children.
l. Ideas of how children develop and learn are based on a number of different **developmental and learning theories and other fields of study** such as the sociology of childhood.

These are just some of the issues you could have raised. There are many more.

> **Something to consider**
>
> Different understandings of what drives good teaching are based, as we have said, on our particular world view or belief system, which should, ideally, be informed by the wide range of theoretical perspectives (ideas that explain something) that underpin early childhood education (ECE).

ECD, including Grade R, is not informed by one particular body of knowledge. Over time, different disciplines such as medicine, education, anthropology, sociology and developmental and other fields in psychology have all added to our knowledge and understanding of how young children develop and learn. You will notice as you study the theories outlined in this book that many of the ideas expressed in the previous pages relate to them. Try, as you read further, to match a specific idea to a specific theory.

In this chapter we are going to look at a number of different theories that all have important implications for how we can promote optimal (the best) growth, development and learning in young children. All of them must be viewed against the sociocultural context in which the young child develops and learns, and this key factor will be discussed at the end of the chapter to deepen our understanding of how theory impacts practice.

Each theory presented will be looked at from three perspectives:
1. What the theory proposes
2. What the implications of this theory for teaching and learning are
3. Something to consider – which will include possible limitations of the theory.

DEVELOPMENTAL AND LEARNING THEORIES

Before we can unpack these theories, we need to explore briefly the meaning of the words *growth*, *development* and *learning*.

What are growth, development and learning?

Growth means an increase in physical size, whereas **development** means an increase in functional capacity – in other words, in what the child is able to know and do (the knowledge and skills that he/she acquires). **Learning** refers to a deepening of knowledge and understanding, and is closely linked to a change in behaviours.

Growth, development and learning are most rapid in the early years of life before formal schooling. During these years (from birth to the age of six), children should slowly acquire (obtain) the **skills** (the abilities), concepts (ideas) and **attitudes or dispositions** that prepare them for success in the formal schooling environment. To do this, children require many and varied experiences over a long period of time. **Play**, where the teacher identifies and utilises the 'teachable moment', is an important way of helping children develop these skills, concepts and attitudes. We will look at play in some depth in Chapter 10.

Holistic development

Holistic development is a viewpoint that considers the interrelationship between the various aspects of a child's development: physical, social, emotional, cognitive, language, perceptual-motor, creative and moral/spiritual. It also includes a child's history, present status and relationships with others. When we study the young child in order to better understand who the child is, we look at individual aspects or areas, or domains of development, but no one aspect can be studied in isolation. No domain is independent of the other domains of development. They are, in reality, closely interrelated and all domains should also be considered in terms of the child's different contexts.

A concept of whole-child development

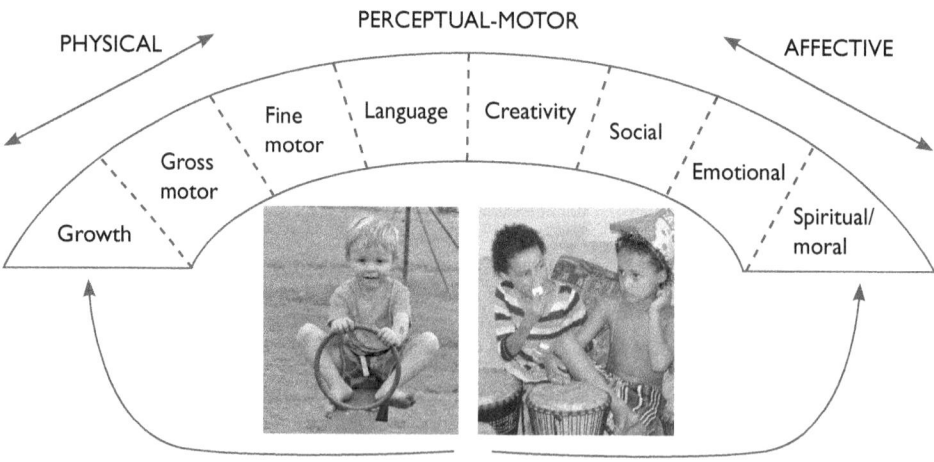

Figure 2.1 Concept of whole-child development

These aspects in the diagram (see Figure 2.1) describe a child who moves, communicates, thinks, relates to people, feels and behaves in a way appropriate to his/her contexts.

Though many developmental theories focus specifically on one aspect of development, when viewed together a holistic perspective emerges. Before we consider specific developmental theories, we first discuss two theories that carry a particularly holistic message: Maslow's hierarchy of needs and Bronfenbrenner's bioecological systems perspective.

SPECIFIC THEORIES
Maslow's hierarchy of needs
What the theory proposes

As human beings we all have needs. Abraham Maslow studied people and developed what is known as a hierarchy (like a ladder) of needs. His theory is shown in the form of a triangle (see Figure 2.2).

Figure 2.2 Maslow's hierarchy of needs

The needs at the base (bottom) of the triangle must be met first because they are basic human needs. After the basic needs for air to breathe, water to drink, food to eat, clothes to wear and a shelter to protect us, we have the need to feel safe and secure, to feel we are loved and that we belong. We also need a healthy self-esteem (feeling good about ourselves) and to receive respect from others. After these needs are met, a person is in a position to fulfil his/her personal potential and achieve self-actualisation. Self-actualisation refers to what gives a person meaning and satisfaction in life. Maslow himself said very few people reach this level. Examples of people who are said to have reached this stage are Gandhi and Mandela. Children must have their basic needs met at level one and two before they can begin to strive for fulfilment on the higher levels (Gordon & Browne, 2008; Charlesworth, 2004).

The implications for teaching and learning

The Grade R child is eager to learn. If a child is not showing this eagerness, you must ask yourself whether the answer can be found in Maslow's theory.

> **Something to consider**
>
> In South Africa we face a vast range of socio-economic and other challenges. Some of these could be seen in the light of Maslow's theory. Is this perhaps a factor in your class?

Bronfenbrenner's bioecological systems perspective
What the theory proposes

Bronfenbrenner describes how child development is influenced by a number of environmental and 'people' factors, for example the temperament of the child. All people have different experiences, and these will influence how they develop and learn. These influences are both inherent (from within) and environmental (factors outside the person) (Donald, Lazarus & Lolwana, 2006). No person therefore develops in isolation. The environment is seen as a system of circles nested inside each other with the child at the centre (see Figure 2.3). The circles or systems interact with and influence each other. Similarly, the interaction between the circles or systems will influence the development and learning of the child.

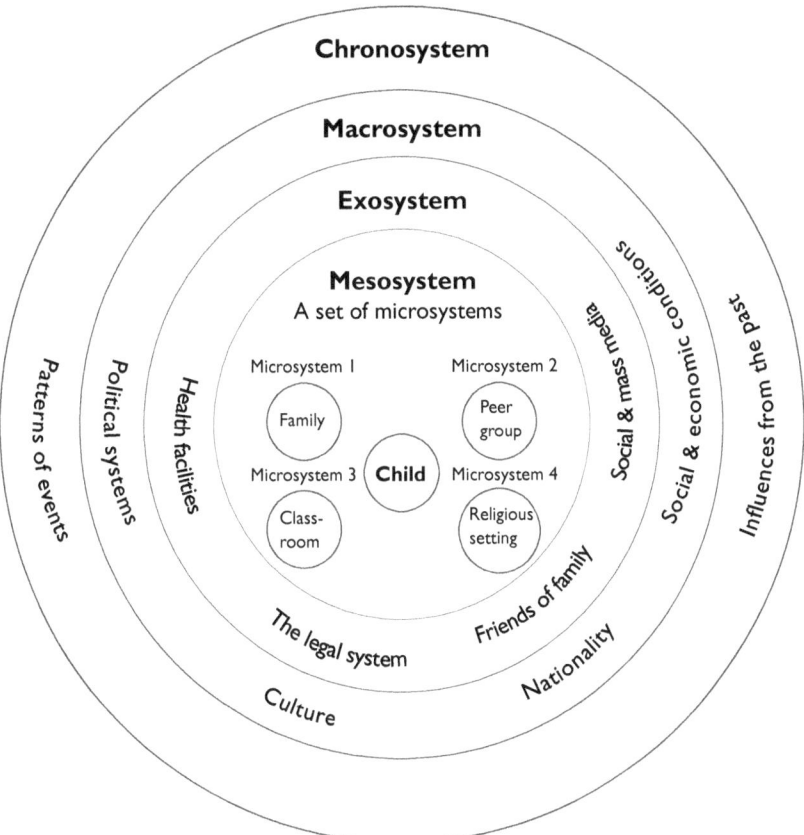

Figure 2.3 Bronfenbrenner's bioecological systems perspective

Find out more

In 2006 he revised his original 1979 theory, adapting the name to Bioecological Systems Theory, emphasising the active role of the individual in the developmental process (Ettekal & Mahoney, 2017).

The *microsystem* is the system closest to the child. It refers to the immediate everyday environment. A child will usually have a number of different microsystems, for example the family, peers, the classroom and religious settings. An example of a disturbance in the microsystem could be domestic violence.

The *mesosystem* is the next level in the ecological environment. Bronfenbrenner and Morris (2007: 817) define this system as 'comprising the relationships existing between two or more settings; in short, it is a system of two or more microsystems'. The interaction between different microsystems can impact development. For example, when parents/caregivers have a close relationship with a child's teachers, the impact on development and learning is positive.

The *exosystem* follows the mesosystem as shown in Figure 2.3. The exosystem includes friends of the family, social and mass media, the neighbourhood and local community, as well as social and legal systems. Aspects of this system can filter down and affect the child's development even though the child is not directly involved in the system. An example could be an unsafe neighbourhood. Can you think of other examples?

The *macrosystem* forms the next outer circle, and these factors are more distant from the child's specific life world. They include broader-based social and economic conditions such as poverty, cultural values and political philosophies. An example is the continuous changing of school curricula.

The outer circle is called the *chronosystem* and refers to events over time that could be far distanced from the child but could still exert an influence on the child's development. Patterns of events such as a continual influx of immigrants from neighbouring countries and historical conditions over time are examples of this system.

The implications for teaching and learning

Study Figure 2.3. You will see that there is a close relationship between the two innermost circles (micro- and mesosystems). This close relationship must always be borne in mind by a teacher. However, you must also pay close attention to factors in the exosystem and the support that you could access, such as making use of a community library and educational supplement from newspapers. As the circles become further removed from the child's everyday life, the direct influences from those systems become less noticeable, but it is still possible that they will be able to influence what happens in the life of the child and influence the microsystems. However, it might be difficult to see how aspects such as the global economy and political philosophies influence the child's life.

We need to acknowledge that each child develops and learns within a particular environment or context that is unique to him/her. Bullying or other social difficulties, or home factors based on gender differentiation, for example girls having to do certain jobs that may be time consuming and tiring, may all impact the physical, emotional and other 'well-being' elements experienced by the children you teach.

> **Something to consider**
>
> How well do you know the background or contextual features impacting the lives of the children who enter your class? If your answer is 'very little', then think how you can plan to enquire further so that you begin to understand what is motivating – or holding back – the children in your care. Only then will you be able to optimise the learning opportunities these children are offered.

Maturational theory: Gesell
What the theory proposes
Arnold Gesell was a paediatrician (a doctor who specialises in children) who compiled a table of developmental norms or milestones for various domains of development (such as physical, cognitive and emotional) based on close observation of children. However, maturational theory strongly emphasises the physical aspects of growth and development.

These milestones or norms give us an idea of what we can expect from children at different ages and/or stages of development. They begin at birth, and describe the behaviours that can be expected at different times during early childhood. In South Africa, some of these milestones for younger children have now been set out in the National Early Learning Development Standards (NELDS), which was compiled by the Department of Social Development. The idea of 'norms' is useful as a guideline. You must, however, look at the whole child in his/her particular sociocultural context before drawing any conclusions about a particular child's behaviour.

Development is informed by a number of principles, which have been influenced by maturational theory and are known as **developmental principles**. Some of these principles are the following:
- Development starts at the head and works downwards towards the feet. For example, children first learn to control their head, then they learn to sit, then crawl, and then walk.
- Development follows the same sequence (pattern) for all children, but the rate differs. For example, all children will first sit, then crawl and then walk. Some might sit at five months, others at seven months. Some might walk at 10 months, others at two years. There is a wide range of normal behaviour.
- Development is dependent upon the growth of the nervous system. Children will not be able to do certain things until the specific part of the nervous system has matured (developed). This means that development cannot be rushed. Children will not, for example, be able to hold a pencil properly until the nervous system has matured enough to enable them to do this. It also means that children need many different experiences in order to master this task. Experts now tell us that the nervous system only reaches maturity in early adulthood. Current research in neuroscience points to the importance of play and kinaesthetic movements in establishing complex neural pathways in the developing brain. We explore new advances on neuroscience later in this chapter.
- Certain aspects of development happen at specific times. These are called critical periods, sensitive periods or windows of opportunity. The term sensitive periods refers to developmental phases at which the individual is more likely to acquire a new behaviour pattern than at other times. For example, if children do not develop their language before the age of six (because, for example, they are hard of hearing and this has not been discovered), they will not acquire the same language competence as their hearing peers.

The implications for teaching and learning

Stages of development are only guidelines as each child's growth and development are unique. Development depends on each child's internal makeup as well as the child's context (circumstances). There is no such thing as a 'universal child', so we cannot generalise milestones and expect all children of similar age to reach them at the same time. Children will reach specific milestones at slightly different times, so we must therefore be culturally and contextually responsive when considering milestones of development (see chapters 3 and 4). In short, it is necessary to know about the developmental milestones, but they should never be used for evaluation in isolation.

> **Something to consider**
>
> An awareness of developmental norms and principles allows us to identify possible learning difficulties. If children do not reach their expected milestones, there could be a possible problem with which we have to deal. Early intervention (help) is essential if the problem is to be effectively managed. That is why we need to be continually observing and assessing our children (see Chapter 9), have an idea of their strengths and weaknesses, and offer appropriate help if necessary. If you are running a well-planned, high-quality programme, it becomes easier to manage children with barriers to learning because your programme will already contain many elements of differentiation, variety and free choice.

Find out more

One of the biggest criticisms of developmental norms is that they were standardised on white middle-class American children. Given the current awareness of the importance of culture and context on ECD, these norms cannot be generalised and said to apply to all children universally. Assessing children according to these 'Western norms' has thus presented some challenges to the South African context. In response to these challenges, Early Learning Outcome Measures (ELOMs) have been developed for South African children. 'The ELOM is an age-normed, standardised instrument for use with children in two age groups: 50–59 months and 60–69' (Dawes et al, 2016: 5). Children in both these groups could be in Grade R. Although it is not a tool for assessing school readiness because it covers a range of developmental domains, it could be used to identify children who are significantly behind the standard expected for their age. For further information, consult the following websites: elom.org.za/; and https://www.google.com/ search?q=elom+technical+manual&oq=elom+technical+manual&aqs=chrome.69i 57j69i60l2.33217j1j7&sourceid=chrome&ie=UTF-8.

Theory of behaviourism and learning
What the theory proposes
Behaviourism is a theory of learning focusing on observable behaviours. Learning is simply defined as the acquisition of new behaviour (Pritchard, 2005: 7).

Behaviourists call this method of learning 'conditioning'. For BF Skinner, 'operant conditioning' involves reinforcing a desired behaviour, such as taking turns during a discussion ring, by rewarding this behaviour. He maintained that rewards and punishments control the majority of human behaviours, and that the principles of operant conditioning can explain all human learning (Pritchard, 2005). Reinforcement, one of his central concepts, refers to anything that has the effect of strengthening a particular behaviour and makes it likely that the behaviour will happen again.

The implications for teaching and learning
A teacher identifies the behaviours that are desirable and those that would be best discouraged. They decide on a reward, for example a star, for desired behaviour. When the desired behaviour is displayed, for example a child sits quietly or does not shout out, the child is rewarded.

> **Something to consider**
>
> **Possible limitations of the theory**
> It is a very limited view of man and cannot give us all the answers in relation to, for example, language development. However, behaviourism has a place in teaching and learning. What do you think?

A further perspective on conditioning
Conditioning, according to Skinner, is central to learning. Another form of conditioning is observational learning or modelling. This perspective, which grew out of S–R (stimulus–response) learning traditions, was put forward by Albert Bandura, and is known as social and/or observational learning. Children learn appropriate social behaviours by observing and imitating other people, usually 'significant others', with whom they come into contact, for example a parent, teacher or superhero. The type of behaviour imitated is frequently that which is perceived to be valuable in the child's culture. Imitation of role models is an important element in how children learn language, deal with aggression, develop a moral sense and learn gender-appropriate behaviour (Bandura, 1986; Papalia, Olds & Feldman, 2006). MacNaughton (2003: 36) contends that, through this passive process of socialisation, 'social behaviours are caught not taught'.

MacNaughton (2003: 35), for example, comments: 'They [supporters of social learning theory] believe that since children learn attitudes that directly reflect a culture's value, manipulating a child's environment creates desirable gender role outcomes', and no consideration is given to the fact that children might (and sometimes do) reject the role models and social expectations they might encounter. If equity issues and social justice are to be promoted, MacNaughton (2003) stresses that teachers should become more than just 'good' role models. Children should be actively encouraged to interact meaningfully with equity-related issues and question so-called norms.

COGNITIVE DEVELOPMENT

Cognitive development refers to the mental or intellectual development of the child – the development of thought. Thinking refers to mental activity, reasoning, problem solving and decision making; in other words, how children come to know, understand and live in their world.

There are two theorists who can help us understand the development of thought: Jean Piaget and Lev Vygotsky. Piaget developed a theory of cognitive development that provides a comprehensive description of the cognitive changes people experience and the mental processes that are responsible for them. He gives us, in other words, extensive accounts of how children think at different times in their lives (McCown, Driscoll & Roop, 1996). Vygotsky offered a theory for understanding cognitive development as a process of learning influenced by the sociocultural environment of the child (McCown et al, 1996).

Piaget: cognitive development

At the age of six months, babies playing with a toy will not search for it after it is hidden under a pillow. At 18 months, however, they will follow the movements of the toy and continue to search for it after it has disappeared from view.

A four-year-old child is shown two identical glasses filled with the same amount of fruit juice. After the juice from one glass has been poured into a taller, thinner glass, the child is asked: 'Which has more?' The child points to the tall, thin glass; in his opinion, the amount of juice is equal to its height.

A five-year-old can learn to walk four blocks from her house to her school, but she cannot trace the route she takes with a pencil on a map. A nine-year-old can trace his route, as well as give people directions without referring to his map. A 12-year-old can do that, and also think about other ways and shortcuts to get to school (Singer & Revenson, 1996: 1).

Insight from Piaget's research

Piaget's research provides insight into how children think, reason and perceive the world (Singer & Revenson, 1996). For Piaget, a child's increase in understanding only happens as the child actively interacts with and discovers the world. Children do not passively receive their knowledge – they are curious and self-motivated (Hill, 2001), and construct (build) their understanding of the world. As teachers, we, according to Piaget, are simply facilitating that construction.

How children construct understanding

According to Piaget, children construct increasingly complex mental 'maps' of their world in an attempt to organise, understand and adapt to it. He suggests that this happens through three continuously interacting processes: assimilation, accommodation and equilibration.

Assimilation is a process whereby new objects, situations or ideas are understood in terms of the mental 'maps' the child already has.

Then something else happens; for example, a cat, considered up to then to be a furry, cuddly creature, suddenly scratches the child. The fact that cats can hurt contradicts or conflicts with the child's mental 'map' of a 'cat' and so a process of **accommodation** needs to occur. During this process the child's existing 'maps' have to be expanded or new ones created to make room for new situations, objects or information. In this case, the new mental map is that cats can be furry and cuddly, and yet still hurt you.

Equilibration is a Piagetian term for the process by which we maintain a balance between assimilation (using old learning) and accommodation (changing behaviour, learning new things). Equilibration is essential for adaptation and cognitive growth (Lefrancois, 2000).

Piaget's account of the processes, experiences and structures involved in cognition describes how people come to know about their world. The experiences they have and the schemes (that is, the generalised ways of acting on the world that provide the basis for mental operations) they use for understanding those experiences change as we mature (McCown et al, 1996).

Piaget formulated four stages of cognitive development that reflect the dominant schemes of thinking children use and the ages at which they use them to organise and interact with their environment.

Table 2.1 Summary of Piaget's stages of cognitive development

STAGE	APPROXIMATE AGE	NATURE OF SCHEMES/ CHARACTERISTICS OF THE STAGE
Sensorimotor	birth–2	Simple reflexive behaviour gives way to ability to form schemas and to create patterns and chains of behaviour.
Preoperational	2–7	Illogical (mental) operations. Children are essentially egocentric and unable to consider events from another's point of view. The use of symbolic thought begins, and the imagination also starts to develop.
Concrete operational	7–11	Children begin to use logical thought about physical operations; they are able to conserve – that is, they realise that two equal physical quantities remain equal even if the appearance of one changes.

STAGE	APPROXIMATE AGE	NATURE OF SCHEMES/ CHARACTERISTICS OF THE STAGE
Formal operations	11 – adult	Children are able to think hypothetically (based on a supposed idea) and abstractly.

Sources: Drawn from McCown et al (1996) and Pritchard (2005)

The implications for teaching and learning

The majority of Grade R children will be at Piaget's preoperational stage where they acquire the ability to represent ideas and engage in mental images. In particular, they do this through the medium of language. They find it difficult to consider situations from another's perspective. A programme rich in language, story and other forms of language use is essential.

> **Something to consider**
>
> **Possible limitations of the theory**
> Of the many hundreds (or thousands) of studies that have attempted to replicate Piaget's findings, the majority agree that the sequence of intellectual stages is much as Piaget described. However, many of these studies suggest that Piaget drastically underestimated the cognitive achievements of pre-schoolers; other indicate that he overestimated the formal operations capabilities of adolescents (and even of adults) (Lefrancois, 2000: 98).

Piaget was a constructivist. He viewed learning as the result of mental construction – that is, learning takes place when new information is built into and added onto an individual's current structure of knowledge, understanding and skills. We learn best when we actively construct our own understanding (Pritchard, 2005). Piaget, therefore, focused more on the individual's learning in contrast to Vygotsky, who proposed that learning happens best in a social context.

Vygotsky: a social constructivist theory
What the theory proposes

Lev Vygotsky was a Russian psychologist. His theory proposes that children are active participants who can construct (build) their own knowledge and understanding with help and support from adults, thus they are able to take charge of their own thinking as they interact and collaborate (share, exchange, take part) with others in meaningful cultural activities. Central to Vygotsky's theory is the idea that, as children participate (take part) in cultural activities with the guidance of more skilled partners, they internalise (take in and understand) the tools for thinking, and move to higher levels of mental processing (Vygotsky, 1978). Thinking is mediated by signs or cultural tools, the most important of which is language.

Social context plays an important role in what children think about and how they think. Social context refers to everything in the child's environment that is influenced by culture (ways of life), which includes the circumstances and culture of the family, the family's values and the school. It is through culture and social relationships that children learn and are able to make meaning. Unlike Piaget, who stated that children's cognitive development is strongly dependent on their maturational stage, Vygotsky believed that social experiences, and interactions with and expectations from peers, older children and adults help to shape children's learning.

According to Vygotsky, interactions that enhance learning and development happen in the child's zone of proximal development (ZPD). We can think of the ZPD as the ideal teachable space. It is the space between what children can accomplish on their own and what they can accomplish with the help of a more knowledgeable other, for example the teacher. Children, working within their ZPD, operate at two levels. At the lower or performance level, they complete a task, for example a 20-piece puzzle, without assistance from a more knowledgeable peer or adult. At the higher or potential level, they show that they can achieve something more, for example the completion of a 40-piece puzzle with the help of a more capable peer or adult. The gap between these two levels of operating is the ZPD. 'Proximal' in this context refers to the next level.

For Vygotsky, language is an important part of children's development and learning as it is central to thinking. Language, he maintained, is a tool for the mind (a psychological tool) that enables us to make meaning of the world in which we live and to increase our knowledge base. Language mediates understanding in a social context and allows us to build relationships between people (Vygotsky, 1978; Berk & Winsler, 1995). As humans we use language as a tool for solving problems and exchanging ideas.

The implications for teaching and learning

In Grade R children, language is developed as they communicate with more competent speakers, especially the teacher, thus it is important that teachers communicate often with children and that they make use of correct language. The interactions that children have with adults are of vital importance if learning is to be optimised (made the best of). Grade R teachers therefore play a central role in children's learning and development as they help children construct meaning. As adults speak with children, they help them understand and find personal meaning in the activities in which they are involved.

Vygotsky's theory also focuses on the importance of children's social and cultural contexts for learning. In other words, the child's family and culture must also be invited into the programme. In Grade R classes there will be children that come from diverse cultures and backgrounds. When planning for teaching and learning, teachers need to consider the inclusion of all the different cultures represented in their class. This includes the different beliefs, celebrations, dress, language, foods and other aspects of cultural importance.

> **Something to consider**
> - What could you do to ensure that children optimise learning through your interactions with them?
> - Understanding that children come from different social and cultural backgrounds, which factors would you consider when planning to teach?

In summary, social constructivist theory proposes that children construct their own knowledge and understanding as they interact with more knowledgeable others and receive suggestions and the support of adults. Culture and social context also play an important role in children's development of knowledge and understanding. As children take part in meaningful cultural activities with more skilled partners such as the Grade R teacher or a peer, they are able to internalise (take in and understand) the tools for thinking, and begin to use more mature (higher) levels of mental processing to solve problems. Language is also important as it is used as a tool to communicate and exchange ideas, and is seen as an important factor of thinking.

AFFECTIVE DEVELOPMENT

We are now going to look at another very important area of development. It relates to affective development and refers to the development of emotional, social and personality characteristics.

Affective development begins early – some would say while the baby is in the womb. Children begin to form bonds or attachments with caregivers, and this becomes the basis for future independence. Like all aspects of development, affective development is a process that is ongoing throughout life, but we do know that it is in the early years that the building blocks (or foundations) for positive affective development are put in place.

Erikson's theory of psychosocial development
What the theory proposes

Psychosocial development, according to Erikson, is the process whereby relationships with others influence one's search for one's own identity. His theory describes and explains the development of the human personality (McCown et al, 1996). Erikson viewed psychosocial growth as consisting of critical periods when the 'parts' of the individual's personality develop. It is these critical periods that define Erikson's eight stages of psychosocial development, each of which identifies the emergence of a part of an individual's personality (McCown et al, 1996).

Furthermore, each stage in Erikson's framework is structured as a dichotomy (a division into two) – for example trust versus mistrust, initiative versus guilt – indicating the positive and negative consequences for each stage. Each dichotomy defines a developmental crisis, a psychosocial issue that will be resolved by the child in interaction with his/her environment in either a positive or negative way (McCown et al, 1996).

The implications for teaching and learning

For the Grade R child, two stages are particularly important:
- Stage 3: Initiative versus guilt (3–6 years)
- Stage 4: Industry versus inferiority (6–12 years).

At Stage 3, children are attempting to develop a sense of initiative – that is, that they are operators on the environment. In Stage 4, the developmental crisis focuses on the child's ability to win recognition through performance. Industry refers to an eagerness to produce, for example, a drawing that captures the teacher's request.

> **Something to consider**
>
> How can your words, said and unsaid (that is, verbal and non-verbal messages), convey to your children how they are viewed as valuable members of your class?

Gardner's theory of multiple intelligences (MI)

Gardner believes that we all have an overall intelligence that is made up of several parts, each contributing to the whole. He defines intelligence as the ability to solve problems, or to create products, that are valued within one or more cultural settings (Swartz, De La Rey & Duncan, 2004). Each intelligence describes a particular talent that a person displays. The development of these intelligences is context dependent. This means that family, culture and community influence the development of intelligences, the value placed on various intelligences, and the way they are expressed. According to Gardner, there are at least eight different areas or categories of intelligence, as explained in Table 2.2.

Table 2.2 Gardner's eight different areas/categories of intelligence

Area/category	Definition
Logical/mathematical intelligence	Being able to think in a logical way, understand and work with objects, for example blocks, and use them to count, order, sequence.
Linguistic intelligence	Being able to use language to express thoughts, ideas and feelings, and the ability to understand other people and what they say.
Musical intelligence	Being able to think in music; to be able to hear patterns, and recognise and remember them.
Bodily-kinaesthetic intelligence	Being able to use one's body and handle objects skilfully, for example move rhythmically or kick a ball.

Area/category	Definition
Spatial intelligence	Being able to represent what and how you see the world through, for example, drawing and painting.
Intrapersonal intelligence	Being able to recognise and express inner feelings, for example happiness and sadness.
Interpersonal intelligence	Being able to recognise and acknowledge other people's feelings, moods and intentions – 'tuning' into, in other words, the feelings of others.
Naturalistic intelligence	Being able to recognise important differences in the natural world and manmade world, for example the differences that exist in the plant and animal world or between objects such as cars or shoes (observation skills).

Sources: Adapted from Catron & Allen (2008); Charlesworth (2004); Gordon & Browne (2008)

Gardner has more recently proposed additional intelligences, for example moral and spiritual, but for the purposes of this book we will focus on the eight in Table 2.2. In Gardner's judgement (Davis, Christodoulou, Seider & Gardner, 2017: 488), none of the other proposed intelligences sufficiently meet the criteria for identification as a unique intelligence. Despite additions and adaptations to the eight recognised intelligences, no other intelligences have been formally added to the recognised eight (Davis et al, 2017).

Find out more
Linking the theory to practice
There is no one right way to enhance multiple intelligences. Gardner makes the point that a daily programme must offer children a wide range of opportunities to foster development in all areas of intelligences (Catron & Allen, 2008). In addition, intelligence, as defined by Gardner, should not be confused with a learning style, which is how a child learns. Furthermore, it is worth noting that formal schooling seems to emphasise two of these intelligences – linguistic (language/literacy) and logical-mathematical (numeracy) – which can be problematic, particularly in Grade R where the emphasis is on whole-child development.

CASE STUDY

In the mornings when the children arrive, they are offered a variety of different activities to choose from. These include blocks which the children can build on the veranda or an audio story that they can listen to in the reading corner where there are also a number of age-appropriate books which can be 'read'. Children can also build puzzles, draw or mould with play dough.

Question
What types of intelligence do you think each of these activities is addressing?

What if ...
What if a second teacher supervised outdoor play where children were able to swing, climb, play with a ball and crawl through hoops? What types of intelligence would be addressed here?

If there was an argument between two children on who could use the swing first, which intelligence do you think would be important in this situation?

Something to consider

Think of your daily programme. Are you offering a variety of activities that will enable children to develop different types of intelligence? Or is your programme one that focuses on linguistic and logical-mathematical intelligences alone? If the answer is 'yes', start thinking of how you can offer a more varied programme that enhances all the different intelligences so that each child has an opportunity to display ability.

Find out more

Researchers in early childhood are consistently bringing new ideas and possibilities in relation to the young child's development and learning. Once such area of research is neuroscience.

EARLY CHILDHOOD AND NEUROSCIENCE

Neuroscience is a field of study exploring optimum conditions for brain development; how different parts of the nervous system function and what can go wrong (Conbayir, 2017). It makes use of imaging technology to take 'pictures' of the brain, which then have to be interpreted. Imaging technology has enabled us to more easily identify the effects that early childhood experiences have on the developing architecture of the brain – both positive and negative.

Neurons are the building blocks of the brain. The growth of new neurones – neurogenesis – begins after conception and continues throughout an individual's life. A neuron consists of three parts (see Figure 2.4) – a cell body and two different extensions called dendrites and axons. Dendrites carry information to the cell body and this is passed on from the cell body by the axon. Information passes from the axon of one neurone to the dendrites of another. The connection between axon and dendrite is called a synapse across which the information is transmitted (conducted) with the help of chemical transmitters. The axon is covered in a white fatty substance called myelin, which helps with the transmission of the information.

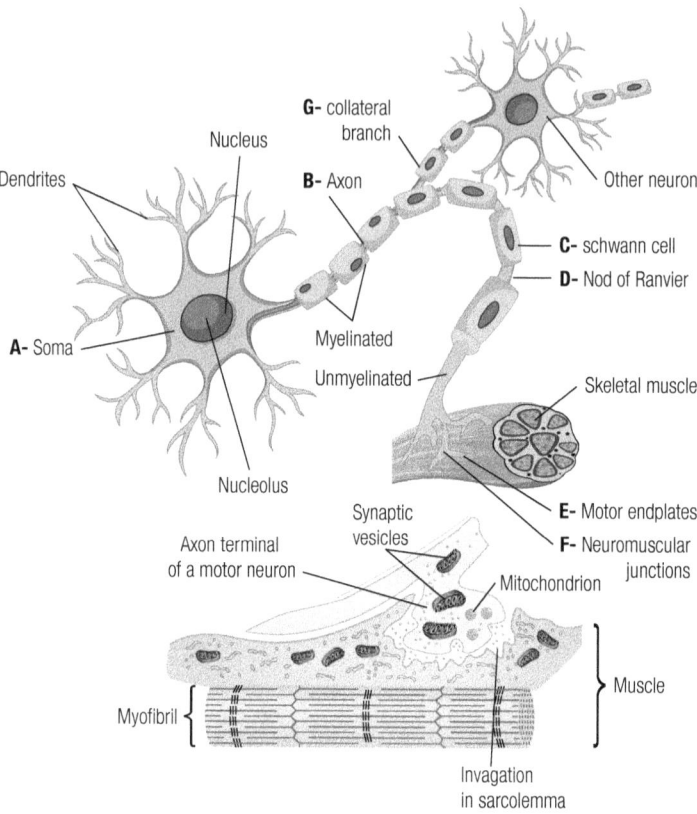

Figure 2.4 A diagrammatic representation of a neurone

At birth, the brain contains approximately 86 billion neurones, and this number continues to grow during our lifespan. Each neurone has about 2 500 synapses, and this number increases to about 15 000 by age three (Conbayir, 2017). This ability to increase the number of neurones and to change the structure and function of the brain is called neural plasticity. The minimal connections between neurones at birth rapidly increase so that by age six they are 'richly connected' (Bergen, Lee, DiCarlo & Burnett: 2020: 11) This rapid increase during early childhood is influenced by environmental experiences and interactions, both positive and negative. These experiences, good and bad, become the neuro-archaeology of the individual's brain (Perry, 2001). We know repetition of experiences not only strengthens the existing synaptic connections, but also leads to neurones creating pathways in different parts of the brain based on experiences.

Implications for teaching and learning

Favourable childhood experiences promote the growth and strengthening of neural connections, therefore brain-enhancing opportunities to engage in quality play should always be identified. These opportunities include exploration and communication with others and enjoying secure, responsive relationships. Possibilities for repetition for ongoing mastery of skills are essential.

Neuroscience has also confirmed that there are sensitive periods or distinct phases in early childhood, specifically between birth to five years, when learning of specific skills appears to be more readily mastered. During this time, the brain is best able to receive and use information gained from experience in order to learn a specific skill. When Grade R teachers know their children and work with them in their areas of interest, the children are being supported in the refinement of skills. In short, as Bergen et al (2020: 79) state, children are being assisted to continue to 'grow their brains'.

A CRITIQUE OF DEVELOPMENTAL THEORIES

In recent years, many of the developmental theories have been criticised for a number of reasons. An important one is that many of these theories foreground a biological account of childhood, and the emphasis has been placed on ensuring that children reaching specific developmental milestones at specific ages. This seems to be the way in which children's development and learning are measured. A troubling consequence has been that little, if any, consideration been given to social and cultural influences that might shape children's learning. According to James and Prout (1990), all children are viewed through a similar lens (a point to who have already referred). Children and childhood have come to be viewed in a very particular way, and this is dominated by a Western perspective on how children develop and learn. We have created an image of the 'normal child', who is a child who meets prescribed milestones and follows specific norms of development. All children are expected to follow this 'development and learning recipe' and if they do not meet the stated norms, they are 'in need' and require help. In addition, the adult has placed him/herself as the knowing elder from whom all knowledge flows.

To counter this narrow understanding of children and childhood, a movement called the sociology of childhood where children are valued as human beings in their own right is gaining ground.

THE SOCIOLOGY OF CHILDHOOD: THE SOCIOLOGICAL CHILD

Sociology is the study of society and human social interaction. It examines 'why we do things, the way we do things, what are the reasons for doing specific things or engaging in specific activities and adopting certain behaviours' (Ferrante, Seedat-Khan, Kaziboni & Uys, 2016: 3). A useful way to study early childhood is through the lens of relational sociology, which focuses on how children see themselves in relation to other people both younger and older. These other people are usually parents, teachers and other significant adults, as well as peers with whom they are friendly and siblings.

Young children are born into interdependent relationships that may already exist between parents, and between parents and other children. To grow as a social being, young children need to learn from their elders and other significant people in their lives. These learnings are historically and culturally shaped and influenced by time, space and aspects of power. The notion of power affects society at every level. For example, in a Grade R context the Foundation Phase HoD usually has more power over decisions taken than the Grade R teacher does. Adults, for example, have power over children and this can be used positively or negatively.

> **Something to consider**
>
> How do power relationships influence decision making in your Grade R classroom? Are decisions about the children's learning and development taken collaboratively? Is it a consultative process between you and the parent, and you and the other relevant staff members? Or do you sometimes feel that you have little or no say in the decisions made? Likewise, are children's interests and choices considered when planning the daily programme? Another example of power relationships is when we consider developmental norms and whether or not children's abilities align (are in keeping) with these norms. For instance, can a child be assessed as being developmentally delayed because he/she cannot cut out a figure on a page. The child might have never practised this skill before because there is no pair of scissors in the home. In this case, the reason for not being able to cut along all the edges is probably a socio-economic or cultural factor and not because of physiological (biological) factors. This points yet again to the importance of context and sociocultural issues when trying to understand a particular issue.

Sociocultural context

All children grow within specific sociocultural contexts. Culture refers to the ideas, customs and social behaviour of a particular people or society. A sociocultural approach focuses on how values, beliefs, skills and traditions are transmitted to the next generation. Children are embedded in the family and culture of their community, and a number of aspects of their development are therefore culturally specific (Gordon & Browne, 2017).

As previously mentioned, a sociocultural approach draws on the work of the Russian psychologist Vygotsky (1978), who argued that we become ourselves through others. In short, culture and family influences impact the development of the whole child. As Rutgers points out (see Chapter 3), Vygotsky held the view that children develop within their social world and that interactions with peers and elders are important in fostering (encouraging) higher levels of cognitive and social development.

Wyness (2012) also points to the importance of environmental factors when he argues that the environment plays an influential role in pushing the child along the developmental pathway. Families, of course, are an integral (essential) part of this environment. Each family will prioritise certain skills and values and beliefs, for example vocabulary development, cooperation with siblings, self-care and independence. In each sociocultural context, therefore, there will be similarities and differences that will inform the unique role that a child plays in the family.

> **Something to consider**
>
> As a teacher you create your own sociocultural context, and the children for whom you are responsible will be part of this context. Is there a 'fit', you must ask yourself, between each child's home and school context? Is there an emphasis on similar roles, attitudes and values? Are the literacy practices similar? Or are the two contexts (the home and your Grade R) a mismatch? For instance, what is important in one context, for example turn taking, may be considered irrelevant in the other. Perhaps a home belief is that children should be seen and not heard while in the Grade R context the child's active participation in decision making is encouraged. These differing views about the role of the child could fan conflict between the school and the home.

The child as an active participant

The new sociology of childhood stresses the importance of children as active participants in the making of decisions that affect them. It acknowledges that children do know things and they do have ideas that should be acknowledged. In other words, according to Prout and James (1997), children have agency and voice, therefore it is important that adults listen to them as this forms an important part of understanding what they are feeling and experiencing (Pascal & Bertram, 2009). Additionally, listening to children can make a difference to understanding what is important to them, what their interests are and what their concerns are (Pascal & Bertram, 2009). Children should be valued and respected for who they are now rather than for who they will become in the future. Childhood is an important space, as children's own opinions and feelings about what happens in their lives have value. In other words, from the perspective of a sociology of childhood, we learn about the concept of agency, which tells us children are, in fact, very competent (able, skilled) in making meaning and contributing (giving) towards their understanding of life.

The implications for teaching and learning

Grade R teachers should realise that although Grade R is considered to be a formal space controlled by the teacher, it is important that teachers invite children to be participating agents in their own learning. As active participants, children can influence what happens in the Grade R context. We, as adults, need to realise that although children are dependent on us, they are capable of making decisions and completing tasks based on their own strengths and on their own. This does not mean that there is no place for adult guidance, but it is not always necessary.

Teachers should not consider children as helpless, unable to perform tasks or voice their own opinions, because they are very capable of making a positive contribution to their lives. Adults should listen to children and value their opinions. In other parts of the world, for example in the United Kingdom and Australia, children are asked to contribute their own opinions about various issues. Some examples are when children are asked their opinions about what they would like to learn and types of equipment they would like in the playground. In other words, children should be given the opportunity to make some choices and decisions. Grade R teachers are partners with the children, not adults who know more dealing with children who know less.

Questions for reflection and discussion

How can we, as Grade R teachers, value the voices of children in the Grade R context? How do we invite their opinions and then value and act on what we have heard?

We will now consider another particular perspective – the constructions of children and childhood through an African lens.

African perspective

As we have repeatedly mentioned, many of the dominant theories on child development and learning offer a predominately Western or European perspective on childhood. Though many of the claims put forward by these theories appear to be valid regardless of race, colour or creed, theory has to be revisited to take into account different competing perspectives. One of these is exploring constructions of children and childhood from an African perspective. We do not claim to be able to accurately represent the cultural beliefs and child-rearing practices of the many different groups of people who live in South Africa, but we do offer some thoughts drawn from eminent African philosophers and educationists on constructions of children and childhood.

Try this out

Think about your own cultural beliefs and practices. Can you identify specific practices in your culture that might differ from other cultures' practices? Consider, for example, different child-rearing practices and attendant norms and values. Think about the about the naming of children – how are names chosen and why that specific name? Is there a particular child-naming ceremony? Do these names change as the child grows older? What are the approaches to feeding children? Are certain types of foods avoided or encouraged? What is the approach to supervising and looking after young children?

»

Is it the mother's responsibility or does this task fall to older siblings who sometimes might only be in Grade R? What, if any, are tasks that young children are expected to do around the home? How are play and play-based learning in Grade R viewed? Are children expected to be seen and not heard, or is their view sometimes welcomed?

> **Something to consider**
>
> You may be able to think of many more culturally specific practices. Share your ideas with your colleagues and start thinking about how these different practices might impact education in Grade R. Do your cultural practices conflict with the cultural practices of others? If conflict does occur, how might it be resolved in a Grade R setting?

Early education: an African perspective

As noted by Pence and Nsamenang (2008), African ECE has not been sufficiently theorised. Penn (2005) claims that Western ECD approaches do not consider culture, context and diversity specifically from an African perspective. We are only now recognising the need for a local, indigenous, community-sensitive approach to child development, learning and well-being.

Child-rearing practices within traditional African philosophical thought should provide a political and social space for children to develop and to perpetuate the cultural legacies of their ancestors (Boakye-Boaten, 2010). In indigenous African societies, children are educated through taking part in family life and being immersed in their traditional customs and values. Spiritual values stem from religious rituals and practices. These values lay the foundations for the respectful governance of the community and the love, respect and obedience which the children are expected to show their parents and elders. Moral and ethical codes of behaviours as well as social relationships are taught to children by the elders through traditional tales and myths. Children in traditional African culture are perceived to be human beings in need of help and direction (Boakye-Boaten, 2010). It is the responsibility of the society to ensure the protection and proper socialisation of children while simultaneously respecting them. This resonates with the African proverb that it takes a village to raise a child.

According to Boakye-Boaten (2010), the social construction of children has two distinctly different elements. The biological element sees children as vulnerable beings in need of protection and nurturing. The sociological element prescribes social functions and relationships for all family members. Fathers are the providers of the family and the mothers the nurturers. Children in traditional Africa philosophy have a fundamental role as a future insurance for their families.

> **Something to consider**
>
> According to Nsamenang and Lamb (1994) and Boakye-Boaten (2010), tension exists between traditional African education ideas and practices, and more contemporary approaches. They claim that traditional child-rearing practices often sit uneasily with expectations of the more economically privileged African families who want their young children to have a Western education, including access to well-resourced schools, experienced teachers, smaller class sizes, an authentic curriculum and engaging pedagogies. Many other African families are now making similar demands.

Find out more

Aubrey (2017) states that within South Africa today there is a very distinctive political and socio-economic climate with competing discourses (conversations) specifically around indigenous knowledge and the discourse of decolonisation. In other words, topics like indigenous knowledge and decolonisation are hotly debated. An example of an indigenous African practice (Masuku & Ndawi, 2001) is young boys going to herd cattle and through this gaining early counting and life skills. Can you think of other traditional practices and discuss what you see as their strengths and limitations?

SUMMARY

This chapter has considered the complexities that surround child development and learning. It has emphasised that knowledge about development is necessary but not sufficient (Walsh, 2005) if we are to understand the developmental trajectory (pathway) of the children in our class. Children cannot be viewed without considering their particular circumstances – that is, the context in which they are growing. This context is cultural, social, economic, political and historical. There is no such thing as a universal child and therefore a one-size-fits-all approach towards teaching and learning is not appropriate. Arguments made from a sociological perspective on childhood offer an important way to understand and address the complexities involved in early childhood education.

BIBLIOGRAPHY

Aubrey, C. 2017. 'Sources of inequality in South African. Early child development services'. *South African Journal of Childhood Education* 7(1): 1–9.

Bandura, A. 1986. *Social foundations of thought and action: A social cognitive theory.* Englewood Cliffs: Prentice Hall.

Bergen, D, Lee, L, DiCarlo, C & Burnett, G. 2020. *Enhancing brain development in infants and young children.* New York: Teachers College Press.

Berk, EL & Winsler, A. 1995. *Scaffolding children's learning. Vygotsky and early childhood education.* New York: Delmar Publishers.

Boakye-Boaten, A. 2010. 'Changes in the concept of childhood: Implications on children in Ghana'. *The Journal of International Social Research* 3(10), Winter.

Bransford, JD, Brown, AL & Cocking, RR (eds). 1999. *How people learn.* Washington: National Academy of Sciences.

Bronfenbrenner, U & Morris, P. 2007. 'The bioecological model of human development', in *Handbook of child psychology.* Wiley online library: 795–828. childhelp.org/wp/content/uploads/2015/07/Bronfenbrenner/U.-and/P (Accessed 8 January 2021).

Catron, CE & Allen, J. 2008. *Early childhood curriculum: A creative play model.* Saddle River, NJ: Pearson/Merrill Prentice Hall.

Charlesworth, R. 2004. *Understanding child development.* New York: Delmar.

Conbayir, M. 2017. *Early childhood and neuroscience: Theory, research and implications for practice.* London: Bloomsbury.

Crain, W. 2005. *Theories of development. Concepts and applications.* 5th ed. New York: Pearson Education International.

Davis, K, Christodoulou, J, Seider, S & Gardner, H. 2017. 'The theory of multiple intelligences', in *Cambridge handbook of intelligence*, edited by RJ Sternberg & SB Kaufman. Cambridge: Cambridge University Press. 485–503.

Dawes, A, Biersteker, L, Girdwood, E, Snelling, M & Tredoux, C. 2016. *Early Learning Outcomes Measure (ELOM) technical manual.* Innovation Edge. file:///C:/Users/Lorayne/Downloads/2016-elom-technical-manual.pdf (Accessed 9 January 2021).

Donald, D, Lazarus, S & Lolwana, P. 2006. *Educational psychology in social context.* Oxford: Oxford University Press.

Ettekal, A & Mahoney, JL. 2017. 'Ecological systems theory', in *The SAGE encyclopedia of out-of-school learning*, edited by K Peppler. Thousand Oaks: SAGE Publications. 239–241. https://www.researchgate.net/publication/316046039 (Accessed 8 January 2021).

Ferrante, J, Seedat-Khan, M, Kaziboni, A & Uys, T. 2016. 'The sociological imagination', in *Sociology: A South African perspective,* edited by M Seedat-Khan, ZL Jansen & R Smith. Andover, UK: Cengage.

Gallahue, DL. 1982. *Understanding motor development in children.* New York: John Wiley.

Gallahue, DL & Donnelly, PL. 2003. *Developmental physical education for all children.* Champaign, IL: Human Kinetics.

Gesell, A. 1974. *The first five years of life: A guide to the study of the pre-school child.* London: Methuen.

Gordon, AM & Browne, KW. 2008. *Beginnings and beyond: Foundations in early childhood education.* 8th ed. New York: Thomson Delmar.

Gordon, AM & Browne, KW. 2017. *Beginnings and beyond. Foundations in early childhood education.* Boston, MA: Cengage Learning.

Hill, S. 2001. *Developing early literacy: Assessment and teaching.* Victoria: Eleanor Curtain Publishing.

James, A & Prout, A (eds). 1990. *Constructing and reconstructing childhood. Contemporary issues in the sociological study of childhood.* London: The Falmer Press: 216–238.

Karpov, Y. 2005. *The neo Vygotskian approach to child development.* New York: Cambridge University Press.

Lefrancois, G. 2000. *Psychology for teaching.* Belmont, USA: Wadsworth.

MacNaughton, G. 2003. *Shaping early childhood.* Berkshire: Open University Press.

MacNaughton, G. 2005. *Doing Foucault in early childhood studies.* London: Routledge.

Masuku, J & Ndawi, O. 2001. 'Incorporating local folklore into the school curriculum in southern Africa'. *Education as Change* 5(1): 85–103.

McCown, R, Driscoll, M & Roop, PG. 1996. *Educational psychology. A learning-centered approach to classroom practice.* 2nd ed. Needham Heights, MA: Allyn & Bacon.

Nsamenang, AB & Lamb, ME. 1994. 'Socialization of Nso children in the Bamenda Grassfields of Northwest Cameroon', in *Cross-cultural roots of minority child development,* edited by PM Greenfield & RR Cocking. Lawrence Erlbaum Associates, Inc: 133–146.

Papalia, DE, Olds, SW & Feldman, RD. 2006. *A child's world. Infancy through adolescence.* New York: McGraw-Hill.

Pascal, C & Bertram, T. 2009. 'Listening to young citizens: The struggle to make real a participatory paradigm in research with young children'. *European Early Childhood Education Research Journal* 17(2): 249–262.

Pence, A & Nsamenang, B. 2008. 'A case for early childhood education in sub-Saharan Africa. Early childhood development', in *Beyond quality in early childhood education,* edited by M Garcia & J Evans. New York: UNICEF.

Penn, H. 2005. *Unequal childhoods.* London: Routledge.

Piaget, J. 1964. 'Piaget rediscovered', in *Readings in learning and human abilities: Educational psychology,* edited by RE Ripple & VN Rockcastle. Ithaca: Cornell University Press: 7–20.

Piaget, J. 1997. 'Development and learning', in *Readings on the development of children,* edited by M Gauvin & M Cole. New York: Scientific American: 20–28.

Pritchard, A. 2005. *Ways of learning. Learning theories and learning styles in the classroom.* London: David Fulton.

Prout, A & James, A. 1997. 'A new paradigm for the sociology of childhood? Provenance, promise and problems', in *Constructing and reconstructing childhood. Contemporary issues in the sociology of childhood,* edited by A James & A Prout. London: Falmer Press: 7–34.

Santrock, JW. 2003. *Psychology.* Boston: McGraw-Hill.

Singer, DG & Revenson, TA. 1996. *A Piaget primer. How a child thinks.* New York: Penguin.

Swartz, L, De La Rey, C & Duncan, N. 2004. *Psychology: An introduction.* Oxford: Oxford University Press.

Vygotsky, L. 1978. *Mind in society. The development of higher mental processes.* Cambridge, MA: Harvard University Press.

Vygotsky, LS. 1986. *Thought and language.* Cambridge, MA: MIT Press.

Walsh, D. 2005. 'Development theory and early childhood education: Necessary but not sufficient', in *Critical issues in early childhood education*, edited by N Yelland. Berkshire: Open University Press.

Wyness, M. 2012. *Childhood and society*. 2nd ed. Hampshire: Macmillan.

GLOSSARY

Agency – the active participation of individuals to bring about change as they shape and influence their daily life

Bioecological systems theory – Bronfenbrenner's theory that human beings always develop in a particular context, which is embedded in a cluster of systems that interact with each other (see Chapter 2)

Environment – the world around us

Kinaesthetic – regarding movement and one's ability to control bodily movements and to handle objects skilfully

Nervous system – a very complex system in the body made up of the brain, spinal cord and nerves, the main job of which is to carry the information from the body to the brain and send out instructions

Sociocultural approach – an approach that considers the influence of cultural and social environments on children's development

Sociology – the study of the social behaviour of humans, which also explores the meanings that they make from their lives

Voice – a concept which, when used with children, indicates that they are knowledgeable and competent, and what they say can and should be highly valued and respected

Chapter 3

Guiding principles of the Grade R curriculum, teaching and learning

Linda Rutgers

In this chapter we consider

- a curriculum and what it entails in Grade R
- the guiding principles of early childhood education (ECE)
- the value of each principle
- the domains of holistic development
- the awareness that children have a voice and agency, and should be active participants in decision making that affects them
- appropriate teaching and learning activities in the Grade R classroom that are based on the different principles of ECE.

INTRODUCTION: THE GRADE R CURRICULUM AND THE PRINCIPLES THAT GUIDE IT

This chapter considers the role of the guiding principles in the implementation of a quality curriculum in Grade R. A curriculum in terms of this book is defined as everything that happens in the school day: the teaching, the learning and the understandings children gain from their experiences in class. The curriculum therefore is made up of the following:
- The learning environment: the layout of the classroom, the outdoor play area
- The learning materials
- The teaching content, and the methods the teacher uses to mediate it
- The assessment strategies.

This is influenced by the teacher's knowledge of children (see Chapter 4) as well as factors such as socio-economic realities that impact learning and teaching (see Chapter 2, Bronfenbrenner). The curriculum is realised through the daily programme. This is made up of three parts, namely teacher-guided activities, child-initiated activities and routines (see Chapter 7).

The guiding principles are meant to be a compass for the Grade R teacher. The six principles provide a backdrop against which curriculum planning, in teacher education settings and in schools, can be done and against which the nature of Grade R classroom practice can be showcased. They guide Grade R teachers in understanding the elements and the nature of the Grade R daily programme, to select their strategies and teaching and learning materials, and to determine the nature of their roles as mediators, facilitators and teachers. The principles that are highlighted in this chapter were compiled using research-based content from different national and international sources that focus on ECE.

PRINCIPLE 1: EMPHASISE HOLISTIC DEVELOPMENT
What does this principle entail?

ECE subscribes to a holistic perspective of child development. This means that teachers and caregivers working with young children (and their families) value and intentionally address the following key domains of children's education, growth and development: physical, perceptual-motor, social, emotional, cognitive and moral/spiritual. Development and learning in each domain influence the other domains, which is the rationale behind the holistic development of the young child.

The physical domain

This involves the development of the whole body, as well as the gross and fine motor skills, nutrition and basic needs such as clothing and hygiene. The five senses – eyes (visual), ears (auditory), skin (tactile), nose (olfactory – smell) and tongue (gustatory – taste) – play an instrumental role in the development of perceptual skills in young children, which are essential for their later literacy and mathematics progress. Young children use all of their senses to explore and perceive their environment.

One of the most important physical changes in the preschool years is the growth and development of the brain (see Chapter 2). Grade R children are in control of their general gross motor movements, such as walking, running, jumping and climbing. They have better control over their gross motor movements than their fine ones. Movement is very important during the preschool phase, because it is through movement that children expand their experiences, increase their awareness of both their body and its capabilities, and deepen their knowledge of the world around them. Opportunities must be created to develop both gross and fine motor skills (see Chapter 4).

The cognitive domain

This refers to the intellectual functions of the young child, which includes intelligence, perception, linguistic development and communication, thinking, reasoning and information processing. Ninety per cent of the brain's growth occurs in the first five years of the child's life. The brain is made up of neurons (nerve cells) which connect to each other through neural pathways.

Appropriate movement experiences stimulate and develop the neural pathways. These allow us to take in information from the world (sensations), interpret them (in the brain) and respond (motor movements). Appropriate learning experiences enhance the interconnectivity between the neurons (different nerves) and establish many different neural pathways (Excell & Linington, 2011).

One of the important ways to enhance the child's cognitive development is to create an environment where the child is stimulated to do things, to experiment, and to listen and learn from each other and adults.

The emotional domain

The child develops a greater awareness of his/her emotions, and feelings such as joy, fear and happiness as well as an enhanced ability to self-regulate these emotions. The young child's emotional development is influenced by different factors, such as his/her sociocultural background, types of educational experiences, parents' socio-economic status (for example total family income) and the rules of the community. Through meaningful interaction with the environment, experiences and people, the child learns understanding and develops a positive self-image. A stable learning environment is required for successful learning.

The social domain

This is the development of the child's awareness of his/her social side. The child develops a sense of self as a social being in a social world that includes the broader community. The young child develops a sense of identity, strong interpersonal relationships and awareness of self in relation to others. Young children's egotistic behaviour decreases as they grow older (see Chapter 2), and more acceptable behaviour and attitudes develop. They learn, for example, responsibility, turn taking and the ability to make good choices where necessary.

The moral/spiritual domain

This refers to the child's increasing understanding of what is right and wrong, good and bad, and acceptable and unacceptable behaviour. Children should be active participants in the decision-making process, and their voice and opinions acknowledged. Young children are guided by the teacher or other adults to make the best choices possible and to take responsibility for them. The teachers'/caregivers' aim is to develop a strong moral sense in them.

Characteristics of moral and spiritual development include the following:
- The ability to differentiate between good and bad
- Appreciation and respect for others
- The ability to control behaviour
- Knowledge of oneself, and one's values and beliefs.

> **Something to consider**
>
> Norms will differ from culture to culture, and perhaps even from home to home. Consideration therefore must always be given to each child's specific context.

How is this principle manifested in the classroom?

Physical development

Physical development and movement education are important during early childhood as children continue to expand their repertoire of physical skills. Development in the psychomotor domain involves learning to coordinate gross and fine motor movements, and demonstrates physical capabilities appropriate to the child's stage of development and context. During early years, the fine and gross motor skills of children are developed and they become interested in performing well in activities like handwriting and mathematics. The ECE curriculum should therefore provide guidelines for the development of physical skills that include fine and gross motor development and coordination to assist the promotion of early handwriting skills such as patterns and letter formation.

Aspects of perceptual and fine motor development are of particular significance in helping children acquire the readiness skills for later formal literacy and mathematics competence (see chapters 4, 11, 12 and 13). Many of the skill areas of the creative and physical motor domains overlap, such as dance, movement and physical exercise (see Chapter 14). Overlapping of activities of the different domains is a characteristic feature of the integrated Grade R curriculum. Children learn as they move around and explore their environment. They experience the world through physical activity such as walking, running, jumping and climbing. Children from birth onward must therefore have regular opportunities to use their muscles and thus develop their gross and fine motor skills through play in well-planned spaces, both outdoors and indoors (see Chapter 7). A simple dance activity or playing with sand and water stimulates, in a fun play context, physical growth, cognitive activity such as language development, and emotional stability.

Emotional development

An ECE curriculum should recognise the central importance of emotions in a child's development. Curriculum goals, activities and teacher–child relationships need to take this into account. In a child-centred curriculum, children approach materials and activities with enthusiasm, and are optimistic about their ability to figure things out and to be assisted in their learning experience by adults and other children whenever they need it. With a child-centred curriculum, the teachers create relationships that support the emotional development of a child. Planned activities, where children are encouraged to play freely, draw and discuss important issues help to build a strong link between affective and cognitive development. Activities that promote emotional expression, like music and creative art, should feature prominently in a well-planned ECE curriculum (see Chapter 14).

Social development

Research shows that children prefer to work in cooperation with one another and to get help from peers rather than teachers (Vygotsky, 1978). Vygotsky held the view that children develop within their social world and that peer interactions are important in fostering higher levels of cognitive and social development. This results, it is claimed, in more turn-taking behaviours, which generates closer bonds with peers and also increases participation in educational and cooperative play activities. Thus to enhance social development, a skilful teacher should be guided by a curriculum that allows for social interaction such as opportunities for conversations and working in pairs. In the Grade R classroom, teachers should encourage children to develop an awareness of healthy lifestyles (see Chapter 14). They should also help children create strong, positive self-images through affirming their acts of kindness, perseverance and sharing.

Cognitive development

Children do not only grow physically during early childhood, but intellectually as well. Children of this age continue to advance their skills in observing via the senses and interacting with the world around them. They also improve their skills of processing, storing and using information. There is an appropriate prescribed curriculum that guides teachers in how to assist young children in the development of emergent literacy and mathematics skills. The Grade R daily programme provides opportunities, activities and materials that can integrate and enhance physical, social and emotional as well as cognitive domains, and thus provide a holistic development, which ensures overall enrichment and growth (see Chapter 7). Much of cognitive development occurs while Grade R children are involved in different types of educational and play activities during their day programme.

Moral/spiritual development

Teachers of young children create opportunities throughout the day to develop a sense of right or wrong. The introduction of classroom rules very early in the year creates an awareness of acceptable and unacceptable classroom behaviour. Young children from diverse sociocultural and economic backgrounds participate in cooperative activities where they learn to respect each other's cultural habits and traditions. A consistent and positive approach to the classroom management system helps to develop a strong character in young children.

> **Something to consider**
>
> **What is the value of this principle?**
> Giving emphasis to cognitive and physical development is very important, but neglecting emotional and social as well as moral aspects would be harmful to young children. Neglecting any one of the holistic domains would lead to an unbalanced developmental process. Children who are physically ill or malnourished are unlikely to feel very good about themselves emotionally. They may experience self-doubt, which is likely to impact negatively on their intellectual and creative performance. It is therefore essential to emphasise holistic development and integrated curriculum approaches that allow children to express themselves creatively, using the whole body and all their senses to acquire new knowledge, skills and abilities as well as the necessary attitudes and values to engage in independent learning (see Chapter 2).

PRINCIPLE 2: A THEMATIC AND INTEGRATED CURRICULUM

What does this principle entail?

Learning is guided by a planned, integrated curriculum with identified developmental outcomes that are age and stage appropriate, culturally responsive and take into account the development of the 'whole' child. The idea of a 'whole child' carries with it the understanding that the child's voice and agency (see Chapter 2) must be included in the choice of a theme. To provide conceptually rich teaching and learning opportunities, a thematic approach to teaching and learning is suggested in the Grade R classroom. Teachers, preferably in negotiation with children, select age- and developmentally appropriate and culturally sensitive themes that can be used as a framework for teaching and learning that integrates literacy, mathematics and life skills. Educational methods and activities are based upon themes in which children are interested and which are appropriate for young learners. The themes are reflected in the different learning corners/areas, on classroom walls and through the resources. Teachers act as facilitators and/or mediators of the learning process, and support the children's initiatives. The teaching–learning methods are based on a participatory child-centred pedagogy, which follows a developmentally and contextually appropriate and culturally responsive approach. These place the child at the centre of planning with the understanding that the learning content should reflect what is appropriate and of interest to the child.

How is this principle manifested in the classroom?

Teaching and learning strategies used in the Grade R classroom include child-initiated play opportunities (unstructured play) as well as teacher-guided (more structured) play. Teacher-guided activities could include storytelling, songs, rhymes, poetry, drama and other forms of art. Suitable themes are selected and covered throughout the year. Each theme is usually covered over one to two weeks and should include, quite naturally, opportunities for the promotion of emergent literacy and mathematics as well as life skills activities.

> **Something to consider**
>
> **What is the value of this principle?**
> Learning is not seen as an isolated activity. Each young child has a unique sociocultural background and ongoing experiences that can support the learning process. Context-focused learning experiences support learning through association, experiential learning and child-centred learning approaches. If young children's school learning experiences are matched with their home learning experiences where possible, they have more confidence and are more comfortable in participating in the learning experiences offered by the teacher.

PRINCIPLE 3: LANGUAGE AS A TOOL FOR LEARNING AND THINKING IN A STRUCTURED AND STIMULATING LEARNING ENVIRONMENT

What does this principle entail?

The stages from birth to six years of age are critical for language development and thinking. Language knowledge, skills and vocabulary allow children to respond actively to learning opportunities. Language development is usually associated with the cognitive domain as it involves much mental activity. The more interaction children have with language, the more quickly they will learn to understand, think and use it. From birth, young children gradually learn language by listening, imitating sounds, interpreting meaning, speaking and producing relevant sounds in context. The youngest infants respond to words and sounds with a turn of the head even when they are unable to reproduce an equivalent sound. Oral language development improves the young learners' ability to concentrate, think, pay careful attention and engage in meaningful conversations. By modelling and practising correct language in context, learners' thinking and communication ability is enhanced.

If there is a mismatch between the home language and the language of learning and teaching in schools (LoLT), this presents specific challenges to the teacher (see Chapter 12). Parents of Grade R children should be informed about the benefits of mother tongue instruction in the Foundation Phase (see Chapter 11). The reality is, however, that many children are, through parental choice, learning through a second or third language.

Language is best learned by young children in 'language-rich' and 'print-rich' environments. Such enriched learning environments stimulate young children to observe and respond through language to the learning and teaching materials that they see in the classroom. Emphasis in Grade R should be on children making meaning as opposed to producing the standard or 'correct' form of the LoLT.

A variety of teaching and learning materials will allow the young learners to explore, experiment, interact and construct new knowledge and learning experiences. Teaching and learning materials should consist of concrete materials that can be manipulated, such as real objects for discussion (literacy) and counting (mathematics), and semi-concrete materials such as pictures and cut-outs for interactive learning. Activities that include colour and texture are recommended to stimulate visual and tactile development.

The integrated thematic curriculum approach provides various opportunities for children to practise and develop their cognitive skills as they acquire and relate new information about their environment. It also provides opportunities for the teacher to model correct language usage, which is an important component in language development whether it occurs during free outside play, organised play indoors or reading aloud. Story time is possibly the most enjoyable and valuable listening activity during the Grade R daily programme. Effective communication between the teacher and the children is the basis of all the activities done in Grade R (Davin, 2013).

How is this principle manifested in the classroom?

The Grade R daily programme offers many opportunities for interaction during every activity that the children are involved in, both inside and outside the classroom. Children's existing vocabulary is expanded through regular communication and effectively planned discussions. Teachers should strive to introduce as many new words as are relevant to the theme every day, especially when the theme or sub-themes are introduced and discussed in the discussion ring. Daily storybook reading, interesting theme discussions and deep conversations with learners will definitely improve young learners' classroom language and thinking. Strategies such as 'show and tell' and impromptu storytelling offer informal speaking opportunities.

> **Something to consider**
>
> **What is the value of this principle?**
> The young child's language is part of his/her being. Being able to speak a language promotes a sense of identity and adds to the development of self-esteem. The Grade R curriculum typically centres on language – not only reading, writing, speaking and listening, but also the language of numbers, spatial relationships, thinking out problems, and expressing oneself through the arts. Children's effective use of oral language can improve their self-confidence and socialisation skills. The language needs of children from diverse cultural and linguistic backgrounds must be acknowledged and accommodated in the classroom.

PRINCIPLE 4: LEARNING THROUGH PLAY
What does this principle entail?

Play is central to the curriculum, allowing children to be active learners, interacting with a wide variety of materials and engaging with projects and learning areas/corners in the process. Play involves cognitive thinking processes, such as creativity, communication, imagination and problem solving. Children learn best through their play and interaction with the environment. According to Wood (2009), play gives young children the freedom to address their needs and follow their interests through exploration and discovery. The different domains of play include construction play, adventure play, creative play, physical play, imaginative play as well as technological play, which has become more prevalent in the past few years.

Play is central to constructivist, developmentally appropriate pedagogy, as it is during both teacher-guided and free play that children engage in 'hands-on' interaction with objects and act out real-life experiences. As young children of different ages manipulate things, interact with people and participate in various events, they are able to engage in critical thinking and construct their own understandings and knowledge of the world. Play is a natural activity and through spontaneous play, learning is usually enhanced. Through child-initiated play, children orientate themselves in the real world of space, time, people and structures, without the help of the teacher. The Grade R classroom environment is structured to include learning spaces and corners to model real-life experiences. The fantasy play area, such as a street scene, the garden, the shop corner and the 'toy' house are examples of such learning spaces that form part of the Grade R classroom. During play, children refine their motor skills, learn how to deal with their own feelings and emotions, think critically about a range of new experiences, learn to interact sociably with others and resolve conflicts in negotiated and often appropriate ways. Children also develop their imagination and creativity as they experiment, discover and dramatise what they see happening around them. A word of warning, however – specific forms of play can marginalise some children and reinforce gender and other stereotypes (see Chapter 10).

Play is the main vehicle through which children integrate knowledge in a meaningful way, learn self-expression and gain a sense of competence. Play is an enjoyable activity and therefore promotes a positive disposition and love of learning in children. The activities followed in a quality play-based curriculum should represent a rich resource of culturally responsive, developmentally appropriate ideas that teachers can use to interest and engage children in learning through play. Play reflects children's own cultures, values, rules and norms of society (see Chapter 2).

How is this principle manifested in the classroom?

The Grade R learning environment is organised to facilitate play in a number of ways. The fantasy area (see Chapter 7) is equipped with resources that allow for imaginative play and learning. Cognitive games allow the child the opportunity to manipulate educational toys and games, and to develop fine and gross motor skills, and reasoning and problem-solving skills. Outside games with balls, hoops and beanbags develop perceptual-motor skills and coordination. The outside play area, such as a mini-town and cycle track, highlights the importance of road safety and safety in general (see Chapter 14).

> **Something to consider**
>
> **What is the value of this principle?**
> During play activities, the Grade R teacher acts as the facilitator and mediator of learning. Although the children have the freedom to select the type of play activities that they want to participate in, the teacher carefully selects the play resources for an exciting learning space for children. The teacher provides a wide variety of opportunities for individual and group exploration and different interpretation of activities. Play allows young children to enjoy, to participate and to communicate freely with others, and to work together in a group.
>
> *What if ...*
> You are appointed as the new Grade R teacher at a primary school. At the first parents evening you have to explain to them the value of play-based learning in Grade R. Which aspects will you highlight in your presentation to the parents? (See Chapter 10 for possible ideas.)

PRINCIPLE 5: CHILD-CENTRED APPROACH
What does this principle entail?

Child-centred pedagogy supports the view that children's ability and enthusiasm are important in learning. The child is seen as the point of departure in the planning of teaching and learning programmes. Teachers should acknowledge what the children bring to the learning process and extend their current learning. Intellectual challenges and a safe space are important in child-centred pedagogy.

Some teachers work in challenging circumstances with more children in a group than is desirable. However, in such circumstances, making each child feel that he/she is a special individual is not an impossible task. Getting to know each child well allows the teacher to meet individual particular needs. Some children are happy with a simple acknowledging touch or smile from the adult, whereas others need further reassuring hugs and conversation. Recognising and responding to children's individual needs is particularly important for young infants, toddlers and children with special developmental and learning needs. Differences in learning styles, and performance and motivation levels must always be borne in mind. Girls and boys alike must be encouraged to pursue their individual interests and engage in learning activities without the limitations imposed by gender stereotyping (see Chapter 10).

How is this principle manifested in the classroom?

The individual child's needs, interests, style and pace of learning are important and must be respected and considered in planning learning experiences and assessment. Children learn more effectively when:
- they are actively involved and engaged in the learning process
- teaching and learning allows for experimentation, exploration and discovery learning
- the daily programme is flexible and can be adapted to the learning needs of individual children
- a variety of teaching and learning strategies is applied during the learning experience
- they can exercise choices in the learning content and procedures
- the emphasis on the teaching approach is on process rather than product.

> **Something to consider**
>
> **What is the value of this principle?**
>
> When children are taught in ways that match their learning styles, the learning outcomes are likely to improve. It is also important to engage children in learning contexts where the style adopted is different from their preferred learning style. For example, a visual learner should also have exposure to listening activities.

PRINCIPLE 6: DIVERSITY, EQUITY AND CULTURALLY RESPONSIVE PEDAGOGY

What does this principle entail?

Culturally responsive pedagogy recognises the reality of diversity and equity and how important it is to consider this in our teaching practice. The school and the classroom are a microcosm of society. This means that the school and its professional practice acknowledge the culture of the community and appreciate the learners as individuals. They welcome those from diverse backgrounds and adapt teaching to their needs to ensure equitable learning opportunities. Issues of socio-economic disparity, race, class, gender and sexuality are part of our children's lives and as teachers we need to address possible inequalities and respond to them appropriately.

How is this principle manifested in the classroom?

A number of strategies to encourage cultural awareness and inclusivity are suggested here:
- *Recognise and get to know each individual child as a unique human being worthy of respect*
  Teachers should try to understand each child in their class. This will include knowing their personal and socio-economic backgrounds, strengths and weaknesses, preferred learning style, interests and fears. Create a safe space where the children can voluntarily share their stories and participate in daily discussions.

- *Acknowledge and embrace children's funds of knowledge*
  The Grade R learners are individuals who each bring a myriad of own experiences and knowledge into the classroom. It would be beneficial for learners if teachers could avoid having an authoritative approach to teaching and acknowledge the funds of knowledge of the learners when planning and presenting lessons. Funds of knowledge can be described as the background knowledge and skills that young children accumulate through their cultural, family and home experiences (Hedges, 2007). Funds of knowledge develop when children 'read' books, play and participate in family activities such as eating together, going on holiday or watching television programmes.
- *Practise a strong sense of cultural awareness and sensitivity*
  Teachers should reflect on their own knowledge and understandings of diversity and broaden their sensitivity to every child's culture. Teachers should try and ensure that all children see themselves as equally important members of the class despite their different culture, beliefs and language usage.
- *Carefully consider cultural diversity in activity plan content*
  Activity plans, discussions and the choice of resources and activities must be relevant and appropriate for all the learners. Where practical, use real-world issues and examples to allow all the children to connect to and understand the content, and benefit from the learning experience. Invite speakers from diverse communities to address and/or present content to the learners.

Something to consider

What is the value of this principle?

All children can benefit from culturally responsive teaching because it encourages multicultural awareness and acceptance of difference which will help them thrive in a diverse society. When teachers get to know their young children and understand who they are and what has shaped them, they are in a better position to identify the children's strengths and needs.

When teachers create a learning environment that recognises and encourages children's individual identities, funds of knowledge, sense of belonging and agency, their motivation to learn is increased. Teachers validate these funds of knowledge when they use them as a resource to enhance young children's learning. Teachers practising diversity and culturally responsive teaching see children for who they are and affirm their uniqueness as children who deserve equal opportunities.

Questions for reflection and discussion

Discuss how the ECE principles that are mentioned in this chapter can be used to:
- plan a relevant and responsive ECE curriculum
- determine effective strategies for facilitation
- select appropriate teaching and learning materials
- plan and set out the Grade R classroom and outdoor learning environment
- enhance learning for the young child across many areas.

CASE STUDY

This case study provides an idea of how the school day might be structured in a particular Grade R classroom and a few of the activities which may take place throughout that day.

Lively five-year-olds from diverse cultural backgrounds enter the Grade R classroom first thing in the morning. They greet one another, put away their belongings, and begin another exciting day in school. The teacher greets the children and gives them an opportunity to talk about what happened on the way to school. A variety of activities occurs during the morning activity time, such as a discussion on a topic, 'reading' books, singing a song related to the theme, and working with manipulatives while the children are sitting on the mat. You can hear lots of productive conversation. The theme which the children have been learning about for the week is plant and animal life. Later, some of the children work together to create a mural. Some children paint the sky and the ground. Others use sponges to paint the grass and the ponds. While the mural is drying, the children draw pictures of their favourite plants and animals. The children cut out their drawings and paste them onto the mural. The snack routine follows with children sitting quietly at their tables and enjoying their sandwiches. The day continues to be a mixture of small and large group work, and activity centre and individual activities. Activities range from quiet listening to active moving. The children participate in movement education which incorporates balance, flexibility and using their bodies to form shapes of letters which they have been learning. Later in the music ring, the children move to the music and create flowing movements with their bodies and colourful scarves. There is much laughter and enjoyment. The teacher encourages the children to be responsible, to clear away their materials when finished and to take pride in their work. Storytime marks the end of the school day. As the teacher reflects on how the daily programme has unfolded, she gains satisfaction from the children's obvious joy in learning.

Question

Discuss the suitability of the structure and the activities that are described in the case study in relation to the guiding principles of ECE.

SUMMARY

A quality Grade R curriculum follows all the principles discussed in this chapter. These have stressed that a teacher must consider linguistic and other diversity issues at each stage of planning and implementation. Teachers must also reflect on the curriculum they will follow and whether the choices they make support holistic development and developmentally and culturally responsive practice. The principles discussed in this chapter ask the teacher to think in a particular way about the focus of ECE. They stress the importance of ensuring that all children are provided with age- and developmentally appropriate and culturally responsive and sensitive learning opportunities that will provide a solid foundation for future learning success. The principles discussed provide a framework that informs early childhood education, Grade R programme development, culturally and contextually appropriate classroom practice, and the planning of learning experiences.

BIBLIOGRAPHY

Cazden, CB. 1988. *Classroom discourse: The language of teaching and learning.* Portsmouth: Heinemann. (ERIC Document no ED383404).

Davin, R (ed). 2013. *Handbook for Grade R teaching.* Cape Town: Pearson Education South Africa (Pty) Ltd.

De Witt, M. 2010. *The young child in context.* Pretoria: Van Schaik.

Excell, L & Linington, V. 2011. 'Moving to literacy: Fanning emergent literacy in early childhood education in a pedagogy of play'. *South African Journal of Childhood Education* 1(2): 27–45.

Hedges, H. 2007. *Funds of knowledge in early childhood communities of inquiry.* Doctoral dissertation. Palmerston North, New Zealand: Massey University.

Joubert, I, Bester, M & Meyer, E. 2008. *Literacy in the Foundation Phase.* Pretoria: Van Schaik.

Miller, L & Pound, L. 2011. *Theories and approaches to learning in the early years.* London: SAGE.

Morrow, LM. 2007. *Developing literacy in pre-school.* London: The Guilford Press.

Neaum, S. 2012. *Language and literacy for the early years.* London: SAGE.

O'Carroll, S & Hickman, R. 2012. *Narrowing the literacy gap.* Cape Town: Wordworks.

Pahl, K & Rowsell, J. 2012. *Literacy and education.* London: SAGE.

Palaiologou, I. 2013. *The early years foundation stage. Theory and practice.* London: SAGE.

Vygotsky, LS. 1978. *Mind in society: The development of higher psychological processes.* London: Harvard University Press.

Whitehead, M. 2010. *Language and literacy in the early years 0–7.* London: SAGE.

Wild, M & Street, A. 2013. *Themes and debates in early childhood.* London: SAGE.

Wood, E. 2009. 'Developing a pedagogy of play', in *Early childhood education: Society and culture,* edited by A Anning, J Cullen & M Fleer. London: SAGE: 27–38.

GLOSSARY

Domain of development – a broad area or dimension of development, each equally important to the child's learning, health and well-being, and including social, emotional, language, cognition and physical aspects

Emergent literacy – the gradual development of literate skills and behaviour as children are exposed to a literacy-rich environment before they start formal learning in schools

Fine motor development – the development of the small muscles, for example hands, fingers, toes, tongue, cheek, eyes

Gross motor development – the development of the large muscles, for example those in the legs or arms

Instrumental – important in contributing to the development of young children

Learning styles – a particular way of learning that works best for the individual, for example through a visual medium, through listening (auditory), through movement (kinaesthetically) or through hands-on activities

Pedagogy – the methods and practices of teaching

Process approach – an approach which emphasises the processes involved in the activity rather than the finished (or end) product

Product approach – an approach which emphasises the end product (ie the final goal) rather than an approach which values the actual engagement with the activity

Self-image – one's opinion of the self

Show and tell – a chance for preschool children to bring an object to class to show the other children and explain what it is all about, an activity which allows them to use language, conceptual thinking and storytelling skills

Chapter 4

Knowing the Grade R child

Annemarie Loubser

In this chapter we consider

- the transition to both Grade R and formal schooling, and the needs of children in both contexts
- the holistic development of the Grade R child with particular reference to perceptual-motor development
- the child from both a developmental and sociological perspective.

INTRODUCTION: WHO IS THE GRADE R CHILD?
A developmental and sociological perspective

One can think of children in different ways. One way, which this book supports, is to view them through a lens of being, belonging and becoming.

A *being child* in his/her current phase of development is seen as capable and competent. Children's competencies and capabilities are acknowledged, and their voice and agency are recognised, as is the contribution they can make as young citizens in their own right. Teachers following this perspective should identify children's strengths and use them as a base for learning and teaching. This does not mean, however, that possible difficulties are ignored.

The idea of a *belonging child* is not new, as the importance of emotional and social development has always been highlighted in early childhood education (ECE), but the focus has shifted. The notion of a belonging child focuses on the importance of respecting children for who they are at this point so that they feel comfortable and accepted in their current context without their gender or culture influencing this acceptance. This view, which reinforces a positive view of identity, informs a contextually appropriate and culturally responsive perspective on childhood.

The idea of a *becoming child* places much more emphasis on developmental norms and what the child still needs to achieve. As a result, the focus has often tended to be on what the child cannot yet do as opposed to what he/she can. This focus on what the child cannot do has given rise to a lot of criticism about developmental theories, developmental norms and developmentally appropriate practice (see Chapter 2 for criticism on the idea of the universal child). However, developmental theories and developmentally appropriate practice (DAP) cannot be ignored and should inform teachers' practice, but, as we have already argued, they are not enough on their own. The idea of a being and a belonging child must also be taken into consideration when decisions are made about the child's development and learning. As the child refines developmental skills and concepts, the teacher should promote the concept of a being and belonging child who will be gaining in independence as he/she acquires self-help skills, builds self-esteem and is recognised as a powerful player in his/her own right.

All young children can be viewed through these lenses. Grade R children, as we have already mentioned, are those who will enter formal schooling in Grade 1 in the following year. First, however, we need to consider their entry into Grade R. You can draw on the idea of a being and belonging child to begin to understand the needs of a young child entering Grade R, and perhaps any form of schooling. This supporting framework is now widely accepted. It emphasises relationships, both with the self and others. In fact, the Early Years Learning Framework for Australia is called *Belonging, Being and Becoming*.

Find out more

Consult the following website for further insights into this informing framework:

https://www.acecqa.gov.au/sites/default/files/2018-02/belonging_being_and_becoming_the_early_years_learning_framework_for_australia.pdfhttps://

WELCOMING THE CHILD INTO GRADE R

It is natural for the Grade R child to be terrified and/or excited on the first day of school. While Grade R is an exciting time, it can also be quite stressful for both the child and the parents/caregivers. To remove the first day's jitters/anxiety and uncertainty, it is a good idea to have an open day at the end of the previous year to ease the transition from home or an early childhood development (ECD) site/centre to school. On this day, children and their parents/caregivers can visit the school in advance. School open days give children and their parents/caregivers the opportunity to see the school in action. The parents/caregivers should have a chat with the principal and their child's future teacher, and gain as much information as possible so they can familiarise the child with the context and begin to understand the school culture. The child and the parents/caregiver can both become familiar with the location and the layout of the school. Attending an open day will add to children's confidence when they arrive on their first official day in Grade R, and ensure that they will see some familiar faces such as that of their teacher.

It is a good idea, if possible, to include in the open day some 'independent' activities for the children, such as play dough that does not require supervision from the teacher. Another idea is to give each child, if possible, a 'take-home bag' that includes a fun activity for the child to do during the holiday. Included in the take-home bag could also be a letter from the teacher inviting the child to his/her class the following January.

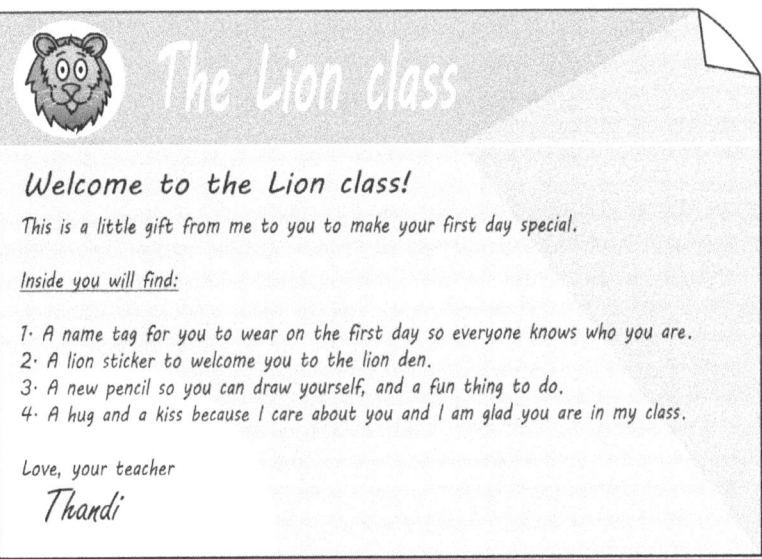

Figure 4.1 Invitation to class next year

Find out more
Also include a letter to the parents with information about the first day of school, the daily programme, and the date and time the school starts.

Advice to parents to help their child adjust to Grade R
While the children are doing their independent activities, you can talk to the parents/caregivers and begin to form a partnership with them in relation to the education of their child. You could suggest that their child is encouraged to become increasingly independent before they come to Grade R, particularly when it comes to dressing, feeding, going to the toilet and washing hands. Make sure the children can undress and dress themselves properly again, such as buttoning a shirt or tying shoelaces. Mastery of these activities will give children the confidence to perform these tasks on their own in Grade R. If possible, let each child spend time with other children entering Grade R so that he/she can begin to establish a friendship base. Another suggestion to parents could be that they encourage their child to role play being in Grade R. Through role play, children begin to explore some of the issues that might be bothering them about the new school year. Advise parents to spend some concentrated time doing activities with their child. These could include reading a book together

for 15 minutes or playing a board game to help the child become mentally prepared for Grade R.

Tell parents that on the first day of school they should plan to get up early to avoid a last-minute rush. They might plan a celebratory breakfast for the child, and/or present the child with a small gift, such as a new bag or lunch box. Pack a change of clothes in the child's bag so that if needed the child has something of his/her own to change into. If the child has a special comfort object such as a favourite stuffed animal or blanket, it should be allowed in class on the first day or two so that the child can feel more comfortable in his/her new surroundings. As the child adapts to the new environment, the comforter will lose importance and may be put in the child's locker and later even left at home.

Tell parents that on the first day of the new year they must take their children into the classroom, show them where to put their belongings and introduce them to the teacher. Parents should arrive at school early so that their child has time to settle down before the school day begins. When parents leave, they should give their child a hug and say when they will be back ('I'll pick you up after lunch') and then the parents MUST leave. Tell parents not to turn around if their child starts crying, as it has been shown that almost as soon as the parent is out of sight, the child will stop. Parents must not linger or sneak out when the child is not looking as this can affect a feeling of trust and weaken the child's sense of belonging in Grade R. Many Grade R teachers allow (or even encourage) parents to stay in the classroom for all or part of the first few days. This can make the child feel more secure. Suggest that parents talk to their child about what happened at school. They should be interested and ask questions which encourage the child to express his/her own ideas.

FIRST DAY IN GRADE R: SUGGESTIONS FOR THE TEACHER

The first day in Grade R may be the first school experience for many children and their first experience of a structured environment. Familiarise children with the indoor and outdoor environment to help them feel safe and comfortable. Show them, for instance, the different areas of the classroom: lockers for bags and lunch boxes, the carpet for ring time and the areas for fantasy play, creative art, etc. Also take them on a tour of the school and show them the bathroom, the office and the outdoor play area. Explain what is considered to be appropriate behaviour in the school context, for example taking turns on swings. After a few days at school when the children have settled, the teacher can include their voices in the choice and implementation of classroom rules.

Ideas for the teacher to keep in mind

Coming to school for the first time is often a traumatic experience for the child. The teacher should ensure that first experiences are both pleasant and challenging. The following should form part of a teacher's checklist:
- The teacher should have an alphabetical list of the names of the children in

his/her class. The register should not be completed before the end of the first week, because changes can occur.
- The teacher should make sure he/she knows which name the child uses and make copies of that name – one for a nametag to pin onto the child, and one for the art wall, the birthday chart and the learner's locker. These nametags form part of incidental 'reading' or environmental print.
- Allocate a specific symbol/picture to each child, which will assist the children in identifying their own space on the wall as well as their own locker. Putting the child's symbol next to the name will also help the child to identify his/her name and might enhance visual literacy. The correct Grade 1 handwriting font should be used at all times.
- An alternative approach, and one that would celebrate a child's identity and create a sense of belonging in the classroom community, is to use a photograph of each child instead of a symbol. A photograph does add a particularly personal touch.

- Get an information book where important information such as observations can be recorded.
- Ensure the classroom is clean, attractive and inviting.
- Design a poster to welcome the newcomers.

- A few bright and appropriate pictures may be put on the walls – any old, faded pictures from previous years should be taken down.
- Plan activities and get ready for the first day beforehand.

Guidelines for teachers' practice

Grade R children can easily become anxious, and therefore the following are important:
- Be kind but firm, fair and consistent when dealing with children. Respect each child's individuality while encouraging group cooperation.
- Assist children in refining essential social skills such as listening, sharing, compromising and turn taking.
- Help them to build mutual trust and respect. One way of doing this is for the teacher as a role model to actively recognise and acknowledge the range of backgrounds of the children and the family's role in their education. This must not be confused with labelling, which often refers to attaching unkind labels such as 'fat', 'stupid' or 'dull' to particular children.

- Be friendly towards all the children, but also keep a little personal 'distance' to try to remain objective about the child and his/her family.
- Quickly establish the patterns and routine for the day at school but remain flexible and sensitive to necessary changes such as a teachable moment.
- Negotiate classroom 'rules' with which everyone agrees, while at the same time leaving these rules open to renegotiation if necessary.
- Reassure children that parents/caregivers/older siblings/taxi drivers will come and fetch them at the agreed time, for example after story time or aftercare.

> **Something to consider**
>
> What would you do to make the transition from home to Grade R easier for the child?

MILESTONES FOR THE GRADE R CHILD

Teachers must both know and acknowledge developmental milestones that align with the 'becoming' child, but they cannot optimise learning for children if they only take note of the 'becoming' child. As we have already mentioned, teachers must know and draw on the different aspects of holistic development (see chapters 2 and 3) and the developmental milestones if they are to optimise learning for every child.

While the stages of development are the same for all children, the ages at which they reach these stages can differ. While the exact developmental timeline differs from child to child, there is a general order and optimal time (window of opportunity) in which milestones should be achieved. Although milestones have been identified for each developmental domain or area, they must be viewed with caution. As we said in previous chapters, there is no such thing as 'the universal child'. Each child is unique, and contextual factors must be taken into account. In this chapter, the milestones for physical, social emotional and cognitive are briefly revisited before exploring perceptual-motor development in depth.

Physical development

Physical and mental health is a state of well-being which increases a child' ability to assimilate knowledge, thus leading, in time, to emotional stability and a positive self-image (Lupua, Elenac & Niculescu, 2014).

Physical development refers further to physical changes in the body and involves changes in bone thickness, size, weight, gross motor, fine motor, vision, hearing and perceptual development. As each physical change occurs, the child gains new abilities. Grade R children should be able to, for example, increase running speed, walk on a thin line and tie their shoelaces. They start to ride a bicycle, often without training wheels, catch a ball with two hands, and drop and catch a bouncing ball. They can balance on one foot for a short period of time, and possess sufficient strength to lift and support their own body weight for a variety of activities (hopping, jumping and hanging). They can skip with both feet, and hop more smoothly. They enjoy physical activity. Acquisition of these skills is, of course, dependent upon the exposure that they have had to particular activities, for example bicycle riding.

Social and emotional development

Being ready for school includes the social and emotional maturity levels of a child.

Social and emotional development is an aspect of child, adolescent and, in fact, lifelong development. It consists of how individuals develop the social skills and emotional maturity to build relationships and relate to other people. Research shows that social and emotional development and behaviour are initially influenced by the home environment and through parental interaction, especially with the mother. Where there are or have been home-based difficulties, early intervention can ease the situation and possibly prevent further social problems such as child neglect and abuse.

Cognitive development

Early childhood is not only a period of amazing physical growth, but it is also a time of remarkable mental development. Cognitive abilities associated with memory, reasoning, problem solving and thinking continue to emerge throughout childhood. By the end of Grade R, children should be able to write their own name and draw a detailed person. They should be able to match most colours, understand numbers and draw with precision and detail. They love to tell longer stories on the same topic, and share jokes and riddles, and begin to understand death and ask many questions about it. They copy an adult's writing and colour pictures carefully, and their attention span increases. They build steps with three to four cubes, copy geometric shapes, and know right from left and their number of fingers.

Table 4.1 Child development milestone chart

AGE	PHYSICAL DEVELOPMENT	SOCIAL AND EMOTIONAL DEVELOPMENT	INTELLECTUAL DEVELOPMENT	LANGUAGE DEVELOPMENT
4 years	• Physically agile, energetic. • Sits with knees crossed. • Skips with alternate feet. • Hops and stands on one foot.	• Plans games cooperatively, especially in groups of two or three children. • Attends to own toilet needs.	• Counts by rote up to 20 but only understands number concept of three or four. • Asks meanings of words.	• Talks fluently. • Uses correct grammar most of the time but still makes errors, eg 'I drawed a picture'.

AGE	PHYSICAL DEVELOPMENT	SOCIAL AND EMOTIONAL DEVELOPMENT	INTELLECTUAL DEVELOPMENT	LANGUAGE DEVELOPMENT
4 years (cont)	• When running, changes direction and can turn a corner. • Goes downstairs one foot per step. • Ball games skills improving – especially aiming. • Throws largish ball with increased body rotation and transfer of weight on feet. • Rides tricycle rapidly, steers smoothly. • Copies a cross. • Builds a tower of 10 cubes. • Can cut out shapes. • Can dress and undress self. • Holds pencil in fist grasp.	• Plans games cooperatively, especially in groups of two or three children. • Attends to own toilet needs. • Starts developing a sense of humour. • Wants to be independent. • Argues with other children if does not get own way. • Can be bossy. • Affectionate towards family and friends. • Exaggerates; tells 'tall stories'. • Has a vivid imagination.	• Counts by rote up to 20 but only understands number concept of three or four. • Asks meanings of words. • Draws a recognisable house. • Still confuses fact and fantasy. • Has an understanding of immediate past and future events. • Starts developing a sense of humour. • Makes up riddles.	• Talks fluently. • Uses correct grammar most of the time but still makes errors, for example 'I drawed a picture'. • Enjoys songs and rhymes. • Vocabulary increases rapidly. • Consistently asks questions. Asks when, why, how questions.
5 years	• Has adult-like posture. • Physically very active. • Well coordinated. Can walk on along a thin line and balance on a beam. • Increases running speed. • Has well-developed ball skills. • Uses whole-body to throw and catch – catches a ball from a distance of one metre. • Can copy an adult's writing.	• Increasing self-confidence. • Chooses own friends. • Dresses and undresses without assistance. • Shows caring attitudes towards others. • Copes well with personal needs. • Accepts and respects authority. • Enjoys group play. • Seldom sees things from another's point of view (remember Piaget in Chapter 2).	• Is very curious. • Sorts objects by a single characteristic/criterion. • Writes name. • Knows address. • Draws a detailed person. • Matches most colours. • Has an increasing understanding of numbers – can count 10 objects. • Gives age. • Understands concepts such as 'more than', 'less than', etc.	• Fluent speech with few infantile substitutions in speech. • Talks about the past, present and future with a good sense of time. • Takes turns in conversations. • Uses about 1 500 words. • Tells a simple story.

AGE	PHYSICAL DEVELOPMENT	SOCIAL AND EMOTIONAL DEVELOPMENT	INTELLECTUAL DEVELOPMENT	LANGUAGE DEVELOPMENT
5 years (cont)	• Colours pictures carefully. • Builds steps with three to four cubes. • Handedness is evident. • Builds steps with 3-4 cubes. • Handedness is evident.		• Has an increasing attention span – approximately 20 minutes. • Draws a man. • Copies a triangle.	
6 years	• Basic gross motor, fine motor and perceptual-motor skills are developed – need refinement. • Boisterous, enjoys physically challenging him/herself. • Learns to skip with a rope. • Rides a bicycle with training wheels and sometimes without. • Copies a diamond. • Knows right from left but is still sometimes hesitant. • Ties shoelaces.	• Tends to be a know-it-all, and freely gives advice. • Is stubborn and demanding. • Is eager for fresh experiences. • May be quarrelsome with friends, which are easily gained and lost. • Increasingly has friends of the same sex. • Believes in rules but not always for him/herself.	• Eager, curious and enthusiastic. • Draws with precision and in detail. • Is developing the skills required to master reading. • May write independently. • Can consider another's point of view. • Sometimes makes use of logical thinking. • Can rote count up to 100. • Has an increasing concentration span. • Likes to work but often does so in spurts.	• Has fluent speech. • Can pronounce majority of the sounds of his/her own language. • Talks fluently and with confidence. • Chatters incessantly. • Often talks with adults rather than to them – able to hold a conversation. • Enjoys jokes and guessing games.

Sources: Adapted from Brewer (2007; Charlesworth (2004); Gordon & Browne (2008); Positive parenting-ally (nd)

Something to consider

Although Table 4.1 categorises the milestones according to developmental domains, it must be noted that many of these milestones could be placed in several domains, which supports the view of holistic development. Milestones are a guide to the stages and ages of behaviour but cannot be seen to be fixed. Remember cultural and contextual factors will always impact development in some way.

Why do you think developmental milestones are important?

PERCEPTUAL-MOTOR DEVELOPMENT AND THE GRADE R CHILD

Perception refers to the process of organising, taking in and interpreting sensory information. Perception is multimodal, with multiple sensory inputs contributing to motor responses. In other words, when input is received through two or more senses, the motor responses are enhanced, for example when an infant turns his/her head in response to the visual cues of the sight of a face and the auditory cues of the sound of a voice. When two or more senses provide overlapping information this is known as intersensory redundancy (California Department of Education, 2020).

The sensory input triggers a specific motor response or type of motor behaviour. The term 'motor behaviour' describes all movements of the body, such as the infant's development of head control and the movements of the eyes (as in a gaze). Gross motor actions include the movement of large limbs or the whole body, as in walking. Fine motor behaviour includes the use of fingers to grasp and manipulate objects. Motor behaviours such as reaching, touching and grasping are forms of exploratory activity, and are dependent on motor development (see Chapter 2 on holistic development). As we have already mentioned, motor development refers to the ongoing, improved ability of children to control their body movements. Infants initially make involuntary random jerking movements such as waving their arms or kicking their legs. They gradually develop voluntary control, which becomes increasingly refined over a period of time. For example, a child progresses from walking at about 13 to15 months, to kicking a ball and then in middle childhood developing complex sports skills (California Department of Education, 2020).

Perceptual-motor development is therefore the ability of the child to take in information through the senses, interpret this information (in the brain) and respond appropriately (a motor response). For example, the child hears a joke, processes the information in the brain and responds by laughing. In this example, the sense is hearing (auditory perception) and the motor (muscle) response involves movement of facial and other muscles. This three-part process (perception, interpretation, response) is central to a child's refinement of his/her perceptual-motor integration and coordination (which is the ability of different body parts to work together rhythmically, for example hand–eye coordination). By the age of six or seven, the perceptual-motor behaviours are generally refined (Gallahue & Donnelly, 2003).

Find out more

According to Ayers (2005), the sensations we experience provide three different sets of information. The first set tells us where our body is in space and how it is moving. This set of information is provided in two ways – first by *proprioceptors*, which process the input about body parts and the body's position in space. This information is received through the muscles, ligaments and joints. For example, we see a step and know we have to move our lower body appropriately. The second way is by the vestibular receptors, which process input about movement, gravity and balance, and receive this input through the inner ear (Kranowitz, 1998).

One must always bear in mind that perceptual-motor development is complex, and draws on many different developmental areas and their related skills. Two key areas are gross and fine motor development.
- **Gross motor (large muscle) development (GMD)** refers to the development of and increased control over the large muscles – the legs, arms, back and shoulders, for example – which are used for walking, sitting, running, jumping, climbing and riding a bike, etc. Both balance and posture are supported by GMD.
- **Fine motor development (FMD)** refers to the development of the small muscles of the fingers, hands, toes and eyes, for example, which are used for activities such as grasping objects, holding, cutting, drawing, buttoning, writing or focusing the eye. These skills are sometimes only refined during Grade 1.

Perceptual-motor activities enable the child to develop greater levels of body control. Young children who possess well-developed perceptual-motor skills are better coordinated and have greater body awareness. This is described by Lundsteen and Tarrow (1981: 213) as 'the recognition of the ways in which the body or parts of the body can be controlled, moved and balanced upon, which can lead to a more positive self-image'. It can also support the development of later school-based skills, for example handwriting. In contrast, children who lack these skills often struggle with coordination and can possess poor body awareness, and therefore feel less confident.

Perceptual-motor behaviours

In addition to the proprioceptors and the vestibular receptors, there are three broad categories of perceptual-motor behaviours that are more commonly foregrounded in studies of early childhood development. To understand this area of development, one should see it as a whole, similar to a tightly woven tapestry where the effect comes from the close weave. The interdependence conveyed by the metaphor of a weave is an integral feature of perceptual-motor development and the refinement of the skills and concepts in this domain that are essential for academic success.

The three categories to which we have referred are as follows:
- Spatial awareness and orientation behaviours, which refer to children's understanding of their bodies and what they can do. They include body awareness and body image, which are, of course, closely related. Body image involves knowledge of the physical structure, movements and functions of the body and its parts, as well as of the position of the body and its parts in relation to one another, to other people and to objects. Awareness of the physical body

is important in the development of the concept of the self as well as in the development of coordination (Lundsteen & Tarrow, 1981: 213).
- Temporal awareness, which refers to children's ability to develop an inner and outer sense of time. An outer sense of time refers to a child's growing awareness of changes in time. An inner sense of time includes coordination and rhythmic movements.
- Sensory awareness behaviours, which refer to children's ability to respond to sensations perceived through the five senses. For successful academic learning, the development of two sensory motor behaviours in particular is crucial, namely auditory and visual perceptual-motor awareness.

Figure 4.2 outlines some perceptual-motor development and behaviours, and illustrates how the acquisition of these behaviours provides a foundation on which more formal academic learning can be based. The example highlights the acquisition of literacy skills. As a result of this, it focuses on only two of the sensory behaviours, namely visual and auditory perceptual-motor behaviours. It does not include tactile, gustatory and olfactory sensory motor behaviours as they play a lesser role in this context.

SPATIAL AWARENESS AND ORIENTATION

Develops through } Gross motor movements: balance, posture, correct sitting position
Fine motor movements: correct pencil grip, turning pages of a book

Position in space: Correct positioning of letters, eg above or below the line
Crossing midline: Being able to write/read across a page
Directionality: Knowing where to start reading/writing – from top to bottom
Laterality: Reading, writing from left to right, identifying and writing letters correctly, eg 'p', 'd', 'h', 'y'

SENSORY AWARENSESS
VISUAL AND AUDITORY
Memory: Being able to remember letters, words and sentences that are seen or heard
Matching/discrimination: Being able to recognise, through sight or hearing, similarities and differences in letters/words
Closure: Being able to close a letter or complete a word, eg an initial 'but' could, depending on the context, lead to 'butterfly'/'butternut'/'butter'
Constancy: Knowing that a letter always represents a specific sound, eg an 'a' is still an 'A'
Figure ground: Being able to pick out a particular letter/word/symbol from a background
Sequence: Being able to put pictures or words in the correct order

TEMPORAL AWARENESS BEHAVIOURS
Rhythm: Fluidity in speaking, reading and writing
Coordination: Hand–eye coordination, etc
Sense of time: Timing of utterances, use of pause, etc

} PROMOTES ACADEMIC LITERACY

Figure 4.2 Perceptual-motor development and behaviours supporting academic learning

The relationship between gross motor development and specific perceptual-motor behaviours, and fine motor development and specific perceptual-motor behaviours is shown in figures 4.3 and 4.7 respectively.

SPATIAL AWARENESS AND ORIENTATION BEHAVIOURS

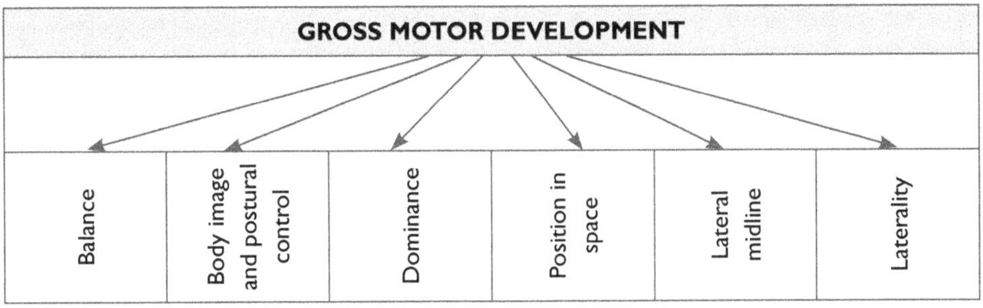

GROSS MOTOR DEVELOPMENT					
Balance	Body image and postural control	Dominance	Position in space	Lateral midline	Laterality

Figure 4.3 Gross motor development

Balance

Balance is how a child is able to keep steady and not fall over when, for example, moving the two sides of his/her body. When children can balance themselves, they begin to realise that the body consists of two parts – a left and a right side. Being able to balance is the first step in the development of other perceptual-motor behaviours such as crossing the midline and laterality.

> **Try this out**
> Use the following activities to help children with balance:
> - Place a balancing beam or a plank of strong wood on the ground or raise it above the ground using, for example, bricks so that the child can walk along the plank.
> - Place a ladder flat on the ground. Let the child walk between the rungs, and then on the rungs only.
> - Children can also be encouraged to walk backwards or to walk on their heels or on tiptoe.

Body image and postural control

Posture refers to how children hold their body when standing, walking, sitting, etc. Good body image and postural control allow them to complete a task in the best body position. Children with postural control problems may struggle to keep their balance when their eyes are closed, and perform poorly in movement activities such as running. They might have poor posture when standing or sitting at a table or on the floor. They might support their head with their hand while their elbow rests on the table, possibly drool excessively and show poor physical endurance. They might be fidgety, rock/move in a chair, and have poor levels of attention or concentration.

Try this out

The following exercises/activities help children with posture and body image problems:
- Encourage children to move by asking them to help with small tasks.
- Offer activities at different levels, for example table-top, carpet and standing activities.
- Encourage children to sit properly, for instance crossed-legged on the floor, not on their haunches or with legs in a w-shape.
- Encourage children to strengthen their jaw muscles by blowing bubbles with soapy water.
- Actively promote outdoor play on large equipment such as swings, jungle gyms and ropes.
- Ask children to touch the part of their body as they are called out, and to show parts of the body on dolls, animals or other children.

Spatial orientation/position in space

Perception of position in space is the understanding children have of their position in relation to another person or object. For example, they know whether an object is behind, in front of, above, below or alongside them. If this understanding is not well developed, their world can appear distorted, and they can become clumsy and hesitant about their movements. They may also not understand concepts such as 'in', 'out', 'up', 'down', 'in front of', 'behind', or 'left' or 'right'.

Children with spatial relation problems may have difficulty with interpreting instructions, for example: 'Write your name at the top of the page'. They will put clothes on upside down or may be unable to turn them the right way around; they may also have difficulty placing cutlery, for example, in the correct position on a table, or copying patterns, for example using Lego bricks.

Try this out

The following exercises/activities encourage children's perception of the position of objects in relation to their own body:
- Give them certain instructions, for example: 'Look in front of you'; 'Walk backwards'; 'Lift your left leg'.
- Play 'Simon says' and leapfrog, crawl under someone's wide legs, play cat-and-mouse games.
- Discuss a picture with a child and ask questions such as: 'Where is the girl sitting?'; 'Where is the house?'; 'Is it near or far away?'; 'Why do you say that the house is far away?'
- Place the arrow chart in front of the child, choose an arrow, and ask the child to point in the direction of that arrow. If the child finds the many arrows confusing, cover the bottom

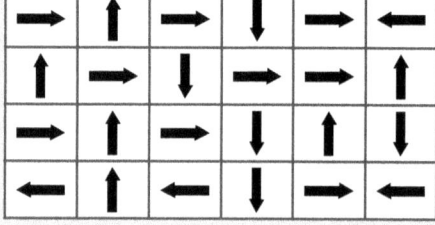

Figure 4.4 Arrow chart

»

three rows with a piece of paper so that only the top row remains visible. As the child progresses, more arrows can be shown (see Figure 4.4).

Lateral midline/vertical midline

The lateral midline is an invisible line that divides the body into a left and a right side. Children need to acquire the ability to cross this midline with their eyes, hands and legs, for example touch their right ear with their left hand. If they are not able to do this, they will have difficulty in reading and writing in formal schooling. When children are not sure of their position in space, they avoid crossing the midline of their body and may develop lateral midline problems.

Figure 4.5 Image of lateral midline

Try this out
The following activities will assist the child with lateral midline problems:
- The child can hit a ball with a tennis racquet or play clapping games, which encourages crossing the midline.
- The child can draw a lazy eight using a wax crayon on a big board or clear A3 paper. The child should only move his/her arms when completing this activity so that he/she has to cross his/her midline to complete the figure. (See Figure 4.6.)

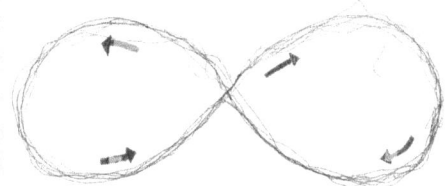

Figure 4.6 Image of a lazy eight

- Alternatively, let the child trace a figure of eight in one continuous line, over and over again without lifting his/her hand or moving his/her feet. To keep the child still, ask him/her to stand on a fixed spot, for example a cross on the floor. The child's body must be kept still, and his/her eyes fixed on the spot where the lines of the figure of eight cross each other.
- The child can draw patterns on a blackboard or easel, and must not move about while doing so.

Laterality

Laterality is an inner awareness of the two sides of the body, namely left and right. A sense of laterality enables the child to be aware of the two sides of his/her body, to know which side is moving, when it is moving and how far it is moving away from the midline or centre line.

Try this out

Do the following exercises/activities to help the child with laterality problems (left-right distinction):

The teacher asks the child to show different body parts, for example: 'Show me your *right* hand', 'Show me your *left* foot'. Constantly use the words 'left' and 'right' in daily activities. Play 'Simon says' or hopscotch, etc. One of the first steps in teaching 'left' and 'right' is to encourage activities that promote a sense of balance, for example asking children to hop on their right foot. They must have a clear concept of the two sides of their body and how they relate to each other. Through such activities, they internalise laterality and can differentiate between a left and a right side, and identify which side of their body is dominant.

Dominance

One of the two sides of the body is usually dominant. The dominant side is more refined and better developed, and is usually chosen by the child to complete an action, for example kicking a ball, drawing a picture with a specific foot or hand, etc.

Something to consider

It does not matter which eye or hand is dominant, as long as the dominance is stable. In other words, it is on the same side of the body.

At 18 months to two years, children will show a hand/foot preference, but actual dominance is only established by five or six years of age.

Mixed dominance, which occurs when a child has no constant preference for using a particular hand, eye or foot (eg right-handed but left-eyed), can seriously affect optimal learning.

Temporal awareness behaviours (an understanding of time)

It is important for children to develop a sense of time and timing. In perceptual-motor terms, we can refer to an inner and outer sense of time. An understanding of an inner sense of time is acquired through the body; for example, we have a rhythmic heartbeat. This sense is further developed as we improve our body coordination and rhythmic movements such as, for example, clapping, stamping, swaying, marching. Children also have to be able to coordinate body movement to a specific tempo and the concepts of 'fast', 'slow', 'start', 'stop', 'now', 'there', etc. Musical activities are a good way of developing coordination and rhythmic behaviours, which are an essential part of temporal or time awareness.

An outer sense of time refers to the idea of time passing. Children need to develop an understanding of time relationships, such as the ability to predict the time of arrival, etc. Routines, such as snack or toilet time, that form part of the daily programme are good ways of helping children build a sense of time because they happen at more or less the same time every day.

Movement that involves gross and fine motor development plays an important role in the refinement of temporal awareness behaviours. The link between fine motor development and some temporal awareness behaviours is shown in Figure 4.7.

FINE MOTOR DEVELOPMENT

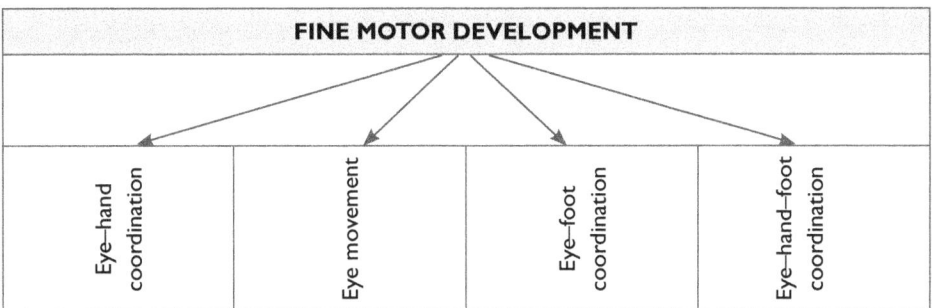

Figure 4.7 Fine motor development

Eye–hand coordination

This refers to the hands and eyes working together when performing a movement, for example throwing or catching a ball. A child who has poor eye–hand coordination has difficulty catching or throwing a ball, and may also find it difficult to draw, colour in, use a pair of scissors and perform all those activities where they use their hands.

Try this out

The following are activities to help develop eye–hand coordination skills:
- Give the child a pipe cleaner and some bottle tops with a hole in the middle of each to make bracelets. The child has to pinch the pipe cleaner with the fingers – the same motion needed for grasping a pencil.
- Let the child mist (spray water on) the plants in the garden with a spray bottle, an activity that can strengthen both writing and scissor skills.
- Scribbling in sand or clay with the fingers is a fun alternative to doing it on paper, and especially helpful for those children who shy away from drawing and writing. A child can practise cutting the clay into small strips.
- Offer writing/drawing utensils in a variety of sizes and shapes. Some people think that fat pencils are easier to hold, but that is not always true. For a child with limited finger strength and flexibility, a smaller, shorter pencil might be easier to manage.

There are many more activities that strengthen fine motor control which contribute to readiness for formal schooling. Can you name some more?

Eye movement

The ability to focus on a particular object and move the eyes in a particular way, for example across a page of text, requires coordinated eye movement. The child must be able to see clearly at close and long range, and adjust eye focus to enable the image which is perceived slightly differently by each eye to come together into a single image. The ability to focus on a moving object is essential in reading and writing. Some of the abilities that should be developed are the following:
- Localisation – using the eyes to find an object quickly in space
- Focusing – the ability to adjust one's focus to be able to see both near and far objects clearly
- Tracking – following a moving object through the visual fields, for example following an aeroplane moving across the sky, or reading a line of print.

Try this out

The following are exercises/activities to help the child overcome eye movement problems. In order to develop the left-to-right eye movement, a toy car can be pushed backwards and forwards across the table. The child follows the movement of the car with his/her eyes, but keeps the head still. The child holds his/her hands up, about 300 mm apart and about 300 mm away from his/her eyes. Put a thimble or a marionette (finger puppet) onto each forefinger.

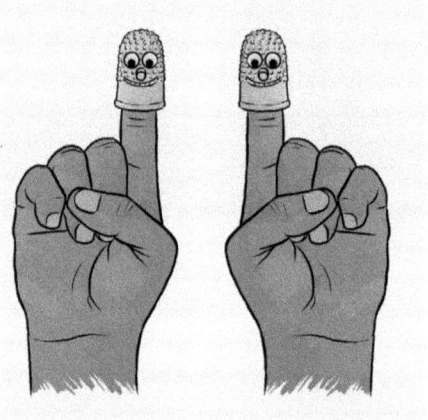

The child must then move his/her eyes from one marionette to the other while keeping the head still.

Eye–foot coordination

This refers to the feet and eyes working together when performing a movement. Children who have not developed eye–foot coordination will find it difficult to kick a ball properly or perform any other action that requires eye–foot coordination.

Try this out

The following activities/exercises will help enhance eye–foot coordination (in all of them the child should use his/her dominant foot first):
- Draw a line or stick tape on the floor, and let the child walk along the line.
- Then encourage the child to take small steps (heel to toe) along the line, walk on tiptoe along it, walk backwards on it, follow it with legs apart keeping the line in the middle, walk over obstacles (eg a schoolbag, a box, a doormat) and jump as in hopscotch.

Eye–hand–foot coordination

Hand and foot movements, guided by the eyes, assist the child in developing a wide repertoire of skills, such as tying bows, cutting with scissors, drawing with crayons, and throwing or kicking objects accurately through the air.

> **Something to consider**
>
> Young children are in Piaget's pre-operational stage of development (see Chapter 2). They are developing memory, imagination and symbolic thought. Their thinking is often still egocentric and based on intuition, not logic. They may not yet grasp complex concepts such as directionality, spatial awareness and speed variance (fast or slow). The brain functions necessary to plan and make decisions ranging from simple to more complex is dependent on the development of perceptual-motor skills and concepts. Refinement of perceptual-motor skills allows children to practise complex and unfamiliar tasks such as stepping back without looking or touching the right hand to the left knee (spatial awareness). The acquisition of refined perceptual-motor skills and concepts sets a foundation for being more active and completing important day-to-day activities independently while preparing to read, write and master more complex skills. Young children need to be taught and provided with opportunities to practise these skills through playful pedagogy – they do not just occur overnight. Waiting until primary school (when specific sports and other physical activities are introduced) to teach motor skills to children contributes to their lack of self-efficacy and consequently their ability to participate successfully. Children who do not develop these skills in their early years may eventually gravitate away from active sports, games and dance towards less threatening sedentary hobbies.

We will now consider the third category – sensory awareness – and in particular visual and auditory awareness behaviours.

SENSORY PERCEPTUAL-MOTOR DEVELOPMENT
Visual perception

Visual perception is the ability of the brain to make contact with the outside world through sight. Accurate visual perception enables the school beginner to read, write, draw and colour in. Good visual perception is necessary for activities such as reading, writing, spelling and mathematics.

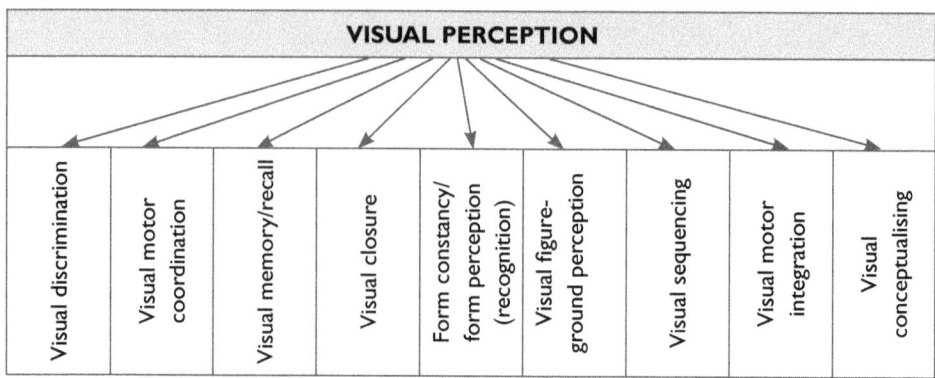

Figure 4.8 Visual perception

Visual discrimination

Visual discrimination refers to the ability to differentiate one object from another. It is the ability to discriminate through sight, for example to recognise similarities and differences between things such as colours and later between letters such as between 'b' and 'd'. Use activity books, for example 'spot the difference'.

Visual motor coordination

Visual motor coordination refers to the eyes and muscles working together in, for example, playing a ball game. Visual motor coordination is central to daily tasks such as dressing, domestic chores, sewing, sport and writing.

Children who suffer from underdeveloped or disturbed visual motor coordination may appear to be clumsy, often bump into things, battle to fasten a button or tie shoelaces, etc. Such children may have difficulty catching, throwing or kicking a ball, and may be unwilling to take part in competitive sport because they fear criticism or ridicule. They might also find it very difficult to write, draw or cut out, or to paste things into books, or take part in any activity that requires a degree of nimbleness with their fingers.

Activities/strategies to help children with visual motor problems include all activities already mentioned in relation to eye movement. Grade R children can also practise writing patterns in sand, gravel, mud, shaving cream or on a chalkboard.

Visual memory/recall

This is the ability to store and recall information perceived with the eyes, for example remembering where an object has been put or recalling details on a picture scene.

Try this out

The following activity will help improve visual recall or visual memory:

Place a few objects on the table in front of the children. When they have had a good look at them, cover them up and ask the children to name what they have seen. Begin with three or four objects and gradually increase them. You could also take away an object and ask the children what is missing. Make sure that the tablecloth is plain so that the patterns do not distract the children. Start with three objects and increase the number of the objects as the children progress.

Visual closure

Visual closure is the ability to complete objects, pictures or drawings from an incomplete visual picture or stimulus – it requires the child to recognise or identify the whole object even though the total picture/stimulus is not presented.

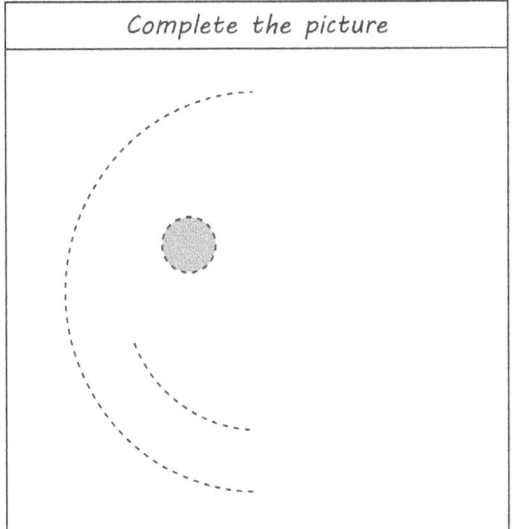

An activity that promotes this skill is doing puzzles.

Form constancy and form perception (recognition)

Form constancy is the ability to distinguish between forms and symbols in one's environment, regardless of their size or position. It is also the ability to observe certain characteristics of objects such as form or shape, colour and clarity, for example recognising a circle as a circle because of its unique shape or that a specific letter of the alphabet is the same whether it is a lower case or capital letter.

Colour in all the shapes that are the same as the first shape.

The following are activities/exercises that will improve form constancy and form perception (recognition):

Make use of every possible opportunity to demonstrate different forms or shapes to the child, for example tell the child that a motor tyre is round or the door is a rectangle. Ask the child to identify other objects in the room which also form a rectangle. Prepare a group of shapes for display on, if available, an overhead projector. Use the shapes to design a pattern. Show the pattern to the children and then switch off the projector while you change the pattern by adding or removing parts. Show the new pattern and ask the children to identify the same shapes or forms in the new pattern.

> **Try this out**
> Include the following activities to prevent problems with figure-ground perception. Let the children set the table, finding the right items in the drawer or cupboard. Let them select pencils/crayons of one colour from a box. Give a picture and ask the children to find particular objects in that picture. Describe a suitable picture.

Visual sequencing

This is the ability to place a series of items in the order they were observed. For example, give children pictures of each part of the daily programme and ask them to place the pictures in the correct order as previously observed by them.

> **Try this out**
> There are activities that can enhance visual sequencing abilities. These include copying a series of body movements; threading beads in a colour or shape sequence; and playing the game 'I went to the market'. Make use of actual items (concrete objects) rather than naming them. Say: 'I bought apples, oranges, bananas', etc, and show children the actual fruit as well and asking them to place it in the order it was bought. Include games such as place swopping where a group of children sit in a row and one child looks at where everyone is seated and then leaves the room. Two children then swap places. The child returns and is asked: 'Who has moved?' Show a row of toys or objects to the children. Mix the objects and ask them to put them back into the order first seen. Start with two or three items and, as the children improve, add more.

Visual motor integration

Visual motor integration measures a child's ability to make sense of visual information and then use it appropriately for a motor task such as writing, playing sports, using tools and utensils.

When a child has a visual perceptual problem, the brain, which has incorrectly recorded or processed the visual information, will probably misinform the muscles during activities that require eye–hand coordination. The child with a difficulty in this area has problems coordinating appropriate motor responses required for both fine motor activities, such as copying a form, and gross motor activities, such as kicking a ball.

Developing visual motor integration is an important skill for handwriting and a significant predictor of handwriting performance. Adequate visual motor integration is necessary to copy movement patterns and images through drawing or handwriting.

Visual conceptualising

This refers to making pictures in the mind based on observations, experiences and data. For example, ask the children to imagine what their favourite bicycle would look like.

Auditory perception

Auditory perception is much more than just hearing. It involves listening to what is heard and interpreting it in a meaningful way. Auditory perception is the ability to interpret the information sent to the brain by the ears and to respond appropriately. Listening in everyday environments can be challenging for children when optimal listening conditions are frequently disrupted. Background noise levels in classrooms often exceed the minimum recommended standards (Nagaraj & Magimairaj, 2020).

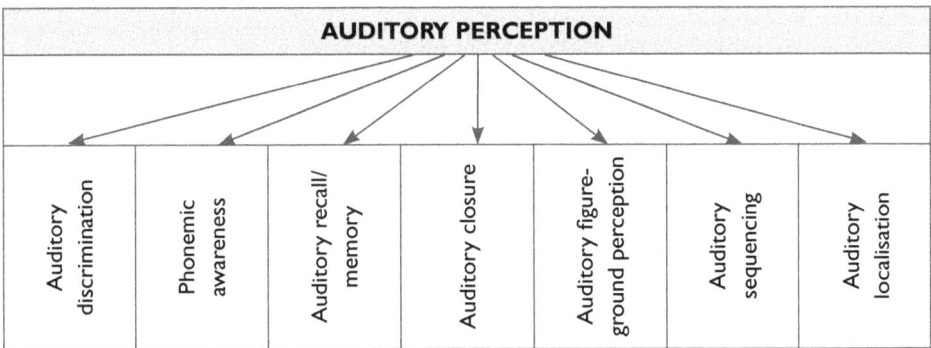

Figure 4.9 Auditory perception

Auditory discrimination

This is the ability to recognise similarities and differences in sounds. For example, 'pig' and 'big' differ in terms of one phoneme: /p/ and /b/.

Phonemic awareness

A phoneme is the smallest unit of sound in a word. For example, the word 'cat' has three phonemes: /c/ /a/ /t/. When children learn to read in Grade 1, they will need to recognise that the words they hear are composed of individual sounds within the word.

Auditory recall/memory

This is the ability to store and recall what has been heard. For example, the child could be asked to do three activities, such as close the window, open the door and place the book on the table. Does the child remember to do all three activities without being reminded? Other activities could be allowing the child to repeat a number sequence after the teacher, such as 6-4-8. Increase the numbers as the child progresses. Play a game: 'I took a trip to the moon and took my spacesuit''. The child repeats the statement, but adds one item, for example: 'I took my spacesuit and my helmet'. The next child says, 'I took my spacesuit and my helmet' and adds another item. In this way, children are encouraged to listen and recall all the additional items.

Auditory blending/closure

Auditory blending is the ability to blend sounds into a complete word. Many children have difficulty blending (eg the phonemes /m/ /a/ and /n/ are blended to make the word 'man'). The teacher can sound a word in parts and the child has to blend these parts to make a complete word: /d/ /o/ /g/ = dog.

Auditory figure-ground perception

This refers to the ability to isolate certain sounds amidst others. For example, a child must be able to follow a conversation while there is background noise. Usually, most people are able to ignore these noises, but a child with problematic auditory figure-ground perception cannot do this. They hear and listen to all the sounds, and this causes confusion and distraction, and they will not be able to concentrate on a conversation. Such children will find it difficult to listen to their teacher in the classroom.

Try this out

Develop auditory figure ground by drawing the child's attention to certain sounds, for example: 'Listen quickly! What do you hear outside?'

Auditory sequencing

Auditory sequencing is the ability to remember the order of items in a sequential list from information that the child has heard. For example, the alphabet, numbers and the months of the year are learned as auditory sequences. This is best done in a singing context.

The child with auditory sequencing problems may have difficulty retelling a story and putting the events therein in the correct sequence. Retelling could be made part of story time. Play the game: 'I went to the market'. Discussing the day's events in order could also help a child with auditory sequencing problems.

Auditory localisation

This refers to the ability to localise sounds in space in relation to oneself, for example hearing a car in the distance.

> **Try this out**
>
> To develop auditory localisation, let the children sit quietly or lie on the carpet with their eyes closed. Present a sound and ask them to identify where it is coming from, for example outside or by the door, etc. To make the listening more interesting, the teacher could cut out paper masks for the children to wear over their eyes.
>
> The child could also be asked to identify various sounds, for example a piece of paper being torn or crumpled, clapping, clicking of the fingers, a knock at the door or a door closing. The ability to localise the sound does, of course, depend on auditory recognition. The child must first be able to recognise the sound.

Tactile and kinaesthetic perception

Tactile and kinaesthetic perception go hand in hand. **Tactile perception** refers to the sense of touch, while **kinaesthetic perception** deals with the sense of body movements and muscle feelings. Together they provide information about body movements and their interelationships, for example you lift your arm and touch a rough surface.

> **Try this out**
>
> To develop the child's tactile perception, put a mask over the child's eyes and place some objects in front of him/her on the table. Then ask the child to feel these objects and say which one is hard, soft, rough, smooth, wet, warm, etc. Make 'feely cards' the size of postcards by pasting a different type of material onto each one, for example wood, sandpaper, cloth, rubber, etc. The child, without seeing the cards, must touch them and describe what they feel like. Put a few well-known objects into a pillowcase. Allow the child to put his/her hand in, feel, identify and describe an object before taking it out, and also say what kind of material it is made of.

Kinaesthetic perception is closely related to gross and fine motor development, and to spatial awareness and orientation behaviours. Kinaesthesis is perception of movement or muscle sense. It is the awareness of body movement and of the body's relative position in space. The more varied movements and positions a child can engage in, the greater the opportunities for developing kinaesthetic perception. We use our kinaesthetic sense whenever we are involved in a physical activity such as walking, running, driving, dancing, swimming, and anything that requires body movement (Cherry, 2020).

Children move to learn and learn through movement. Body movements are therefore essential in the acquisition of all perceptual-motor skills. In fact, all perceptual-motor skills should first be developed through kinaesthetic movements followed by three-dimensional activities (this means using concrete objects, for example blocks). Only when children have demonstrated capabilities in these areas should paper and pencil representations of the specific skill be offered to them (Charlesworth, 2004).

Olfactory perception

This is the ability to recognise and interpret information sent to the brain through the sense of smell. To test this sense, cover the child's eyes with a mask, and ask him/her to smell and identify certain fruit such as bananas or pineapples without touching them. Do the same with vegetables, herbs, etc. Draw the child's attention to specific smells – the smell of rain, newly cut grass, a flower in the garden, etc. The sense of smell can help a child escape danger, for example when smelling smoke or food that is going off.

Gustatory perception

This is the ability to recognise and interpret information through the sense of taste. The tongue identifies five different tastes – sweet, sour, bitter, salty and umami (a strong savoury flavour that makes Marmite and sushi so hard to resist). The sense of smell plays a further role in identifying specific tastes.

Try this out

Once again, this perceptual skill can be enhanced by covering the child's eyes with a mask and asking him/her to taste and then identify different food, such as bread, cheese, cake. Do the same with different vegetables or fruit. An extension of this activity that draws on knowledge of taste is to tell the child that you are thinking of something sour and describe the object. Then ask the child to guess what the object is. Change the item you describe and ask the child to identify it again. Another activity could be to ask questions such as: 'I'm thinking of a lemon. Is it sour, sweet, bitter or salty?' Do the same with other foods (Grové, 1982).

Something to consider

Why do you think is it important to develop perceptual skills? How would you promote the development of perceptual skills in your Grade R class?

Do not worry if some of the children in your class are having a difficult time in one or more of these perceptual areas. What is important is that you are exposing them to activities that lead to improvement. Always remember, children want to have fun and be active! Play participatory pedagogy is now recognised as an important feature in a successful transition to Grade 1.

TRANSITION INTO GRADE 1

One of the main aims of the Grade R year is to foster independence in the young child. Independence is critical in helping the child adjust to the demands of formal schooling. In Grade R, the child has, ideally, refined essential social skills such as sharing, compromising, turn taking and conflict resolution. Holistic development has been given a special focus to help build competence and confidence, not only socially but also emotionally, physically, cognitively, creatively and spiritually. The child has been alerted to environmental print in a fun-based context and, as the curriculum requires, can now recognise most letters by sight, identify number symbols 1 to 10, count 10 objects, differentiate between shapes and colours, and talk to some degree about the passing of time.

It is important to bear in mind that it is just as important for the school to be ready for the child as it is for the child to be ready for school. In Chapter 1, for instance, we spoke of five important learning dispositions. If children display curiosity, perseverance, trust and responsibility, and acquire a positive self-image, they are more likely to succeed in Grade 1 and further schooling.

The late developer

Holding children back for the wrong reasons can be counterproductive. However, it is better to go to school too late rather than too early. A common reason to hold children back is because there are indications that they are not yet mature enough to cope successfully in Grade 1. Sometimes parents of children who just meet the age requirement to start Grade 1 may rethink sending them to formal school because they are not yet 'school ready' (especially if they are boys). If they are not ready for Grade 1, send them to Grade R, even if it is at another school. It is better to send children to school with the expectation that they will pass Grade 1. Within the South African context, children are often sent to Grade R because it is cheaper than sending them to a crèche or an ECE centre, but this is not always in their best interests. They may be just too young or immature to benefit from Grade R. Rather encourage parents to wait another year.

The gifted child

It is important to identify giftedness at a young age. This makes it possible for the teacher to recognise a child's special needs by putting in place the resources to make sure that this giftedness is nurtured. It appears that academic and intellectual giftedness are areas most easily identifiable at an early age, especially in relation to the use of numbers, language and word concepts.

Questions for reflection and discussion
- Briefly reflect on the transition of the learner to Grade R and formal schooling, and the needs of children in both contexts.
- Write down your thoughts on the importance of the development of perceptual skills in Grade R.
- Discuss the developmental and sociological perspective in relation to the Grade R learner.

SUMMARY

This chapter has explored particular aspects of the Grade R child and pointed to particular considerations for the teacher. Each child is unique, but children's needs in relation to success in formal schooling are remarkably similar. We have considered the wide range of perceptual-motor skills and competencies that the child needs to acquire in a fun-based, culturally responsive environment. We have stressed the importance of contextual considerations, and argued that developmental milestones cannot be seen in isolation.

BIBLIOGRAPHY

Arnheim, D & Pestolesi, RA. 1978. *Elementary physical education. A developmental approach.* St Louis: The CV Mosby Co.

Ayers, AJ. 2005. *Sensory integration and the child.* Los Angeles: Western Psychological Services.

Brewer, J. 2007. *Introduction to early childhood education.* 6th ed. Boston: Pearson.

California Department of Education. 2020. *Annual Report: Perceptual and Motor Development.* https://www.cde.ca.gov/sp/cd/re/itf09percmotdev.asp (Accessed 18 January 2021).

Charlesworth, R. 2004. *Understanding child development.* New York: Delmar.

Cherry, K. 2020. *Kinesthesis and physically active learning.* https://www.verywellmind.com/what-is-kinesthesis-2795309 (Accessed 18 January 2021).

Department of Basic Education. 2008. *Foundations for learning.* http://www.education.gov.za (Accessed 3 April 2012).

Department of Basic Education. 2011. *Curriculum and Assessment Policy Statement. Life Skills Foundation Phase.* Pretoria.

Excell, LA & Linington, V. 2011. 'Moving to literacy: Fanning emergent literacy in early childhood education in a pedagogy of play'. *South African Journal of Childhood Education* 1(2): 27–45.

Gallahue, DL & Donnelly, PL. 2003. *Developmental physical education for all children.* Champaign, IL: Human Kinetics.

Grové, M. 1982. *Volgende jaar skool toe.* Kaapstad: HAUM.

Gordon, AM & Browne, KW. 2008. *Beginnings and beyond: Foundations in early childhood education*. 8th ed. New York: Thomson Delmar

Kranowitz, CS. 1998. *The out-of-sync child*. New York: The Berkley Group.

Lundsteen, SW & Tarrow, NB. 1981. *Guiding young children's learning*. New York: McGraw-Hill.

Lupua, E, Elenac, G & Niculescu, G. 2014. 'Education regarding addictions and the impact of leisure time'. *Social and Behavioral Sciences*. 59: 283–287, htpp://www.sciencedirect.com (Accessed 18 January 2021).

Nagaraj, NK & Magimairaj, B. 2020. *Auditory processing in children: Role of working memory and lexical ability in auditory closure.* https://doi.org/10.1371/journal.pone.0240534 (Accessed 18 January 2021).

Positive parenting-ally.com (nd). *Child development from 4–6 years*. http://www.positive-parenting-ally.com/child-development-stages.html (Accessed 30 June 2014).

Riley, J (ed). 2003. *Learning in the early years*. London: Paul Chapman.

GLOSSARY

Auditory blending – the ability to blend sounds into a complete word

Auditory discrimination – the ability to recognise similarities and differences in sounds

Auditory figure-ground perception – the ability to isolate certain sounds amidst others

Auditory localisation – the ability to localise sounds in space in relation to oneself

Auditory memory/recall – the ability to store and recall what has been heard

Auditory perception – the ability to interpret the information sent to the brain by the ears and to respond appropriately

Auditory sequencing – the ability to remember the order of items in a sequential list from information that has been heard

Balance – the ability to keep steady and not fall

Body awareness – the recognition of the ways in which the body or parts of the body can be controlled, moved and balanced on

Body image – subjective picture of one's own physical appearance established both by self-observation and by noting the reactions of others

Cognitive development – the continuous emergence throughout childhood of cognitive abilities associated with memory, reasoning, problem solving and thinking

Dominance – a word used to describe the side of the body that is more refined, better developed and usually chosen by the child to complete an action

Dominant hand – when one hand is consistently used more than the other, and is more skilled at tasks than the other hand

Environmental print – the ability to identify product and company names, signs and logos commonly used in everyday environments

Eye movement – the ability to focus on a particular object and move the eyes in a particular way

Eye–foot coordination – the feet and eyes working together when performing a movement

Eye–hand coordination – the hands and eyes working together when performing a movement

Fine motor development (FMD) – the development of the small muscles

Form constancy and form perception (recognition) – the ability to distinguish between forms and symbols in one's environment, regardless of their size or position.

Gross motor development (GMD) – the development of and increased control over the large muscles

Gustatory perception – the ability to recognise and interpret information through the sense of taste

Kinaesthetic perception – the sense of body movements and muscle feelings

Laterality – an inner awareness of the two sides of the body, namely left and right

Olfactory perception – the ability to recognise and interpret information sent to the brain through the sense of smell

Perceptual-motor development – the ability of the child to take in information through the senses, interpret this information (in the brain) and respond appropriately (a motor response)

Posture – how the child holds his/her body when standing, walking and sitting

Phonemic awareness – the recognition of the smallest unit of sound (a phoneme) in a word, (eg the word 'cat' has three phonemes – /c/-/a/-/t/)

Phonemic awareness – the ability to segment words into phonemes (individual sounds)

Physical development – physical changes in the body involving changes in bone thickness, size, weight, gross motor, fine motor, vision, hearing and perceptual development

Self-image – the way we think about ourselves and our abilities or appearance

Sensory awareness – behaviours that refer to children's ability to respond to sensations perceived through the five senses

Social and emotional development – a child's ability to understand the feelings of others, control their own feelings and behaviours, and get along with peers

Spatial awareness and orientation – behaviours which refer to children's understanding of their bodies

Tactile perception – the sense of touch

Temporal awareness – an understanding of time which in children describes their ability to develop an inner and an outer sense of time

Vertical midline – an invisible line that divides the body into a left and right side

Visual closure – the ability to complete objects, pictures or drawings from an incomplete visual picture or stimulus

Visual conceptualising – making pictures in the mind based on observations, experiences and data

Visual discrimination – the ability to differentiate one object from another

Visual figure-ground perception – the ability to distinguish an object from its surrounding background and to make a meaningful distinction between objects

Visual memory/recall – the ability to store and recall information perceived with the eyes, for example remembering where an object has been put or recalling details in a picture scene

Visual motor coordination – the eyes and muscles working together in, for example, a ball game

Visual perception – the ability of the brain to make contact with the outside world through sight

Visual sequence – the ability to place a series of items in the order in which they were observed

Chapter 5

Who is the Grade R teacher?

Naseema Shaik

In this chapter we consider

- the many facets of being a Grade R teacher
- why certain qualities are important in the Grade R teacher
- the identity of a Grade R teacher through a personal and a professional lens
- how these two lenses contribute to being a successful Grade R teacher
- the role of the Grade R teacher.

INTRODUCTION: WHO IS THE GRADE R TEACHER?

The Grade R teacher is an individual who teaches children between the ages of four-and-a-half and six. Teaching and learning in Grade R ideally occurs through a play-based, integrated approach. Depending on context and qualification, the person teaching Grade R may be described as a teacher/practitioner or educator. The current trend is to use the word 'teacher', and this is the one used in this book. The field of teaching is both challenging and rewarding. Teaching Grade R calls for a high level of responsibility and accountability. The approach the teacher follows should lay the foundations for future lifelong learning. The beliefs, attitudes and values modelled by the Grade R teacher will influence the children for many years.

Something to consider

Possessing such influence means that Grade R teachers must be very aware of the model they provide to the children. They should also be aware that every aspect of their personality and teaching beliefs will impact practice. As Vygotsky (1978) said, 'We become ourselves through others'. This quote immediately alerts us to the importance of the modelling used by Grade R teachers in their interactions with the children. For example, a teacher who sees children's opinions as relatively unimportant will find it difficult to create an interactive teaching and learning context, and will not encourage them to ask questions and to exercise their agency.

We will now explore the identity/identities of the Grade R teacher through two particular lenses,[1] a personal and a professional one. Through each lens we can begin to identify important characteristics of the Grade R teacher. We will use the personal lens to consider the qualities and personality of the Grade R teacher, and the professional one to explore the roles of the teacher, and the ethics that should inform his/her practice. We will also briefly consider a possible career pathway for the Grade R teacher.

The personal lens

There are many different reasons why people want to become Grade R teachers. Many students say it is because they have a love for children. They present as caring and nurturing individuals who want to make a difference in the lives of young children.

Try this out
Together with a friend, list all the reasons that prompted you to become a Grade R teacher. Now compare your reasons with your friend's.

In your discussion, did you consider some of your qualities and personality aspects that might assist you in becoming a good Grade R teacher?

Find out more
Personal qualities and personality of the Grade R teacher
There is no one type of personality that is ideally suited to Grade R teaching. Teachers will have different beliefs, attitudes and values, as well as display different personal qualities. One quality, however, appears constant and important – the Grade R teacher should have a genuine love for children. Loving children, however, is not enough, and one also needs to have caring qualities that enable teachers to empathise with young children. Part of this is to take into account not only the becoming child when we consider his/her physical, cognitive, social and emotional needs, but also the being and belonging child (see Chapter 4).

Try this out
Reflect on the teachers you have known and what made them memorable. Consider also what you also disliked about certain teachers.

---

[1] A lens, like a camera lens, enables us to view a situation from a particular perspective or point of view.

Find out more

Did you mention that the teachers you particularly liked were those who were kind, friendly, patient and compassionate, and those that had a good listening ear? Did you refer to a sound knowledge base of development and learning including pedagogical content knowledge. Were there other qualities that you mentioned or even the possibility that a particular teacher inspired you to want to become one yourself? Perhaps some of the qualities that you disliked in teachers included screaming and shouting, and teachers who were unkind and did not take the time to listen to you.

Although many people can be great Grade R teachers, not all of them find satisfaction and success in this field. So what types of personal characteristics and personality should a Grade R teacher have? Successful Grade R teachers have been described to have the characteristics listed in Table 5.1.

Table 5.1 The qualities of a successful Grade R teacher

THE NURTURING, CARING TEACHER	THE RESPECTFUL TEACHER	THE ENERGISED TEACHER
Caring	Respect for diverse cultures, language, race, gender and disabilities	Curiosity
Nurturing	Respect of the Grade R teacher for him/herself as a valuable contributor to society	Commitment
Warmth	Respect for values	Openness to new ideas
Sensitivity	Respect for education	A sense of humour
Flexibility	Self-awareness	High energy level
Emotional stability	Respect for young children and their families	Physical strength and enthusiasm
Passion	Perseverance	Willingness to take risks
Patience	Integrity (being honest and standing up for moral righteousness)	Positive outlook
Creativity	Love of learning	Trust in children
To be able to empathise	Acknowledging the agency of children	Being open to child participation

Try this out

Tick the characteristics that best describe you and then work with a friend and add any other qualities that may not be in Table 5.1, but best describe you.

> **Every Grade R teacher has a story to share: Vignettes from some Grade R teachers about what prompted them to choose this profession**
>
> **Story 1**
> *Thando lived in the area of Khayelitsha in Cape Town. Being unemployed and seeing the need to start a facility to care for young children while their mothers went to work, Thando decided to open a little crèche. Having started off with just three children, the number soon increased to 10. After a while she found that the children were not being stimulated enough so she decided to join an ECD programme where she could obtain a qualification to teach Grade R and younger children. She completed an initial course and obtained a certificate. She then obtained a degree through Unisa that qualified her to teach from Grade R to Grade 3.*
>
> **Story 2**
> *Leslie worked at a bank for many years but got no job satisfaction. She had three children and always enjoyed working with younger children, so she decided to resign from the bank and do a Bachelor of Education degree that qualified her to teach Grade R as well as grades 1–3. She now teaches at a preschool in Cape Town and enjoys every moment of it.*
>
> **Story 3**
> *While studying law at Unisa, Cayla was asked to fill in for a teacher who had to go on maternity leave. She so enjoyed working with young children that she decided to change her course and qualify to teach in Grade R.*
>
> Now, together with a peer, share what prompted you to become a Grade R teacher.

PERSONAL BELIEFS AND VALUES

Our personal beliefs will also impact our classroom practice. People have beliefs about many things, for example education, religion, peace, etc. Our values, which are also influenced by our beliefs, play an important role in the decisions we make. Both beliefs and values are impacted by our religion, family norms, culture and life experiences. Some values are taught to us directly while others are learnt in an indirect way. Values influence our choices and partially inform, for example, the house we choose to live in, the car we choose to drive, the food we eat, and the education we seek for our children. Our intention to teach may be based on how we value education and the role we think it has in building a new South Africa.

> **Try this out**
> - Reflect on the values that you have and list them.
> - What were the factors that helped you develop those values?
> - Have your values remained the same or have they changed over time?

We will now move to the professional lens where we will consider the roles of teachers in their professional capacity, and briefly examine issues relating to professional development and qualifications, as well as ethical considerations.

THE PROFESSIONAL LENS
The roles of the Grade R teacher
The Grade R teacher as teacher

Grade R teachers often have many different roles to play, one of the foremost of which is to engage children in meaningful interaction and thus provide rich learning experiences for them in a culturally responsive and contextually appropriate environment. These experiences will guide children in the development of their knowledge, skills, values and attitudes. Effective teaching requires careful planning at all times. To do this effectively he/she needs both subject content knowledge as well as pedagogical content knowledge.

The Grade R teacher as mediator

The Grade R teacher and the children in Grade R take on roles as mediators interacting with each other through language, the most important psychological tool. Grade R teachers and children use language to make meaning and thus enhance learning.

A different understanding of mediation is when conflict between children remains unsolved and the teacher intervenes as mediator. He/she may also adopt the role of social worker when problems need to be solved between parents/caregivers and their children, and even perhaps between a child in the class and an older sibling.

The Grade R teacher as parent/caregiver

The Grade R teacher may also have to take on the role of parent/caregiver to some children who might need some emotional support during the absence of their own parents/caregiver.

The Grade R teacher as nurse

At times, the Grade R teacher might also have to play the role of nurse when children injure themselves or become ill during the school day.

The Grade R teacher as secretary and principal

A Grade R teacher can, in specific contexts, be called on to be teacher, secretary and even a principal, all at the same time – three different hats and three different sets of responsibilities, all making different demands on time and insight. In some small, privately run ECD sites or preschools, the Grade R teacher might need to take on all these responsibilities.

The Grade R teacher as supporter

If unexpected accidents occur in the Grade R classroom, the Grade R teacher might also have to support children. Sometimes young children may unexpectedly mess their pants or themselves for any reason. Grade R teachers should be sensitive to these issues and should understand that these types of occurrences are inevitable considering that they are working with very young children. The Grade R teacher should therefore be prepared and willing to deal with such issues.

The Grade R teacher as reporter

Another role that Grade R teachers have to play is that of reporter to all interested stakeholders such as curriculum advisors, paediatricians, educational psychologists, occupational therapists, etc. This requires close observations, detailed recording and a range of report-back contexts. It is part of the role as a team player.

The Grade R teacher as team player

The role of a Grade R teacher also means being part of a team working with other teachers and personnel in the school or ECD centre. Every person will bring their own strengths and limitations to the educational context. The teacher will need to recognise these strengths and limitations, some of which could be challenging, and will also at times have to deal with differences, which might require negotiation. To work in a team means having team spirit and respecting the positions/points of view of other members. Working collaboratively is the key to achieving success in a group. Working in a team provides support and a platform for sharing ideas. It can also strengthen the teacher's sense of belonging, which is as important for him/her as it is for the children. In fact, it can truly open the doors to learning as teachers should share ideas and learn from other teachers, adults and children.

As already stressed, it is important in the teacher's role as a team player to respect the views of others and to deal with differences in a respectful manner. Just because somebody else's views are different does not necessarily mean that they can be ignored or labelled as wrong. Importantly, too, is that the teacher is modelling active listening, respectful negotiation and collaborative decision making to the children in the class.

> **Try this out**
> Can you think of any other roles that the Grade R teacher might have to play? List these roles and discuss with a friend why they are important for the Grade R teacher to fulfil.

Find out more
What type of Grade R teacher does South Africa need?
Ebrahim, Verbeek and Mashiya (2011) provide an alternative on how to position teachers. Teachers, they argue, need to claim a position of agency. When we speak of teachers as agents, we are referring to their ability to influence their practice and bring about positive change. Teachers who exercise agency are those who are proactive (take initiative) as part of their commitment to critical reflection and appropriate change. They will critically reflect (honestly and insightfully) on their current practices, and ask what is it that they need to change. There is a body of research that is urging teachers to transform their practice. To achieve this transformation, teachers need to claim their space as agents of change.

According to Ebrahim et al (2011), teachers can position themselves in one of three roles, namely a deliverer, an adaptor or a creator of the curriculum. Ebrahim et al suggest that many Grade R teachers are currently positioned as deliverers of the curriculum and have to be supported to shift their practice to become adaptors, and ultimately creators. Each position will now be briefly outlined.

Teachers as deliverers
- They implement the curriculum as it is prescribed.
- They take on the role of deliverer.
- They follow the curriculum like a recipe.

In other words, such teachers do as instructed by others who have designed the curriculum. Their creativity and the power are therefore minimised, and are limited in the planning potential of their lessons as they follow prescribed lesson plans designed by others (Kavanoz, 2006).

Teachers as adaptors
- They take on a reflective and more powerful role.
- They become more knowledgeable, flexible, responsive and adaptive (Gambrell, Malloy & Mazzoni, 2007; Hoffman & Pearson, 2000; International Reading Association, 2003).
- They become more knowledgeable and can think meta-cognitively about how and when to adapt their teaching (Lin, Schwartz & Hatano, 2005).
- They are able to adapt lesson plans in the process of delivery to suit the particular teaching context and the learning styles and abilities of their learners.

Through this role, the teacher is able to reclaim some agency and become a proactive member of the teaching profession.

Teachers as creators
- They develop a sense of creativity, and their imaginative drive is not stifled by prescribed curriculum plans.
- They do not remain in their comfort zone. They are ready to take risks and work outside what they see as being safe and comfortable (Ebrahim et al, 2011).
- They claim their space as creators when they believe in their own professional agency and pedagogic autonomy. Only then will they realise that they have the power to shape the curriculum (Ebrahim et al, 2011).
- They work collaboratively, which results in an increased sense of collegiality which in turn also enhances creativity.

Try this out
Together with a friend, discuss which type of teacher would you like to be and why. What do you need to do in order to shift your position if this becomes necessary?

To be a successful creator, a teacher must pay attention to self-care, which is an important element of well-being. Committed effective teaching can leave a teacher feeling emotionally and physically drained. The curriculum and other mandates from the education department as well as negative attitudes of some colleagues and parents might all contribute to this 'burnout'. To address this state of exhaustion, teachers need to balance their personal and professional lives and ensure that they are looking after themselves as well as others for whom they care.

There are, of course, things you can control such as your attitude towards teaching, the quality of your teaching and the enthusiasm that you bring into the classroom. These strengths should be nurtured as they have the potential to make a difference to learners' lives. Meeting personal and professional demands requires self-care.

What is self-care?
Self-care for teachers implies intentionality. As Ray (2019) notes, factors that are under our control such as having sufficient rest or exercise can be self-initiated and regulated by ourselves, thereby consciously contributing to our own state of health. Ray (2019) has identified the importance of holistic self-care which includes physical, emotional, spiritual, intellectual, social and sensory development. In addition, teachers should consider work and financial demands.

When you take care of yourself, try to pay attention to all areas of self-care as mentioned above. Improve the areas in which your self-care is lacking and be committed to making it a regular practice. Reflect on all these areas and ensure they are addressed.

Practising self-care entails lowering the risks of teacher ill health, anxiety, stress, burnout, depression and as such supporting and protecting your holistic well-being. It is about building your strengths and resources to succeed during the challenging times of teaching.

> **Try this out**
> Read the following suggested strategies and habits to practise intentional self-care.
> - Establish healthy physical routines and habits.
> - Focus on the positive aspects of what you can contribute as a teacher.
> - Build enough rest and sleep into your daily routine.
> - Plan regular and nutritious meals. Include lunch breaks.
> - Have a regular exercise routine to stay fit.
> - Take time to socialise with other adults.
> - Include activities that you enjoy and help you relax, such as listening to music or reading a book.
>
> Without taking care of yourself, you will not have the energy to help others. Teachers, like most people, are encouraged to set personal and professional boundaries. Paying attention to self-care and a growth mindset enables teachers to achieve more in their personal and professional lives. People with a growth mindset believe they can get better at something with time, effort and energy.

QUALIFICATION PATHWAYS FOR THE GRADE R TEACHER

Grade R teachers and Grade R teaching do not have a high professional status. Many individuals consider the Grade R year to be little more than a babysitting service. A commonly held belief is that Grade R teachers take 'care' of children rather than 'teach' them. This idea is inaccurate, and currently there is a strong drive from the Department of Higher Education and Training to ensure that all individuals who teach in Grade R hold suitable qualifications. Relevant qualifications will go some way toward improving the status of the Grade R teacher, but this will only be effective if Grade R teachers implement quality Grade R programmes. An important aim of this book is to help teachers improve their Grade R classroom practice by furthering their qualifications and deepening their knowledge so that their professional practice can reflect their commitment to child-centred, contextually adaptable pedagogy. To be a professional requires one to have specialised knowledge of and experience in a particular field. Professionalism is a complex issue. According to Feeney, Moravcik, Nolti and Christensen (2010), a qualified professional Grade R teacher would fulfil the following criteria:

1. Has undergone prolonged training in the field of early childhood education. Prolonged training refers to studying towards a qualification in Grade R and gaining teaching practice experience.

2. Has a specialised body of knowledge.
3. Fulfils a gatekeeping function that ensures that only competent people may practise.
4. Has adopted a particular mission that includes commitment to the public good, and a set of shared values with other interested stakeholders including teacher colleagues and professionals such as educational psychologists and parents.
5. Demonstrates his/her belief in agreed-upon standards created for the public good, and a set of shared values with teacher colleagues and professionals such as educational psychologists and parents.
6. Displays autonomy and self-regulation (Feeney & Freeman, 1999, adapted from Gordon & Browne, 2008).

Once you are qualified as a Grade R teacher you will be seen as a professional. This implies that you have had appropriate education and training in the field. Sometimes individuals have had plenty of experience with young children, but their qualifications are in other fields. They may think that they are qualified to teach Grade R without attaining an appropriate qualification. This is not the case. Irrespective of the experience that one may have had working with young children, one is not viewed as fully equipped with the necessary knowledge and skills required to teach in Grade R without an appropriate qualification. To be professionally qualified requires a recognised qualification coupled with appropriate teaching experience.

> **Try this out**
> With a colleague, discuss what it means to be a professional. What types of knowledge, skills and values do you think you would need in order to become a qualified professional Grade R teacher?

ETHICAL CONSIDERATIONS IN A SOUTH AFRICAN CONTEXT

The word 'ethics' refers to knowing what is right and good in our teaching practice. It is associated with acting in a way that is morally defensible – that is, our conduct in many different contexts can be seen as illustrative of our clear understanding of what is right and what is wrong. Within the South African context, all qualified teachers have to be registered with the South African Council of Educators (SACE). This requirement also applies to qualified Grade R teachers. It is important to register teachers as this is one way to enhance the status of the teaching profession. In addition, the SACE sets out a professional code of ethics that all registered teachers need to follow. This has the potential to promote quality professional practice.

SACE upholds strong values, which are composed of the following:
- Being service oriented to the development and education of young children
- Openness and transparency
- Quality
- Professionalism.

Every registered teacher in South African should be familiar with the code of professional ethics in South Africa. This code is available on the SACE website, which is http://www.sace.co.za.

FURTHER TEACHING REQUIREMENTS IN SOUTH AFRICA

The Department of Higher Education and Training has developed policy guidelines that set out the minimum requirements for teacher education qualifications. The guidelines include some of the basic competences a beginner teacher should have, among which are the following:
- Sound subject knowledge
- Knowing how to teach subjects and select appropriate content
- Determining the sequence and pace of learning offered in accordance with both the subject and children's needs
- Knowing children, how they learn and how to tailor teaching accordingly
- Being an effective communicator
- Having highly developed literacy, numeracy and IT skills
- Being knowledgeable about the school curriculum
- Understanding diversity in the South African context in order to teach inclusively
- Being able to identify learning and social problems, and work in partnership with professional service providers to address these.

It is hoped that you will acquire many of these competences if you engage fully with the subject matter included in this book.

SUMMARY

This chapter has unpacked on the professional and personal identity of a Grade R teacher. The personal and professional lenses help Grade R teachers to shape how they engage with children. Additionally, the different roles that Grade R teachers play are extremely important as they also contribute to the development and education of young children. Choosing to become a Grade R teacher requires thoughtful insight, commitment and hard work, as such teachers are positioning themselves to educate and nurture the future of our country – our children.

A FINAL CONSIDERATION

This chapter raised the question of teaching inclusively. Elizabeth Walton elaborates on this as she considers inclusion in the current South African educational context.

Inclusive education

Over the centuries, education has seen various differences among children as important enough to educate them separately. Think, for example, of gender. Often boys and girls were, and still are, taught separately. Or consider race – in South Africa during apartheid, children of different races went to separate schools with separate curricula. We still regard age as an important difference, and carefully divide children up and teach them in separate age cohorts. Another difference that many people think necessitates separation of children is ability and disability, but in the second half of the 20th century, there was a growing sense that the educational segregation of children with disabilities was neither beneficial nor necessary. Separate special education was criticised for a number of reasons, including the ways in which children were labelled as 'abnormal', and the lowered expectations that people had of children in separate settings.

People began to realise that education can and should be inclusive of all children, but also realised that there was a lot that was built into the way we do things in education that works to marginalise and exclude certain children, so an important shift in thinking has been that teachers need to make pedagogical choices that result in learning for all children. Previously, a teacher might have said, 'Jabu doesn't understand instructions. There must be something wrong with him. He should go to a special school.' Now, knowing what we do about the benefits for children to learn with peers who are different from them, the teacher might say, 'Jabu doesn't understand instructions. He's possibly not the only one. Let me see how else I can explain what I want learners to do, perhaps with more examples and demonstrations.' Also, we have begun to understand that there are many reasons why some children experience difficulties at school, and it is not because there is something wrong with them. They may be a number of explanations, including anxiety about family problems, hunger or lack of sleep, language barriers, or even teaching that is not as effective as it could be.

The United Nations supports inclusive education, as does South Africa's education policy. This does not mean that there will be no more special schools, but it does mean that only children with high support needs, like those with multiple and severe disabilities, should be in special schools. Ordinary schools and teachers need to see how they can change to be more inclusive of all learners, and work to understand what they need to do so that they all can learn effectively. This requires us to consider how we can ensure that every child enjoys his/her right to education, free from discrimination on any grounds. To learn more about inclusive education, read White Paper 6: Special Needs Education, published by the Department of Education in 2001.

BIBLIOGRAPHY

Ebrahim, HB, Verbeek, C & Mashiya, JN. 2011. 'Enabling roles for teacher agency: Insights from the Advanced Certificate for Education (Foundation Phase)'. *Perspectives in Education* 29(4): 58–65.

Feeney, S, Moravcik, E, Nolti, S & Christensen, D. 2010. *Who am I in the lives of children? An introduction to early childhood education.* 8th ed. Upper Saddle River NJ: Merrill.

Gambrell, LB, Malloy, JA & Mazzoni, SA. 2007. 'Evidence-based best practices for comprehensive literacy instruction', in *Best practices in literacy instruction*, edited by LB Gambrell, LM Morrow & M Pressley. 3rd ed. New York: Guilford Press.

Gordon, AM & Browne, KW. 2008. *Beginnings and beyond: Foundations in early childhood education.* 8th ed. New York: Thomson Delmar.

Hoffman, JV & Pearson, PD. 2000. Reading teacher education in the next millennium: What your grandmother's teacher didn't know that your granddaughter's teacher should. *Reading Research Quarterly* 35(1): 28–44.

International Reading Association. 2003. *Standards for reading professionals.* http://wwwreading.org/General/CurrentResearch/Standards/ProfessionalStandards.aspx (Accessed 18 September 2010).

Kavanoz, SH. 2006. 'An exploratory study of English language teachers' beliefs, assumptions and knowledge about learner-centeredness'. *The Turkish Online Journal of Educational Technology* 5(2): 1–7.

Lin, X, Schwartz, DL & Hatano, G. 2005. 'Toward teachers' adaptive metacognition'. *Educational Psychologist* 40: 245–255.

Moll, C. 1990. *Vygotsky and education.* Cambridge: Cambridge University Press.

Ray, JB. 2019. *Crumbling foundations: The case for prioritizing self-care among educational leaders.* Theses and dissertations. https://scholarworks.uark.edu/etd/3275

Vygotsky, L. 1978. *Mind in society. The development of higher mental processes.* Cambridge, MA: Harvard University Press.

GLOSSARY

Attitude – a fixed way of thinking about something

Belief – accepting that something exists or is true

Ethics – the principles of decent human conduct; doing what is right and good

Professional – describes individuals who have gone through different levels of education and training in a particular field that equip them with the necessary knowledge and skills to perform in that field

Psychological tool – something (such as language) that helps make meaning of memory, perception and attention in ways that are appropriate to culture

Values – one's judgement of what is valuable or important in life

Chapter 6
A transdisciplinary approach: an enhancement of positive community engagement

Lorayne Excell, Vivien Linington, Linda Rutgers

In this chapter we consider

- the transdisciplinary approach
- the value of indigenous knowledge systems and indigenous knowledge
- unpacking understandings of community
- school/community partnership
- possible types of interaction that a teacher should consider having with the community and the kind of relationships that could flow from such interactions
- ways of maximising these relationships so that all stakeholders benefit
- the notion of a child-friendly school (UNICEF, 2009) and how such a notion would impact partnerships
- professional commitment to outreach and partnership formation
- how to begin to form partnerships
- how to choose with whom to partner
- managing and sustaining partnerships – dealing with possible tensions.

INTRODUCTION

Indigenous knowledge (IK) is referred to as traditional knowledge, traditional ecological knowledge or local community-based knowledge. It reflects the commonly held norms and values of a society.

The term 'indigenous knowledge systems' (IKS) refers to a broad body of knowledge embedded in African philosophical thinking and social practices that have evolved over thousands of years (DoE, 2003). It includes many aspects such as culture, skills and various bodies of knowledge including child-rearing practices, agricultural practices and education approaches.

THE CHILD IN COMMUNITY

The African proverb 'it takes a village to raise a child' is probably even more relevant today than it was yesteryear. If early education is going to be contextually appropriate and culturally responsive, it must take cognisance of indigenous knowledge systems and recognise the way of life of the communities who support the development and learning of the Grade R child. Early education provisioning needs to draw on relevant and appropriate indigenous knowledge systems (IKS) and indigenous knowledge (IK). IKS and IK should inform the curriculum that children follow, the relevant education infrastructure supporting the Grade R year and also who the multiple stakeholders are and what their functions are in relation to holistic learning and the development of children. This means we should recognise the ongoing contributions of various stakeholders in knowledge production and draw on their insights when relevant. In this way, we would be adopting a transdisciplinary approach to successful Grade R provisioning.

A transdisciplinary approach is one that goes beyond a specific discipline or subject area and recognises that collectively parents, community members and other stakeholders should work together to ensure the holistic and successful development and learning of the child (Moodly, Phatudi & Mavusa, 2019). In a transdisciplinary approach, the essential roles of various community members and organisations as well as the parents/caregivers are acknowledged, and their involvement encouraged in the education of the child.

We first explore the place of community involvement and then that of parents or caregivers.

WHAT IS A COMMUNITY?

The word 'community' has a number of different meanings such as all the people living in a specific locality, a fellowship of interests or a body of people united by a common interest.

In all cases it refers to people who have something in common. Within the schooling context, this common interest is surely the child. Who, then, in the context of Grade R, would comprise the community and who is responsible for ensuring that the school and community work together to promote the interests of the child?

> ### Something to consider
> Spend a few minutes thinking about the school community and who is responsible for establishing a working relationship between the school and the community. Write down your responses on a piece of paper and then read further.

School leadership is very important. The principal has a key role, but so does the teacher. Active family/community involvement benefits the teacher and the school. The teacher is the person who is with the child every school day and may therefore be in a key position to interact with many of the community members. These community members could include the following:

- The parents and/or caregivers
- Members of the extended family
- Members of the school – teachers, auxiliary staff, volunteer workers (who may help, for example, with the school feeding scheme), school management team
- School governing body
- Members of the education department – district officials, school support services and others
- Members of other government departments – Department of Health (school health services, for example, who may be involved in the screening or referral of sick children) and Social Development (in relation to, for example, child grants)
- Members of the local community – clinic staff, private sponsors (who might subsidise/supply resources, buildings, etc)
- An array of health professionals such as doctors, nurses, physiotherapists, speech therapists etc
- Traditional healers
- Members of various community organisations – for example the Sunshine Centre Association, which focuses on early intervention and support for children who have difficulties with learning
- Non-governmental organisations (NGOs) – READ, Molteno, etc, sometimes also known as non-profit organisations (NPOS)
- Ward councillors.

Add to this list yourself; the available community resources will vary from school to school and from location to location.

A functioning school will ideally have built partnerships with many different community members, and staff will be able to interact with their organisations if, and/or when, the need arises. In this way, a transdisciplinary approach is optimised, and teachers can ensure a strong support system that may enable children to gain additional benefit from their education.

ESTABLISHING COMMUNITY PARTNERSHIPS

In order to promote a functioning school where the best interests of the children are paramount (ie of utmost importance) and where effective teaching and learning are always promoted, partnerships with the community are essential. These are, however, difficult to establish, especially if the school is not functioning effectively.

To help promote and implement quality schooling, UNICEF introduced the idea of a child-friendly school (CFS), which is one where the needs and interests of the child are prioritised and where members of the teaching staff work together with the community to make sure that quality teaching and learning happen.

Find out more

What is a child-friendly school?

Three principles underpin the idea of a CFS. These are as follows:
- Child-centredness – the child is at the centre of the education process.
- A democratic approach where the question arises: 'How do we teach for democracy through democracy?' The term 'education for democracy through democracy' presents particular challenges for the teacher. It means we must educate our children about the principles of democracy through the use of democratic practice. We cannot, for example, exclude certain children from participating in discussions while teaching about the importance of open communication in a democracy. A democratic approach would therefore support the idea of a being child where he/she is already regarded as a citizen with a voice to be heard and agency to exercise (see Chapter 2).
- Inclusiveness – do we consider all the children and their particular contexts and challenges? Remember inclusiveness embraces diversity of every kind, for example language, gender and shifting identities, culture, learning styles and difficulties, socio-economic challenges, religion, class and chronic illnesses, as well as mental and physical disability. In a CFS, the unique nature and circumstances of each child are considered. We do not adopt a 'one-size-fits-all' approach.

Contained in these three principles are six identifiable characteristics of a CFS. As you read the list of identifiable characteristics, ask yourself: 'How child friendly is my school/classroom?' The six characteristics are as follows:
1. A rights-based and inclusive school
2. An effective school
3. A safe, protective and supportive school
4. A health-promoting and health-seeking school
5. An equity- and equality-promoting, and gender-sensitive school
6. A community partnership-building school.

Can you see how the three principles are included in one or more of these characteristics? The idea of a CFS is very broad. If you study these six characteristics, you will begin to see the advantages of promoting a CFS. It involves the construction of an interdependent relationship – that is, a child-friendly school builds community partnerships, and community partnerships promote the development of a CFS; in other words, a truly transdisciplinary approach.

Successful and effective education is based on strong community partnerships. They are part of the bioecosystemic 'web' of influence that was referred to in our discussion of Bronfenbrenner in Chapter 2. Teaching and learning that promotes holistic development does not happen in isolation.

Now we will briefly consider each of the six characteristics or indicators of a CFS. As you read, again consider: 'How child friendly is my school/classroom?'

A rights-based and inclusive school

- Is informed by the values of dignity, respect and responsibility. In addition, the rights and responsibilities of all staff members are acknowledged.
- Promotes social justice.
- Respects and responds to issues of violence and abuse, and also to those of diversity, which includes HIV/AIDS, gender and shifting identities, disabilities, language, religion, and cultural and economic differences.
- Ensures equal opportunities for all.
- Embraces diversity, which is not viewed as a disadvantage.
- Encourages participation of all children and their families – regardless of social, cultural, economic or family background.

Something to consider

Consider the following questions:
- How do you ensure equal access to school for all Grade R children in your community?
- How can you ensure a democratic quality learning process?
- How can you ensure that all children have access to adequate learning support?
- How do you ensure all children have access to appropriate resources?
- What could you do to promote a rights-based and inclusive school?

An effective school

Ensuring this means the following:
- Quality education is provided that is relevant for the children's needs for life and for survival and growth (see Maslow, Chapter 2). Children also need to develop knowledge, skills and attitudes that encourage them to reach their potential.
- All decision making is based on the notion of child-centredness to ensure that the interests of the child are safeguarded.
- A range of basic minimum requirements for creating enabling conditions is identified, which include the following:
  - Skilled, motivated and well-trained staff supported by good conditions of service
  - Strong leadership and management capacity
  - Access to ongoing professional development

- Understanding and implementing an appropriate curriculum
- Provisioning of adequate physical resources
- Understanding the role of the hidden curriculum. 'Hidden' in this context refers to everything that is learnt at school, some of which might not be intended.

> **Something to consider**
>
> Consider the following questions:
> - In your current circumstances, what are the challenges you face in implementing an appropriate curriculum?
> - What type of community partnerships should you establish to help ensure that you can implement an effective Grade R programme?
> - What indicators could you use to show whether the transdisciplinary approach is being used in your school/classroom?
> - How can you ensure that the rules and regulations are fair, transparent and non-discriminatory, and promote positive behaviour?
> - How can you ensure you use strategies for including children with mental and physical challenges?
> - How can you create open learning environments characterised by group cooperation?

A safe, protective and supportive school

This characteristic is very important. Think back to Chapter 2 and Maslow's hierarchy of needs. Children's motivation to learn will be negatively affected if their physiological needs are not met and if they are not in a safe, protective and supportive school. Many basic aspects of the physical and social environment need to be considered in relation to this characteristic:

The physical environment (see Chapter 7)

- *The indoor environment*
    - Design of building, positioning of playrooms, office, bathrooms, etc
    - Room arrangement and monitoring – tables, chairs, carpet, shelves, storage, placement of resources, floor covering, heaters, ventilation, cleanliness, etc
    - Bathrooms and kitchen – water, availability of toilets, etc.

- *The outdoor environment*
    - Perimeter security fence, wall, gate, parking, etc
    - Natural environment – ground covering, trees, shade, etc
    - Positioning of equipment – safety, state of repair, etc
    - Storerooms.

Both environments should be constructed in such a way that disability is accommodated.

The social environment
- Rules
- Attitudes and values informing the classroom culture (part of democratic practice)
- Discipline, aggressive behaviour, the handling of conflict, and resolution of possible differences of opinion

In summary
A safe, protective and supportive school is one:
- where children can learn and teachers can teach in a warm, welcoming and secure environment
- that provides adequate supervision
- where the behaviour of all the stakeholders helps in maintaining order and the safety of all children and teachers, and other people in the school
- that has well-qualified teachers and supportive parents/caregivers and school community.

A health-promoting and health-seeking school (see chapters 7 and 14)
- The government has a legal responsibility (is obligated by law) to provide secure and safe environments which promote effective learning – Children's Rights Charter (CRC).
- Teachers require deep insights into health-promoting and health-seeking schools. They should do the following:
  - Assess the state of the school in relation to health issues.
  - Know how to include health-promotion measures in the curriculum and the school as a whole.

These measures could include the following:
- Ensuring a healthy environment
- Drawing up school health policies in relation to environmental hygiene and safety, management of ill health and accidents, and emergency evacuation, to name a few
- Health education – which can be woven, quite naturally, into routines, rings and free play as the teacher both models and promotes healthy ways of living (see Chapter 14)
- Health maintenance – particularly in relation to nutrition (making healthy choices about what you eat), managing ill children, screening, etc.

> **Something to consider**
>
> Do you think that it is the sole duty of the teacher to ensure a safe, protective and health-promoting school? If not, who could you approach for assistance and guidance?

An equity- and equality-promoting and gender-sensitive school

A CFS actively engages with issues relating to equity (fairness), equality and gender sensitivity. This thread is interwoven throughout this book.

Try this out

What is the difference between equity and equality?

Look for examples of equity, equality and gender-sensitive behaviour throughout this book and in your own classroom practice. The concepts of equity, equality and gender-sensitive behaviour inform the notion of a being and belonging child (see Chapter 8).

What could you begin to do differently to ensure that your practice addresses these issues?

A community partnership-building school

This acknowledges the following:
- Schools are part of the community.
- Teachers have an important role in establishing and maintaining school–community partnerships, but do they have to do this on their own?
- The community should also provide a safe and caring environment.

CASE STUDY

Riverside Primary School is in an area where unemployment is high, and service delivery is often problematic. The school has limited resources but has established a strong partnership with the community. As a result, parents and other community members keep a constant lookout for waste materials that could be used for teaching and learning in Riverside's new Grade R classes and outdoor play area. The school community has already provided the following:
- Six old, abandoned tyres that are used during outdoor play
- Planks of wood that have been sanded and are now used as balancing beams
- A stainless-steel basin for water play together with a number of empty containers such as yogurt cups to enhance water play
- A sandpit, with sand donated by the local hardware shop.

This case study illustrates some of the features of what could be termed a child-friendly school.

Something to consider

- Is your school part of the community? If so, how?
- If not or only to a small extent, what first steps could you take to try to become part of the community?
- Distinguish between family-focused and community-based partnerships.
- How do you establish relationships and network with the community? Whom would you approach first?
- If partnerships are already in place, how could they be strengthened?
- What is important if partnerships are to grow and develop? What do you need to consider?
- Who should be responsible for what? What should be a matter of joint responsibility? Where do equity and equality come into the strengthening of partnerships?

In summary

A CFS should be a place where children can grow, develop and learn. It should also be a place that provides a safe, secure and healthy environment for children. A CFS does not exist in isolation; it works together with the community and promotes community/teacher/school partnerships. It supports the notion of a being child.

ESTABLISHING PARTNERSHIPS

The word 'partnership', as we have already suggested, refers to a joint business or a sharing and working together towards the realisation of a common goal – in this instance, quality education for the children. Community involvement in the setting-up of a stimulating play-based Grade R environment is one example of this. Within the school environment, one of the most desirable partnerships is between school/teachers and parents/caregivers.

A parent–teacher partnership implies that both parties have something to offer and are equally important. However, they bring different competencies to the partnership. The parent is the primary educator, knows a lot about the child and has firm beliefs about what should happen to the child during the school day. The teacher, on the other hand, has (or should have) expert pedagogical knowledge. Together they should ensure that the child is immersed in the best possible education environment.

How to establish partnerships

Establishing successful partnerships takes a lot of work and requires a professional commitment (see Chapter 5). It requires more than simply being in the classroom.

It requires a teacher to actively demonstrate the following:
1. Knowledge and skills (knowledge of child development, subject content knowledge, knowledge of pedagogy and the skills to apply this knowledge in an effective way to ensure high-quality learning and teaching)
2. Abiding by a code of ethics
3. Continuing educational and professional development
4. Professional affiliations, such as support of the SACE
5. Cultural responsiveness and inclusivity, and constructive management of diversity issues
6. Advocacy (to promote, support, uphold and champion quality early-years education – in this case Grade R).

> **Something to consider**
>
> Can you see how closely the characteristics of a CFS and proactive professional practice can complement each other? As we revisit professionalism in the context of this chapter, we will be touching on points introduced in Chapter 5.

As a Grade R teacher, bound by professional ethics, you may have to consider issues that are different from those considered by teachers at child-friendly primary and high schools.

> **What if ...**
>
> A child in your class always cries and hangs onto the parent/caregiver when they arrive at school. How would you handle this?

The professional and ethical conduct of the early-years teacher is believed to be so important in some countries that professional 'early-years' associations have drawn up a special code of ethics for their members, all of whom are early-years teachers.

For example, the National Association for the Education of Young Children (NAEYC), a professional organisation based in the US, has drawn up such a code. This code sets out in detail the professional responsibilities of an early-years teacher, and is made up of four sections, namely the teacher's relationship and work with:
1. children
2. families
3. colleagues
4. the community.

Becoming aware of how to relate professionally to children, colleagues, families and the community is a good first step in the establishment of partnerships.

Something to consider

Some of the roles of a teacher that help establish strong partnerships are the role of communicator, team member and advocate (these and other roles have been discussed in Chapter 5). We suggest that the teacher as communicator, team member and advocate can provide a structure for the establishment and maintenance of teacher–parent/caregiver partnerships.

ROLE	TEACHER'S FUNCTION
Communicator	Interacts respectfully with children Forms a *partnership* with parents/caregivers
Team member	Works as part of a team – this includes other colleagues, parents/caregivers and other community members
Advocate	Advocates for rights of young children (teachers need to uphold what they know is appropriate and optimal for this age group). This means they have to be able to communicate and to work as a member of a team; in other words, they should be forming varied types of partnerships

THE TEACHER–PARENT/CAREGIVER PARTNERSHIP

The three above-mentioned roles offer one way of establishing and maintaining teacher–parent/caregiver partnerships.

Something to consider

One way of considering whether you already fulfil these three roles is to reflect on all aspects of your professional practice including your relationships with parents/caregivers. These relationships should be ones of acceptance and support.

Try this out
Use the following checklist as a reflective tool.

A checklist for making your Grade R class parent/caregiver friendly and promoting parent/caregiver partnerships

Do you
- ✓ know the children in your class and see each child as a unique individual
- ✓ observe the children and note how they relate to other children and adults
- ✓ share your observation with parents
- ✓ suggest ways of guiding children's behaviour

»

- ✓ remain open to parents'/caregivers' concerns
- ✓ encourage parents/caregivers to ask questions and to express their concerns
- ✓ invite parents/caregivers if they have a concern to come to the school at a time convenient for all parties?

In addition, do you
- ✓ create a space, for example a notice board, for communication between parents/caregivers and yourself
- ✓ encourage parents/caregivers to know what goes on in the classroom and include them in decisions affecting their children's education
- ✓ provide childcare at the school when parents/caregivers come for meetings
- ✓ establish a book and/or toy lending library
- ✓ visit or telephone families where possible, especially to share a child's success
- ✓ gather information about families' particular interests and needs
- ✓ demonstrate a strong commitment to supporting families and parents/caregivers
- ✓ provide opportunities for families to volunteer assistance, for example maintenance of class resources?

Are you
- ✓ respectful of social, ethnic and religious backgrounds of families
- ✓ considerate of issues of diversity (for example, not all parents/caregivers might speak the LoLT of the school, and translators might need to be provided)
- ✓ fully informed about possible links to health and social support services
- ✓ able to explain referral procedures if required
- ✓ able to offer information on how to create learning opportunities at home
- ✓ aware that misunderstandings can occur and that they need to be dealt with as soon and as sensitively as possible?

The home/school partnership is a foundation that points the way to motivation and pride. Children visibly 'grow' in stature when their families are seen as an integral part of the school, and teachers acknowledge the value of this partnership.

What if ...
Your reflection has shown that there are gaps in your relationship with parents and the community? How could you go about addressing this?

Find out more

The checklist has focused on your relationship with parents/caregivers and the community. Equally important, however, is your relationship within the school context. This means working collaboratively with the principal or supervisor, other teachers, the administrative staff and the support staff (caterers, general staff, gardeners, etc).

Being part of a team does not happen by accident. One way is to commit yourself to getting together and sharing ideas with your colleagues. Collaboration can lighten your load, deepen your insight, enrich learning for all the children, and improve communication with parents/caregivers.

Finally, as an advocate promoting the rights of young children, you will be serving your children, their parents/caregivers, the school and the broader ECE community. As an advocate promoting the rights of young children, you will engage in debates about the importance and quality of ECE, including Grade R. Grade R is often marginalised as many people do not fully understand the importance of quality education during the early years. Even fewer people understand how to implement a developmentally informed, contextually appropriate programme that foregrounds a play-based approach towards the education of young children and acknowledges each child's specific context.

Young children are not able to fight for their own rights – not on a broader, societal level. We, the teachers of these children, need to lobby for appropriate and meaningful education. This is part of advocacy. An additional factor is that many principals, HoDs and Foundation Phase teachers as well as parents/caregivers do not have deep insight into appropriate Grade R teaching and learning programmes. It has not been part of their life experience, which therefore places teachers in a vital informative role.

One way of promoting quality Grade R teaching is through understanding the developmental and learning needs of the child, implementing an appropriate, culturally relevant curriculum, and establishing strong relationships with parents/caregivers and other members of the school and broader community in a contextually appropriate way. This is one way for teachers to use their agency to broaden understanding of the unique nature of Grade R pedagogy and the unique opportunities this year presents in the education of young children.

SUSTAINING PARTNERSHIPS

Even partnerships that are collaborative and open to differences of opinion can run into difficulty. It is far better to acknowledge these difficulties and work through them in a respectful atmosphere than to ignore them. Democracy and democratic practice do not ignore voices in opposition. They work with them as a stimulus for growth and insight for all involved.

SUMMARY

This chapter explored the important role of the community in ensuring successful teaching and learning. It showed that effective schooling cannot occur in isolation. Community–school partnerships provide an essential source of support for teachers and parents. Successful partnerships are those where the strengths of all members are recognised and their contributions positively acknowledged.

BIBLIOGRAPHY

Bredekamp, S (ed). 1987. *Developmentally appropriate practice in early childhood programs serving children from birth through age 8.* Washington: NAEYC.

Broadfoot, P, Osborn, M, Gilly, M & Bûcher A. 1993. *Perceptions of teaching. Primary school teachers in England and France.* London: Cassell.

Christie, P. 2008. *Opening the doors of learning.* Johannesburg: Heinemann.

Department of Education. 2003. *National Curriculum Statement Grades 10–12 (General): Life Sciences.* Pretoria: Department of Education.

Excell, L, Linington, V & Helsby, M. 2010. *Grade R practitioner's course.* University of the Witwatersrand: Johannesburg.

Gordon, AM & Browne, KW. 2008. *Beginnings and beyond: Foundations in early childhood education.* New York: Thomson Delmar.

MacNaughton, G & Williams, G. 2004. *Teaching young children. choices in theory and practice.* Maidenhead: Open University Press.

Moodly, A, Phatudi, N & Mavusa, M. 2019. 'Early childhood education and care: A South African context and transdisciplinary approach', in *Childhood care and education (0–4). A transdisciplinary approach*, edited by Cape Town: Oxford University Press: 1–20.

National Association for the Education of Young Children. (NAEYC). 1997. *Code of ethical conduct.* Washington, DC. NAEYC.

South African Council of Educators (SACE). (nd). *Code of ethics for educators.* Pretoria: SACE.

UNICEF. 2009. *Child-friendly schools. A human rights approach.* Nairobi.

Yelland, N, Lee, L, O'Rouke, M & Harrison, C. 2008. *Rethinking learning in early childhood education.* Maidenhead: McGraw Hill Open University Press.

GLOSSARY

Code of ethics – guidelines for behaviour that is morally appropriate and justifiable

Cultural responsiveness – sensitivity in cross-cultural communications on the part of the teacher and a world view that is willing to be open, flexible, curious and non-judgemental about different perspectives and issues

Democracy – a form of government where a constitution guarantees basic personal and political rights, fair and free elections, and independent courts of law

Democracy – an approach to teaching and learning that attempts to acknowledge and include everyone's rights and perspectives. It emphasises respect for different points of view and differences of every kind. In short, its focus is the inclusion of the voice of all stakeholders in Grade R, including that of the child

Early childhood education (ECE) – a term used to refer to the education of young children from birth to nine years of age

Equality – in a social justice context, the equal distribution of resources and ways of overcoming economic and other disparities among people

Equity – fairness, impartiality and fair play – an important component in social justice and enshrined in our Constitution

Pedagogical knowledge – knowledge about the art and science of teaching

Proactive professional practice – in summary, the teacher's qualities

Professionalism – in education, doing things well at the right time and for the right reasons and taking responsibility for decisions made (all professions have a particular set of beliefs and practices)

Professional affiliations – belonging to a professional body, which in South Africa could be SADTU and NAPTOSA

Chapter 7

An optimal learning environment

Lorayne Excell, Vivien Linington

In this chapter we consider

- the curriculum in the learning environment
- what a Grade R learning environment is
- how to create an interactive play-based Grade R environment
- how to ensure a safe and secure learning environment
- planning and structuring the physical indoor learning environment
- planning and structuring the physical outdoor learning environment
- the temporal environment
- planning for diversity and inclusion
- appropriate contextual resourcing of the learning environment
- the role of the teacher in managing the environment and ensuring optimal learning and teaching opportunities including using the environment as a third teacher.

INTRODUCTION: THE GRADE R LEARNING ENVIRONMENT

We have already discussed who the Grade R child is and how best this child learns. How learning is planned and what happens in the learning environment is determined by the curricular approach. Curricular approaches differ, and tend to be based on our philosophy (what we know and believe) about children and how they learn. In this book we have adopted a more informal play-based approach to the implementation of the Grade R year. Though this approach is open to critique, it is an approach which has gained wide acceptance and is also the approach endorsed by the National Curriculum Statement and the CAPS documents (DBE, 2011).

THE PURPOSE OF THE CURRICULUM

The curriculum answers questions about what to teach and how to teach by providing an overall guideline based on assumptions on how children develop and learn. The curriculum informs decisions about how to organise the learning environment, how to choose appropriate content and how to implement the learning and teaching day. The curriculum is related to the overall quality of the programme.

Find out more
What is a curriculum?
A curriculum is an *organised framework* that sets out what children are to learn (content, skills, attitudes and values), the process through which children achieve these learning goals or outcomes, *what teachers do* to help children achieve these goals, and the *context* in which teaching and learning occurs. The curriculum has also been described as everything that happens in the school day (Gordon & Browne, 2008). A teacher needs to consider educational theories, approaches and models which inform curriculum development and implementation.

A curriculum is made up of many aspects:
- It is everything that happens in the school day.
- It is what is planned and what is not planned.
- It is what is prepared and what is not prepared.
- It is what is visible and what is not visible, for example your inclusion or not in your daily programme of the children's different cultural contexts.
- It is the messages that are sometimes unwittingly sent through everything that happens at school. For example, the common perception that boys are more likely to misbehave at school is often enforced by a teacher's attitude. This is sometimes called the hidden curriculum.
- It is all the learning that takes place.

It is, in other words, the what, the why and the how that frame all a child's learning experiences in Grade R. Bear in mind that what you teach may not be what all the children learn. Their interpretations of events that occur can be very different from adults.

Something to consider
In order to ensure appropriate learning experiences for children, the teacher implements a developmentally appropriate and culturally responsive programme that takes into account each child's sociocultural context. A developmentally appropriate and culturally responsive programme considers the following:
- The children's ages and stages of development
- Their interests, experiences and needs: Are there known learning problems? What is their home language? Is it different from the LoLT? etc
- What experiences they have already had
- What knowledge and skills they already have acquired in each of the developmental domains (physical, cognitive, emotional, social, creative)

»

- Cultural values, diversity issues
- What parents/caregivers want, and their concerns
- The community context – relations with other people
- The overall goals and aims of the programme
- The different activities and learning experiences provided, and the available resources for these
- Democratic and inclusive classroom practice, which would include the voice of the child in decisions made
- The creation of a safe and dynamic learning environment which draws on all available resources in the school, the community as well as those that are supplied by the Department of Basic Education (DBE).

Find out more
Planning an appropriate learning environment
A safe, dynamic learning environment is an essential first step in planning to teach and in implementing a quality Grade R programme.

A **learning environment** is made up of three parts:
1. the **place** – where we learn: the physical environment
2. the **people** – who is with us: the interpersonal environment
3. the **programme** – what we learn, and how and when we learn it: the temporal environment refers to the when (how time is allocated in the daily programme).

In previous chapters we have already mentioned the people – the children, the teachers, the parents/caregivers and a variety of other people who will be involved in the implementation of the Grade R year. In this chapter we are going to concentrate on the place (the physical environment), and introduce the programme (which includes what and how we learn as well as the temporal environment). Specific aspects of what we learn will be the focus of other chapters.

In order to explore how the day comes together from a perspective of time, we will now consider the temporal or time environment.

THE TEMPORAL ENVIRONMENT: GETTING IT RIGHT, PLANNING FOR THE DAY

The Grade R day comprises three aspects. These are:
1. Routines – events or rituals that happen every day at more or less the same time
2. Teacher-guided activities/rings (small and large group activities)
3. Child-initiated free play (indoor and outdoor).

These three aspects are realised through the daily programme.

The daily programme

The daily programme is what happens in the class every day. It provides a structure and sequence for the events of the day. In primary school it is called the timetable. We prefer to call it the daily programme as this suggests a more informal approach towards teaching and learning. This programme should be balanced, flexible and varied.

> **Something to consider**
>
> Place an illustrated copy of the daily programme on the classroom wall so that the parents and children can 'read' this programme. You could also take photographs of children participating in the different aspects of the programme and display them in sequence, in or outside your classroom.

Find out more

An example of a daily programme

Study the example of a daily programme. You will see that it includes:
- Routines (beginning and ending of the day – arrival and departure; tidying up after activities; toilet time; snack time; rest and possibly health checks)
- Child-initiated activities (indoor and outdoor free play with equipment and learning support materials (LSMs)
- Teacher-guided activities:
  - Small-group teaching – the teacher does an activity with a small group of children (eg main creative art activity or a perceptual, language, mathematics or life skills activity)
  - Large-group presentation – the teacher takes the whole group together (eg planned rings – theme discussion, music, movement, perception, science, dramatisation, language, story, mathematics, life skills).

Times have been suggested but these might have to be adapted to suit your specific context. Remember to provide a lengthy period of time for free play so that the children's play can be a meaningful learning experience. We have also shown how each aspect of the daily programme can be linked to learning criteria set out in CAPS.

Daily programme/timetable – Grade R

From approximately 07:30 to 13:30

Time	Activity
30 mins	Arrival and free play
15 mins	Morning greeting, register
30 mins	Teacher-guided activity – for example morning discussion ring, science, perception, etc
45 mins	Creative art activity (every day) – main + three supporting activities + indoor free play
15 mins	Tidy-up time
30 mins	Teacher-guided activity – music, movement, show and tell, etc
30 mins	Toilet routine, snack (Life Skills)
45 mins	Free play OUTSIDE
15 mins	Tidy up (outside) Toilet time (Life Skills)
30 mins	Teacher-guided activity – story (every day)
15 mins	Rest/departure

Life Skills
Mathematics
Language

Indoor free play
Fantasy play
Construction
Blocks
Educational toys
Perceptual games
Puzzles
Quiet area
Book corner
etc

Outdoor free play
Water play
Sand play
Role play
Balls
Jungle gym
Cycle track/wheel toys
Tyres
Swings
etc

MATHEMATICS (90 MIN)
Meeting the CAPS criteria through:
Display table
Number songs and music
Finger rhymes
Counting rhymes
Stories
Perceptual activities
Science
Weather
Sand and water play
Outdoor free play
Indoor free play
etc.

LANGUAGE (90 MIN)
Meeting the CAPS criteria through:
Display table
Theme poster
Parent poster
Wall charts
Discussion
Show and tell
News
Dramatisation
Stories
Poems/rhymes/songs
Music/movement ring, etc
Perceptual activities
Indoor/outdoor play
Routines
etc.

LIFE SKILLS (70 MIN)
Meeting the CAPS criteria through:
Display table
Stories
Poems and rhymes
Music
Movement activities
Routines (toilet, snack)
Indoor freeplay
Outdoor freeplay
etc.

Routines

Routines can be thought of as rituals that provide the child with a sense of predictability and give a child a sense of belonging.
- They are a constant – certain events are repeated, which provides a structure to the day.
- They give children a sense of safety, security and emotional well-being because they know what is going to happen next.
- They encourage a certain amount of independence.
- They foster a sense of responsibility in children.
- They reinforce good health and social habits.

Teacher-guided activities

These are periods of time when the teacher mediates learning, usually with the whole class. In South Africa we usually call this ring time. Another name is circle time.

Rings should usually last between 20 and 25 minutes as the Grade R child does not have a longer concentration span. These activities will be described in more detail in chapters 11, 12, 13, 14.

Individual child-initiated activities

In general, a large amount of time is given to free play. We know that children learn best through an interactive, play-based approach towards teaching and learning. Important questions therefore become the following:
- How do we set up a learning environment that promotes free-choice activities?
- What is the teacher's role in mediating these learning experiences for the children? In other words, can play that is free still include a role for the teacher? If so, what is that role? See Chapter 10.
- How can the teacher identify teachable moments and use these to enhance learning?
- What is the learning value of individual activities?

To answer these questions, we should consider the physical learning environment or place.

The remainder of this chapter will be spent on exploring how best to establish a quality Grade R physical learning environment.

THE PHYSICAL LEARNING ENVIRONMENT: THE PLACE

The physical environment comprises both the indoor and outdoor environment. Children will not be able to learn constructively if these environments are not safe and hygienic. Size should also be a consideration, which we will return to when we discuss the outdoor environment. We have already discussed the

child-friendly school (see Chapter 6) and we remind you of the two important characteristics of such a school which relate directly to the physical environment:
1. A safe, protective and supportive school
2. A health-promoting and health-seeking school.

It is essential to meet the criteria set out by these two characteristics before considering the other factors necessary for establishing and maintaining a quality learning environment. Why? In Chapter 2 we discussed how children learn best. We said, for example, that children are curious, and that they are concrete, interactive learners. For children to explore an environment constructively and safely, certain elements need to be in place:
- The children feel safe and can trust the teacher.
- The learning environment is stimulating and challenging.
- The environment is secure – for example with age-appropriate equipment in a good state of repair.
- There is adequate adult supervision at all times.

In relation to health, children are active learners, therefore they should be healthy in order to maximise their learning opportunities. Ill and/or hungry children do not have sufficient energy or motivation to engage meaningfully with learning activities or to listen attentively to a teacher (see Chapter 14).

Something to consider

How do you ensure a health-promoting safe and protective school?

School policies

A school that meets the above criteria will have a clear health policy. The principal, teachers, parents/caregivers and appropriate community personnel will help draw up this policy, which should be filed in the office and be available to all parents/caregivers and other interested people.

The **policy** should consider the following:
- The maintenance of a safe and healthy school environment through cleanliness of the classrooms, offices, ablution blocks (toilets), school kitchen or cooking area; the prevention of the spread of infectious diseases; maintaining a safe indoor and outdoor learning environment
- The provision of emergency care, for example first-aid procedures
- The provision of health screening, for example the weight and height of children, visual (eye) screening, auditory (hearing) screening
- Procedures for the referral of children, where necessary, to relevant support services

- The management of ill children in the school in relation to communicable and chronic illnesses, or those children who become ill during the school day
- Adequate nutrition of children, for example the provision of a feeding scheme or advice to parents/caregivers where children bring their own food to school
- Appropriate emergency evacuation procedures, for example in the event of a fire
- The promotion of health education for children, staff and parents/caregivers. Parents/caregivers are included because what is taught in the school should be followed through in the home. Parents are the primary educators and they ought to know what their children are being taught with regard to health-related matters. Contextual sensitivity in this regard is important.

Find out more

Policies should always be open to adaptation as circumstances alter. For example, at the time of writing the Covid-19 pandemic requires a number of policy changes in relation to school hygiene, personal safety and distancing.

Try this out

How did the Covid-19 pandemic impact your school policies? What changes were made to these policies?

Classroom rules

A classroom should also have set procedures in relation to rules. Appropriate rules will have been negotiated with all parties – staff, parents and children. They are then taught to children and displayed on the classroom wall. These rules should be as follows:

✓ Simple and easy for children to understand and follow
✓ Illustrated as well as written – remember that Grade R children do not read
✓ Worded in a positive way – for example 'We only run outdoors' instead of 'No running in the classroom'
✓ Few in number – no one can remember too many rules
✓ Consistently reinforced (remind children from time to time – if they break rules there should be an appropriate consequence)
✓ Flexible and open to adaptation.

CASE STUDY

An important rule in Mrs Dlamini's Grade R class is that children only run outside. Thabo is a very active child who enjoys playing in the fantasy corner. He keeps on running through the other play areas and has already knocked down the tower that Busi had been building in the block corner. Mrs Dlamini reminds

Thabo that 'we only run outside'. After reminding him three times, she says: 'Thabo, come here! I have reminded you three times not to run inside and you have not listened to me. Now you must go outside and run around there where there is more space. Mrs Sechefo will keep an eye on you.'

Question

This illustrates one way of handling persistent rule breaking. What do you think about the way in which this situation was handled?

THE INDOOR LEARNING ENVIRONMENT

The environment consists of many different areas. The classroom should be arranged in such a way that there are opportunities for large-group work, individual work, as well as small-group work. Large-group work usually happens on a carpet – a large area where children can sit down, sometimes on mats or cushions. Such areas would usually be used for teacher-guided activities (see chapters 11, 12, 13, 14). Near to the carpeted area should be a space for a theme table that can be used as a resource for theme discussions held on the carpet.

The remainder of the room should be covered with a floor covering such as vinyl which is easy to keep clean. In this area there should be child-sized chairs and tables. These tables, ideal for creative art or educational toys and games, would normally seat four to six children.

There should be space for children to place their bags and other personal possessions in a cubbyhole, often called a locker. These should be at the children's height. Each child's locker should be easily identifiable by a symbol, for example a coloured shape placed on the locker. If there are no lockers, plastic or even cardboard boxes can be used. Lockers are usually positioned against a classroom wall, but if there is not sufficient space indoors, they can be placed outside the classroom on a covered veranda or stoep.

Low shelves, made if necessary with bricks and planks, should run along at least one or two of the classroom walls. Much of the play equipment is placed on these shelves so that it can be easily reached by children. Suitable posters and pictures could be placed above these shelves. These are examples of environmental print and they relate to, for example, the theme, language and mathematics or whatever currently interests the children (see chapters 11, 12, 13, 14).

Planning the indoor learning environment

Plan carefully and thoughtfully to maximise teaching and learning opportunities, and to enhance the children's learning potential. There is no one right way of planning the indoor environment. It depends on, for example, the shape and size of the classroom and the position of the door(s) and window(s).

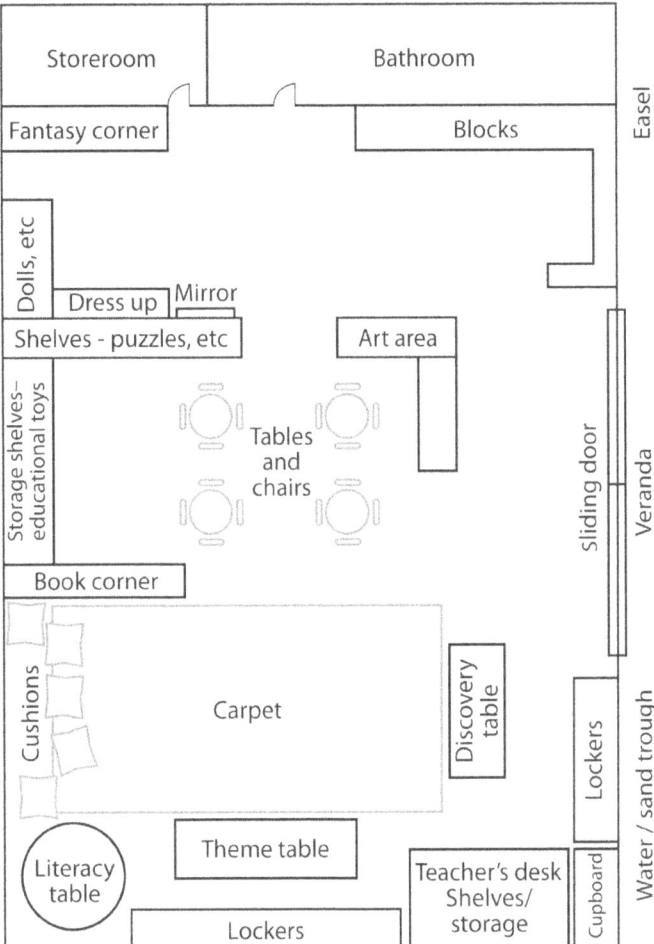

Figure 7.1 An example of an indoor play area

It also depends on available resources.

The teacher should plan different play/activity areas that are easily accessible to the children. There should be sufficient play materials/toys/apparatus so that all children can be meaningfully engaged and have their own play space. These materials can be bought (commercial), but they should also be drawn from the natural environment (pebbles, acorns, differently shaped leaves, sand, etc), and waste material such as empty cereal boxes, egg cartons and cardboard tubes from toilet rolls, etc.

The teacher still has an active role even when children are involved in indoor free- or child-initiated play. The teacher should do the following:
- Provide not less than a 45-minute uninterrupted block of time.
- Decide (sometimes together with the children) what equipment and play materials will be used.

- Ask the children to help with the setting out and tidying of play areas.
- Use language to mediate play where appropriate by encouraging children to play constructively and creatively; to try new ideas; to solve problems; to work together; etc. Mediation might include asking a question or making a suggestion.
- Encourage both girls and boys to play in all the areas, for example the block, educational toy and fantasy areas.
- Supervise play, making sure, for instance, that all areas are visible.

In addition, the teacher must do the following:
- Help children solve any conflicts.
- Assist children to have fun and to enjoy learning.
- Be continually mindful of children who are not being included in group play, and deal with this.
- Observe and record where individual children play, how they play and with whom they play. This includes what they say when they communicate with each other. These observations form the basis of assessment (see Chapter 9).

Setting out the different indoor play areas

If there is enough space in the room, all the play areas (sometimes called 'corners') are set out. If the room is too small or there are too many children, some play areas can be set up outside or on a veranda. All the play equipment and materials should be packed away at the end of the day.

Ideally, all children should have access to the following play areas:
- Block play
- Educational toys
- Fantasy/make-believe/dress-up/pretend or socio-dramatic play
- Book corner
- Creative art.

Other possible play areas could be:
- a science or exploratory corner
- a listening or music area
- a mathematics corner
- a language corner.

> **Something to consider**
>
> What other play areas could you add to the Grade R classroom? What equipment would you need for these areas?

The block play area

When a child plays with blocks, various aspects of holistic development are encouraged (physical, perceptual motor, cognitive, language, emotional, social, moral/spiritual and creative). Block play also promotes learning in the three subjects in the Foundation Phase CAPS documents: Language, Mathematics and Life Skills. Why? It deals with concepts such as 'bigger than' and 'less than', and behaviours such as cooperation.

Ideas for the block area are as follows:
- It should be large enough to accommodate several children and enable them to build a big block construction without being disturbed by others walking in this space. The floor should be smooth and level so that the blocks do not fall over easily.
- It needs to be away from the quieter areas such as the book or educational toy area because playing with blocks can be very noisy at times.
- It can be near the fantasy area to encourage play between these two areas.
- It requires specific rules so that safety is promoted, for example: 'We pass blocks to each other; we only throw balls'.

Try this out
Can you add some more rules?

Blocks are stored in a large container or on storage shelves. Draw the outline of the shapes of the different blocks on the shelves or on paper, and then paste this paper on the shelves. This guides the children to pack the blocks away in the correct place (it is also a visual matching activity).

Encourage creative play by adding new items or toys to the block area. Some ideas are as follows:

Small boxes	Toy food or other shopping items
Plastic or clay animals	Shells, sticks, pebbles
Toy people or superheroes	Short pieces of hosepipe or rubber tubing
Toy houses	Building tools, eg small spades
Puppets made from toilet roll tubes or cotton reels	Pictures, eg old greeting cards, pictures from catalogues and magazines
Cars	Small pieces of carpeting.

If resources are limited, encourage children to make their own toys using, for example, corks or bottle tops. This could become a creative art activity.

The educational toy area

The educational toy area is the area in the classroom where the educational toys, puzzles and games are kept, usually on low shelves. Like blocks, educational toys help the children develop and learn a number of different skills and concepts. You will need to consider the specific learning value of each different toy or game. Educational toys can be bought or homemade. Even pebbles, twigs and leaves, plastic bottles, bottle tops, magazine pictures or a pack of playing cards can be used as educational toys and games. For example, children can sort, group or match bottle tops according to specific criteria including some suggested by them. Educational toys and games should have few rules and not too many pieces or parts so that children can play with them on their own. The games should also be well made and durable. Other considerations are that they must be safe, for example not covered in lead-based paint or have sharp edges; be easy to clean; and preferably be multipurpose so that children can play with them in a number of different ways.

Educational toys include:
- Concept toys and games such as What's in a Square?, memory games, dominoes, Lotto, etc. These help children explore concepts such as colour, size, shape and number while developing skills such as sorting, matching, classifying, seriating and sequencing.
- Construction toys such as Duplo, Lego, Junior Engineer, Mechano, Constructo Straws and Unifix blocks. Construction toys have pieces that the children connect or fit together to make different 'constructions'. Sometimes the construction may be a specific thing such as a car or a house, but sometimes the children just enjoy fitting pieces together without making something specific. Homemade construction toys include clothes pegs, tops of aerosol (spray) cans and pipes of different sizes.
- Manipulative toys, which are toys with pieces that can be manipulated or moved by the children. These include threading and lacing toys and cards, beads, stacking rings, sorting trays and pickup sticks.
- Puzzles which could be put with either the construction or the manipulative toys as they develop similar skills and concepts. Puzzles tend, however, to be placed in their own space. They can be of different sizes, and have a different number of pieces and even shapes. A rough guide is that by age six most children will be able to complete at least a 20-piece puzzle, but again contextual factors will affect this. Different types of puzzles include inset puzzles where the pieces fit into holes, and jigsaw puzzles where pieces fit together.
- Educational games that have rules. The rules are about how the children play the game and what they can or cannot do when playing the game. Snakes and Ladders, Ludo, dice games, Snap and Diketo are examples of educational games. These games can be bought or can be homemade. Can you name some other educational toys/games that are played in your culture?

The fantasy play area

Young children like to take part in make-believe or fantasy play (which is also sometimes called 'dramatic play'), and this is an integral part of early learning. In fact, according to Vygotsky, fantasy or socio-dramatic play is the lead activity for children between ages of three and six, so the notion that fantasy play is not appropriate for Grade R children is incorrect.

Children like to pretend to be adults – mothers, fathers, grandparents, firemen, doctors, nurses, hairdressers, office workers, taxi-drivers, traffic officers, shopkeepers, etc. They also like to adopt other roles such as babies, or superheroes such as characters from *Frozen*, or Catboy, Spiderman and Batman, who remain popular. According to Erikson (see Chapter 2), it is through fantasy play that children start making sense of the complex adult world.

Children will use real objects such as spoons, cups and plates in their games, but these objects can also become symbols (represent something else) where children pretend that objects such as blocks are cars, food, cell phones, etc (see Chapter 10).

All Grade R children should have access to a fantasy play area. This could be in their classroom, a common space used by all children or even, if appropriate, be set up outside. To expose children to a variety of experiences, change the fantasy area regularly. Introduce different props so that different types of imaginative play are consistently encouraged. Where possible, the fantasy area could be an extension of the theme.

The fantasy area does not have to comprise expensive equipment. Many everyday items can be used for fantasy play. Items no longer used in the home, for example a broken but still safe cooking pot. If there is not enough storage space, make use of large boxes, crates or old suitcases to store the equipment enjoyed during fantasy play. Dressing-up clothes could also be displayed on a homemade washing line using sturdy poles and a length of rope. If practical, display a mirror so that body image is naturally reinforced.

Some suggested themes which lend themselves to fantasy play are listed in Table 7.1.

Table 7.1 Themes and props for fantasy play

THEMES/TOPICS	EQUIPMENT AND CLOTHES (ADD TO THIS YOURSELF)
Who am I?	Mirrors, clothes, toys, etc
My family	Dress up as various family members; add items that could be used as jewellery, ties, handbags
The kitchen	Dishcloth, washing-up bowl, drying-up cloth, pots, pans, radio, clock, ironing board, toaster, broom, dustpan and brush, papier-maché or plastic fruit and vegetables, empty food containers, etc

THEMES/TOPICS	EQUIPMENT AND CLOTHES (ADD TO THIS YOURSELF)
My school	Lunch box, water bottle, appropriate food, pencils, paper, easel with board, chalk, scrap paper stapled to make books, crayons, school uniform
The clinic/hospital	Doctor's white coat or old white school shirt, nurse's apron, nurse's cap, stethoscope, bandages, cottonwool, torch, ambulance men's caps, notepad and pencil, clipboard, paper and pencil, crutches, syringes without needles
The office	Desk, old computer, paper, pens, punch, letter/parcel stamp, telephone directory, telephone/old cell phone, appropriate dressing-up clothes for both boys and girls
The fire station	Fire engine (make with box/wagon/chairs), bell, rope, small ladder, hose or piece of hosepipe, buckets, gumboots, jackets and caps, helmets, gloves, first-aid kit, road map, telephone, walkie-talkie or cell phones
The spaza shop/shopping	Different items that could be sold there, 'money', cash register, shelves, bookcase or empty boxes in which to place tins or packets of food, paper bags, shopping bags, shopping baskets, etc
Building	Hardhats, buckets, rope, shovel/spades, tools, pieces of wood, 'bricks' (eg shoeboxes or wooden blocks), etc

> **Something to consider**
>
> Fantasy play encourages holistic development and learning. During fantasy play, children experiment – they move, see, hear, touch and talk. See Chapter 10 for a detailed discussion on play.

If possible, teachers should also promote creative dramatic play by providing the children with enjoyable experiences. Children should be taken on outings or visits, such as to a park or a shop. Teachers could invite interesting people, such as a fireman, to visit the class and talk about their work. Reading and telling stories, showing pictures or short DVDs on, for example, dancing, and planning interesting theme discussions help to stimulate children's imaginations and can thus enrich fantasy play. Children can also make items to add to the fantasy corner during creative art activities, for example modelling salt dough fruit and vegetables, or drawing pictures of food on a paper plate for the 'restaurant' or home.

The book corner

Interacting with books is an important way to promote emergent literacy in young children. There must be a book area in every Grade R classroom, even if it is only a small area.

Planning this area:
- Set up the book area in a quiet part of the room where the children can sit and 'read' (look at) the books and pictures without being disturbed.

- Display books on low bookshelves which can be used as a room divider and easily accessed by the children. If there are no bookshelves, think of alternatives such as placing a plank between two chairs or even using a cardboard box to display the books. Do not place too many books on one shelf.
- Make the book area an inviting one. Place a carpet, mats or carpet samples in the book area. Add cushions, if possible, for colour and comfort. A small table and chairs can also be used in the book area if there is sufficient space. The children can sit at the table and 'read' and discuss their books together. Ideally try to avoid having children sitting on a cold floor.
- Select appropriate books for display in the book area. Books should be provided in the language of instruction used at the school as well as other home languages. Change the books regularly. If possible, choose some books that are associated with the theme as this encourages the children to learn more about the topic. The children can also make their own books to add to the book area. Remember, sometimes you can get books from your local library. Find out what facilities are available in your community.

Something to consider

A teacher says: 'I cannot give the children a book area because they ruin the books. They draw in them and tear the pages'.
What would your response be?

Find out more

Your role is to teach children to look after the books and to encourage them to enjoy 'reading' them. Teach the children how to turn the pages, how to look at them respectfully and how to learn from them. The teacher is the role model. See chapters 11 and 12 for more information.

Remember: A book area or corner is NOT the same as story time. And teaching children how to use books is NOT the same as reading or telling a story. All these need to happen.

Children play in the book corner during free play or child-initiated activities. The story ring (see Chapter 11), usually the third ring of the day, is a whole-group teacher-guided activity.

Other areas/corners

If you have sufficient space in your classroom, you can set up a special area or corner that links to your theme/topic.

> **Something to consider**
>
> **A listening area/ corner**
> This is a corner with specific listening activities that help children to learn to listen and in so doing enhance a variety of auditory perceptual-motor skills (see Chapter 4).

Table 7.2 sets out some of these skills and suggests some activities that could enhance them. Children can do these activities on their own, either in pairs or in small groups.

Table 7.2 Activities to enhance perceptual-motor skills

PERCEPTUAL-MOTOR SKILL	SUGGESTED ACTIVITY
Auditory memory Children must be able to recall what they have heard.	Children can listen to CDs and then describe what they have heard. Reading a story onto a DVD/CD/cassette and allowing children to listen to it and then describe what they have heard.
Auditory discrimination Children can identify differences between the sounds.	They can play with shakers which make different sounds and then identify which shaker is making which noise.
Auditory matching Children can identify sounds that are the same.	Make six shakers with lids, for example tins, plastic bottles or boxes. In two containers place the same number of pebbles; in another two pour the same amount of rice; in the last two pour the same amount of sugar. Mix up the containers. The children shake each container and listen to the sound it makes. They then put the two containers that make the same sound together.
Auditory sequencing Present sound in a specific order or pattern.	Encourage children to sequence sounds – listening to and repeating the sounds in the order they were presented. For example, one child makes sounds with two to three different items without the other child seeing what is happening. The second child waits until the child making the sounds has finished and then says which was the first sound, which was the second and which was the third sound heard.
Auditory association Children learn to match or associate a sound with the correct representation of what/who makes the sound.	Give each child a handful of bottle tops and a card with pictures of things that make a different sound for example a cat, cow, telephone, tractor, car. One child is chosen to be the 'sound maker'. He/she makes one of the sounds represented and the other children place a bottle top on the correct picture. The game continues until each picture on the card is covered with a bottle top (this is sometimes called 'sound bingo'). »

PERCEPTUAL-MOTOR SKILL	SUGGESTED ACTIVITY
Auditory closure When pieces of a spoken word are missing, and children are able to fill in the missing sound.	Children hear the incomplete word 'cater…' and they complete the word: caterpillar.

A music area/corner

Although music rings are teacher-guided activities, the teacher can plan a special music area (corner) for a day, a week or a longer period of time. Use tapes, CDs or even a cell phone, and teach the children how to use the device correctly. Even a radio playing music can be used sometimes for the children to listen and move to music in the music area (corner). Musical instruments can be placed on shelves or hung on hooks in the music area. These can be natural items (eg seed pods), homemade instruments (eg shakers made from empty shampoo bottles, or metal bottle tops threaded on a piece of wire), bought instruments or toys that make sounds. Rules might have to be negotiated to control noise levels (see Chapter 14).

A discovery area/corner

A discovery area/corner is where the children are given apparatus which is placed on a low table to explore by themselves. Listening and music areas/corners are also 'discovery' areas where the children make discoveries about sound and music. In other discovery areas, the children learn about the environment, nature, science, mathematics, etc.

By exploring the objects, children can experience hands-on learning. Pictures or books on their own do not make it a *discovery* area. The children need objects and apparatus that they can see, touch, hear, smell and taste. They learn about the world around them through all their senses. Some ideas for a discovery table include the following:

Nature	Seeds, rocks, stones, soil, plants, insects, animal hides, hard and soft in nature, rough and smooth in nature, etc
Science	Magnets, machines, things that float and sink, things that are used for tying (fastening), things with lids, things with holes, heavy and light things, etc
Mathematics	Beads, pebbles, counters (think of acorns, the ties that keep bread bags closed, etc), sorting trays, scale, tape measure, shapes, etc.

Discovery corners/areas can feed curiosity, and lead to language-rich discussions.

> **Something to consider**
>
> **What other play areas/corners might you introduce to extend curiosity?**
> Corners/areas could be set up to explore the subjects that have to be covered in the Grade R year. These areas could include, as already mentioned, a language area/corner, a mathematics area/corner and a life skills area, such as a visual arts area. See chapters 11, 12, 13, 14 for more information on these areas.

THE OUTDOOR LEARNING ENVIRONMENT

Children are active learners, and outdoor play is activity focused as well as providing opportunities for fresh air and sunlight, and to burn off excess energy. Furthermore, it encourages the child's holistic development and learning, especially physical development which includes gross and fine motor and spatial awareness.

The outdoor environment should be of sufficient space to allow the children to run freely as well as use the equipment. If you have a large enough space, you could cordon off a section to become an indigenous garden area where you let natural grasses grow. Small creatures such as insects would be drawn to such an area. This could offer children, especially those with naturalistic intelligence (see Chapter 2), additional learning opportunities, and could also utilise the environment as the third teacher, which we discuss later in the chapter.

Plan the outdoor area carefully to ensure that the apparatus and activities provided stimulate and challenge the children, and play is both purposeful and creative. Safety must be considered at all times. For example, there should always be adult supervision.

Outdoor equipment

Equipment should be durable (long lasting) and sturdy. It should offer children a multitude of different learning experiences. Outdoor equipment play can be divided into two main categories:

- **Fixed equipment** – this refers to larger pieces of equipment (apparatus) that are fixed into the ground, for example a jungle gym.
- **Moveable equipment** – this refers to smaller pieces of equipment that can be moved or re-organised into different positions or shapes by the teacher or the children, for example hula hoops or old tyres.

> **Something to consider**
>
> **Suitability of outdoor equipment**
> How many children can use a particular piece of equipment at the same time? Is the equipment age appropriate and appealing or might they be hesitant to play on it? If so, why?

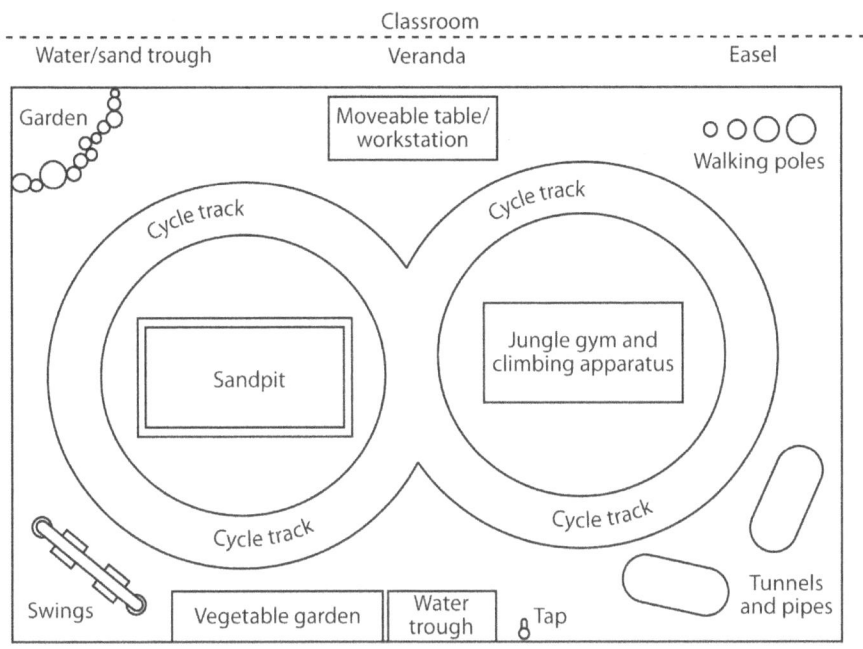

Figure 7.2 An example of an outdoor play area

Find out more

Equipment should be:
- safe
- multipurpose
- easy to maintain
- appealing to children
- able to enhance several areas of development; for example, while playing on a jungle gym, children are developing physical and social skills, and have to take turns as well as balance and climb
- open to imaginative play.

Fixed equipment

This includes the following:
- **Wooden jungle gym**

  Place the jungle gym on a grassy or sandy area and not on concrete or bricks. It is important to use smooth, treated wooden poles which are planted securely in the ground and well attached to each other. There must be no splinters, rough parts, nails or screws that can hurt children. Attach steps, ladders, ropes, rope nets, tyres, a fireman's pole, etc, to the jungle gym to add variety and extend play.

  Maintenance – look after the jungle gym by treating the wood regularly with a linseed oil/turpentine mixture. Check all the joints regularly. Make sure that any ropes are not frayed.

- **Metal jungle gym**
  Place the metal jungle gym in the shade so that the metal does not get too hot and burn the children. The metal piping/tubing must be strong and not too thin (in diameter). The bars/rungs must also not be too thick for children's small hands. They must be able to grasp the bars safely. There should be no rough edges after welding. Have different-sized spaces between the bars/rungs and have one section where children can hold on above their head and stretch and swing their whole body.

  Maintenance – protect the jungle gym from rusting by painting the metal with a lead-free paint. First, apply a suitable undercoat and then use brightly coloured paint on top. Treat any damaged areas with anti-rust and repaint afterwards.
- **Climbing frame**
  Metal climbing frames are like traditional jungle gyms but are made in different shapes, for example an aeroplane, rocket, car, and an A-frame tent. The children enjoy climbing on them, and metal ladders or wooden planks can be hooked onto them to make steps to climb up or down, or platforms to sit on. A climbing frame can also be made into a shelter, den or 'house' by throwing a blanket or old curtain over it. Props (items) can be added for outdoor fantasy (dramatic) play.
- **Tyres**
  Old car tyres can be used in many ways – as a climbing wall, part of an obstacle course, a tyre tunnel or steppingstones (by sinking the tyres into the ground). A large tractor or truck tyre can be placed on the ground and the children can stand or jump on it. Children can also roll tyres, and climb through them or over them, etc. Tyres can also be used to create boundaries and as planters for flowers or vegetables.
- **Swings**
  Swings are very popular with children. They need to be placed out of the way (often in a back corner of the playing area) to prevent children from walking too close and getting hit by them. Swings can be made with strong ropes and hung from a tree. The seats can be made from wood or old car tyres. Rope ladders or ropes knotted at intervals can be used for swinging as well as climbing.
- **Slides**
  Slides must be a suitable height and safe. They can be free-standing or part of a large jungle gym. Metal slides can become very hot so they should be placed in the shade. Wooden slides must be free of splinters and should be treated, varnished, oiled or painted well.
- **Concrete pipes**
  Children enjoy crawling through concrete pipes, sliding over the sides, jumping off them and even sitting inside them and chatting. The pipes must be wide enough to allow children to crawl through and short enough for those passing through to be visible from both open ends. The pipes must be properly secured and, preferably, painted in bright colours.

- **Logs**
  Walking on different-sized pieces of tree trunk or logs encourages children's sense of balance. Bury the wood firmly in the ground at different levels, in groups and in patterns. Use them as part of an obstacle course.
- **Old car, taxi or boat**
  An old car, taxi or boat can be used for creative play. Make sure there are no sharp edges and that the equipment is rust free. Doors and boots must have locks removed to prevent children from getting trapped inside.

Moveable equipment

This type of equipment promotes social interaction, negotiation, sharing and decision making. Because it is moveable, it has to be packed away after use to make sure it does not get damaged, lost or stolen. Encourage children to participate in this tidy-up routine.

- **Wheeled toys**
  Plastic motorbikes, bicycles, tricycles and scooters can help the children develop coordination skills such as pedalling and steering. Concrete bicycle tracks can be laid in a special cycling area. Once the children can ride, the play opportunities can be extended:
  - Use chalk to create unusual pathways for children to follow. Challenge the children by drawing curved lines or zigzag lines, or large shapes.
  - Arrange objects so that the bikes have to travel around and between them without touching them.
  - Make roads and crossroads, and add stop streets, traffic lights, road signs and even a zebra crossing. Plan a weekly theme that focuses on road safety. Teach the children the correct signals and when to use them.

  Wagons (carts) and trucks encourage social play and develop physical strength. The children push, pull and load the wagons and trucks. The children will add their own ideas to their imaginative play using the wagons and trucks.
- **Other moveable equipment**
  These develop many different skills and encourage creative play. They can also be used in teacher-guided activities. Some examples are shown in the following table.

Balancing boards	Blankets	Water trough
Barrels	Carpet squares, car mats	Game skills equipment – balls, bats, beanbags, skittles, hoops, etc
Bottles (plastic)	Curtains	Ropes
Boxes	Cushions	Tyres
Buckets	Ladders and planks	Punching bags
Tubes and pipes	Wooden reels	Empty plastic containers

Sand play

It usually happens outdoors but can take place indoors or on the veranda. Offer both on a regular basis to children. They should be fun, enjoyable activities.

For sand play, a sandpit, sand tray or sand trough can be used.

- **Sandpit**
  - Choose a place where the sandpit will get both sun and shade, but where it will not become filled with falling leaves.
  - Build it near a tap or water supply so that the sand can sometimes be wet.
  - Have a cement, brick or paved area around the edge of the sandpit for the children to sit on, and cement the sides and bottom of the sandpit to prevent soil from mixing with the clean sand. Make sure there is proper drainage.
  - Fill with clean river or specially treated sand. Cover the sandpit when not in use, especially overnight, and treat the sand regularly with a solution of disinfectant such as Jik or Jeyes Fluid or by digging in coarse salt. Use a large fork to turn the sand.
  - If the sand play takes place under a shelter or on a veranda protected from the rain, a large wooden box (without a lid) can be filled with sand. The box should be big enough for a few children to sit in it together. Make sure that the wood is smooth and safe, without splinters. Varnish or paint it.
- **Tyre sandpit**

  A tractor or truck tyre can be used to make an outdoor sandpit. If the top edge is cut away a little, this sometimes helps to prevent insects hiding under it. Check the tyre regularly for spiders and insects, and keep it filled with clean sand which is disinfected regularly.
- **Sand trough**

  Large plastic troughs or basins can be used for sand play. Put the trough on the ground in a suitable area or place it in a securely made metal or wooden stand. Some deep sand trays (troughs) are built as part of the stand and are not separate. They are sometimes called sand tables.
- **Sand tray**

  A sand tray is not as deep as a sand trough. It is often used indoors on the floor (on sheets of plastic or newspaper) or on a low table.

Water play

This can be offered indoors or outdoors near to a sink, a tap or a hosepipe. Different containers can also be used for water play such as a trough, a baby bath, a large basin, a zinc bath, or a piece of a gutter. The water should be changed daily if possible, and water play must be supervised. Protect children's clothing with waterproof aprons and roll up long sleeves before water play. Do not allow children to stay in wet clothes. If it takes place indoors, protect the floor and furniture with heavy sheets of plastic. Special care should be taken in winter so that children do not become wet and cold.

- **Factors to keep in mind in relation to sand and water play**
  - Most equipment used in water and sand play must be strong and durable. Anti-waste equipment, such as yogurt tubs often used in water play, is one exception to this.
  - All equipment must be safe for the children to use.
  - Check the equipment regularly and remove any broken items.
  - Larger equipment is more suitable for a sandpit as small equipment is easily buried and lost. Smaller accessories such as toy animals are suitable for sand trays.
  - Store the equipment in containers such as plastic storage boxes or even a laundry basket. Use containers of a size that the children can carry themselves.
  - Teach the children to shake the sand off the equipment before packing it away.
  - Remind children not to rub their eyes with sandy hands.
  - Keep a hard, grass broom nearby for sweeping the sand from the surrounding ledge back into the sandpit.
  - Cover the floor or table with sheets of plastic or newspaper when using a sand tray indoors.

Suggestions for equipment include the following (many items could be used for both, but some are more suited to either sand or water):

Plastic cups and jugs	Anti-waste items (eg yoghurt tubs)	Toy cars, boats, animals	Sieves and strainers
Spades	Plastic bottles	Measuring cups	Scoops
Rakes	Wooden blocks	Shells	Buckets
Bowls	Ice cream sticks	Eggbeaters	Tubing
Moulds	Pieces of hosepipe	Soup ladles	Toy boats
Variety of spoons	Plastic flowerpots	Spray bottles	Feathers
Funnels	Old pots and pans	Medicine droppers	Tennis balls

Value of sand and water play

Many different skills, attitudes and concepts can be developed through sand and water play. For example, a child can explore the idea of how much a container holds, and how fast water flows through a particular type of sieve or funnel.

Something to consider

What are the developmental and learning opportunities presented in sand and water play?

Find out more

The following table makes some initial suggestions. What other ideas could you add?

SAND AND WATER PLAY		
ACTIVITY	**DEVELOPMENTAL FOCUS**	**CONCEPT FORMATION**
Sand and water play in general	*Physical* Fine and gross motor skills Eye–hand coordination *Social* Negotiation, turn taking, sharing Sensory awareness Spatial awareness *Cognitive* Estimation Prediction Memorisation Differentiation (sorting) Language – finding alternate words to describe items and experiences Language structure – adjectives and adverbs (eg 'coarse sand' and 'sinks quickly') *Emotional* expression through, for example, sensiopathic play that can help with the release of emotions *Creative*, eg children make a landscape in the sand for toy dinosaurs	More, less, heavy, light, on top of, behind, near, next to, number, shape, mass, equal, same as, fast, slow, different textures, coarse, smooth, etc
Water play: floating and sinking using a wide range of different containers	*Cognitive* Estimation Prediction Problem solving Memorisation Differentiation (sorting) Language (eg words that describe how water flows through different objects)	Float, sink, shallow, deep, fast, slow, quickly

ROLE OF THE TEACHER

To make the most of learning opportunities that arise in both outdoor and indoor free play, the teachers do the following:

- Identify the teachable moment and use it, for example, to pose open-ended questions, engage in active listening, model the use of new vocabulary, encourage prediction, and thoughtfully observe and record what children do.
- Debrief the children from time to time – giving them the opportunity to tell others what they did and learned at play.
- Occasionally help a few children evaluate their efforts and plan what they can do tomorrow.
- Communicate to parents/caregivers the value of developmentally appropriate and culturally responsive play.
- Ensure that the equipment is safe and the children are properly supervised.

Find out more

A safety check list

A child-friendly school, to which we referred in Chapter 6, is consistently safety conscious. Following is an example of a safety checklist for an outdoor and indoor environment that could be used by a teacher. This list may be adapted to meet a particular school's context.

Table 7.3 Safety checklist

ITEM	WATCH POINTS
OUTDOOR ENVIRONMENT	
Fence	This must be intact, approximately two metres high, with no breaks, etc.
Protective surfaces under equipment	Avoid compacted soil, uneven surfaces, concrete and tar. Surfaces should be loosely covered with materials such as wood chips, mulch, shredded rubber or soft mats, or, in certain instances, appropriate astroturf.
Playground	Ensure that the surface is safe, for example no dangerous tree roots, no large stones, no litter, no dangerous materials – broken glass; cans; twisted metal; cracked, loose, slippery paving stones; sharp objects; etc.
Climbing equipment	Check for rough surfaces, splinters, rusty areas, peeling paint, sharp points (nails, bolts, etc) missing rungs, broken steps, etc.
Swings	Check for worn bearings that need to be oiled, damaged seats, frayed rope, etc.
Flowers and plants	Ensure there are no poisonous plants, for example oleander, and many types of mushrooms, etc. »

ITEM	WATCH POINTS
INDOOR ENVIRONMENT	
Safety rules that cover outdoor and indoor environment	These must be clearly displayed (pictorially as well as written), and an emergency evacuation plan must be in place and practised at least once a term.
Classroom layout and maintenance	Classroom arrangement must be such that the teacher can see all children at all times; it must be litter free, the equipment must be stored properly, and the tables cleaned after activities, etc.
Floor surfaces	These should be clean and non-slip; carpets must be cleaned daily; spills must be wiped up immediately; and there should be no uneven tiles, etc.
Adequate ventilation	Windows must be intact and able to open, and air vents must be open, etc.
Heating	Heaters must be wall mounted, and there must be suitable fire guards, etc.
Storage of equipment	There must be sufficient shelves that are easy for children to reach; all areas must be labelled properly; poisonous items/hazardous substances must be out of reach, and stored and labelled properly; free-standing shelves and cupboards must be secure, etc.
Electrical appliances	Lights and other appliances must be in good working order, and cables must be clear of walkways, etc.
Bathrooms	Toilets must be cleaned daily and after use; facilities with soap for washing hands must be available; the hand basins must be clean with no dripping taps; clean towels must be provided to dry hands; hand sanitisers must be provided; etc.
Add to this list	

Keep the checklist in your classroom where you file other documents and policies, and use it once a week to ensure a safe environment that will promote learning.

Taking responsibility: making the checklist work

One way to deal with problems identified is suggested in Table 7.4. Note the problem and action required and when the problem was resolved.

Table 7.4 Example of completed checklist

DATE	ITEM	ACTION REQUIRED	ACTION COMPLETED (DATE)	ACTION TAKEN AND BY WHOM
OUTDOOR ENVIRONMENT				
23 Sep 2014	Fence	Repair hole in fence next to swings	Repaired 26 February 2021	Mrs Dlamini
Add ...				

INDOOR ENVIRONMENT				
25 Sep 2014	Bathrooms, toilets only cleaned once a week	Clean after routines and thoroughly at end of day	25 March 2021	Mrs Tshepo

To summarise, therefore, the teacher's role in the design and management of the indoor and outdoor learning environment includes the following:
- Choosing appropriate equipment, and planning its positioning
- Inspecting it every day and making sure it is safe for the children to use
- Supervising the children playing on, and with, the equipment, and ensuring it is packed away safely at the end of the day
- Mediating children's play by rotating (changing) the equipment, adding new equipment, and identifying and utilising teachable moments
- Observing which children use the equipment, how they use it and how often, and which children do not use it
- Recording observations and using them in planning, assessment and report writing
- Involving, if possible, the parents/caregivers and the community in the provision of maintenance of both resources and appropriate learning experiences
- Planning the environment so it can act as a third teacher.

Find out more

The environment as the third teacher

'What children learn does not follow as an automatic result from what is taught, but rather, it is in large part due to the children's own doing, as a consequence of their activities and our resources' (Malaguzzi, 1996).

For Loris Malaguzzi the founder of the Reggio Emilia programme, the learning environment was so important in making learning meaningful that he called it the third teacher. Malaguzzi's philosophy was based on the belief that children are capable and competent learners who can collaborate meaningfully with each other during group activities. He thus believed in social learning and was able to blend theory and practice to enhance learning.

Question

Who do you think are the first and second teachers?
Jot down your ideas, then read further.

For the learning environment to be the third teacher it has to be flexible, and responsive to the needs of the teacher and children in order to learn together.

Such a learning environment should reflect the values we want to communicate to children (think back to the hidden curriculum). Malaguzzi recognised that a supportive learning environment enables children's agency and helps shape a child's identity as a powerful player in his/her own life and the lives of others. For this type of environment to actively promote these values, teachers have to have deep insights into the underlying principles that inform early childhood education and how children learn best. This type of environment encourages curiosity, exploration and discovery, the asking of questions, and reasoning and thinking skills.

According to Malaguzzi (1996), for the environment to be the third teacher the teacher ought to do the following:

- *Create a flexible, relationship-driven learning environment*
  Such an environment will include the other two teachers – the parent and the class teacher. Often assuming the role of researcher, the teacher engages meaningfully with children and intentionally engages them in meaningful work and conversation. The third teacher – the environment – is a setting that is aesthetically pleasing and reflects purposeful learning (see Chapter 10 on playful pedagogies). Such an environment leads to guided learning and the co-construction of knowledge through an emergent curriculum; in other words, teachers become co-learners with the children. Such a curriculum demands a visionary and knowledgeable teacher. Flexible environments allow teachers to be responsive to the interests of the children, freeing them to construct knowledge together. When a sudden event such as a helicopter flying closely overhead occurs, a teacher should feel comfortable moving out of her planned schedule or activity and allow the children to focus on this sudden occurrence that has sparked their curiosity and imagination.

- *Create an environment that reflects our values*
  We need to ask: 'What kind of culture do we want the children to experience in our schools'? The Reggio approach would suggest that teachers engage in creative and reflective thinking about their teaching environments (Curtis et al, 2013). Such an environment is respectful of all, and collaboration and discussion (participatory learning – see Chapter 8 – are valued as an integral part of the learning and teaching practices.

- *Create environments that foster creativity*
  This idea of creativity is captured in the expression 'a hundred languages of children'. The 'hundred languages' refers to communication and emphasises the importance of providing children with 100 ways to share their thinking of the world around them (The Compass School, 2017). These are the multiple symbolic expressions used by children to express their own knowledge and desires through artwork, conversation, early writing (drawing), dramatic play, music, dance, and other outlets. The environment inspires and supports creative thinking and invention. Creativity is the conduit – the instrument that allows us to communicate with and understand others. Teachers should think carefully about resources. Open-ended resources such as clipboards, paper, a variety of writing and drawing tools (pens, crayons, kokis, feathers, etc) are preferred

to ready-made materials such as bought foam shapes or rubber stamps. To further inspire creativity, the teacher makes use of materials and activities that provoke (lead to or encourage) investigation and group learning. Examples of provocations could be the introduction of a special insect such as a dung beetle or a rain spider. According to Malaguzzi (1996), creativity emerges from multiple experiences, coupled with a well-supported development of personal resources, including a sense of freedom to venture beyond the known. Teachers therefore must foster creativity through investigations, explorations and discovery learning.

Try this out

Read the following extract (Biermeier, 2015). Implement this or a similar activity in your classroom. Write a short reflective account of the processes, the learning highlights and challenges for both you and the children.

> In Reggio Emilia-inspired schools, teachers place great emphasis on using materials and activities that provoke investigation and group learning. As expected, being curious and inventive little people, the children are very excited about the new spider addition to their classroom. They closely watch the tarantula [type of spider], using the magnifying glasses to see the details and then drawing what they observe. The conversation is lively and loud as they speculate about where the spider came from, what the spider eats, whether it is a boy or a girl spider, and how the spider compares to the other spiders in the photographs.
>
> When the children ask their teachers what kind of spider it is, the teachers seem uncertain and wonder aloud how the class might figure it out. 'We don't jump at giving them the answers,' explains Jane Barber, classroom teacher. 'Our intent is to focus on the processes of discovery, to teach them how to learn by not only observing but also using resources such as books and the Internet. We act as guides in the hunt for information.' In the weeks that follow numerous drawings of spiders are on display in the classroom, and the children count the legs and eyes, write their names on their drawings, and ask how to spell *tarantula, spinneret, and egg sac*. The children want to write, because the writing is meaningful to them. The scientific inquiry, early literacy, and math opportunities naturally fall into place around the spider investigation (Biermeier, 2015: 8–9).

Find out more

To foster creativity, Reggio Emilia schools have an art centre called an atelier with specialised art teachers. The other teachers have fixed times when they bring their group of children to the atelier, but are welcome to bring small groups of children at any time. Such an environment encourages joyful, meaningful learning (see Chapter 10). The focus is on the process of creating, not the end product.

Celebrating the child's identity

Promoting children's feelings of self-worth is pivotal; it is an important attitude/value to develop in young children. In the Reggio approach, promoting feelings of success in young children by acknowledging who they are and their achievements is paramount. Experiencing success is a strong motivator for further learning.

Ensuring that children 'belong' and feel part of a group is essential (see chapters 4 and 8). One way of promoting this feeling in a Reggio environment is to place photos of each child with their name boldly printed on the wall at the beginning of the school year. These photos are quickly followed by pinning the child's drawings and other artwork next to the photo. If possible, the child's name is written in his/her own hand as well as a quotation about something the child likes.

Try this out

What are some other ways that you can build and celebrate the child's identity?

Did you think of including an 'All about me' book that contains family photographs, and naming the child's locker and making a birthday chart that is displayed on one of the classroom walls?

Implications of the third teacher for teaching and learning

The idea of the third teacher draws on the importance of a quality learning environment that motivates and supports the child's learning through participatory, interactive activities (see Chapter 8). As the teacher it becomes your responsibility to ensure that you implement an optimal learning environment that allows children to feel safe and secure, promotes curiosity and discovery learning through active participation. Such an environment should also encourage you to feel safe and to venture beyond what is already known as you co-construct learning with the children. 'Although good teaching requires organization and routines, it is never inflexible and rarely routine. It dances with surprise. It pursues wonder. It finds joy at every turn' (Biermeier, 2015: 5).

SUMMARY

This chapter has considered how to set up an optimal learning environment. It has been stressed that proper planning and care of the physical environment are fundamental to establishing a successful Grade R day. It also emphasised the importance of variety and creativity in decision making about equipment choice and safety. It considered the role of the environment as the third teacher and the teacher's role in creating such an environment.

BIBLIOGRAPHY

Biermeier, MA. 2015. 'Inspired by Reggio Emilia: Emergent curriculum in relationship-driven learning environments'. *Young Children* 70(5), November. https://www.naeyc.org/resources/pubs/yc/nov2015/emergent-curriculum#mainrces (Accessed 12 January 2021).

Bredekamp, S (ed). 1987. *Developmentally appropriate practice in early childhood programs serving children from birth through age 8*. Washington: NAEYC.

Bruce, T. 2004. *Developing learning in early childhood*. London: SAGE Publications.

Catron, CE & Allen, J. 2008. *Early childhood curriculum. A creative play model*. New Jersey: Pearson.

Crosser, S. 1994. 'Making the most of water play'. *Young Children* 49(5), July.

Curtis, D, Lebo, D, Cividanes, WM & Carter, M. 2013. *Reflecting in communities of practice: A workbook for early childhood educators.* St Paul, MN: Redleaf Press.

Davin, R & Van Staden, C. 2005. *The reception year*. Sandown: Heinemann.

Department of Basic Education (DBE). 2011. *Curriculum and Assessment Policy Statement*. Pretoria: DBE.

Excell, LA, Helsby, M & Linington, V. 2010. *Grade R practitioner's course*. University of the Witwatersrand: Johannesburg.

Gordon, AM & Browne, KW. 2008. *Beginnings and beyond: Foundations in early childhood education*. New York: Thomson Delmar.

Malaguzzi, L. 1996. *The hundred languages of children. The Reggio Emilia approach towards early childhood education.* New Jersey: Ablex Publication.

McEvilly, K & Tiley, J. 1990. *A sound foundation: Education for primary school*. Johannesburg: Hodder & Stoughton.

The Compass School. 2017. *The hundred languages of children*. https://www.thecompassschool.com/blog/the-hundred-languages-of-children/#:~:text=The%20hundred%20languages%20is%20a,of%20the%20world%20around%20them (Accessed 13 January 2021).

GLOSSARY

Environment – the physical surroundings and conditions that affect people's lives

Gross motor – large muscles, for example muscles of the arms or legs

LSM – learner support material

Mediation – the guidance, support and collaboration with others to solve a problem through the use of psychological tools, the most important of which is language

Provocation – a Reggio Emilia term to describe a stimulus that arouses children's curiosity and encourages them to engage with the stimulus in a variety of ways

Sensiopathic – refers to how the senses, in particular the sense of touch, can be used to sooth and calm. Finger painting and play dough are good examples of sensiopathic activities

Spatial awareness – children becoming aware of the space around them and the position they occupy in that space, eg in front of a swing, next to a table, etc

Teachable moment – an opportunity that arises spontaneously where the teacher can introduce new knowledge which could be a different point of view on, for example, a familiar theme such as the family

Voice of the child – providing opportunities for children to make choices, offer opinions and to be listened to

Chapter 8

Teaching and learning

Corné Kruger, Elsabé Wessels, Hasina Ebrahim, Naseema Shaik

In this chapter we consider

- how to deepen the understanding of developmentally and culturally appropriate practice in Grade R
- an understanding of the concept of participatory learning
- how views of children inform the teaching–learning process
- the kind of teacher you are and how this influences participatory learning in Grade R
- the planning of teaching and learning in Grade R
- the role of the curriculum in the daily teaching–learning activities in Grade R
- how to plan learning activities that are informed by the curriculum.

INTRODUCTION

Teaching, learning and assessment are central to activities aimed at promoting the acquisition of knowledge, skills and values. Each activity should be well planned and implemented, as it is an important part of a cohesive dynamic system called the curriculum.

Teaching, learning and assessment are implemented in an integrated way in Grade R. Although this chapter will focus more on teaching and learning strategies, and Chapter 9 will deal in more detail with aspects of assessment in Grade R, the three components are interrelated and will influence each other.

All teaching in the Grade R class should be directed towards effective learning and therefore needs to adhere to the key principles of learning in the Grade R classroom (see Chapter 3). Planning for learning should thus be based on the following question: How does a young child learn?

HOW DOES A YOUNG CHILD LEARN?

Chapter 3 included play-based learning as one of the key principles of teaching and learning in Grade R. Not only do play activities accommodate the fantasy world of a Grade R child, but play also allows for a participatory approach to learning, where the teacher and child are equally involved in the teaching–learning process (see Chapter 10).

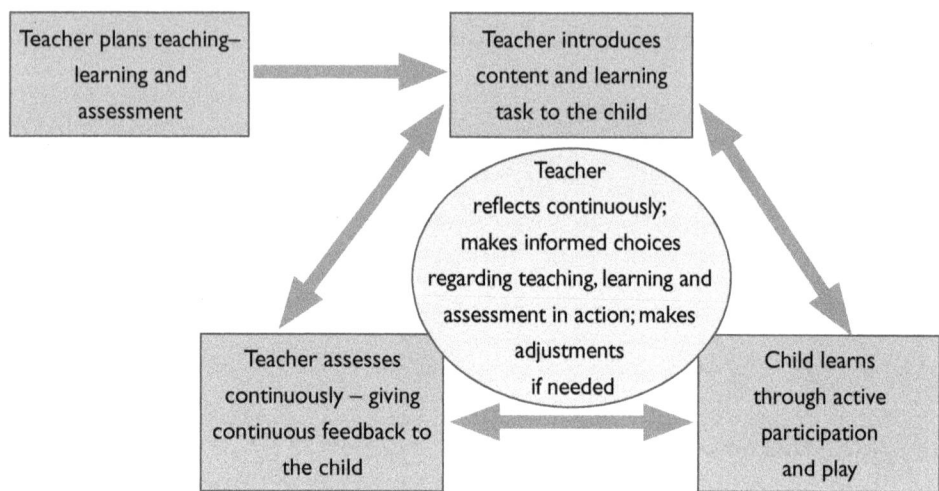

Figure 8.1 Reflective planning for and implementation of teaching, learning and assessment

The teacher:
- plans the teaching, learning and assessment activities in detail
- designs/chooses learning and teaching support material, which includes assessment instruments
- implements the teaching and learning experience while continuously assessing the children's progress
- uses and records information gathered through continuous assessment to inform teaching, and revises teaching and learning strategies should this information show that learning is not effective
- optimises learning opportunities generated by the children
- provides opportunities for children to make choices and give good reasons for them.

A young child learns through participation

Participatory learning is made up of two concepts – participation and learning. Participation is a medium through which children can be involved in meaningful ways to influence decisions that affect them. When children participate, they are actively making sense of their life world. To make their participation meaningful, children should be encouraged to share with others the different meanings they are making. It is important for teachers to invite children to share their views and opinions as participants in the learning process. When this happens, they become valuable contributors to their own education (Lansdown, 2004).

As a Grade R teacher, it is important to understand that participation means more than just taking part. There has to be joint ownership in the decision-making process, and active involvement of all parties (Miller, 2003). A study by Zhang et al (2015) confirmed that, when a curriculum that prioritises decision making in collaborative groups is implemented, children are more able to transfer what they had learned to other tasks in different contexts. Decision-making opportunities thus support the development of self-regulation that again supports generalisable skills.

If Grade R children are to be participants in a true sense, then it means creating a space for them to contribute their ideas. It is important that young learners be included in simple decision making in the classroom (Zhang et al, 2015; Willow, 2002). Children are interested in what occurs around them and are also well grounded in their own experience and therefore have the capabilities to shape processes and products (Lansdown, 2004). The teacher and the child can actively make decisions as partners. For example, children can be invited to suggest spaces for a 'kids' corner' to display what they have produced.

When children are participating in learning, a social process is taking place. The children, through interaction with their peers and teachers, increase their knowledge and understanding of their world, and the teacher also learns from the children. This two-way process is supported by a strong partnership where teachers create opportunities for children to be fully involved.

The case study that follows illustrates participatory learning which involves children and the teacher as partners in learning.

CASE STUDY 1

It is outdoor free play. Tasha goes to the sandpit. She takes a small bucket and a spade. Sandile is seated next to her. The teacher watches them and then decides to join the children.

Tasha:	I'm making my birthday cake.
Sandile:	Me too.
Teacher:	I would like to learn how to make my birthday cake. Can both of you show me how to make it?
Tasha:	But big people know how to make cakes.
Teacher:	Yes, but they struggle to make cakes with sand.
Tasha and Sandile:	(*giggle*) We'll show you.
Tasha:	You must fill your bucket with sand.
Sandile:	I like a little bit of sand.
Teacher:	I think I will take a little more sand than you, Sandile.
Tasha:	(*points to the teacher's bucket*) It's overfull.
Teacher:	Never mind – I want to see how my cake will turn out.
Tasha:	I'll only take so much sand and I got some water (*extends the palm of her hand vertically*).
Sandile:	Okay, now let's make the cake.

The teacher and the children fill their buckets and pat them with the spade. They turn their buckets upside down and wait for each other to show their cake.

Tasha: No one must show their cake now. I'm going to count to five and then we'll all take off the buckets.
Teacher: Must I lift my hands to show which number we are at?
Sandile: No, let me do that. I know my numbers now.
Teacher: Okay, I'm happy to let Sandile count.
Sandile: One, two, three, four, five (*lifts a finger as he calls out the numbers*).

All three of them remove their buckets. Tasha's cake has the best shape. She jumps up and claps.

Tasha: My birthday cake is the best!
Sandile: I saw you put sand and some water in too.
Teacher: Mine was a flop. Tasha, I need to take more lessons from you.

Try this out

- Draw a mind map that outlines six key points about participatory learning.
- Share your ideas with your colleagues.

Understanding the degrees of participation and their influence on learning

Lansdown (2004) developed ideas on degrees of participation which help one understand the different roles of teachers and children. The degrees are consultative, participatory and self-initiated.

If the teacher takes too much control, participation by children is limited. This happens in structured lessons to teach knowledge and skills. Where teachers become partners with children, children's participation increases. The best participation is self-initiated. We see this during free play when the children are free to explore and experiment without the help of the teacher.

Table 8.1 Lansdown's degrees of participation (Lansdown, 2004)

CONSULTATIVE	PARTICIPATORY	SELF-INITIATED
Projects are designed and controlled by adults. Although the process is controlled by adults, children understand the process, and their opinions and views are valued.	Adults initiate and create partnerships with children. This gives children the power to influence or challenge the process and the outcome. Although this degree of participation is initiated by adults, it does give children some opportunity to share power and also an opportunity to shape the processes in which they are involved.	This type of participation is not defined by adult-led agendas. The children take action. Adults act as facilitators rather than leaders, and the process is controlled by the children themselves. During this process, there is genuine respect for the children. Children identify their own areas of interest. Adults are responsive to children's ideas, views and opinions.

The degrees of participation are further illustrated in Table 8.2.

Table 8.2 The degrees of participation

TEACHER DIRECTS	TEACHER AND CHILD PARTICIPATE	CHILD INITIATES OWN ACTIVITIES
All activities are planned and organised by the teacher, but children understand the procedure, and their thoughts are valued and taken into account. The teacher is in control, and input from the children is limited, for example structured lessons to teach knowledge and skills.	The teacher takes the initiative but involves the children – empowering them to influence the learning outcome. Adults initiate and create partnerships with the children. This gives children the power to influence the teaching–learning process and the outcome.	The child takes initiative and may or may not involve the teacher. Children are in control and the teacher may facilitate or respond to their ideas. The teacher respects the children's ideas and allows the development of the children's interests.

Something to consider

- Study the daily programme for Grade R in Chapter 7.
- Share your ideas on how you could apply the degrees of participation in three different components of this programme.

Find out more

In pairs or a group, discuss the challenges you might experience in implementing Lansdown's degrees of participation for active learning in South African Grade R classes.

Children do not learn in the same way

Grade R children come from different backgrounds. It is important to pay attention to differences. You need to consider how you are catering for diversity. The following ideas are helpful to encourage participatory learning in the context of diversity:

- The learning environment must be accessible to all children. Freedom of movement must be considered, for example, for children in wheelchairs.
- Children with barriers to learning need time and support to participate in learning opportunities. Special care should be taken when planning learning experiences for them.
- The nature of the activities may influence how girls and boys will participate. Observations in relation to who participates and preferences shown should be noted by the teacher and reflected on.
- All children should feel valued in the classroom. Their sense of belonging should be reinforced through interactions with the teacher.

- Collect a wide variety of resources, both homemade and commercial. These resources should provide ample opportunities for exploration and experimentation. When collecting resources, consider the interests of all the children in the class. Do not forget to take into account aspects such as gender, race and culture; for example, there should be dolls of different colours.
- The content of the activities must provide opportunities for all children to participate. Themes must be selected with this in mind. For example, themes such as home and family must reflect all the realities of the South African context.
- Avoid stereotyping practices, for example making assumptions that all girls like to play with dolls, all Indian children like eating curry and rice, etc. Let children experience ideas, and explore tools and utensils from different cultures in order to educate them about diversity.

Something to consider

Write down your thoughts on how a prescribed curriculum (like CAPS) addresses, positively and/or negatively, the learning opportunities for children with diverse needs.

Find out more

Do an electronic search and find out more about the 'anti-bias curriculum' by Louise Derman-Sparks. Explain how you could use these ideas in South African Grade R classes to promote participatory learning.

HOW DO WE TEACH FOR OPTIMAL LEARNING IN GRADE R?

Considering the way young children learn, teaching strategies should focus on learning through play and participatory learning. Furthermore, activities should be developmentally appropriate – that is, suit the level of the children's cognitive, emotional, social and physical development (see Chapter 4). Accommodating diversity among children implies that planning for learning will allow for the various learning styles and developmental levels of the children. Teachers should also keep in mind that young children enjoy and learn through movement, and therefore activities that develop children's small and large muscles should be at the core of teaching and learning in Grade R.

Teaching for participatory learning

Participatory learning should be an integral part of Grade R practice. It takes a certain kind of teacher to encourage participatory learning. A 'jug and mug' teacher will not be able to give children opportunities to learn in participatory ways. This happens when the teacher sees him/herself as the 'jug' with all the necessary knowledge that needs to be poured into a child (the 'mug').

Such teachers will use repetition and the drill method to get children to learn by rote (mostly recalling information taught). Children will be passive and the teacher will be active. Learning becomes a one-way process. The children become bored and lose interest easily because what they know and can do are not connected to the new learning experience.

For participatory learning to take place, an intentional teacher is needed. This type of teacher wants the children to be active in the learning process. The teacher is not the 'jug' but a partner in learning, sometimes taking the lead in the learning process, and at other times letting the children take the lead. Both will learn from each other. An intentional teacher therefore:

- thinks carefully about how to encourage participatory learning
- purposefully selects learning experiences that will help children to develop their knowledge, skills, attitudes and values in participatory ways
- makes informed decisions about what and how children should learn
- takes action to help children actively participate in their learning (Oberg & Oberg, 2012).

Something to consider

- Using the information above, draw a table to distinguish between the two types of teachers.
- How would you describe yourself as a teacher in Grade R? Do you think your characteristics are aligned to the jug and mug or the intentional teacher, or are you somewhere in between? Provide examples to explain.
- What do you think would help teachers become intentional? What challenges do you think they might face in their desire to become such a teacher?
- How would you suggest these challenges may be overcome?

Actions of intentional teachers encouraging participatory learning

Since intentional teachers are serious about children's participation in the learning process, they take action in key areas. Figure 8.2 shows what intentional teachers could do to make learning a participatory process.

Find out more

Grade R, as with all teaching, is influenced by the context in which it takes place. What do you think are some of the difficulties teachers in the following contexts may face as they try to teach intentionally?

- Rural sites
- Sites with children from poor socio-economic backgrounds
- Overcrowded Grade R classes
- Teachers in well-resourced classrooms where technological resources are plentiful.

Set up high-quality learning environments	• Motivated teachers committed to learning from children will pay attention to the kind of interpersonal relationships that encourage high participation in learning. • The physical learning environment must be safe, hygienic and secure. • Resources are essential. These are not necessarily expensive, commerically made toys. The natural environment will provide objects and materials. Waste materials can be used to make resources to support early learning. (See Chapter 7 on the optimal learning environment.)
Encourage children to explore and experiment	• Give chidren a variety of open-ended material that allows them to make their own creations. • Allow children to ask questions, collect information, come up with solutions, reflect on them and open themselves up to challenge.
Join in children's activities	• Let children see the teacher as a learner who is interested in their understandings, ideas and experiences, for example use prompts such as 'I would like to know how you ...', 'Can you teach me?' • Listen to the children and respond to their needs for information and guidance. • Encourage them to share their ideas and views. • Responses to children's views and ideas must not be judgemental. Teachers need to see the value in a child's understanding of his/her world rather than judging them. Empathy (putting yourself in their shoes) is needed to understand children's views and opinions.

Figure 8.2 Actions of intentional teachers
Source: Adapted from Epstein (2007)

Try this out

Interview two Grade R teachers – preferably one from the school where you are. Ask the following questions to deepen your understanding of the way participatory learning forms part of Grade R practice:
- What opportunities do your indoor and outdoor environments provide for learning?
- Provide three examples of how you join in the children's activities in order to help them learn.
- Write down your thoughts on whether the teachers interviewed have encouraging or discouraging practices in relation to participatory learning.

Participatory learning impacts on the whole teaching–learning situation. Table 8.3 shows the characteristics of the teacher, children, classroom and learning content.

Table 8.3 The characteristics of the teacher, children, classroom and learning content

CLASSROOMS	• High-quality teaching–learning centres • Safe, clean and secure • Enough resources from the natural environment or recycled materials • Motivated and responsive teachers who encourage participative learning
TEACHER	• Encourages children's natural curiosity and need to experiment and explore • Joins in play/learning activities • Provides a variety of material and allows children to be creative • Encourages questions, guides children to solve their own problems and reflect on their activities • Shows interest and asks questions like: 'Will you show me ...' • Listens to children and respects their ideas; encourages children to share ideas
CHILDREN	• Freely experiment with materials • Solve own problems
CONTENT	• Flexible curriculum • Is influenced and can be changed by children's interest

Teaching techniques to encourage participatory learning

Different teaching techniques can be used to support participatory learning. They involve varying degrees of child and teacher participation, and are summarised in Figure 8.3.

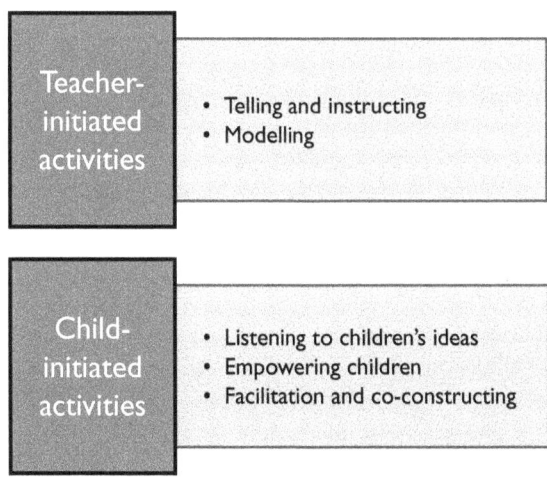

Figure 8.3 Types of teaching techniques supporting participatory learning
Source: MacNaughton & Williams (2004)

Teaching with teacher-initiated support
Telling and instructing

This technique offers children the lowest form of participation in the learning process. It is associated with the 'jug and mug' teacher. This technique is used when information or knowledge is transmitted from a knowledgeable person (teacher) to someone who does not have this knowledge (child). It is also called the conventional, traditional, chalk-and-talk approach to teaching. The teacher selects ideas and concepts, and tells children about them. Children are also instructed how to do something (MacNaughton & Williams, 2004). Although telling and instructing do not encourage strong child participation, both have their place in professional practice, for example when children cannot learn something through exploration and discovery alone.

CASE STUDY 2

This case study provides an example of how telling and instructing is used in a lesson on road safety in Grade R.

Teacher: (*points to a chart showing children waiting to cross the road at a pedestrian crossing*) There are two figures that send messages to the children to help them cross the road. They come on at different times. Do you know their names?

Children: (*no answer*)

Teacher: Okay, let me tell you (*holds up two pictures*). This one is Ronnie Red and the other one is Graham Green. What do you think they make us do?

Jenna: They tell us to do something.

Teacher: Yes, but what is that something?

Children: (*no answer*)

Teacher: Ronnie Red says you cannot walk across the road as it is not safe. When Graham Green comes on, it is safe to cross the road. Now I want you to say after me: 'Ronnie Red tells me to wait and Graham Green tells me it is safe to cross the road'.

Children repeat the above.

Teacher: I want you to sit in a semi-circle with your legs crossed and look at the sentence strip on the board. It says: 'Ronnie Red says you cannot walk across the road as it is not safe.'

Children follow the teacher's instruction and read the sentence out aloud.

Teacher: I will call out a letter. You will listen carefully and try to find the letter on the sentence strip. I must only see hands up if you know the answer. Let's begin.

Find out more
- What would you have done differently to create greater opportunities for children to be active participants in learning?
- When you are teaching a skill or providing children with knowledge, ask them questions to help them understand why you are saying what you are saying. For example: 'You need to put your bags in the lockers provided. Why do you think this is important?'
- Where children have difficulty in figuring things out for themselves, you can provide step-by-step guidance, for example when tying their shoelaces or completing a jigsaw puzzle. As you proceed with the activity, ask children to tell you what they are doing and how they are coping with the activity. When they have completed the activity, you can ask them to reflect and share their feelings.
- Allow children some space to figure out things for themselves before telling them or instructing them how to do something. You can have resources that will give them a clue to the new information that you want them to acquire. For example, in the activity dealing with making fruit salad, give them the topic and then pictures that set out the process to be followed, for example the steps involved in making a fruit salad.

Modelling

This type of technique is also associated with low levels of child participation. Children learn through copying the behaviour of others. They will watch what their peers or the teachers do, and will then reproduce the behaviour. For this approach to work, children must grasp what the teacher wants them to reproduce, remember the key aspects of what needs to be reproduced and turn this into action (Cole & Chan, 1990).

Try this out
Ideas for practice
- It is important to decide exactly what you want the children to learn.
- Think carefully about the children's strengths and needs as these will affect their ability to re-enact the modelled behaviour or skill.
- Plan opportunities for children to acquire desired behaviours and skills.
- Be observant – there might be unplanned opportunities to teach children through modelling; for example, during formal instruction time there might be a chance to model how to work with a partner and share resources.
- Model the behaviour or skill over time.
- Reward and praise children for good performance.

Source: Adapted from MacNaughton & Williams (2004)

Teaching techniques for child-initiated support
Listening and consulting children

This technique allows for strong child participation in learning. It reverses the role of the teacher as the expert who dominates the learning situation.

Listening means that children are given opportunities to share their views, opinions and concerns (Lancaster, 2003). When this happens, teachers see children as capable people. When we listen to children and talk to them, it shows them that we are interested in their understanding of whatever the topic of discussion is. Teachers respond to what the children are saying. When children are asked their views and opinions and there is no real response to their answers, this shows that the teacher has no real interest in their views (Mooney & Blackburn, 2002).

A step that goes beyond listening is consulting children about how they like things done and the resources that support their learning (Lansdown, 2004). When the teacher acts on this information and responds appropriately, children will realise that their views and opinions are taken seriously. Considered feedback can deepen learning.

Try this out
- Make time for children to share their experiences and ideas. This is important when we consider that children spend a lot of time listening to their teachers.
- Be mindful about what they are sharing with you and with other children.
- Children might use terminology and concepts that are unfamiliar to you. Ask them to explain and ensure that you understand what they are saying. Ask questions in a non-threatening manner.
- To show children you have listened to them, use phrases such as 'I hear what you are saying'. Children need to know that you 'connect' with their ideas and views.
- Good modelling can help children acquire active learning skills. Make them aware of the importance of body language, for example how to show feelings though facial expressions. Encourage them to listen carefully.

Source: Adapted from MacNaughton & Williams (2004)

Empowering children

In Grade R classes, the teacher has the power to shape learning experiences. In a classroom where participatory learning features, children are valued as people in their own right, and teachers place trust in their abilities. Children are encouraged to become involved in activities where they have some degree of control; for example, they make choices and solve problems. This often happens during free indoor and outdoor play (MacNaughton & Williams, 2004).

Try this out
- Decide on the skills that children need to develop to allow them greater participation for learning, for example an understanding of the different roles they can take in a group-based activity.
- Set out activities that allow choice and could build confidence.
- Pay attention to the level of challenge that is offered. Tasks that are too difficult might demotivate children and if too easy, they become bored.

»

- Encourage children to cooperate with their peers so that they can learn from each other.
- Encourage children to participate responsibly and then reflect on what they have learnt.

Source: Adapted from MacNaughton & Williams (2004)

Facilitating

Good facilitation, where the teacher is flexible in his/her planning and organisation, promotes strong participatory learning. Space is created for children to share their ideas, views and opinions (Catron & Allen, 1991), and the teacher is sensitive to their strengths, needs and interest.

Try this out
Ideas for practice
- Your choice in time, space and materials can deepen children's knowledge and enhance their skills.
- Allow time for children to experiment with ideas and concepts through hands-on experiences.
- Build in questions that invite children to share their ideas. This will help you to understand the thinking and reasoning behind their actions.

Co-constructing

This technique helps children to develop their knowledge, understanding and skills together with other people. Teachers and children work together as partners in learning. They build an understanding of the world around them together and offer support to each other. The focus is not on getting to know the facts of something, but about how the partners make sense of, understand and interpret what is going on around them (see Chapter 10).

Try this out
Ideas for practice
- As you plan, consider how activities could encourage children to express and share their meanings.
- When activities are given, invite children to share their thoughts and ideas in relation to the activities, for example how they completed the task or solved the problem. Use these report-backs to generate further learning for everyone involved.
- Provide resources which allow children to explore and search for meaning. For example, the fantasy area allows them to demonstrate the understandings they »

have of their life world. Observing children in fantasy play can provide insight into what they have learnt about people, places and objects.

Source: Adapted from MacNaughton & Williams (2004)

Something to consider

Always reflect on the teaching techniques you use and the implications of these for participatory learning.

Try this out

Refer to the CAPS policy document for Grade R.
- Choose a subject, for example Mathematics.
- Select content you wish to cover and the skill/s you wish to focus on.
- Choose a teaching technique for strong child participation.
- Explain how you would go about teaching the content/skill using this technique.
- Write down the resources you will use to support strong child participation.

Find out more

There is a variety of preschool approaches (eg Reggio Emilia) that encourage participatory learning for early childhood education. Consult electronic sources or visit the library to help you to get information. Do or answer the following:
- Write down 10 points on how the Reggio Emilia approach promotes participatory learning.
- Identify two other early childhood education (ECE) approaches other than Montessori that promote participatory learning.
- In what ways do you think they promote participatory learning?

Teaching according to the developmental level and needs of the child

In Chapter 3 developmentally appropriate practice (DAP) and culturally responsive teaching were identified as key principles for teaching and learning in Grade R. A basic knowledge of child development is critically important to plan play-based learning activities in Grade R. To plan a successful learning programme for Grade R, you should be aware of the age-appropriate needs and abilities – what children at a given age should be able to do as well as what they will enjoy doing (see Chapter 4).

> **Implications of a developmentally and culturally responsive practice for the Grade R teacher**
>
> **Pedagogical knowledge**: Know the developmental milestones of the Grade R child. Get to know the individual children in your class as soon as possible, including their home and cultural backgrounds. Determine the individual learning needs of each child through close observation and interaction with each child.
>
> **Content knowledge**: Know the important aspects of the different cultures and religions represented in the group. Know how to choose, organise and present content in a developmentally and culturally appropriate way.

A TIME TO REFLECT

On the following pages you will find summaries of many of the key issues we have addressed so far in this book.

Table 8.4 provides a summary of DAP principles, and indicates how they can be applied in the classroom to contribute to the children's holistic development and learning. Remember, these principles must always be viewed not only in terms of development but also in relation to cultural and other contextual features.

Table 8.4 A summary of developmental principles and practices in Grade R

PRINCIPLE	IMPLICATIONS FOR PRACTICE
Children learn best in a friendly, relaxed atmosphere where their physical needs are met and they feel safe and secure.	Young children learn best while they are having fun. This does not mean that there is no place for discipline as the classroom should be safe and secure. The suggested daily programme (see Chapter 7) allows for routine activities where children's physical needs are addressed (eg snack/lunch time, tidy-up time and toilet routine), free play as well as teacher-guided activities. Furthermore, there is a balance between periods of active play and periods of quiet restful activity. Such a classroom will also contribute to children's emotional development.
Children construct knowledge through engagement with the environment, other children and adults.	Grade R children need interaction with other children and adults, as well as with the environment. They discover knowledge through active experimentation, sparked by their natural curiosity. This implies that children should be able to talk to one another while they are experimenting with water, blocks, puzzles, creative tasks and books, or during fantasy play.
Children learn through play.	This principle calls for hands-on active learning. Children explore their environment through play. Fantasy play provides opportunities to develop creativity. Play contributes to logical thought, and social and emotional development. The Grade R child begins to take turns, wanting to please friends and form friendships. The suggested daily programme allows for two periods of free play, approximately one hour inside as well as one hour outside.

PRINCIPLE	IMPLICATIONS FOR PRACTICE
Interest and curiosity motivate learning.	In a developmentally appropriate classroom, teachers identify children's interests and plan accordingly. Children are encouraged to solve problems individually or with friends. A 'table of interest' where children can see, touch, smell and taste real objects encourages their natural curiosity.
Each child is an individual	Children are influenced by family experiences and cultural background. This contributes to the uniqueness of each child and therefore one cannot expect identical developmental patterns in all aspects of development. A wide range of individual development is normal and should be expected. The teacher should acknowledge individual differences and abilities, but at the same time have grounded knowledge of developmental milestones. This will help the teacher to teach in such a way that each child has opportunities to reach his/her optimum potential.

THE TEACHER'S VIEW OF THE CHILD

How the teacher views the child will influence teaching and learning in the classroom, because people's thoughts influence their actions. Three views held by teachers regarding the child are identified as becoming, being and belonging (see Chapter 4).

The becoming view of the child is the one most commonly held by teachers. Children are seen as adults-in-the-making. Teachers are the experts and children are novices. This view is important as teachers develop the knowledge, skills and values that they deem important for children as future adults. Children's participation in the learning process is limited (Ebrahim, 2007).

The being view of the child allows for children to take the lead in the learning process. This is in keeping with the participatory rights of babies, toddlers, young and school-going children. They have a right to express their views and opinions. They can also participate in decisions that affect their lives. This is, of course, dependent upon age and maturity. This view of the child suggests a strong form of child participation in learning.

The belonging view of the child affords children opportunities to participate in their learning in inclusive ways. Their culture, religion, beliefs, gender, age and abilities are valued. This view affirms children as they are, and promotes self-esteem and interdependence.

Something to consider

Views of the child
How will the teacher's view of the child influence his/her approach to teaching and learning?

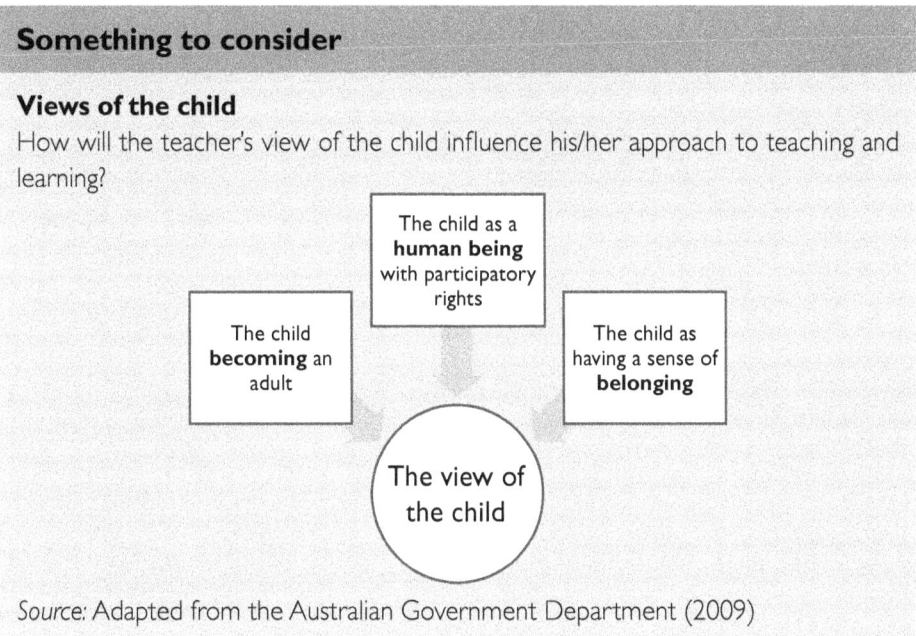

Source: Adapted from the Australian Government Department (2009)

After reflecting on these points, many of which relate to the how of teaching and learning in Grade R, we will move to the what. The Grade R teacher should have a good knowledge of what to teach and how to structure the learning content in a meaningful way.

WHAT DO WE TEACH IN GRADE R?

Earlier in the book we stressed the importance of sensory learning in Grade R. It was also noted that content should be presented in such a way that young children can see, touch and manipulate the object of learning, listen to related sounds and hear about the object in a language they can understand. But what should they hear about and where can this learning content be found?

The national school curriculum, drawn up by the Department of Basic Education (DBE), sets out what children should know and be able to do as a result of teaching and learning. The intention is that all Grade R children will develop the same knowledge, skills and values, master the content at more or less the same level, and attain the same outcomes. The curriculum covers all subjects. Curriculum content for grades 1, 2 and 3 progressively builds on the knowledge, skills and values to be mastered in Grade R, therefore all Grade R teachers should be familiar with the purpose and content of the curriculum to prepare children for formal learning in later years.

In Grade R, as we have said, children are taught three subjects: Language, Mathematics and Life Skills (also see chapters 11, 12, 13 and 14). These subjects should be taught in an interactive, integrated and holistic way (see chapters 3 and 7). In practice, this means that when you are teaching Mathematics, you will also be teaching Language (eg mathematical terms as new vocabulary) and Life Skills (eg learning the importance of accurate measuring or using an hourglass when children take turns doing mathematical activities). Art activities may fall under Life Skills in the curriculum, but discovering symmetry by folding a paper double on blobs of paint develops geometrical concepts. Block play does not only develop eye–hand coordination but also the cognitive domain. This is apparent when children are able to reason that the larger block should be placed at the bottom of the tower to keep it from toppling over.

> **Something to consider**
>
> The teacher chooses a subject as a main focus, eg Mathematics. The learning tasks relating to this subject may, however, include the arts. This is apparent when children pack out a repeating pattern with wooden blocks, make music as they clap the repeating pattern in a song, and use carrot tops to print a repeating pattern. This learning experience is identified as a Mathematics lesson. The time taken to complete it is allocated to Mathematics as is the main focus of assessment – the children's ability to repeat a pattern in a specific sequence (learning aim). Nonetheless, the other two Grade R subjects have been included in this example, namely Life Skills and Language.

The learning content of the three subjects is woven throughout the daily programme. (See Chapter 7 where the possibilities for alignment between the curriculum and the daily programme are shown.) Even the set time allocations in the curriculum for each subject (see Appendix 2) can be met through imaginative planning. Where Grade R differs from other grades in the Foundation Phase is that in Grade R the content and concepts that need to be addressed are done so in a holistic and integrated way. We showed in the previous paragraph how mathematics can include life skills. In addition, topics in Life Skills can also provide a learning context for the teaching of language and mathematics, but content should not be forced into a specific topic (see Appendix 1 for topics).

When choosing a topic, the teacher should keep the developmental level, interest and context of the children in mind. Integration of content and topics should happen in a natural way and only if this contributes to effective learning and understanding. Teachers should therefore use their own professional discretion in the way topics are presented and integrated through the three subjects. It should always be borne in mind that knowledge, skills, attitudes and values are, for the Grade R child, best acquired in a fun and developmentally and contextually appropriate way. Typical teaching activities include singing songs, saying rhymes (with actions), real-life experiences (like outings and baking activities), art activities as well as movement and musical activities (see Chapter 14).

Try this out

Search for controversial newspaper articles that are currently in the news and will be interesting to the children (eg rhinoceros poaching). Reflect on the way such a topic could serve as starting point and basis for Language, Mathematics as well as Life Skills learning experiences. The following table shows how this has been done with rhino poaching. Find your own controversial article and design a similar chart.

RHINOCEROS POACHING		
LANGUAGE	**MATHEMATICS**	**LIFE SKILLS**
Listening Read a newspaper article/story about a rhino. Find useful links to access curriculum-based content on the topic at Juta Passmasters **Story** *iThemba* by Linda 'Lulu' Fellowes at Juta Passmasters **Speaking** Ask open-ended questions based on the article/story, for example: • What do you think we can do to stop poaching? • What are the children in the video doing to help? **Reading** Provide labelled pictures to extend vocabulary. Encourage children to bring newspaper articles/pictures about the topic. **Rhymes/poems** *A Poem about a Rhino, a Giraffe & an Elephant* by Jessica Johnson at Juta Passmasters Also ask children to make their own rhymes.	**Numbers** (Based on the poem: *A Poem about a Rhino, a Giraffe & an Elephant*) **Count** How many friends are there in the poem/story? **Measurement** Which friend is the tallest? Shortest? (Based on a newspaper article on poaching) Make children aware of the weight of a rhino cow or bull. **Data handling** Draw a picture graph showing how many rhinos were killed per day in one week in the Kruger National Park.	**Beginning knowledge** Set up a display on the topic with labelled pictures. **Videos** can also be a useful resource to encourage children to get involved in discussions at Juta Passmasters **Creative arts** Children draw/paint pictures. Children model a rhino with play dough. **Music** Find a very cute song with visuals at Grade R level at Juta Passmasters Guide children to explore the tones and rhythm, for example walk like a big rhino while you sing the song slowly and in a lower tone. Walk like a baby rhino while you sing the song in a higher tone.

The next example is based on the topic 'Water'. See if you can allocate an estimated time for the various activities and then determine what additional activities you could include to make up the time allocated to the three subjects as set out in Appendix 2.

TOPIC: SAVE OUR WATER!

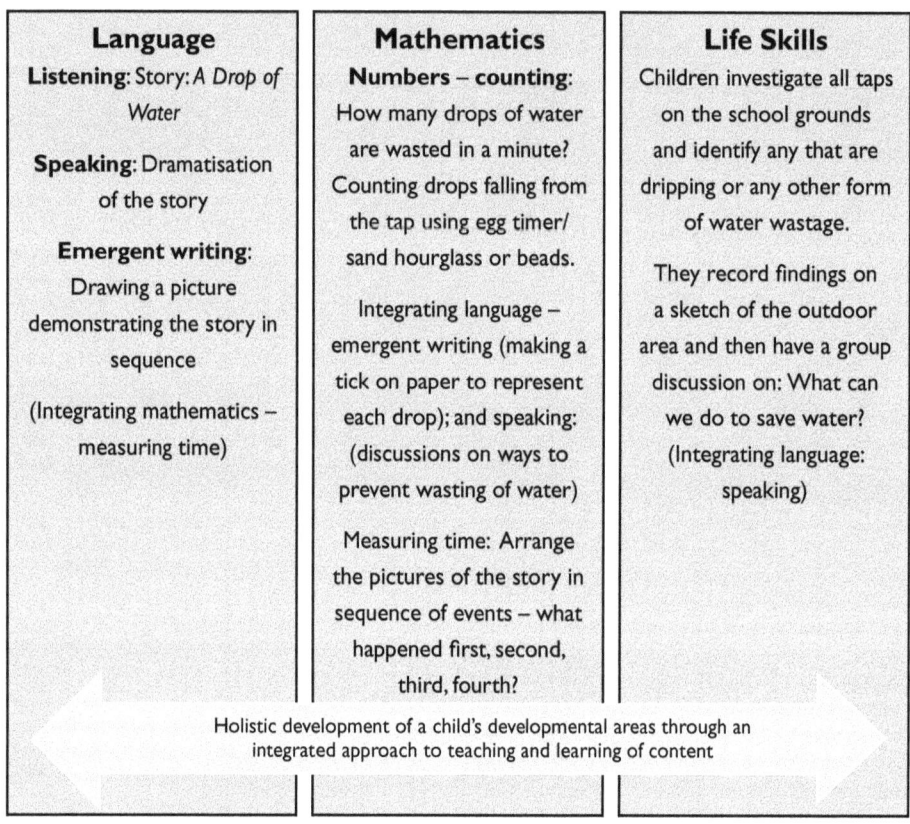

Figure 8.4 Example of integrated and holistic teaching and learning in Grade R

Curriculum realisation

The curriculum outlines the purpose, learning content, assessment as well as the time frame of teaching–learning activities to be implemented in the various grades within the school system. The teacher is guided in purposeful planning by the curriculum, which indicates what to teach (content), why to teach (purpose), and how to teach (teaching activities and time allocation, gives suggestions regarding teaching and learning strategies), as well as how to assess (using particular strategies to determine the learning progress and learning needs of the children).

Although the DBE prescribes a certain curricular approach, it is expected of teachers to interpret the prescribed curriculum and plan all teaching and learning activities according to the curriculum framework.

As noted in Chapter 7, a curriculum is made up of many aspects:
- It is everything that happens in the school day.

- It is what is planned and what is not planned.
- It is what is prepared and not prepared.
- It is what is visible and what is not visible, for example your inclusion or not in your daily programme of the children's different cultural contexts.
- It is all the learning that takes place.

Teachers' views of a particular curriculum, the extent to which it matches their own ideas about teaching–learning and their approach towards curriculum materials in general influence the way they use the curriculum. The curriculum is therefore shaped by the beliefs and commitments the teacher holds. These include the teacher's ideas about the learning content of a subject, how children learn, the teacher's own theory of effective teaching, and his/her role in the curriculum. Because teachers do not implement their plans in a vacuum but in a classroom with children, the curriculum is also shaped by the children's background, behaviour and actions. In addition, it is shaped by environmental factors such as resources, facilities such as school buildings, and support systems, for example parents and paraprofessionals. It is expected of teachers to have the necessary skills and knowledge to adapt the curriculum to best match the children's individual contexts.

Find out more

Make sure you are familiar with the aims of South Africa's school policy, terminologies used, and the formats for planning of learning experiences. Access the CAPS document on the internet should you not have the document (www.education.gov.za). Compare the prescribed learning content of Grade R and Grade 1, and make a summary of the progression from Grade R to Grade 1.

General aims of a curriculum in a South African context

The curriculum aims to give expression to the knowledge, skills and values worth learning in South African schools. This curriculum aims to ensure that children acquire and apply knowledge and skills in ways that are meaningful to their own lives. In this regard, the curriculum promotes knowledge in local contexts while being sensitive to global imperatives.

The curriculum further aims to equip children, irrespective of their socio-economic background, race, gender and physical or intellectual ability, with the knowledge, skills and values necessary for self-fulfilment and meaningful participation in society as citizens of a free country.

Find out more

Read the aims of the curriculum in the CAPS document. Set out the main goals and principles of the current school curriculum in a diagram.

The role of the Grade R teacher in curriculum implementation

The content that Grade R learners need to master as a foundation for formal learning in Grade 1 is provided in detail in the CAPS. However, curriculum knowledge is only one aspect of being an effective Grade R teacher. Effective teaching requires both content and pedagogical knowledge, plus the ability to bring them together in what is called pedagogical content knowledge (PCK) (Shulman, 1986).

Facilitating the mastering of prescribed knowledge and skills set out on the curriculum so that five/six-year-olds benefit optimally requires a special kind of PCK, attitude and vision. One of the core principles of the CAPS is 'active and critical learning that encourages an active and critical approach to learning, rather than rote and uncritical learning of given truths'. Among several learning aims the CAPS lists is the ability to identify and solve problems and make decisions using critical and creative thinking. Competences such as working effectively as individuals and with others; organising and managing themselves and their activities responsibly and effectively; collecting, analysing, organising and critically evaluating information are listed as learning aims (South African Department of Basic Education, 2011). Keeping these aims as well as the curriculum content in mind, the teacher applies pedagogical content knowledge to make informed choices about teaching and learning actions. These informed choices apply to every aspect of the Grade R day (teacher-guided and child-initiated activities as well as routines). Choices made will also draw on knowledge of the children, their context, child development and other relevant factors.

Good teachers are strong on PCK. They have a good understanding of which methods are most appropriate for teaching specific content as well as promoting the relevant skills, attitudes and values in the young child.

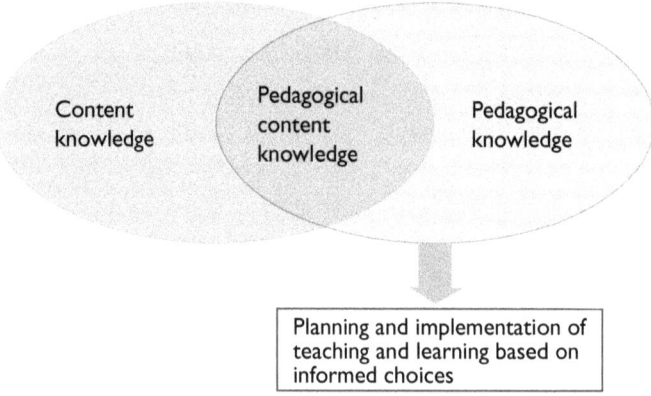

Figure 8.5 The teacher's knowledge

It is important to remember that the curriculum content is not taught to learners through direct transfer of knowledge to them, but that the Grade R teacher takes on the role as facilitator and mediator of learning. Mediation and facilitation of learning are often regarded as synonyms in the context of education. Although both approaches to teaching draw on constructivism, facilitation is an overarching term while mediation of learning specifically refers to the way a teacher creates a learning process where learners are challenged to move to higher cognitive levels. Rahim, Hood and Coyle (2009) explain that 'mediation is a combination of creating a supportive learning environment that challenges the learners yet facilitates their learning'. Toress Vigoya (2005) explains that, when a teacher mediates learning, learners learn to think by setting goals for themselves and to find ways to reach those goals. The teacher provides opportunities for learners to use strategies such as problem solving and investigations to enable them to realise their potential (Toress Vigoya, 2005). Learners are encouraged to take a leading role in their own personal and academic growth and thus become 'more effective, independent, and critical people' (Toress Vigoya, 2005: 179). In this sense a critical person does not merely accept information but asks questions such as: How do I know if this is true? What is the evidence? What is the meaning of this for me in my context?

In a world where children are bombarded with information on social media platforms, developing critical awareness in the early years becomes even more important. This approach to learning reflects the traits of self-directed learners who are resourceful and can independently take initiative, to identify their learning needs. They can, formulate learning goals, identify necessary human and material resources, select and implement appropriate learning strategies, as well as evaluate learning outcomes (Knowles, 1975). During the Covid-19 pandemic when schools had to shut down worldwide for long periods, educationists realised too late the crucial role self-directed learning could have played in upholding education standards and quality learning outcomes (Mahlaba, 2020; Wai-Cook, 2020; Zhu & Liu, 2020). Learners who are guided to adopt these skills early on in their lives will be more able to flourish academically and personally, irrespective of challenges such as teacher absence.

Teachers' PCK will play a crucial role in the way they facilitate and mediate learning of the curriculum content.

Something to consider

Do you apply your pedagogical content knowledge to support struggling children?
Are you strong in both knowledge areas, or do you need to strengthen one of them?
Are your teaching–learning activities developmentally appropriate?
Are your teaching–learning activities contextually responsive?
Are you mediating learning or simply transferring knowledge to children?
How are your teaching strategies supporting children to develop as self-directed learners?
How do you as a teacher use critical reflection to develop your skills of self-direction?

Planning for learning

Planning involves the 'thinking through' of the coming event(s). The planning of the teaching–learning process involves the purpose of the learning experience, learning content and assessment as well as classroom management strategies. Thought must also be given to what are age-appropriate activities for Grade R.

Planning teaching–learning activities in Grade R can be compared to planning a party – it should be fun, and certain preparations should precede the actual day of the event. Imagine inviting 30 people to your home without any prior planning or knowing who your guests are! In the very same way, teaching–learning activities should be well thought through and prepared in detail to ensure success. Remember, in Grade R you will not only be planning teacher-guided activities but also considering with the children what should constitute the indoor and outdoor learning environment (see Chapter 7). Before the implementation of the teaching and learning activities, the teacher should reflect on each aspect of planning by asking the following questions:

- What will the children gain through this activity/task– that is, what knowledge, skills, and attitudes and values?
- How will these gains align with the Grade R curriculum? What value will this learning have for the children in their everyday lives?
- Why would they want to take part in this task and find it enjoyable? The teacher should acknowledge children's prior knowledge and background. New knowledge should be built on what children already know as this enhances understanding. Meaningful learning implies that children will view what they have learnt as useful and worth knowing.

Something to consider

How do you know if the children in your class enjoy the teaching–learning activities?

THE PLANNING PROCESS OF TEACHING–LEARNING AND ASSESSMENT IN GRADE R

WHY?	WHAT?
• The purpose or goal • Supports the Grade R curriculum • The purpose/goal will be the focus of teaching–learning and assessment	• What knowledge, skills, attitudes and values will I teach/co-construct with children? • What are the key concepts/skills to be understood/mastered or learned? • What content will I use to reach the goal?

»

HOW?

TEACHING	ASSESSMENT	CLASS MANAGEMENT
• What is the logical order to teach the concepts? • At what level of difficulty should I teach? • How long can I expect the children to concentrate? • Did I consider learning styles? • What teaching strategies will I use? • How will I settle the children and introduce the new concepts in a way that gains their attention? • What will the children's role be? • How can learning be deepened and newly learnt knowledge/skills reinforced?	• How will I assess the children's prior knowledge? • When will I assess? • What methods of assessment will I use to determine the progress of the children? • How will I use the information obtained from the assessment to adapt, if necessary, further learning experiences?	• What time is allocated to this subject? • What knowledge do I need in order to teach the new content/concept/skill effectively? • Is the learning and teaching support material (LTSM) readily available? What alternatives can be used if necessary, for example anti-waste? • How will I use the space available to its best advantage? • Is there ample opportunity for participatory learning for each child?

The sequence of planning teaching–learning and assessment activities in Grade R

Planning is done on different levels. The teacher needs to consider what content will be covered over a year through the different themes or topics (see Appendix 1). Teachers also need to consider a weekly plan (see Appendix 4), a daily programme (see Chapter 7) and an activity/lesson format (see Appendix 5).

Planning for the grade

It is a good idea to collaborate with other Grade R teachers so that ideas can be shared and teaching capacity strengthened. If there is only one Grade R class at the school where you are teaching, try to find teachers at neighbouring schools or use the internet to collaborate with fellow teachers. Social networks such as Facebook and Twitter provide an opportunity to interact with other Grade R teachers – not only nationally but also internationally. Many early childhood teachers create their own blogs where they share knowledge, new teaching strategies that work for them, and even resources such as pictures or ideas for creative art activities.

Find out more
A blog is a personal website through which people share their knowledge and experiences. This can also take the form of a thematic site sustained by a number of people. A number of blogs can be linked to form a community that shares information in a specific field.

Try this out
Search for early childhood education teacher blogs on the internet and create your own. This is not only a showcase for your own professional competence but also provides parents with a window into your classroom and allows them to share in their children's learning experiences. Find links to various blogs, and instructions to start your own one, at Juta Passmasters.

Planning for Grade R will be influenced by various aspects. These are available resources (eg electricity, infrastructure, parental involvement, number of staff), the teacher–child ratio, the competence of the teachers (new teachers need more support and mentoring) and important events on the national and school calendar. These aspects may influence learning time and should be taken into consideration when planning for the grade.

The curriculum structures learning content in a progressive way, but teachers will have to decide on the best way to present it. Answers to the following questions will influence decisions in relation to time and topics:
- Which available resources will be most appropriate?
- Should some limited resources be rotated between teachers?
- What content will be most appropriate for an outing, etc?

Drawing up a year plan for the grade according to school weeks will guide both weekly planning and lesson/activity planning.

Annual planning for a subject
The school curriculum provides a framework for the content to be covered for each subject in Grade R. A year plan of the learning content for each subject is useful in providing the teacher with a summarised overview of all learning content of each subject. This can also serve as a basis for your assessment plan. The template in Appendix 3 sets out a yearly plan for each subject, and shows how the content can be integrated into a sound Grade R theme-based approach.

A word of warning – no planning should be set in stone. Children's voices and interests must always be taken into account, thus there is a place for an emergent curriculum – one that can be changed or adjusted as children share their current interests with you.

Lesson/activity planning (planning a teacher-guided learning experience)

Lesson/activity planning is focused on a specific aspect of learning such as a skill or an aspect of subject content knowledge. This subject content may well be linked to the week's theme. To identify the steps in planning the lesson/discussion/ring, consider the points raised in the 'Something to consider' box on page 178 (on the process of planning teaching and learning in Grade R).

In summary, teachers will consider why they should teach this specific content/skill to the children, what should be taught, and how this teaching–learning should take place so that all children are heard.

The teacher will be guided by the children. Their language, ability and diversity as well as the type of content will influence the choice of teaching and learning strategies. For example, some skills need to be mastered through exploration and manipulation of resources or material by the children, such as the mixing of different colour paints to discover 'hands on' what happens when primary colours are mixed. The mastering of other content may require step-by-step demonstration by the teacher, such as following a recipe to bake biscuits. The teacher will consider teaching strategies as well as learning styles.

Alternatively, the teacher could structure this baking activity by setting out, in sequence, recipe cards that the children can follow. Furthermore, the teacher should give careful consideration to class and time management to ensure that learning is optimised within a certain period of time. Remember that although time allocation needs to be borne in mind, teachers do not have to adhere rigidly to a timetable in Grade R but should use their discretion.

Small-group versus whole-group teaching and learning strategies

Maintain a balance between working with the whole class, small groups and individuals. The International Reading Association (IRA) (1998) indicated that the teacher–child ratio can influence the quality of education. Because there is such a wide range of differences among individual children, young children benefit most from being taught in small groups or individually. In other words, small-group teaching is preferable to accommodate children's diverse abilities and interests, strengths and needs.

Although some activities such as music, listening to stories or a language/discussion ring work well when the whole group participates and interacts, learning is sometimes more effective in small groups. This particularly applies to the South African context where there can be classes of 50 or more children per teacher. In small groups, children are more likely to ask questions spontaneously and interact naturally with one another as well as the teacher.

Divide the class into small groups of ± six children. For example, in a class of 54, there would be nine groups of six children each. During the planning process, the teacher has to provide for a variety of activities (eg painting, drawing, puzzles, cutting and pasting, play dough, numeracy games, block play, books, fantasy play, threading) as well as the main activity (eg collage with basic shapes). How the teacher organises the rotation between activities is not fixed. Teachers should not force a group to stay with a specific activity until the whole group has completed the activity/task as this may become a source of frustration and boredom for some of the children. In other words, children should be able to exercise a choice and move freely between activities.

The small-group approach with a number of different activities offered at the same time allows for children to make certain choices, promotes learning though play and gives the teacher an opportunity to observe children and mediate learning.

The teacher should guide children during group activities and ensure that every child knows what is expected of him/her in relation to each activity. Before the group activities start, the teacher should describe to the whole group what is on offer at each activity centre. Once the children are in their smaller groups and at the various stations, the teacher can move from group to group, supporting and mediating where necessary. The main focus, however, should still be on the main activity and the teacher should try to ensure that every child completes the main activity, noting if a particular child is reluctant to engage in a specific activity and trying to find out why.

The children's concentration span, however, must be kept in mind when deciding how long each group should be involved in an activity. Concentration span can be calculated by multiplying the child's age by three – that is, a five-year-old child can concentrate for about 15 minutes.

Often in the daily programme the creative art and indoor free-play times are integrated. The time allocated is more or less 80 minutes, as suggested by the daily programme. If, for example, the class consists of nine groups of six children each, then the main art activity could be presented over two or three days to allow each child to complete this activity.

Schools may make alternative arrangements; for example, one day per week the 'indoor free play' is given a mathematics focus and children participate in different mathematical games and activities. This gives the teacher an opportunity to support and assess, in a small-group context, children's understanding of a particular mathematical concept.

All the planning we have discussed can be seen as part of a pathway leading to what you hope to achieve. Assessment will, of course, provide insight into whether the children have learned what you intended them to learn and any misunderstandings that might have occurred.

During the teaching–learning phase, the teacher should assess the understanding of the children through ongoing observation, and adapt the teaching–learning activities if necessary, even if it means a deviation from the initial planning. In Grade R, as we have said, teaching–learning and assessment happen simultaneously in an integrated way, and each impacts the other.

Observation and the recording of your observations as a basis for reflection are central to Grade R teaching and inform future planning. It is a cyclical process where teachers reflect on their own teaching, and consistently revise and replan where necessary.

Phases in the lesson/activity presentation (ring planning)

Lesson/activity plan (see Appendix 5) formats may vary as teachers and schools develop a format which suits their teaching style or circumstances best, but the three phases in Table 8.5 almost always form part of any learning experience.

Child support

The teacher should indicate in the lesson/activity plan how learning activities can be adjusted to accommodate the different ability groups in Grade R. Ability groups imply that learners with the same ability will be grouped together – they are also, at times, called homogenic groups. On the other hand, if the teacher organises groups to include learners with different abilities, these may be called heterogenic groups. These are also sometimes referred to as 'same' ability and 'mixed' ability groups. Consideration must be given to ensuring that the activity is sufficiently challenging for the more able child and will at the same time provide for the less able child. Remember that learning styles as well as developmental levels differ and that some children need more time to understand a new concept, develop a specific skill or complete an activity.

Learning and teaching support material (LTSM)

LTSM refers to teaching–learning material, and includes diverse teaching material such as posters, pictures, three-dimensional (3D) objects, theme tables, computers (possibly), apparatus for experiments, worksheets, etc. The main purpose of LTSM is enhance teaching–learning. All LTSM should be mentioned in this plan, for example pictures, poems, stories, etc. Storing of these LTSMs in plastic sleeves or large envelopes together with the lesson/activity plan will save you time and effort when you use them again in years to come.

In Grade R it is preferable not to use worksheets. This is particularly applicable in the early part of the year. If worksheets are used, they should be developmentally appropriate in terms of content, the size of pictures and the font used for text. They should be approached with caution as they are, in fact, the third phase of learning. Learning and understanding occurs in a sequence: first through movement (kinaesthetic), and second through handling 3D objects, which is the concrete level. Children need to be supported when taking the next step to the two-dimensional (2D) level (worksheets), where they represent their mathematical thinking on paper. Children should be allowed to use their fingers or counters when they are expected to complete worksheets.

Something to consider

A way of representing this learning sequence is set out below. One stage is missing, which is it and how could you include it?

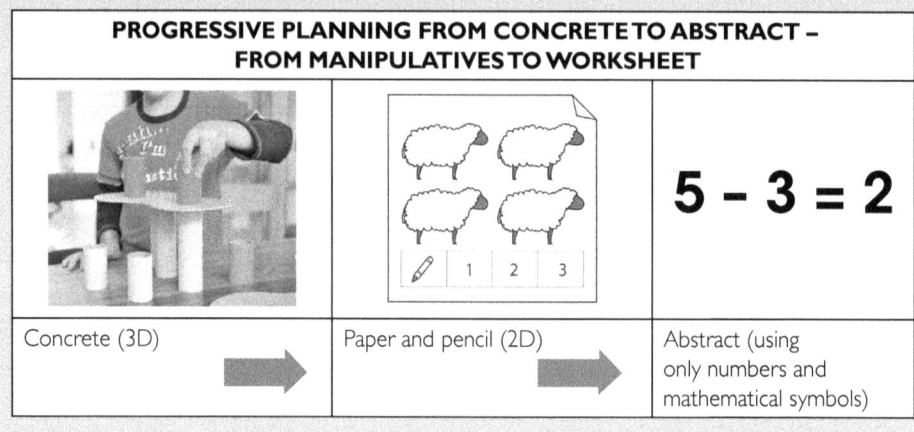

PROGRESSIVE PLANNING FROM CONCRETE TO ABSTRACT – FROM MANIPULATIVES TO WORKSHEET

| Concrete (3D) | Paper and pencil (2D) | Abstract (using only numbers and mathematical symbols) |

Table 8.5 Phases in lesson/activity preparation

LESSON/ACTIVITY PHASE	TEACHER'S ACTIVITIES	CHILDREN'S ACTIVITIES
1. The introduction This is the WOW! moment of a lesson/activity where the teacher makes sure that all children are interested in the learning that is to follow. This is the 'make or break' moment, and will largely determine if effective learning will take place (Chapter 3). (See the note on the information processing model (IPM) that follows.) Without children's full attention, knowledge cannot play an important role in new learning as well as recalling ideas from previous discussions. Recall can be done before the introduction to determine if the children are indeed ready for this new learning experience. In this phase, children are also invited to reflect on their own	Get children's undivided attention by creating interest and involving the senses of the child in the learning process. Example: '*Close your eyes and listen carefully – what do you hear?*' (Teacher pours water into a glass as the introduction for a natural science lesson/activity on fluids). The teacher may also start with a relevant story or interesting rhyme/riddle that will focus the children's attention on the content to follow. In contextualisation, the teacher helps children recall what they already know about the topic, which will enable them to identify gaps or misconceptions in their current knowledge, and determine if specific skills are in place or not. For instance, the teacher could ask questions	Children's response to this invitation to learn will depend on the type of introduction and the way the invitation stimulates their curiosity. Children may be motivated to use their senses such as touch, visual, auditory, smell or taste to engage with new content. The children may talk about what they already know about the topic. They may answer questions, give a definition or discuss estimations or expectations. If, for example, a new mathematical concept is to be investigated, the children may estimate what the answer might be before proceeding to the next phase of the activity. They may be asked to comment on a story or rhyme. This could give the teacher a sense of their current understanding. »

LESSON/ACTIVITY PHASE	TEACHER'S ACTIVITIES	CHILDREN'S ACTIVITIES
experiences in relation to the learning content. The purpose of this phase is to ensure the child's interest and attention.	to establish what the children already know about a concept.	
2. Teaching–learning phase This is also known as the input and implementation phase, as activities are used to present the new content/skill. Children engage with new content. If teaching is participatory, the children will engage actively with the content and express opinions. Different methods can be used to achieve this.	The teacher mediates learning of the new content by questioning and guiding children through an experiment, engaging them in an educational game, etc. Other methods of engaging children with new content include discussion, group work, research projects, art activities, finding new solutions to problems, etc. The Grade R teacher will observe children continuously during this stage to enable them to guide children and adapt the activity if necessary.	The children, following guidelines, participate in discussions, engage in experimentation or play, and are invited to ask questions about the new content, practise the new skill or reflect on a value that has been discussed.
3. Conclusion This is the AHA! moment, a summarising activity where the children are given the opportunity to discuss what they have learnt with each other and the teacher. They can reflect on the new knowledge, skills and attitudes they have explored during the lesson/activity. This phase plays an important role in the way content is sent to the long-term memory (LTM).	The teacher evaluates the children's understanding of the learning experience. They can show this orally or draw a picture to demonstrate what they have learnt. Children could also retell a story, organise the pictures of the story in the right sequence or provide an alternative solution to a problem, etc.	The children reflect on what they have learned through orally summarising the content, drawing a picture, retelling a story or offering a different solution to a problem, etc.

Find out more

Why is the information processing model (IPM) so important?

The way young children process new information should determine the what and the how of the teaching actions. Knowledge of learning theories as well as critical reflection on the implications of these theories and models for effective teaching and learning, such as the IPM and the constructivist model of learning (see Chapter 2), should guide you in the planning and implementation of learning experiences.

The IPM has specific implications for the teacher of young children. Learning has to be supported by teaching and learning support material that children can see, feel (touch), smell, hear or taste (see chapters 2 and 4). Merely telling children what they should know is meaningless. This is the main reason why so many teachers do not support the focus on worksheet-based tasks in Grade R as worksheets only accommodate the visual senses on a two-dimensional (2D) level. If teaching strategies negate sensory learning, new information will not pass through the sensory zone en route to interpretation and memorisation in the brain, and little or no learning will take place.

The following diagram illustrates the way information is processed by children according to the IPM. This model consists of three main components, namely the sensory memory, working memory and long-term memory.

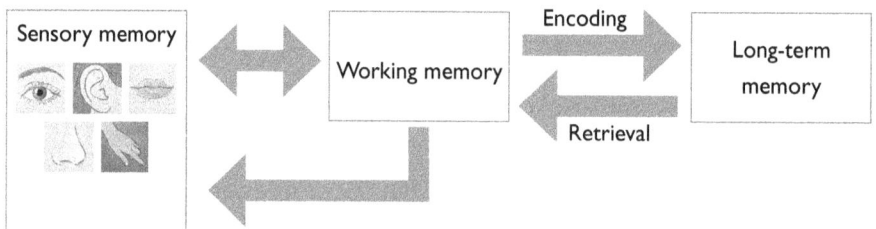

According to this model, in order for children to remember new information, it has to be sent to the long-term memory (LTM). New information has to get through the sensory zone of a child before it can be stored in the LTM. You have gathered by now that young children learn primarily though their senses, and activities that include touching, listening and seeing as well as opportunities to talk about the new content will motivate the child to pay attention to the learning activity and content. The more senses involved in the learning process, the greater the chance for knowledge to get past the sensory zone and thus to move on to the working memory for interpretation and accommodation, and to be stored in the LTM. Once knowledge is stored in the LTM it can be recalled by the child as needed, for example to solve similar problems in real-life situations. Knowledge that does not pass this sensory zone may be lost unless the teacher realises the knowledge gap through continuous assessment and provides children with other opportunities for the mastering of new content knowledge (Thadani, 2010).

> **Something to consider**
>
> What is the role of computers and other IT in Grade R? When should these be used? Will the lack of expensive LTSM hamper learning readiness of the Grade R child? What else could you use to replace expensive, bought LTSM? Elaborate.

Try this out

Google the following words:

'Resources', 'early years', 'free downloads of [insert a topic]'. Choose a topic from a subject to find specific resources that you can use in your classroom, for example 'resources, early years, measuring weight'.

SUMMARY

This is an important chapter because it outlines the pedagogical imperatives to be considered by all Grade R teachers. It highlights how the Grade R teachers' views about children, teaching and learning, their insights into culturally responsive and developmentally appropriate pedagogies and their mastery of content knowledge as well as pedagogical content knowledge will determine their success in the classroom. It stresses the value of becoming an intentional teacher who foregrounds participatory learning. Specific guidelines on how to plan and prepare for all teaching and learning events are highlighted. The National Curriculum Statement (NCS) is unpacked and drawing on the recommendations made in this document, examples of planning templates and their practical application in the classroom are discussed. Teaching strategies that foreground participatory learning are made explicit and the sequence of planning teaching-learning and assessment activities in Grade R are clearly illustrated. A detailed interrogation of assessment will follow in Chapter 9.

BIBLIOGRAPHY

Australian Government Department of Education, Employment and Workplace. 2009. *Belonging, being and becoming. The early years learning framework from Australia*. https://www.coag.gov.au (Accessed 13 September 2014).

Catron, C & Allen, J. 1991. *Early childhood curriculum*. New York: Macmillan.

Cole, P & Chan, L. 1990. *Methods and strategies for special education*. New Jersey: Prentice Hall.

Department of Basic Education (DBE). 2011. *The Curriculum Assessment Policy Statement*. Pretoria: Government Printer.

Ebrahim, HB. 2007. *Constructions of childhood for and by children in two early childhood centres in the province of KwaZulu-Natal, South Africa: An ethnographic study*. Unpublished dissertation. Durban: University of KwaZulu-Natal.

Epstein, AS. 2007. *The intentional teacher: Choosing the best strategies for young children's learning*. Washington, DC: National Association for the Education of Young Children.

International Reading Association (IRA); National Association for the Education of Young Children (NAEYC). 1998. 'Learning to read and write: Developmentally appropriate practices for young children'. A joint position statement of the IRA and the NAEYC. *Young Children* 53(4): 30–46. http://www.naeyc.org/about/positions/pdf/PSREAD98.PDF (Accessed 23 August 2009).

Knowles, MS. 1975. *Self-directed learning.* New York: Association Press.

Lancaster, P. 2003. *Listening to young children.* Berkshire. Open University Press.

Lansdown, G. 2004. 'Participation and young children'. *Early Childhood Matters* 103: 4–14.

MacNaughton, G & Williams, G. 2004. *Teaching young children. Choices in theory and practice.* Berkshire: Open University Press.

Mahlaba, SC. 2020. 'Reasons why self-directed learning is important in South Africa during the Covid-19 pandemic'. *South African Journal of Higher Education* 34(6): 120-136. doi:https://dx.doi.org/10.20853/34-6-4192

Miller, J. 2003. *Never too young: How young children can take responsibility and make decisions.* London: Save the Children Fund.

Mooney, A & Blackburn, T. 2002. *Children's views on childcare quality.* Institute of Education for DFES, University of London. http://webarchive.nationalarchives.gov.uk/20110506183305/https://consumption.education.gov.uk/publications/eOrderingDownload/RR482.pdf (Accessed 24 November 2014).

Oberg, C & Oberg, F. 2012. *Intentional preschool teaching.* www.caheadstart.org/2012Conference/Oberg.pdf (Accessed 25 January 2014).

Rahim, FA, Hood, P & Coyle, DO. 2009. 'Becoming experts: Learning through mediation'. *Malaysian Journal of Learning and Instruction* 21. doi:10.32890/mjli.6.2009.7610

Shulman, L. 1986. 'Those who understand: Knowledge growth in teaching'. *Educational Research* 15(2): 4–14.

Shulman, LS. 1987. 'Knowledge and teaching: Foundations of the new reform'. *Harvard Educational Review* 57(1): 1–22.

Thadani, R. 2010. *Information processing theory.* www.buzzle.com/articles/informationprocessingtheory.html (Accessed 24 November 2014).

Toress Vigoya, FS. 2005. 'The mediated learning experience and the mediator's implications'. *Profile Issues in Teachers` Professional Development* 6: 177–186. http://www.scielo.org.co/scielo.php?script=sci_arttext&pid=S1657-07902005000100016&lng=en&tlng=en

Wai-Cook, MS. 2020. 'The reality of home-based learning during Covid-19: Roles of parents, teachers, and school administration in promoting self-directed learning'. *Journal of School Administration Research and Development* 5(S2): 86–92. http://ojed.org/jsard

Willow, C. 2002. *Participation in practice: Children and young people as partners in change.* London: The Children's Society.

Zhang, X, Anderson, RC, Morris, J, Miller, B, Nguyen-Jahiel, KT, Lin, T & Hsu, JY. 2016. Improving children's competence as decision makers: Contrasting effects of collaborative interaction and direct instruction. *American Educational Research Journal* 53(1): 194–223. doi:10.3102/0002831215618663

Zhu, X & Liu, J. 2020. Education in and after Covid-19: Immediate responses and long-term visions. *Postdigital Science and Education* 1–5. doi:10.1007/s42438-020-00126

GLOSSARY

Abstract level of thinking – develops after concrete level of thinking: children are able to think about things that are removed from the 'here' and the 'now'; children are able to reflect on concepts and on attributes of objects as well as the relationships between objects even in the absence of the specific example or concrete object; for example a concrete thinker can see that a shape is round while a more abstract thinker can think about shape in general. While a concrete thinker can count five crayons; a more abstract thinker can think about numbers in general

Assessment – the process which involves gathering information about what children know, understand and can do, and using this information to further enhance learning

Blog – a personal website or web page on which an individual records opinions, links to other sites, etc, on a regular basis

Classroom management – the wide variety of skills and techniques used by teachers to organise the teaching and learning environment (in the Grade R context this implies that teachers are able to manage all learning activities in and outside of the classroom in such a way that effective learning is mediated)

Cognitive development – the development of thought, focusing on problem solving, remembering and the ability to make decisions

Concentration span – the time a child is able to concentrate, estimated by multiplying the child's age by three

Content area – a now-preferred term for subject or subject area among teachers, referring to a defined domain of knowledge and skill in an academic programme

Content knowledge – the body of information that teachers teach and that children are expected to learn in a given subject or content area

Culturally responsive teaching – teaching which draws on the cultural knowledge, prior experiences and the performance styles of diverse students to make learning more appropriate and effective

Developmental principles – patterns of change over time which begin at conception and continue throughout the lifespan

Developmentally appropriate – an approach to teaching that respects both the age and the individual needs of each child, the idea being that the programme should fit the child and not the other way around

Diversity – the wide range of individual differences among children

Emotional development – the attainment of emotional capabilities, an increased understanding of emotions, the causes and consequences of emotions, as well as the emerging ability to reflect on and describe emotions

Fantasy play – where young children create stories and act them out (also called 'pretend' or 'imaginary' play)

Free play – a time slot in the daily programme where children have a choice regarding the activity, either indoors or outside, they want to do

Grade R daily programme – a programme followed daily in the Grade R class, accommodating the various facets of the learning programme in an integrated way, which includes play-based learning activities, snack time and toilet routine

Information processing model (IPM) – a systematic model of memory, cognition and thinking that consists of three main components, namely the sensory memory, working memory, and long-term memory

Integration (in the context of curriculum) – teaching and learning of language, mathematics and life skills in all activities

Interaction – when two or more people communicate with or react to each other

Kinaesthetic learning – learning through body movement, an important way in which to introduce new knowledge or skills to young children and enable them to begin to internalise this new information or skill

Learning and teaching support material (LTSM) – resources (commercial and/or self-designed, and often made from anti-waste materials)

Learning centres or activity areas – different areas within the classroom where children work alone or cooperatively with one another, using a variety of different learning materials to explore and expand their knowledge and skills

Learning readiness – having prerequisite cognitive, socio-emotional and physical attributes, skills and dispositions to allow benefit from formal learning opportunities

Logical thinking – the process of rational thought

Long-term memory (LTM) – cognitive function of the brain whereby knowledge is stored for later recall

Main activity – an activity planned and implemented by the teacher that usually forms part of the organised play-based learning programme and mediates learning

Meaningful learning – understanding new knowledge or mastering new skills, and viewing this as useful and worth knowing

Mediated learning – stimuli experienced in the environment which are selected, enhanced, focused and organised by a mediator, usually a parent or teacher, to support learning by the child

Observation – the act of careful watching and listening in order to get information

Optimal learning – the acquisition of skills and/or knowledge and values in a supportive environment that meets a child's needs as far as possible

Participatory approach – an approach to teaching and learning where the child is guided to actively take part in his/her own learning through first-hand experiences and interaction with people and objects

Pedagogical content knowledge – the ability to blend content knowledge and pedagogical knowledge – a prerequisite for effective teaching involving an understanding of how particular topics, problems or issues are organised, represented, adapted and taught in a way which accommodates the diverse interests and abilities of children

Pedagogical knowledge – deep knowledge about the processes and practices or methods of teaching and learning and how they encompass (among other things) overall educational purposes, values and aims covering all issues of child learning, classroom management, lesson plan development and implementation, as well as assessment

Physical development – the progress of a child's control over his/her own body

Progressive learning – a form of learning that occurs gradually through discovery and experience

Ratio (teacher–child ratio) – the number of children in the class divided by the number of teachers (regardless of their teaching assignment)

Recording – keeping a record of assessment data gathered on children's performance and progress, either in writing (assessment sheets, recording sheets) or electronically

Reflect – the action whereby a teacher analyses experiences in order to learn from them

School policy – a set of procedures that has been agreed upon by the school board/management, the main aim of which is to set out the responsibilities of teachers, parents and children to ensure the well-being of all

Search engine – tool for finding information, especially on the Internet or World Wide Web

Teacher-guided activities – a learning approach in which the teacher is primarily in charge of the teaching and learning activity, for example a language ring, art activity and story time

Three-dimensional (3D) – an object that has height, width and depth, for example blocks, tables, chairs, etc

Two-dimensional (2D) – a shape that has only width and height and no thickness or depth, for example pictures drawn on a flat surface or a worksheet

APPENDIX 1: THEMES/TOPICS FROM CAPS: LIFE SKILLS
Themes/topics for Grade R – Suggested distribution of topics per term

FIRST TERM	SECOND TERM	THIRD TERM	FOURTH TERM
Me	Home	Winter	Spring
At school	Safety	Transport	Reptiles
In the classroom	My family	Jobs people do	Dinosaurs
Days of the week	Weather	Water	Wild animals
My body + healthy living	Autumn	Fruit	One wild animal
Summer	Sound, sight, touch	Vegetables	Sport
Shapes and colours	Taste and smell	Dairy farming	
Festivals and special days		Wool farming	
		Healthy environment	

APPENDIX 2: TIME ALLOCATION PER SUBJECT FOR THE FOUNDATION PHASE (HOURS PER SUBJECT PER WEEK ACCORDING TO PRESCRIBED CURRICULUM)

SUBJECTS	GR R	GR 1–2	GR 3
Home Language	10	8/7	8/7
First Additional Language	N/A	2/3	3/4
Mathematics	7	7	7
Life Skills • Beginning knowledge • Creative arts • Physical education • Personal and social well-being	6 (1) (2) (2) (1)	6 (1) (2) (2) (1)	7 (2) (2) (2) (1)
Total	23	23	25

APPENDIX 3: YEARLY PLANNING GRADE R
Annual planning

DATE	LANGUAGE					LIFE SKILLS	
	THEME	STORY	SONG	SKILL	CONCEPT	STUDY AREA	SKILL/ KNOWLEDGE/ VALUE
	Me						
	At school						

DATE	LANGUAGE					LIFE SKILLS	
	THEME	STORY	SONG	SKILL	CONCEPT	STUDY AREA	SKILL/ KNOWLEDGE/ VALUE
	In the classroom						
	Days of the week						
	My body + healthy living						
	Summer						
	Shapes and colours						
	Festivals and special days						
	Home						
	Safety						
	My family						
	Weather						
	Autumn						
	Sound, sight, touch						
	Taste and smell						
	Winter						
	Transport						
	Jobs people do						
	Water						
	Fruit						
	Vegetables						
	Dairy farming						
	Wool farming						
	Healthy environment						
	Spring						
	Reptiles						
	Dinosaurs						

»

DATE	LANGUAGE				LIFE SKILLS		
	THEME	STORY	SONG	SKILL	CONCEPT	STUDY AREA	SKILL/ KNOWLEDGE/ VALUE
	Wild animals						
	One wild animal						
	Sport						

APPENDIX 4: WEEKLY PLANNING GRADE R
Weekly planning Grade R

ACTIVITY	MONDAY	TUESDAY	WEDNESDAY	THURSDAY	FRIDAY
Teacher-guided activity (1)					
Creative arts Indoor free play					
Teacher-guided activity (2)					
Toilet routine					
Refreshments					
Free play outside					
Toilet routine					
Tidy-up time					
Teacher-guided activity (3) Story time					
Departure					

APPENDIX 5: LESSON PLANS FOR GRADE R
Lesson plan (Format A)

Subject: Grade: R
Topic: Duration:
Purpose/goal: (from curriculum)   Integration:

CONTENT	TEACHER ACTIVITY	CHILDREN'S ACTIVITY
Introduction		

CONTENT	TEACHER ACTIVITY	CHILDREN'S ACTIVITY
Teaching–learning		
Conclusion		

Assessment (should correspond with the purpose/goal)

Learning and teaching support material

Children's support

Reflection

Lesson plan for Mathematics (based on the CAPS document) (Format B)

Subject: Mathematics	Date: Duration:		Parents notice	
Topic				
Grade:	Term:	Week:	Day:	
LEARNING COMPONENT	Numbers, operations and relationships	Patterns, functions and algebra	Space and shape	Measurement	Data handling

»

Integration (where relevant):				
LOOKING BACKWARDS AT:		**LOOKING FORWARD TO:**		
Teacher and children's activities	Learning content/concepts/skills to be developed during each phase of the lesson	Assessment: Who, what, when, how?	Resources	Teacher reflection
Introductory phase				
Teaching and learning phase: Unfolding of content areas/knowledge/skills	Content	Assessment	Resources	Teacher reflection
Closure phase				

This planning form is designed for the subject of Mathematics. You would have to adapt this format if you want to use a similar lesson/activity plan for a Language or Life Skills lesson/activity. Consult the relevant CAPS documents for suitable headings.

APPENDIX 6: SOME RESOURCES FOR STORIES

Juta Passmasters

Write your own story, such as the following.

Splish and Splash and their adventurous journey
by Corné Kruger and Elsabé Wessels

Two drops of water called Splish and Splash were friends who lived in a big dam on a farm in Africa. One day, while floating in the dam, they felt the heat of the sun and became very, very hot. They looked up in the air and saw a big white cloud – it looked cool up there. 'Maybe we should go to the cloud,' said Splish. As soon as the words were spoken, the two friends realised that they were floating to the cloud – they were evaporating!

As they climbed higher and higher, it became cooler and cooler. Splish and Splash were so happy. At last they reached the cloud. They landed among many other drops of water. 'Isn't this beautiful?' asked Splash. 'Maybe we will be able to touch the stars.' They were surprised by all the beautiful views up in the sky. They saw a lot of other clouds around them, which began to grow darker and darker. They heard loud thunder. 'I'm afraid,' said Splish. 'Hold on to me,' whispered Splash, also feeling doubtful.

All of a sudden they began to fall off the cloud. They tumbled downwards. They saw sheep, cows, trees and green grass – things they had never seen before. Then they fell with a thud onto the ground next to a maize plant. Splish said, 'I want to go home.' He looked as if he was going to cry. Splash whispered, 'Hold on to me.' He also did not know what to expect. All of a sudden they heard a friendly voice saying: 'Hallo you two, my name is Droppy. What has happened to you?' Splash said, 'Maybe you can help us to get home?'

Droppy smiled a friendly smile and asked, 'Was this your first time?' 'First time of what?' replied the two friends, who were very confused. 'Nothing to worry about,' said Droppy, still smiling. He explained, 'Rain is what just happened. The clouds could not hold all the drops of water together anymore. That's why they let us go. We fell down from the sky.'

Splash asked, 'Can we go home now?' But just as Droppy was about to answer, they were pulled to the ground and were absorbed by the roots of the maize plant nearby. Splish and Splash were really terrified now. Droppy calmed them and said, 'We are on our way back to the cloud, but there is something we have to do first.'

The three friends went through the plant's roots to the leaves and Droppy said, 'Hold on guys, the sun will soak us up again, and we will form another cloud!' Splish and Splash waited and then they suddenly realised that they were floating again. They were on their way back to the clouds! Droppy explained, 'This is the water-cycle. It will continue forever – a never-ending adventure!'

Splish and Splash were not uncertain or troubled anymore! Being drops of water means they have a never-ending adventurous journey!

Chapter 9

Assessment

Corné Kruger, Susan Greyling

In this chapter we consider

- the integrated role of assessment in all teaching and learning in Grade R
- fundamental principles of contextually and culturally responsive as well as developmentally appropriate assessment in Grade R
- the aims of assessment in Grade R
- the assessment cycle
- the different types of assessment implemented in Grade R
- assessment strategies and instruments relevant to Grade R.

INTRODUCTION

In Chapter 8 we discussed the integral nature of teaching, learning and assessment. In this chapter we focus on assessment, and explore the various ways in which a teacher can meet the assessment criteria set out in the curriculum while at the same time promoting the growth, development and learning potential of all children in the class.

One of the first questions we have to ask ourselves is: 'What is assessment and how is it best handled in a Grade R context?'

The Department of Basic Education defines assessment as follows: 'Assessment is a process of collecting, analysing and interpreting information to assist teachers, parents and other stakeholders in making decisions about the progress of learners' (National Protocol for Assessment Grades R–12) (South African Department of Basic Education, 2011b). Effective teachers monitor children's progress in appropriate ways to assist in making informed decisions about teaching and learning.

Assessment in Grade R must be informal, and children should not be subjected to a 'test' situation. For this reason, assessment activities have not been included in the Grade R curriculum documentation. *Informal or daily assessment* is the process of collecting information on the child's progress through observations, discussions, practical demonstrations and informal interactions. It allows the teacher to make daily instructional decisions and provide feedback to the children, and it informs the teacher's planning. In Grade R most of the assessment takes place through observation, with the teacher recording the assessment findings using, for example, various forms of documentation such as a photograph, video clip as well as checklists and charts. We will discuss these in more detail later in this chapter. As the year progresses, a full picture of each child, complete with challenges and strengths, is gradually built. This allows for challenges to be addressed and strengths to be maximised.

Although formal assessment strategies such as tests are not used in Grade R, the teacher includes *formal and informal assessment tasks* in the planning of learning experiences. Formal assessment tasks provide opportunities for children to demonstrate their knowledge and competency regarding specific content and skills as set out in the Curriculum and Assessment Policy Statement (CAPS). For example, a formal task may entail the children sorting concrete objects according to shape. In this task, sorting is the main focus of the assessment, and the teacher assesses the children's sorting skills through observation. Data gathered through observation on the children's skills, knowledge and attitude is then recorded on assessment sheets. However, this sorting task also provides opportunity for assessing informal tasks such as counting the round shapes, comparing the number or objects in each group, and using mathematical vocabulary such as 'more than', 'least', 'bigger', 'smaller', etc. Both *formal* as well as *informal assessment tasks* provide valuable opportunity for teachers to assess whether children have mastered content and/or skills, and take note of areas where they may need additional support (see Appendix 2 for a copy of an assessment sheet that provides for assessment of both formal as well as informal tasks). Although assessment strategies are always informal, the teacher records children's progress in a structured way. They will use an assessment or recording sheet or some other form of documentation to capture the children's progress regarding the specific knowledge or skills that are being demonstrated.

ASSESSMENT AS PART OF TEACHING AND LEARNING

Teaching and learning have a reciprocal relationship – that is, they influence each other. Continuous assessment needs to be done to monitor the success of the teaching and learning process, and to revise or adapt teaching strategies to support children's development and learning. This approach to assessment is called formative assessment. This means that assessment forms an integral part of each component of the teaching and learning cycle, and cannot be separated from the teaching–learning process. In Grade R, formative assessment is the preferred assessment strategy. Formative assessment is not done to children, but rather for them to guide and improve their learning. Formative assessment is an ongoing process where the teacher, through a variety of different ways, collects information or evidence about each child. Through reflection on the evidence, the teacher can make further decisions about teaching and learning. Aspects that may constrain effective learning could include ineffective teaching strategies, the child's current level of competence, learning style preference or contextual features. If the assessment results suggest that the child did not learn as anticipated, the teacher, based on this information, revises his/her teaching strategies. In cases where assessment shows that most children did not master the target skill or knowledge, it may be that that resources or language used during the teaching process were not appropriate.

It is senseless to carry on with a lesson/activity as planned if the continuous assessment shows that the anticipated learning has not occurred and therefore there may be conceptual misunderstandings and confusion.

Find out more

Why assess?

'The intended use of an assessment – its purpose – determines every other aspect of how the assessment is conducted' (Shepard, Kagan & Wurtz, 1998: 6). Grade R teachers need to determine children's developmental and learning status at a given time and their progress and change over time.

An assessment cycle can help them do this.

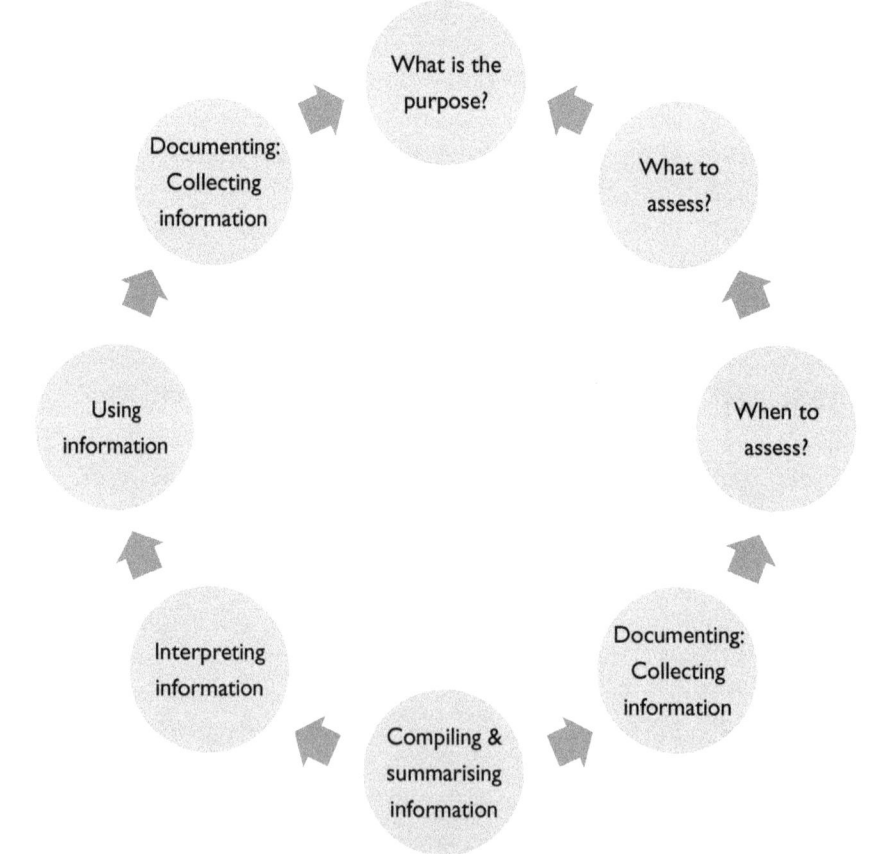

The assessment cycle enables the teacher to do the following:
- Observe Grade R children's development and learning.
- Guide classroom planning and decision making in order to help Grade R children learn effectively.
- Recognise Grade R children who might have barriers to learning.
- Give and communicate information about children's learning to, for example, the parents/caregivers.

THE AIM OF ASSESSMENT

The aim of assessment is not to group the children into 'can/cannot' groups for Department of Basic Education (DBE) grading or for writing reports for parents/caregivers. Assessment in Grade R should be primarily focused on gathering evidence to help make decisions about how best to support the child in his/her learning. The assessment process should be systematic and based on everyday tasks/activities undertaken by the child. This implies that assessment happens throughout the school day, not during special 'test periods'.

The main aim of assessment is to help children to reach their full potential. Assessment should be transparent and clearly focused; integrated with teaching and learning; based on predetermined criteria or standards; varied in terms of methods and contexts; and valid, reliable, fair, correctly paced and flexible enough to allow for expanded learning opportunities.

> **Something to consider**
>
> Assessment is generally conducted to do the following:
> - Determine children's strengths and areas of difficulty.
> - Make informed decisions about interventions that might be teacher-based or involve referral.
> - Determine the children's progress over time.
> - Evaluate teaching – is teaching supporting the children to master the required knowledge and skills?
> - Provide information for a report on the child's progress which is given to parents/caregivers.

Find out more

We use various assessment strategies to find out what a child knows and understands (knowledge). Various forms of assessment can also provide a window into what skills the child has acquired (ie can do) as well as the attitudes and values a child has developed. The information you wish to gain will guide your choice of assessment strategies and the instruments you use. The teacher integrates assessment into her planning and implementation of the teaching and learning programme.

According to Grinder and Kochanoff (2007: 6), assessment is:
> … NOT conducted to classify the child's 'readiness' for inclusion in an educational setting; NOT conducted to exclude the child from a grade (such as Grade R or Grade 1) because of an erroneously presumed lack of readiness. But assessment IS conducted to plan beneficial learning opportunities for each child.

The following are some of the various forms/types of assessment that could be used by the Grade R teachers:
- Performance-based assessment
- Practical exercises/demonstrations
- Projects
- Role plays
- Aural/oral questions
- Pedagogical documentation
- Observations.

These forms of assessment are described later under the heading 'Assessment strategies'.

CASE STUDY 1

The Grade R children are busy with a drawing activity and the teacher is observing their pre-writing skills to assess if they have established hand dominance. The teacher notes on the observation sheet that one child has not yet done so. This is evidenced by the child continually moving the crayon from one hand to the other. The teacher interprets the evidence as the child not yet having developed an inner awareness of hand dominance, and recalls that this behaviour has previously occurred. It is important for the child to develop hand dominance, so the teacher suggests that the child chooses and uses his/her dominant hand. The teacher may use various strategies such as placing a sweet in the non-dominant hand and asking the child to hold onto it until the picture is completed. The child's progress is recorded and followed up on during a next drawing, painting or cutting activity. This is done not only for recording and reporting purposes, but specifically to support the child to develop an inner awareness of hand dominance. Behaviouristic strategies such as praise or other rewards may also be used to motivate young children to develop such skills. Children should never be punished for using their non-dominant hand to hold a writing tool. A more constructive approach is to show the child the difference in the end product when the dominant hand is used.

TYPES OF ASSESSMENT

Assessment can be either formative or summative.

Formative assessment

Formative assessment (also called informal assessment) is *assessment for learning* – a process of continuously collecting information on a child's achievements.

Children are also able to assess themselves through guided reflection in their work. This is called *learning as assessment* and will be elaborated upon later under the heading 'Assessment strategies'. In relation to the teacher, he/she assesses informally through observations, discussions, practical demonstrations and informal classroom interactions. This implies that the teacher will assess during the daily teaching–learning activities and utilise alternative teaching strategies to ensure effective learning. The purpose of formative assessment is to support children and provide feedback on their progress. Data gathered on the children's progress through formative assessment is recorded for reporting back. An important report-back purpose is to inform parents/caregivers of their child's progress and how they can partner with the teacher to assist the child and promote success.

Children should be given a number of different opportunities to display their competence in an assessment area. Conclusions drawn when reporting back cannot be based on just one assessment activity as many factors may play a role in a young child's performance at a specific time, such as the emotional and physical well-being of the child.

> **Something to consider**
>
> Formative assessment is ongoing and takes place whenever a suitable situation arises. This, as we have said, might be done by the teacher or the child. When assessment is undertaken by the child, this is referred to as assessment as learning. In this type of assessment, children are encouraged to evaluate their own learning, and if necessary adapt what they are doing to improve their learning experiences. Self-assessment involves teaching children the metacognitive – that is, thinking about their thinking processes – to evaluate their own learning and make the necessary adjustments. Learning as assessment is briefly discussed under 'Assessment strategies'.
>
> Formative assessment will often involve continuous assessment.

Continuous assessment

- Takes place over a period of time and is ongoing. Learning is assessed regularly, and the records of children's progress are updated throughout the year.
- Supports the growth and development of children. Children become active participants in learning and assessment. They understand to a degree the criteria that are used for assessment activities, and can be involved in

self-evaluation. They can also set individual targets for themselves, reflect on their learning and, as a result, increase their confidence and self-esteem through participation in this process.
- Provides a window into the effectiveness of teaching and learning.
- Allows for integrated assessment. This may include assessing a number of related outcomes within a single activity. For example, in creative art a child may demonstrate that he/she has established hand dominance, can cut along a line and can share ideas with others in small-group discussion. The acquisition of a particular skill can be demonstrated in many different ways, and thus a variety of assessment methods and opportunities must be provided through which children can demonstrate their competence.
- Allows for flexibility. As a result, teachers can meet children's individual needs and learning styles, and take developmental pace into account. This flexibility also allows children to be assessed at different times and, if appropriate, in different ways.
- Continuous assessment can also be used to inform summative assessment.

Summative assessment

Summative assessment is sometimes known as assessment of learning as it is often used to compare individual children's learning and to report on the child's progress. It thus provides an overall picture of a child's progress at a given time. Summative assessment, which is usually implemented at the end of a term or a year, is more formal than formative assessment. In the Grade R year, summative assessment must be used very carefully. We need to be very sure of what we are assessing and why we want to assess in this way. Tests and examinations are good examples of summative assessment, but they should not be used in the Grade R year, because Grade R children are still refining many of the basic skills and concepts that underpin successful formal learning. Summative assessment does not always give us reliable and valid information about the children (Excell, Linington & Helsby, 2010). In addition, formal assessment creates a stressful learning environment that can hamper the young child's actual levels of competence.

> **Something to consider**
>
> Can you think of any instances where summative assessment might be useful in Grade R?

APPROPRIATE ASSESSMENT PRACTICE IN GRADE R

Formative (informal) ongoing assessment is preferable in Grade R because young children are not yet ready to cope with the demands of summative assessment. In fact, emotional barriers, such as being scared of the test situation, may constrain children's ability to demonstrate the knowledge and skills they have mastered. Assessment must be fair and reliable, and adhere to ethical principles. Making incorrect inferences regarding a young child's abilities and knowledge, possible misinterpretation of the evidence and, as a result, incorrect reporting to parents will not only impact negatively on the child's development and learning but will also harm relationships between the teacher, the child and the parents/caregivers.

Assessment practices must be culturally responsive and compatible with the anticipated developmental level of the children. Young children learn by doing, first using their bodies and moving (kinaesthetic learning) and then through manipulating concrete objects (three-dimensional learning). They should therefore have the opportunity to demonstrate their knowledge, skills and understanding through actions using these approaches. Paper and pencil assessment (often called two-dimensional tasks) such as worksheets or workbooks should not be the first choice of an assessment strategy. Although worksheets are often used as a way of gathering evidence of children's progress and serve as proof of knowledge or skills mastered, many learning goals included in the Grade R curriculum cannot be demonstrated on paper. Different learning criteria will require different strategies and assessment instruments to show if they have been attained.

Something to consider

Remember that there are no formal assessment tasks in Grade R. Assessment is based mainly on observation, and on oral and practical activities.

Find out more

Useful information relating to assessment can be found through accessing the following site: ecap.crc.illinois.edu/eecearchive/digests/1997/katz97.html

At this site you can access the following information: *A developmental approach to assessment of young children* by Lilian G Katz.

PLANNING ASSESSMENT

As we have said, planning of assessment should be included in the plan for the teaching–learning activities (see Figure 8.1 in Chapter 8). The Grade R teacher will choose assessment strategies that will best determine the mastering of new content or skills. If the activity is hands-on, such as creative art, where the learning aim is the development of the child's fine motor skills, dominancy, use of colour, ability to explore new techniques, imagination, etc, the assessment strategy needs to include continuous observation while the child completes the activity. The completed product on its own cannot provide sufficient insight.

Assessment strategies must be specific and clearly indicated, if appropriate, in the lesson/activity plan. Free play or routines would not follow this format. A substitute teacher should be able to implement these strategies as planned should you not be able to present the learning experience yourself. Aspects that form part of your planning for assessment include the following:
- Who will assess?
- What skills, knowledge, attitudes and values will be assessed?
- Which strategies will be implemented to determine if the children have mastered the required learning?
- How will assessment data be recorded and reported to the stakeholders?

ASSESSMENT STRATEGIES

In Grade R, the main assessment strategies or methods used by the teacher, as we have said, are observations, pedagogical documentation, oral discussions and practical demonstrations by the children (eg art activities, constructions, puzzles). The teacher can also introduce self-assessment (assessment as learning) or peer assessment as a means to begin to develop critical evaluation skills. It must be remembered, however, that young children are not yet able to assess in an unbiased manner when assessing themselves or their peers. They should nonetheless begin to compare and evaluate the different methods applied by their peers to solve a specific problem. They can, for example, motivate why they agree or disagree with the solution of a peer, or why they view their own solution as the best. This is in line with participatory learning. Peer, group or self-assessments should not, however, be used to gather data to be recorded and reported to the parents regarding their child's progress. Children's ability to begin to reflect on the learning of others and themselves should be recorded and reported where appropriate to other stakeholders.

As we have already discussed, continuous observation is usually the most appropriate to gather evidence of a child's competencies, knowledge and attitudes. Daily teacher-guided activities such as news time, music and movement rings, and routines are all valuable sources of information regarding the child's development and learning. Child-initiated activities as well as creative arts can also provide valuable information in the teacher's assessment of holistic development in relation to the physical, cognitive and socio-emotional domains.

Assessment is neither rigid nor fixed. Flexibility and spontaneity are important. Just as an unplanned teachable moment can arise spontaneously, so too can an assessment moment. Be alert to such moments and use them. For example, if a fight breaks out in the sandpit, this can give a teacher insight into the socio-emotional development of the children involved.

Some useful assessment strategies

- Performance-based assessment – this is a system of learning and assessment that allows children to demonstrate their knowledge and skills in a learning environment that embraces their higher-order thinking skills, as well as relating it to real-world situations. Children would be given a task and be expected to complete it. Block construction, visual art activities and movement/music rings are all examples of this type of assessment strategy.
- Practical exercises/demonstrations – this is similar to performance-based assessment. Children are encouraged to demonstrate a particular skill through doing.
- Projects – the children work together to complete a particular learning task. For example, they do a group creative art project.
- Role plays – children have an opportunity to act out or dramatise, for example, a story, a rhyme or a particular poem.
- Aural/oral questions – children are either encouraged to ask or to answer questions. This strategy enables the assessment of listening skills, thinking skills as well as speaking.
- Pedagogical documentation – this is a more recent assessment strategy introduced in the 1970s and 1980s by proponents of Reggio Emilio (Edwards, Gandini & Forman, 2012). Pedagogical documentation refers to making children's thinking and learning visible in many different ways. These include written or audio recordings of what children have said or done, videos or other digital traces, appropriate texts and transcripts of children's words (ideas, thoughts), photos of the process, artifacts and any other interesting evidence of children's work, even a small significant moment (Wien, nd; Stacey, 2015).

Find out more

According to Rinaldi (2005), pedagogical documentation is the process of gathering evidence of children's learning through observations, work samples and conversation transcripts. Children's and teachers' reflections are then analysed, interpreted and shared in a co-construction of knowledge. The role of the child in his/her own learning is recognised and valued. All players are encouraged to listen to children, create meaning from that listening, and together interpret children's ideas about their competencies and the world (Wein, nd). Pedagogical documentation extends the idea of assessment being predominantly focused on development; it enables teachers to reflect upon many more aspects of children's learning experiences and understandings of the world. These documented traces of lived experience, when shared with others, become a tool for thinking together. Through this collaborative approach and the sharing of each other's thoughts, we come to realise there are many viewpoints (Wien, nd). As Wien (nd) acknowledges, pedagogical documentation creates a new phase of thinking and wondering together between the act of observation and the act of planning a response. Rather than looking for what is known through assessment, pedagogical documentation invites the creativity, surprise and delight of teachers who discover the worlds of children.

Teachers revisit experiences and reflect together with children on their thoughts about their work. Teachers facilitate conversations with parents and through reflection think about their teaching, raise appropriate questions, and provide the next steps in the learning and teaching journey.

Observation

Observation means to perceive, to watch, to take notice, become conscious of. This should be ongoing, but teachers also need to set specific times for specific observations as one cannot observe everything all the time. When planning an observation time, consider the observation tools you are going to use and the place where the observation is to happen. Teachers should observe children in different contexts – indoors, outdoors, during routines, and in teacher-guided and free play. Finally, you need to consider what you plan to observe. Decide on the aspect of behaviour that you wish to focus on (eg social interactions) or the specific developmental areas you want to observe (eg an aspect of fine motor development).

There are different types of observations – each one has a place in the Grade R classroom. These include:
- Narratives – written descriptions
- Time sampling – observing what happens during a specific time
- Event sampling – identifying an event and then observing when and where it happens (eg aggressive behaviour)
- Modified child studies
    - Checklists

Table 9.1 A summary of observation strategies

METHOD	OBSERVATIONAL INTERVAL	RECORDING TECHNIQUES	ADVANTAGES	DISADVANTAGES
1. Narratives				
Diary description	Day to day	Use a notebook and pencil; itemise activity or other ongoing behaviour; can see growth patterns	Rich in detail; maintains sequence of events; describes behaviour as it occurs	Open to observer bias; time consuming
Specimen descriptions or running record	Continuous sequence	Same	Less structured	Sometimes need follow-up
Journal	Regular, preferred daily/weekly	Log, usually with space for each child; often a summary of child's behaviour	Same as diary description	Difficult to find time to do; possibly subjective

»

METHOD	OBSERVATIONAL INTERVAL	RECORDING TECHNIQUES	ADVANTAGES	DISADVANTAGES
'On-the-hoof' anecdotes	Sporadic	Ongoing during class time; make use of notepad and/or sheet of paper at hand	Quick and easy to take; short-captured pertinent events/ details	Lack detail; needs to be filled in at a later time; can detract from teaching responsibilities
2. Time sampling	Short and uniform time intervals	On the spot as time passes; prearranged recording sheets	Easy to record; easy to analyse; relatively bias free	Limited behaviours; loss of detail; loss of sequence and ecology of event
3. Event sampling	For the duration of the event	Same as for time sampling	Easy to record; easy to analyse; can maintain flow of class activity easily	Limited behaviours; loss of detail; must wait for behaviour to occur
4. Modifications				
Checklists	Regular or intermittent	Use prepared recording sheets; can be during or after class	Easy to develop and use; can record information for a number of children at any one time	Lack of detail; tell little of the cause of behaviours
Rating scales	Continuous behaviour	Same as for checklists	Easy to develop and use; can use for wide range of behaviours	Ambiguity of terms; high observer bias
Shadow study	Continuous behaviour	Narrative-type recording; uses prepared recording sheets	Rich in detail; focuses in depth on individual child	Bias problems; can take up too much of a teacher's time and attention

Source: Adapted from Gordon & Browne (2008: 247)

Observations can be problematic, so teachers should watch out for possible pitfalls. These are frequently related to poor observation techniques or poor recording methods, and include:
- errors of omission – leaving out important details
- errors of commission – misinterpretation of observations
- errors of transmission – mistakes in the actual recording of information, which could include the length of time between the observation and the recording of it.

Find out more

Access different examples of observation templates such as a check list, rating scale and event sampling schedule that you think could guide your observations in your Grade R classroom.

ASSESSMENT CONTEXT

Observations of play-based learning activities provide a starting point for further inquiry. These play-based learning activities – both teacher guided and child initiated – provide the most reliable opportunities to gather evidence of children's holistic development and learning. During these activities, children are demonstrating their knowledge, skills, values and attitudes in an everyday context on an ongoing basis. It is in these informal contexts that assessment is most worthwhile.

CASE STUDY 2

During outdoor free play, the teacher observes that Mpho is not socialising. He is sitting on his own while the other children are playing. The teacher, who has previously made similar observations, starts to think that Mpho may have some difficulty in socialising with other children. The teacher walks over to Mpho, sits down next to him, and starts an informal conversation:

Teacher:	What do you feel like doing today, Mpho?
Mpho:	I don't want to play.
Teacher:	What do you usually do on days when you do feel like playing?
Mpho:	I play with Tommy.
Teacher:	And what is Tommy doing today?
Mpho:	He is playing with Sipho today. He doesn't want to play with me. I don't like him anymore.
Teacher:	Well, why don't you all play together then?
Mpho:	No! I only want to play with Tommy.
Teacher:	There are other boys who would like to play with you …
Mpho:	No, I don't like them!

Without putting words in the child's mouth or supporting his 'blame game', the teacher obtained some valuable information regarding Mpho's inability to handle conflict, to socialise with more than one child at a time, and to play in a group. This one opportunity, however, would not be sufficient reason to record that Mpho seemingly cannot socialise. The teacher's observation should, though, be noted on the observation sheet. The teacher should continue to observe Mpho during other instances of free play or group activities in order to provide reliable evidence which could be used in a report to parents/caregiver. Only if such problematic behaviour persists will the teacher report it as a developmental area that needs attention. The teacher should both model appropriate social behaviour and use specific strategies to promote social development. Methods that the parents/caregiver could implement at home to address the problem, such as inviting new friends to play, motivating new friendships and modelling positive social behaviour to the child, could also be employed.

To bystanders, this initial interaction between Mpho and the teacher may have seemed like a meaningless conversation, but the teacher utilised the opportunity to gather information regarding Mpho's social development. A skilled teacher will act on this information and support the child in his/her social development by, for example, choosing a story for story time with a title such as: 'Will you be my friend?' After the story, the teacher will ask Mpho probing questions based on the story to support social development: 'What did you like about the story, Mpho? How did the story make you feel?' And to the whole group: 'I wonder if there are children in the class who feel the same as the boy in the story? How does making new friends make you feel?' Note that the teacher is not asking 'Yes' or 'No' questions, as he/she wants to encourage Mpho and the other children to express their feelings and to develop their social skills.

Find out more

The teacher in the case study used a teachable moment and informal interaction to gather evidence, and used the information to design learning opportunities (story) to support the child's social development and learning. In this instance, the teacher is also encouraging the children to provide reasons for choices made. The development of reasoning skills is one of the aims of education.

Capturing real-life examples of children's problem-solving, language, literacy, mathematics, motor, social and various life skills may seem like a daunting task. However, dedicated and passionate Grade R teachers who integrate teaching, learning and assessment in an ongoing and meaningful way will soon find that these authentic assessment opportunities become an integral part of their own teaching style. The whole child is assessed in his/her natural learning environment.

In short, as discussed earlier, worksheets, standardised tests and other types of 'table-top testing' are not appropriate for a variety of reasons. Specific learning dispositions such as curiosity, self-esteem and perseverance that can be linked to social and emotional development are required for successful learning in Grade 1, and these cannot easily be measured on paper or through highly structured one-to-one assessment tasks.

ASSESSMENT PROCESS

Schools often have their own assessment procedures, which may include the prescribed frequency of assessment, the structure of recordings, and when and how to report to parents or other stakeholders. Teachers are expected to compile progress reports based on continuous observation for every child at least three times each year. Each child's progress and growth should be documented during the year and compared with previous performance (if available). This serves as a reference point for the child's progress. Watch, observe and record each child's strong and weak areas through daily/weekly observations.

It is important to follow up on observations as children may change considerably throughout the year. The teacher should keep in mind that a parent usually knows the child well, and indicating that 'Billy cannot tie his own shoelaces', a task which he recently mastered quite well, may lessen the parents' confidence in the teacher and lower her credibility.

> **Something to consider**
>
> Why is it important to follow up on observations in Grade R?

ROLE PLAYERS IN ASSESSMENT

Although the teacher manages the assessment process, the parents/caregivers, as partners in the child's development, also play a critical role in assessment. Not only does the teacher have to report evidence of the child's performance to the parents/caregivers, but the parents should also be informed and guided on how to assist their child to develop and learn optimally. This partnership applies not only to cases where children may be lacking certain skills or knowledge, but also where assessment indicates giftedness that requires additional stimulation and support.

Interviews with parents/caregivers may also provide valuable information that will help the teacher to better understand the child's progress. Parents have knowledge of the child's progress to date and difficulties that might have occurred, such as biological, psychological or socio-economic barriers. They can also provide insights into the child's out-of-school behaviour, which may assist the teacher in understanding why certain developmentally appropriate knowledge, skills and attitudes are not in place.

In some schools, other role players may include class aids or caregivers who know the child well and who have the opportunity to observe the child's physical, cognitive and socio-emotional development on a daily basis.

In cases where the teacher suspects there may be more serious problems that require specific expert help, the child should be referred for specialist support such as occupational or speech therapy. These therapists play an important role in addressing barriers and need to be consulted on a regular basis regarding the child's progress. In these instances, a partnership should be formed with the teacher, therapist, parents and child so that they can work together as a team to support the child. This is, of course, an ideal that not all families may be able to access for a variety of reasons. In some instances, school support services may offer assistance.

RECORDING AND REPORTING

Recording is a process in which the teacher documents the current level of a child's competence and ongoing progress. Records of a child's competence should provide evidence of the child's progression within a grade and, at the end of the year, their preparedness for the next one.

Reporting is a process of communicating a child's competence to parents/caregivers, schools and other stakeholders. A child's competence levels can be reported in a number of ways. Firstly, report-backs on individual children can be shared through report cards, parent–teacher conferences, phone calls, as well as letters. The information shared in this type of reporting should remain confidential and only discussed with the support team. General information about whole class performance that identifies patterns of behaviour or competence can be shared through parents' meetings, school visitation days, open days and class or school newsletters, etc.

The CAPS document (South African Department of Basic Education, 2011a) provides a rating scale against which children' competence levels can be assessed. This scale goes from 1–7, with 1 representing 'not achieved' and 7 'outstanding achievement' (see Appendix 2 for more details on this). In Grade R, children are not given a percentage mark. However, in some instances the teacher may find that their competence level (as represented by the 1–7) can be equated with a percentage range (see Appendix 1).

The way reports are written is an indication of your professionalism. Language used should be simple but informative with an invitation for parents to contact you if they do not understand a point you have made or if they would like further information from you about their child. It should be emphasised that reports are confidential and, apart from specific school personnel, a child's progress should not be discussed with anyone else without the parents' consent. Make sure there is always a copy of the report for the school.

Something to consider

'Reporting to the parents after the first term is the most important report in Grade R.' Do you agree? Motivate your answer.

CULTURE AND LANGUAGE FAIRNESS IN ASSESSMENT

Assessment should always consider the influence of cultural and/or language differences on learning. Children from different cultures may well have different communication styles, as well as hold different value systems. For instance, one cultural group may hold the view that young children are allowed to speak only when they are spoken to, while another group views the child as having the same rights as adults to participate in conversations. Teachers should also reflect on their own perspectives, influenced by their cultural background, and acknowledge these as well as recognise the diversity children bring to the class. This diversity should be accommodated in assessment strategies, and each child's cultural context taken into consideration. Cultural dynamics that may influence teaching and learning should be part of the teacher's discussion at the beginning of the year with parents/caregivers.

Children coming from a home where the mother tongue is different from the language of learning and teaching (LoLT) may also find it difficult, especially initially, to demonstrate their understanding, knowledge or skills. They may, as a result, be inattentive and distract others. 'Communication barriers' can also impact the emotional as well as the social well-being of a child. According to Saneka and De Witt (2019), children with language barriers in relation to the LoLT could be seen by the teacher as being not motivated, not ready for formal schooling, or even suffering from a developmental delay. Saneka and De Witt suggest that assessment of children with a home language different from the LoLT should be conducted in a comfortable, familiar, interesting setting, and rely less on the child's current language ability in the LoLT.

ASSESSMENT AND CURRICULUM

Assessment should align with the learning aims as set out in the curriculum. Lesson/activity planning should clearly indicate what the child is expected to know and can do as a result of the learning experience, and how assessment strategies will allow the teacher to assess the progress the child has made in the learning process.

Assessment should also serve to inform future planning. For example, when assessment shows that most children cannot use a pair of scissors properly, more cutting experiences are built into the daily programme. Assessment may also indicate that your teaching strategies need to be revised or the knowledge base you are co-constructing should be broadened. You may also need to think about whether the resources you are using are appropriate.

> **Something to consider**
>
> **Assessment of children with barriers to learning**
> Assessment must address children's language, mathematics and life skills development. This is especially important in the early stages of the Grade R child's development where the teacher needs to recognise possible barriers to learning and address them appropriately.
>
> Inclusion in your class of Grade R children with barriers to learning has assessment implications. You may need to adjust your approaches to teaching and assess differently, as suggested by the principles of integrated curriculum and assessment (ICASS).
>
> The principles of integrated curriculum and assessment enhance individual growth and development, monitor the progress of children and facilitate learning. In addition, they help you find out what a child knows, understands and/or can do, and make

»

judgements based on valid and appropriate evidence. These judgements should then enable you to make well-informed decisions about what a child needs to learn next and give an indication of successful learning. The administration of ICASS should include a variety of techniques that encourage children to go beyond simple recall of data or facts and close the gap between the classroom and the real world. It should include opportunities for children to perform tasks and solve problems, and make provision for adaptive methods of assessment.

Find out more

Further useful information can be found through accessing the following sites:
   http://www.osepideasthatwork.org/toolkit/index.asp
   http://www.circleofinclusion.org

Self-assessment by the teacher

Teachers should continuously evaluate their own teaching. At the end of the activity/lesson, the teachers determine to what extent their expectations have been met. This can apply to planned lessons and/or activities, routines as well as free play. If their practice has not been successful, they should adapt the next lesson and/or activity so that the outcomes can be attained. It is thus important for teachers to note which aspects worked well and which did not. This assists your progress towards optimal teaching and learning. Table 9.2 shows an example of a self-assessment rubric.

Table 9.2 An example of a self-assessment rubric

SELF-ASSESSMENT RUBRIC FOR THE TEACHER	☹	😐	☺
Question 1			
Did you use all three subjects?			
Are you planning according to the CAPS document?			
Are activities planned in the context of this planning?			
Will the activities provide opportunity to meet your anticipated outcomes?			
Question 2			
Did you indicate who will be doing the assessment: teacher, child or peer group?			
Did you indicate what skills, knowledge, attitudes and values will be assessed?			
Did you implement various assessment strategies?			
Did you indicate all assessment tools/instruments?			

The following two documents (available at: http://www.education.gov.za) provide useful information regarding assessment in Grade R:
- National policy pertaining to the programme and promotion requirements of the National Curriculum Statement Grades R–12.
- The policy document, National Protocol for Assessment Grades R–12

We will now look at a specific example of assessment in one of the subject areas: Life Skills.

Find out more

Assessment in Life Skills happens mainly through regular and systematic observation of children participating in various activities such as whole-group discussions related to themes, games and activities. The creative arts, including visual arts, dance, music and drama, and oral and practical demonstrations such as role play and 'show and tell', etc, are also useful assessment strategies. Pedagogical documentation which entails taking photographs or short video clips of children participating in various activities is becoming a popular methods of recording assessment. These photographs and/or video clips can be shared with parents and provide visual evidence of what the child is doing. However, a word of caution. Assessment must be ethical. Assessment results should be confidential and not shared with other parents. Thus, parental permission must be obtained before children are photographed or videoed. If you share images with parents of their child, but other children are also captured in the frame, parental permission from all parents whose children's images are captured needs to be obtained. Furthermore, if you acknowledge that children should have voice and agency (see Chapter 2), you should also obtain their permission before videotaping or photographing them. Obtaining parental permission might be something you discuss with all parents at a meeting held at the beginning of the year. You could then request blanket permission to share non-sensitive information that has possibly been captured through digital means. However, should a particular image contain evidence of one child behaving in an inappropriate fashion, this image should not be shared with other parents.

The National Policy encourages the use of a comprehensive checklist/holistic rubric to track and monitor children's progress in Life Skills every term (see Appendix 3). Assessment in Life Skills during the Foundation Phase is largely informal, and is ongoing.

Table 9.3 shows some of the competences that could be observed and assessed.

Table 9.3 Some of the competences that could be observed and assessed

Beginning knowledge and personal and social well-being	• The child's contribution to the lesson and/or activity (level of knowledge and awareness)
	• Participation in the lesson and/or activities (oral, practical, written component) for example:
	  ▪ Draws or paints pictures to convey a message
	  ▪ Copies known letters in own name to represent writing
	  ▪ Writes from left to right and top to bottom
	  ▪ Contributes ideas for a class news book by means of drawings
	  ▪ Makes an attempt to write letters using squiggles, scribbles, etc
	  ▪ Talks to own writing, for example 'reads' what squiggles 'say'
	  ▪ Makes own books and contributes to class book collection)
	• Application of concepts and skills, etc

Other classroom skills that can be observed	• The child's classroom behaviour (following routines, showing respect, time on task, responsibility and care) • Participation in classroom activities • Cooperative skills (interaction with peers and teacher)

The following aspects can be used as guidelines to monitor the children's progress:
- Their perceptual-motor abilities (see Chapter 4)
- Their ability to express their ideas visually and verbally
- How successfully they can include elements of art such as shape and form (see Chapter 14)
- If they possess good manipulative skills (how they are using tools such as a paintbrush or a pair of scissors)
- If they are creative and can solve particular problems in an interesting and original way.

These aspects could be assessed by the teacher during visual art activities.

Find out more

http://artswork.asu.edu/arts/teachers/assessment/performance2.htm

SUMMARY

Assessment is a process of collecting, analysing and interpreting information to assist teachers, parents and other stakeholders in making decisions about the progress of children. Assessment in Grade R must be informal, and children should not be subjected to a 'test' situation. For this reason, assessment activities have not been included in the Grade R curriculum documentation. Each activity used for assessment should be carefully planned so that it integrates a variety of skills. Assessment of knowledge and attitudes must also be taken into account.

Continuous assessment is preferable as it allows teachers to revise or adapt their practice to better support children's learning.

Assessment in Grade R should be primarily focused on gathering evidence to help the Grade R teacher to make decisions about how to best support the Grade R children in their learning. The assessment process should be systematic and based on everyday tasks/activities undertaken by the children. This implies that assessment happens throughout the daily programme and not during special 'test periods'. Child-initiated play can provide rich opportunities for assessing socio-emotional development and other aspects of holistic development. The key elements of assessment are to help Grade R children to reach their full potential.

BIBLIOGRAPHY

Edwards, C, Gandini, L & Forman, G. 2012. *The hundred languages of children: The Reggio Emilia Experience in transformation.* 3rd ed. Santa Barbara, CA: Prager Press.

Excell, LA, Helsby, M & Linington, V. 2010. *Grade R practitioner's course.* Johannesburg: University of the Witwatersrand.

Grinder, EL & Kochanoff, A. 2007. *Revised report and guidelines on early childhood assessment for children from birth to age 8 (Grade 3).* Pennsylvania: Early Learning Standards Task Force and Kindergarten Assessment Work Group.

Kellough, RD & Kellough, NG. 1999. *Secondary school teaching: A guide to methods and resources; planning for competence.* Upper Saddle River, NJ: Prentice Hall.

Rinaldi, C. 2005. *In dialogue with Reggio Emilia. Listening, researching and learning.* London: Routledge.

Saneka, NE & De Witt, M. 2019. 'Barriers and bridges between mother tongue and English as a second language in young children'. *The South African Journal of Childhood Education* 9(1): a516. https//doi.org/10.4102/sajce.v9i1.516

Shepard, L, Kagan, S & Wurtz, E (eds). 1998. *Principles and recommendations for early childhood assessment.* Washington, DC: National Education Goals Panel.

South African Department of Basic Education. 2011a. *Curriculum and Assessment Policy Statement (CAPS).* http://www.education.gov.za (Accessed 12 April 2012).

South African Department of Basic Education. 2011b. *National Protocol for Assessment Grades R–12.* http://www.education.gov.za (Accessed 29 October 2012).

Stacey, S. 2015. *Pedagogical documentation.* https:/www.earlychildhoodwebinars.com/wp-content/uploads/2015/01/PowerPoint-Slides-1.15.2015-Susan-Stacey.pdf

Wien, CA. nd. *Making learning visible through pedagogical documentation.* http://conference-handouts.s3.amazonaws.com/2019-nctm-san-diego/pdfs/378-1020.pdf

GLOSSARY

Continuous assessment – assessment which takes place over a period of time and is ongoing

Developmental approach – an approach that considers the 'normal' developmental pattern of children

Fairness – treating people in a way that does not favour some over others

Flexible – easily changed; able to change/adapt or to do different things

Formative assessment – assessment for learning, a process of continuously collecting information on a child's progress (also called informal assessment)

Metacognitively – allowing individuals to think about their thinking, including using different ways to learn and to problem solve

Reliable – describes assessment findings that make sense, and are consistent and dependable

Reporting – the process of communicating the knowledge and understanding gained from assessing a child's learning and progress to various stakeholders such as parents/caregivers, other teachers and/or departmental officials

Summative assessment – more formal assessment (eg a formal test or examination) which provides an overall picture of a child's progress at a specific point in his/her development and learning

Validity – ensuring an assessment covers what it was intended to assess; in other words, how close the findings and interpretations are to what was observed

APPENDIX 1: CAPS ASSESSMENT

Codes and percentages for recording and reporting rating code description of competence percentage (South African Department of Basic Education, 2011a)

CODES AND PERCENTAGES FOR RECORDING AND REPORTING

RATING CODE	DESCRIPTION OF COMPETENCE	PERCENTAGE (%)
7	Outstanding achievement	80–100
6	Meritorious achievement	70–79
5	Substantial achievement	60–69
4	Adequate achievement	50–59
3	Moderate achievement	40–49
2	Elementary achievement	30–39
1	Not achieved	0–29

APPENDIX 2: GRADE R MATHEMATICS – ASSESSMENT SHEETS

Example of an instrument that can be used to record the Grade R child's mathematics learning. (A similar format should be used for assessment of Language and Life Skills learning.)

ASSESSMENT SHEET (Example A)

MATHEMATICS   GRADE R

va	Numbers, operations and relationships	Patterns, functions and algebra	Space and shape	Measurement	Data handling	

Content knowledge: ....

Learning task: ....

	Children (alphabetically)	7 Outstanding achievement/ exceptional competence	6 Meritorious achievement/ progress is fast	5 Substantial achievement/ progress is consistent	4 Adequate achievement	3 Moderate achievement	2 Elementary achievement/ progress is slow	1 Not achieved/ unable to do task
1								
2								
3								
4								
5								
6								
7								
8								

GRADE R MATHEMATICS – ASSESSMENT SHEET (Example B)

Content area: Numbers, operations and relationships (Formal assessment task)	**Content:** Whole numbers
Activity: Decorating cupcakes 1. Children mix icing sugar (four teaspoons of icing sugar, one teaspoon of margarine, one teaspoon of milk) 2. Each child receives 10 Smarties to decorate their two cupcakes. They count out how many Smarties they have, and share them equally between the two cupcakes	**Objectives and minimum requirements:** Count to at least 10 everyday objects Problem solving involving whole numbers using the following techniques: • Building up and breaking down of numbers • Doubling and halving • Using concrete apparatus (eg Smarties)
Informal assessment task: Children measure ingredients for icing sugar using a 5 ml measure (teaspoons). What is the shape of the cupcake/Smarties?	**Formal assessment task:** Children answer the following questions: How many Smarties do you have in total? How many Smarties can you put on each cupcake if you share the Smarties equally between the two cupcakes? (10 ÷ 2 = 5). If you eat one cupcake, how many Smarties are left?

Children	Informal assessment tasks			Formal assessment task																		Comments
	Colours	Measurement: Estimates, measures, compares 3D objects using non-standard measures (teaspoon)	Space and shape (geometry): Recognise, identify and name 2D shapes and 3D objects – circle	Counts to at least 10								Building up and breaking down of numbers								Doubling and halving
				1	2	3	4	5	6	7		1	2	3	4	5	6	7		1	2	3	4	5	6	7
	✓	✗	✓	✗	✗	✓	✗																			
Katlego																										
Tshephang																										
Steven, etc																										

Legend: ✓ achieved   ✗ fairly achieved   ✗ not achieved at all

APPENDIX 3: COMPREHENSIVE CHECKLIST/HOLISTIC RUBRIC

The National Policy encourages the use of a comprehensive checklist/holistic rubric.

Life Skills

Term 1 Grade R Performing arts – music, dance and drama: Creative games and skills Name of learner:	7 Outstanding achievement/ exceptional competence	6 Meritorious achievement/ progress is fast	5 Substantial achievement/ progress is consistent	4 Adequate achievement	3 Moderate achievement	2 Elementary achievement/ progress is slow	1 Not achieved/ unable to do task
• Warming up and breathing using everyday actions, such as waking up and getting dressed – stretching, curling, twisting, shaking, crossing the midline							
• Developing spatial awareness: freeze games, finding own space, no bumping							
• Keeping a steady beat: playing rhythmic games such as clapping, stamping, percussion using different rhythms and tempos							
• Exploring music, movement and voice: focusing on tempo – fast and slow							
• Singing action songs using different parts of the body to interpret the song							≫

APPENDIX 3 continued

Term I Grade R Performing arts – music, dance and drama: Creative games and skills Name of learner:	7 Outstanding achievement/ exceptional competence	6 Meritorious achievement/ progress is fast	5 Substantial achievement/ progress is consistent	4 Adequate achievement	3 Moderate achievement	2 Elementary achievement/ progress is slow	1 Not achieved/ unable to do task
• Spontaneous use of voice and movement in participatory rhymes and stories							
• Cooling down the body and relaxing (eg ice-cream melting activity)							
• Improvising and interpreting							
• Improvising stories based on fantasy or own life experiences using voice (singing/speaking), movement, music, props/objects and drama techniques							
• Expressing moods and ideas through movement and song (eg an angry lion, a hungry mouse)							
• Exploring the senses through dramatising stories, rhymes and songs (eg 'leading the blind', feeling different textures of objects)							

APPENDIX 3 continued

Term 1 Grade R Visual arts: Create in 2D Create in 3D (constructing) Name of learner:	7 Outstanding achievement/ exceptional competence	6 Meritorious achievement/ progress is fast	5 Substantial achievement/ progress is consistent	4 Adequate achievement	3 Moderate achievement	2 Elementary achievement/ progress is slow	1 Not achieved/ unable to do task
Create in 2D • **Drawing:** Draw and give own interpretation of drawings using the week's topic using wax crayons, oil pastels and other drawing media							
• **Painting:** Use pre-mixed tempera paint or coloured inks or dyes in primary and secondary colours to respond to the week's topic							
• **Art elements:** Informal experience and use of shape in drawing and painting							
• **Design principles:** Informal use of contrast (big/small, long/short) in drawing and painting							
• **Variation of paper size and format:** Encourage working in different scales							⟫

APPENDIX 3 continued

Term I Grade R Visual arts: Create in 2D Create in 3D (constructing) Name of learner: _____	7 Outstanding achievement/ exceptional competence	6 Meritorious achievement/ progress is fast	5 Substantial achievement/ progress is consistent	4 Adequate achievement	3 Moderate achievement	2 Elementary achievement/ progress is slow	1 Not achieved/ unable to do task
Create in 3D (constructing) • **Fine motor and sensory coordination (eye–hand–mind):** Manipulation of scissors and other tools and equipment. **Visual literacy** (to be covered throughout the term)							
• Naming shape in own work							

Chapter 10

Learning and teaching through play

Lorayne Excell, Vivien Linington

In this chapter we consider

- theories about play
- the value of play in early learning and teaching, and opportunities lost if play is not appropriately utilised
- features of play that enhance learning
- play as classified according to different age-related stages
- different types of play from a practical perspective
- a pedagogy of play
- the play continuum
- the role of indigenous play in the Grade R classroom.

INTRODUCTION

Play has been described as a cornerstone of learning for young children (Gordon & Browne, 2008; Jenson et al, 2019) as it is one of their first steps towards discovering their world and making meaning of it. However, everyone appears to have a slightly different understanding of what this word 'play' means and how it can become a meaningful learning and teaching strategy. The exact nature of play and what teachers mean by a play-based approach is an area of debate and differing interpretation.

In this chapter we explore different theoretical understandings of play, the value of play, the features of play, play as classified according to stages, and different types of play from a practical perspective. We also consider play in a decolonising context. We will ask the questions: 'Do all children necessarily play?' and 'Is play always a positive occurrence?' We also explore how play can become a meaningful teaching and learning tool in the Grade R classroom.

What does the word 'play' mean?

Read these meanings of the word 'play', taken from three dictionaries.

> *Chambers Twentieth Century Dictionary*
> To operate; to move about freely; to have some freedom of movement; to take part in a game

> *Pocket Oxford Dictionary*
> To have free movement within limits

> *Reader's Digest Illustrated Oxford Dictionary*
> To occupy or amuse oneself pleasantly with some recreation, game, exercise

Something to consider

Is there a similarity between the dictionary definitions? Are there any common words? Compare the dictionary definitions with your own understanding of play.

If your understanding of play is similar to the definitions given above, the chances are that as you read this chapter you are going to develop a very different understanding of this word. You are going to realise that it is loaded with many different meanings. Within the early childhood education (ECE) context, play means *much more* than what is implied in the dictionary definitions. Play is a rich, complex and multifaceted activity undertaken by most children. But do all children play, do all children want to play and are all children given equal opportunity to play? Does play in fact exclude some children?

PLAY FROM A THEORETICAL PERSPECTIVE

Throughout the ages, the importance of play in promoting growth, development and learning has been recognised by various theorists. Some examples include the following:

- **Froëbel**, founder of the kindergarten (which today is often referred to as Grade R) suggested that play is the highest level of child development. It is the spontaneous expression of thought and feeling. It is never trivial. It is serious and deeply significant, not only for what children learn about the world, but also for the spiritual significance of play (Kerry & Tollitt, 1987). Froëbel argued that children should play until age seven as it is only then that they are ready for the demands of formal schooling.
- **Freud**, the father of psychoanalysis, felt that play was a means of expressing and releasing emotions and tensions (Monighan-Nourot, in Branscombe, Castle, Dorsey, Surbeck & Taylor, 2003).

- **Vygotsky**, a social constructivist, claimed that play was important for children's adaptation to the social world through the learning of cultural norms and the growth of language. Vygotsky viewed play as a key factor in learning. He saw play as 'creating a zone of potential development in which children operate at their highest level of functioning, beyond their present-day possibilities so that they become ahead of themselves' (Bruce, 2004: 142). According to Vygotsky (1978: 129), 'in play a child is always above his average age, above his daily behaviour, in play it is as though he were a head taller than himself'. He also claimed that during play, while imitating their elders in culturally patterned activities, children generate opportunities for intellectual development (Vygotsky, 1978). Howard (2017) maintains that, according to Vygotsky, symbolism during imaginative play represents children's first experiences with systems they will later apply in numeracy and literacy. For example, blocks in the home corner can, through the use of imagination, represent a sandwich. One of the children, pretending to be the 'mother' gives the sandwich to 'one of her children'. This use of a symbol (block) to represent a concrete object (the sandwich) can be linked to the emergence of number concept where the written number 1 will represent a single object. This example also shows how children begin to master abstract thought through play; through using their imaginations and understanding the progression of a game. Vygotsky argues that play leads to development and learning. In fact, for Vygotsky, play, in particular socio-dramatic (fantasy) play, is the most important activity for children between the ages of three and six years (Karpov, 2005). Because 'they are only playing', they are free to take risks, doing things they are not yet confident to do well. In social play children interact with each other, make sense of their world and create meaning.
- **Piaget's** view of play aligns with modern research on the early development of the brain which 'suggests that play involves the senses and movement as well as developing the imagination and rule behavior' (Bruce, 2004: 143). Piaget is a stage theorist who identified different kinds of play which developed in order, and we shall be returning to these when we discuss the classification of play.
- **Bruner**, a cognitive theorist, showed that children who first interact with materials in free play were better problem solvers with the same materials in later tasks than were children who had not played with the materials (Branscombe et al, 2003).

Current conceptions of play examine it though a critical lens, and challenge a number of accepted beliefs and assumptions about the nature and purpose of play. The idea that all children benefit from and learn through play has been questioned. Attention has been paid to how factors such as race, gender and socio-economic conditions influence children's ability to play meaningfully. Furthermore, traditional beliefs about free play and choice, and the role of the teacher in free play have also been questioned. The concept of play has also been broadened to explore not only how children learn through play but also to examine how teachers teach through play. These ideas will be explored in greater depth towards the end of this chapter.

THE VALUE OF PLAY

Research continues to show that play and playful forms of activity are essential to support and promote early learning. Play-based activities promote children's understandings of complex forms of knowledge, skills and understanding, particularly in the social and cognitive areas of development (Wood, 2009). There is general agreement that play is a universal phenomenon; it happens throughout the world, in all communities. However, what children play and how they play is determined by their specific cultural context. For example, many children play 'wedding, wedding' but the form the play takes will depend on their experiences of a wedding in their community. According to many educationists, play is a self-satisfying activity through which children come to understand life and gain control over their world. Play behaviour is spontaneous and requires the active engagement of the players. Through playing, children achieve a sense of personal motivation. It is the activity itself rather than the goals that are important. Children supply their own meaning to play activities and control these activities themselves. Play is relatively free from outside rules and if they do exist they can be modified by the players. Play is useful to children because it helps them to understand their world, both cognitively and affectively. Bruce (2004) further notes that play allows the mind to become flexible, adaptive and imaginative, and suggests that if imaginative types of play behaviours are encouraged, they will help children to become more creative in adulthood.

In other words, play is important in the holistic development and learning of young children because, through play, children do the following:
- They take steps to explore, investigate and test their ideas.
- They develop concentration, perseverance and problem-solving skills.
- They develop and practise many of the skills, knowledge, attitudes and values that prepare them not only for success in the formal schooling situation but also for life. This includes, for example, aspects of motor, social, cognitive and emotional development.
- They make sense of the adult world.
- They have an opportunity to make choices and decisions.
- They come to terms with a problem that is troubling them, for example the arrival of a new baby in the home.

Play therefore has certain defining characteristics:
- Play is open-ended; it is a process that focuses on the activity rather than the end product – it is an end in itself.

- It is universal, and common to all children. However, the kinds and types of play will be determined by the children's particular contexts and cultural values.
- It is intrinsically motivated – children play because they want to play, not because they have to (unlike many other forms of learning).
- It is relatively free of rules – except those which children create themselves.
- It is generally controlled and led by the children.
- It is about choices. Children play in areas and with equipment of their choice.
- It is enjoyable, and should always have an element of fun.
- It is possibly therapeutic for the child. It can be a way of helping children deal with stressful situations that they find difficult to verbalise.

Find out more

Evidence (Liu et al, 2017) has shown that play is most beneficial when it is characterised by joy, meaning, active engagement, iteration (repetition) and social interaction. These characteristics stimulate neural connections and enhance learning and development. Joy is said to enhance memory and attention as well as creativity and motivation. Meaningful play helps children make connections between familiar and unfamiliar stimuli, which makes learning easier. Active engagement promotes agency and decision making because children are active participants in the activity, and has been linked to self-regulatory behaviours. Iterative or repetitive play encourages perseverance and enables flexible thinking which can begin to consider alternative points of view. Social interaction fuels healthy emotional development and promotes plasticity in the brain, which can help with challenges later in life.

Should you wish to read further about these new understandings of play go to the following website: https://www.google.com/search?q=Neuroscience+and+learning+through+play%3A+a+review+of+the+evidence&oq=Neuroscience+and+learning+through+play%3A+a+review+of+the+evidence&aqs=chrome..69i57.2060j0j7&sourceid=chrome&ie=UTF-8

Something to consider

Although all these characteristics may apply, there can still be negative aspects that prevent children from playing or from enjoying playing or from experiencing play as a beneficial activity. These are discussed later in the chapter.

Try this out

After reading this section, answer the following questions:
- How would you respond to a Grade 1 teacher who thinks the children spent too much time playing?
- What would you say to a parent who thought too much time was spent on play and questioned its value?

PLAY CLASSIFIED ACCORDING TO AGE-RELATED STAGES

We have seen there is substantial agreement about the value and characteristics of play. However, when it comes to stages or classifications in relation to play, there is less agreement. Modern thinking around play still notes the stage factor but questions the age/stage relationship.

Parten's classification (cited in Bruce, 2004) is one of the oldest and illustrates how the age/stage relationship can be questioned. Parten describes the stages of play as follows:

- **Solitary play** – children play alone and are absorbed in their own play. They are unaware of what other children are doing. According to Parten, babies and toddlers engage in solitary play, but modern theory would question the age range because children who might play this way include the following in addition to the very young child:
  - The older child who is egocentric
  - The child who is not able or ready to share and cooperate during play
  - The older child who is emotionally and socially immature
  - The older child who is not immature but who chooses to play alone.

> **Something to consider**
>
> Can you think of one example of a child in your class who is at this stage? Give your own example of solitary play.

- **Parallel play** – children play alongside other children, notice what they are doing but continue with their own activity. They do not interact socially with other children. In addition to toddlers, children who play in this way include those who are perhaps shy and would like to become more involved with other players but are not sure how to do this.

> **Something to consider**
>
> Think of your own example of parallel play that you have observed in your class.

- **Associative play** – children play together developing interactions through imitating what other children are doing or playing with similar equipment. Though this type of play is most frequently seen in three- to four-year-old children, it could be observed in older children, possibly in those who are new to the group or who might be a little shy to join a group uninvited.

> **Something to consider**
>
> Describe one example of associative play that you have observed in your classroom.

- **Cooperative play** – children are ready to share and cooperate with others. They might, at first, only play cooperatively for a short while. Later they might want to join in a group game or want to do what the group is doing. They are ready and prepared to put aside their own desires and interests in order to follow those of the group. Children usually play cooperatively at about five years of age.

> **Something to consider**
>
> Give some examples of cooperative play that you have observed in your classroom.

A Grade R child could at different times choose to follow all these different forms of play depending on a wide range of personality and contextual factors.

Piaget also classified play according ages and stages. Knowledge of this classification is still relevant today. These stages are the following:

- **Sensory-motor/practice play** – this begins in infancy and today it is acknowledged that this form of play continues throughout life. Much of this play is just for the pleasure of exploring the senses. It involves a lot of repetition, for example swinging on a swing or kicking a soccer ball.
- **Symbolic (make believe, fantasy or pretend) play** – this begins somewhere towards the end of their first year when children start to give a different meaning to an actual object. For example, the swing could now become a rocket ship travelling into space. A block could become a cellphone. Wadsworth (1989: 60) points out that in 1967 Piaget wrote that 'its [symbolic play's] function is to satisfy the self by transforming what is real into what is desired'. Today it is also acknowledged that this type of play can continue throughout childhood.
- **Games with rules** – children begin to make and agree to rules that will govern their play. They might invent their own games and make up the rules as they go along. This form of play is typical of Grade R children.

CASE STUDY 1

Raj is on the jungle gym climbing across the monkey bars. He is pretending to be Spiderman and moving very slowly, taking a long time to get to the other side of the bars. John standing below becomes restless and shouts out, 'Come on, Raj, it's my turn to be Spiderman. We all agreed to have one turn each before we have to go inside.'

What types of play do you identify in this case study? Was Piaget right in the way in which he ordered the three types of play? Could they happen at the same time? What do you think?

DIFFERENT TYPES OF PLAY FROM A PRACTICAL PERSPECTIVE

Play can also be described according to the different types in which children become involved. This is perhaps a more practical description of play and one with which you are more familiar. These types of play often feature in a quality Grade R daily programme. We could describe the following types of play:

Functional play

- Is simple and repetitive.
- Emphasises the physical aspect of play.
- Involves movement and large muscle development (running, jumping, climbing, etc).
- Encourages small (fine) muscle development (cutting, tearing, squeezing, etc).
- Involves movement control (hand–eye coordination, etc).
- Involves the use of the senses.
- Occurs in the practising and mastering of skills.
- Promotes a sense of achievement in the child.

> **Promoting functional play**
> Provide outdoor equipment such as jungle gyms, swings, cycle tracks.
> Provide indoor resources such as toys, puzzles, drawing materials, etc.
> (See Chapter 7 for planning related to functional play.)

Constructive play

- Occurs when the child's physical movements become more controlled.
- Involves constructive, creative and imaginative use of play materials.
- Is play with a purpose.
- Involves the use of building blocks, playing with Lego or building with cardboard boxes (eg cereal, washing powder or toothpaste boxes), etc.

> **Promoting constructive play**
> Provide blocks, cardboard boxes, Lego or other construction toys. (See Chapter 7.)

Manipulative play

- Involves mostly small muscles.
- Children manipulate (use, work with) objects such as lacing cards or pegboards.
- Also promotes the development of cognitive (intellectual) and imaginative skills.
- Sand play and water play are good examples of manipulative play.

> **Promoting manipulative play**
> Provide lacing cards, pegboards, sand play and water play and creative art activities. (See chapters 7 and 14.)

Fantasy play (socio-dramatic play)

- The children develop their imagination.
- They create an inner world within which they can make things happen in whatever way they wish.
- They act out frightening situations, putting themselves in control.
- They learn to understand their behaviour and feelings, and how to come to terms with them.

> **Promoting fantasy play**
> Provide appropriate props. (See Chapter 7.)

Games with rules

- The children play in groups.
- They are mature enough socially to play cooperatively.
- They are mature enough intellectually and emotionally to understand and follow the rules.
- They are able to cope with the physical skills involved in the games.
- They are able to work out their own rules, which may differ from the actual rules of the game.
- They enjoy this type of play from about five to eight years of age and upwards.

> **Promoting games with rules**
> Provide cards, or homemade or bought games such as board games. Examples include Snap, Ludo, Snakes and Ladders, and Diketo. Games with rules can also be played outdoors, for example catch, hopscotch, hide-and-seek and soccer.

THE ROLE OF THE TEACHER

The teacher's role is key. As mentioned in Chapter 7, teachers must ensure that children are offered developmentally and contextually appropriate, meaningful play opportunities. These should also be joyful and meaningful, and nurture active engagement and social interaction if children are to have purposeful learning experiences. Refer back to Chapter 7 on where the environment takes the role of the third teacher. However, teachers cannot assume that child-initiated play alone will meet all the child's developmental and learning needs. See the discussion of playful pedagogies later in this chapter.

> **Something to consider**
>
> Think about your classroom. Do you think you provide sufficient stimulating play opportunities for the children? Write down exactly what you do (or do not do). Now read further.

Find out more
The teacher **provides a balanced programme** where child-initiated play, teacher-guided activities and routines are all recognised as suitable and appropriate ways of achieving the desired learning outcomes (see Chapter 7).

To provide appropriate play opportunities, teachers should:
- Show an interest in and understanding of the importance and value of play.
- Support play by showing an interest in what children are doing.
- Set the stage for play considering both the time allocated and space available.
- Provide appropriate resources to enhance both indoor and outdoor play using their partnership with the community to fill possible gaps in the resources.

Interest and understanding
Teachers learn about children by listening to and observing spontaneous play activity and planning a curriculum that encourages play. They discover each child's individual personality, learning style and preferred mode of play. They create spaces for children who might wish to play cooperatively but appear reluctant to join a group. Genuine interest is one way teachers show their approval of the play process. Another way is to create a safe environment where children feel physically and emotionally secure and included.

A difficult task for teachers is knowing when to join children at play and when to remain outside the activity. The teachers must ask themselves whether their presence will support what is happening and extend learning, or whether it will disrupt play so that it loses some of its benefits.

> **Read the following, which is an incident observed in a fantasy corner**
>
> Thokozani, the shopkeeper, is discussing how much change he should give to Jabu who has come to buy bread and bananas at the 'spaza shop'. Jabu feels he should be getting more change, but Thokozani is insisting that he has given Jabu the right amount of money.

Something to consider

Do you as a teacher interrupt the flow of play and explain the concepts involved to the children or do you continue to observe quietly from the sideline? Sometimes, these are not easy decisions to make. As you consider this dilemma, think back to Chapter 2 and Vygotsky's argument that learning is social in nature and there is a definite mediating role for the teacher.

Setting the stage for play: structuring the environment and encouraging play

There should be an uninterrupted time in the daily programme (at least 45 minutes to an hour) for child-initiated play. This gives children time to explore and discover. It is frustrating for young children to have their play cut short just as they are getting deeply involved. In free play, the child's right to choose what to play, how to play and how often should be the guiding principle – guiding, but not necessarily prescribing. The teacher should ensure that new play materials and resources are added to stimulate interest. They should also ensure that the materials and resources chosen appeal to all children's needs, interests and emotions. Issues to consider include the following:

- Is there sufficient space? The classroom layout can either encourage or restrict play. For example, if the block corner is next to the book corner, an extended block construction and/or the noise levels could interfere with the 'reading' process.
- In fantasy play, props are required for a variety of roles:[1] Men, women, babies, doctors, nurses, shopkeepers, postmen, teachers, firemen, etc. See Chapter 7 for examples of suitable props.
- Props that represent aspects of the child's daily life are important; children require many opportunities to act out their life stories. For younger children, teachers make sure there are duplicates of popular materials as sharing might be difficult and group play should be encouraged. For example, social interaction is enhanced when there are three firemen's hats.
- Play is further enhanced by materials that are *open-ended* – that is, they can be used in many ways, for example blocks.

In short, the teacher's role in play is to balance the facilitation of play with the utilisation of the teachable moments that could enhance further learning.

---

1 Choosing materials to place in a classroom should be done with an awareness of exposing children to images of diversity (eg male nurses, female construction workers, African doctors, etc), rather than reinforcing existing stereotypes.

> **Something to consider**
>
> As you reflect on your role in the facilitation of play, ask yourself the following:
> - Do I show excitement and enthusiasm for play?
> - Is the environment a safe and secure one where children are eager to play, explore and discover?
> - Are there sufficient play spaces? Do children have enough opportunities and time to be able to play meaningfully and do they have sufficient resources (play materials)?
> - Do they have opportunities to play indoors and outdoors?
> - Am I offering a variety of indoor and outdoor play opportunities?
> - Are children given sufficient choice and the opportunities to make their own decisions about what and with whom to play?
> - Do I have sufficient resources and if not, how could I get more?

A CRITIQUE OF PLAY: IS PLAY ALWAYS BENEFICIAL?

If play is not sufficiently challenging for the children, it can become repetitive, a waste of time and have little learning value because children become bored and lack focus.

In recent years, a number of early educationists have been examining play from a sociocultural perspective (see Chapter 2). They agree that, if properly offered, play has immeasurable value in promoting early learning, but these benefits can only be realised if the specific contexts of each and every child are recognised and taken into account. Play does not necessarily benefit all children at all times. For example, play is not always a spontaneous activity in all cultures.

Though little has been written about play in the African early childhood education (ECE) context, Nsamenang (2008) suggests that although play is an important part of African children's childhoods, in an African context the emphasis is on peer involvement and learning. The issue of peer involvement has not been particularly foregrounded in the traditional Western approach to ECE where the focus has been on the individual. Cultural norms must always be borne in mind.

For example, many black children do not come from homes where it is the norm to take a toy off a shelf and start playing with it. They wait for permission to do so or wait until the toy has been given to them. In a school situation they may do the same thing – wait. The traditional classroom practice of promoting self-help activities and free play is thus not necessarily beneficial for these children as they might miss out on learning opportunities because they are not aware of the behavioural codes or 'norms' of the class. Another example is related to gender preferences in play. Teachers should ask themselves to what extent the play options that they provide support or present a barrier to children's learning. Are boys, for example, allowed to play in the home corner, and can girls do woodwork? In fantasy play, a teacher who observes children role playing very stereotypical male/female roles could suggest to the children that there might be other ways of enacting these roles.

CASE STUDY 2

A teacher observes a boy in the role of a father reading the evening newspaper while a girl in the role of his wife rushes in from work and starts cooking dinner. The father shouts out, 'Get me a drink, I have been waiting for a long time. When will I get my dinner?' In line with participatory learning, you want to get children to think about what are appropriate male and female roles in the 21st century. At the same time, you do not want to undermine their family norms, so you could ask in a querying way whether this role play and the allocated roles are fair in a family context today. This is what we mean by identifying a teachable moment and mediating possible change.

> **Something to consider**
>
> Once again, think about your own classroom situation. Can you recall particular instances when either boys or girls were at a disadvantage during free play, when perhaps they were displaying stereotypical behaviours? If so, can you think of some reasons why this might have happened? And most importantly, do you think it would have been appropriate in this instance to tackle the stereotypical behaviour? If so, how could you have gone about this?

Find out more

MacNaughton (2005) argues that play always involves a power relationship between children, and each child's opportunities to play freely need to be examined in the light of them. Imbalances in power relationships are caused by many factors, which include, for example, racism, sexism, homophobia and classism.

We have considered in this chapter complex and different understandings of play and a play-based approach to early learning. These different understandings stem from differing interpretations of children and childhood, and of teaching and learning in the context of ECE. In addition to what we have discussed, we now consider a further interpretation of play which extends some of the earlier ideas and shows how playful learning can be used cross curriculum through the day.

A FURTHER INTERPRETATION OF PLAY: PLAYFUL PEDAGOGIES

A traditional developmentally appropriate approach to ECE strongly suggests that growth, development and learning are supported by play. The focus in this approach is on *how children learn through play*. In this traditional model, the emphasis has been on free play and free choice. Much has been said about the role of teachers and how they can support this view of play, but a growing field is on *how the teacher can teach through play*. Linking these two concepts, teaching (pedagogy) and play, is not easy because of the implications for practice. Wood (2009) suggests that we also need to focus on how teachers teach playfully, an approach which she has called a pedagogy of play. In a pedagogy of play, the teacher has a more definite role, and becomes an active part of a playful process instead of merely supervising the children's play (Wood, 2009).

Something to consider

Can free play be truly free when a teacher purposefully intervenes to enhance learning? These are some of the considerations and tensions that are currently being debated because of a renewed focus on the purposes of play in education and the role of the teacher in both free play and teacher-guided activities. Part of this approach is an analysis of different phases of play and the degree of participation in the different phases by the children and the teacher.

Find out more

Wood (2009) suggests, as we have already mentioned, that it is time to explore not only how children learn through play but also how teachers teach through play. This, she argues, would be a way to counter the increasing formality that appears to be creeping into early childhood (Grade R) classrooms. If teachers could teach effectively through play and playful activities, their reliance upon paper and pencil activities and workbooks/sheets would be lessened. Furthermore, they would be able to make use of appropriate play-based teaching and learning strategies that support quality teaching and learning. Wood (2009) claims that alternative strategies for implementing an effective play-based curriculum in ECE could be explored through a **'pedagogy of play'**, which she defines as follows:

> The ways in which early childhood professionals [teachers] make provision for play and playful approaches to learning and teaching, how they design play/learning environments, and all the pedagogical decisions, techniques and strategies they use to enhance learning and teaching through play (Wood, 2009: 27).

Four broad strands inform a pedagogy of play. These are how learning and pedagogy are understood; the nature of knowledge; assessment and evaluation; and quality in the early years (see Figure 10.1).

As with participatory learning, this approach requires teachers to think about their practice in a different and new way. It recognises the importance of teachers seeing themselves as having a definite role in planning an interactive learning environment that offers challenging and stimulating choices to children, and promotes holistic development and learning (see Chapter 7 on the environment as the third teacher). In a pedagogy of play, the teacher has a distinctive role in mediating play as well as identifying and constructively handling the different sociocultural contexts that might be represented in the class.

In particular, it demands that teachers have excellent content/subject knowledge and a deep understanding of playful learning, and asks them to work much more closely with the children. How and what teachers say to children is particularly important. Do you remember our reference to the hidden curriculum in Chapter 7)?

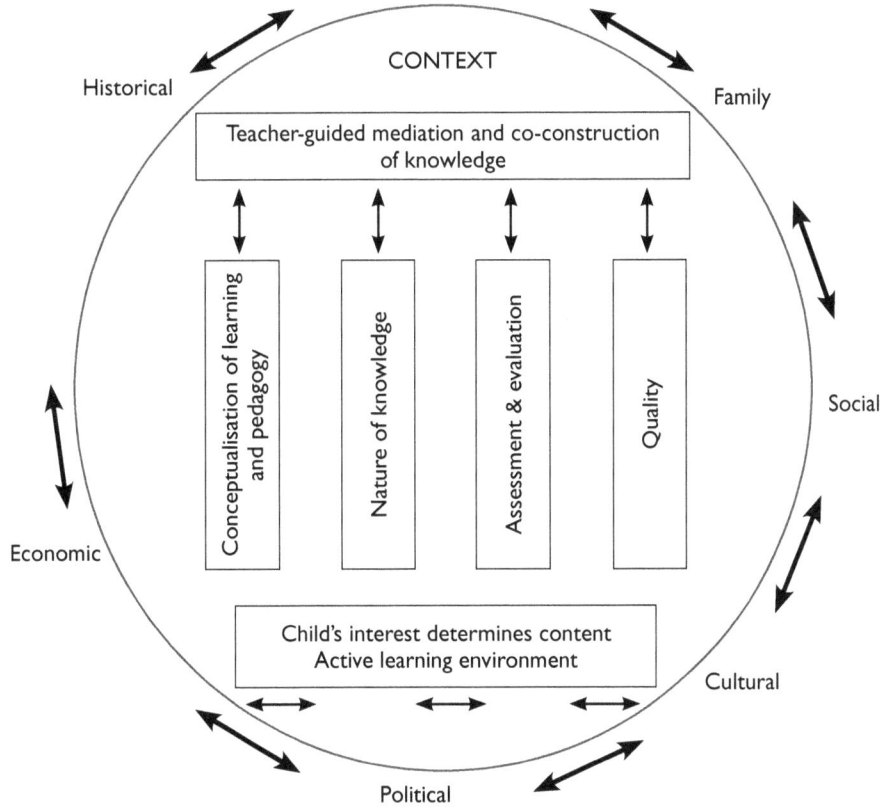

Figure 10.1 A diagrammatic representation of a pedagogy of play

Something to consider

How do you as a teacher encourage and support children in their thinking? How do you as a teacher encourage your children to explore and discover information during free play? Teachers have to think about when and how they ask children questions, » the type of language they use and suggestions they make (ie how they mediate the children's learning). Teachers and children co-construct knowledge. This co-construction has been called 'sustained shared thinking' (Fleer, Anning & Cullen, 2007). In this approach, children are increasingly being recognised as powerful players in their own learning. They are viewed as capable, competent and unique human beings who are able to make and co-construct meaning together with responsive adults, such as the teacher, as well as their peers. This view supports the idea of a 'being' child (see Chapter 8).

Find out more

Co-construction of meaning and understanding requires that teachers become aware of what children know and are thinking and understanding so that they can help them make sense of their findings. To do this, teachers need to gain insight into a topic before sharing their thoughts with the children. 'Co-construction requires that teachers are willing to find out more about content knowledge as well as develop excellent dialogue [conversation] skills' (Jordan, 2009: 43). The teacher takes a leading role in creating play/learning environments, as well as being responsive to children's choices, interests and patterns of learning (Wood, 2009). It should not be an either/or teaching and learning environment. In other words, it is not a question of either free or teacher-guided play, but rather a thoughtfully planned integration of both, and this takes the ability to read the moment and the children's activities at that time. A way to represent these different facets of play and playful learning and teaching is through a play continuum.

Something to consider

Teachers are expected to make informed choices about how to incorporate play into their practice. The play continuum provides an alternative lens through which to view playful teaching and learning, and recognises that there are many ways to play, each with different roles for adults and children. The play spectrum encapsulates the different phases of play and presents them on a continuum moving from high teacher control to minimal teacher engagement where children gain voice and agency. In other words, children are free to make their own choices. The boundaries between these phases are fluid. During the school day teachers can facilitate movement between these phases in order to best meet the interests and learning needs of the children.

See Table 10.1 for the range of the play continuum, the key features, the role of the adult, benefits to children, and other features.

Table 10.1 The play continuum

	INSTRUCTION/ TEACHER DIRECTED	**TEACHER GUIDED**	**GAMES WITH RULES**	**FREE PLAY (CHILD-INITIATED PLAY)**
Key features	Adult initiates and directs. Child follows. More structure and less choice. The adult sets goal(s) attuned to perceived children's learning needs and interests. Explicit instruction through telling and scaffolding. Children may (or not) be actively engaged.	Adult initiates, child directs. Balanced structure and choice. The adult sets goal(s) attuned to children's learning needs and interests. Children should have some choice in what to do and how; the adult is present and interacting with children, but cannot direct their actions. Children should be actively engaged.	Context provides structure and choice within game rules. Game rules set goals and scaffold interactions between players. Children play by game rules (which they might make up); this way, the game directs the activity. Children have agency and choice in the game and how to play it. Active engagement and participation.	Child initiates and directs. Less structure and more choice. Children set own goals in the play, following their interests. They are often very active: exploring, asking what if, re-inventing ideas and creating new meanings. Children actively engaged and participating.
Adult role	Prepare environment and materials in line with learning goal(s). Guide and scaffold children's attempts, explain, observe their efforts and support when they struggle to master the intended learning goal or skill.	Create a play context, with or for children, with an embedded learning focus (eg a spaza shop with signs, appropriate props and paper money). Observe, build on and extend children's thinking and ideas.	Get children started by setting up a game, or help them choose a game to play together. Support children in understanding and practising rules of the game (taking turns, for example). Help children join a game with peers.	Child initiates and directs. Less structure and more choice. Children set own goals in the play, following their interests. They are often very active: exploring, asking what if, re-inventing ideas and creating new meanings. Children actively engaged and participating. Observe, listen to and acknowledge children during play. »

	INSTRUCTION/ TEACHER DIRECTED	TEACHER GUIDED	GAMES WITH RULES	FREE PLAY (CHILD-INITIATED PLAY)
				Support when children struggle, for example, to join peer play, explain their ideas or needs, make plans or regulate their emotions. Ensure a safe and secure learning environment.
Child benefits	Well-planned and intentional instruction with use of effective techniques can lead to improved academic outcomes and socio-emotional skills.	Guided play can lead to higher gains on literacy, numeracy, social skills and self-regulation skills than instruction or free play alone.	Well-designed games can lead to literacy and numeracy skills (digital and physical games) as well as social skills. Music games can lead to improved self-regulation.	Free play is linked to executive functions (cognitive reasoning, etc), self-regulation, social skills, self-esteem, health and well-being. Physical play is linked to spatial skills and mathematics.
Other features	Structured approach; high teacher control. There is a time for explaining and telling children what and/or how to do something. Instruction forms an integral part of practice.	Balanced and flexible approach. Degree of teacher control varies according to the situation. Teacher requires deep insight to know when to offer children choices and when to stand back.	Balanced and flexible approach. Slightly less teacher control – teacher 'reads children' and intervenes only when and if necessary, or if invited to join game.	Child makes the choices and should be encouraged to practise his/her agency and voice. Teacher supervision is necessary but there is minimal teacher control.

Source: Adapted from Jenson et al (2019)

Try this out

Think about your own practice. Can you identify instances when you have facilitated playful pedagogy in relation to each indicator on the play continuum?

Find out more

The idea of the play continuum also opens a space for teachers to re-examine their practices from a contextually bound perspective which in South Africa must include an African perspective. How and to what extent do you include indigenous knowledge in the curriculum, and incorporate indigenous games and rhymes as part of your teaching strategies? An indigenous approach foregrounds knowledge embedded in the cultural traditions of regional, indigenous or local communities. Nyota and Mapara (2008) acknowledge that indigenous knowledge is expressed in a variety of ways including stories, legends, folklore, rituals, songs, games and even laws. Semali and Maretzki (2012) define indigenous knowledge as an emerging area of study that focuses on the ways of knowing, seeing and thinking that are handed down orally from generation to generation, hence the importance of language and story in the transmission of indigenous knowledge.

Language is integral to culture which encapsulates value systems. As Mji, Kalenga, Ned, Alperstein and Banda (2020) suggest, some of Africa's indigenous roots and value systems might include specific sayings such as:

- *umntu ngumntu ngabantu* (a person is a person because of the contributions of other people)
- *ubude abuphangwa* (you cannot hurry to be tall – in other words, do not try to be what you have not achieved)
- *uhambo alunqgitywa ngemini enye* (you do not finish a journey in one day – in other words, be patient – do not try to achieve it all in one go as you might miss some learning lessons on the way as you are hurrying it all up).

In the Grade R context, these sayings and their origins could be explored in language or story rings and integrated with the teaching of Life Skills and themes such as 'Who am I?', or 'My family and the community'. If one places these activities on the play continuum, they could fall under 'Instruction' (ie in the teaching of the actual saying) and 'Teacher guided' as you tell the story related to the saying and invite children to actively participate.

Returning to the play continuum, the next category, which is games with rules, can also be promoted through indigenous games and rhymes. Examples of games with rules include Diketo (a counting game played with stones, called Jacks in English); *tsoro* (the Shono equivalent of a board game know as draughts in English); and *chamuvandevande* (hide-and-seek) (Mutema, 2013). The examples mentioned highlight how children across different cultures play similar games – even though the names may be different, the rules are similar.

When planning free play, the home and community context should be taken into account. Consider, for example, the type of shops and health services used by the community you are serving. Resources should also reflect the child's home world. However, children also need to be offered new insights into ways of being and living. A balance between the known and unknown/familiar and unfamiliar should always be sought. For example, the fantasy corner in a health theme could provide resources that reflect a township clinic and a doctor's surgery.

Try this out

If you had the theme 'health' and needed to set up a fantasy corner to support the theme further, what resources would you provide to reinforce the familiar and introduce the unfamiliar?

Can you think of particular indigenous games, rhymes and stories that you could include in your Grade R practice? Share your identified activities with colleagues with whom you are in touch. In this way you could increase your resource 'bank' and possibly enrich your programme.

SUMMARY

This chapter has considered the complex nature of play and questioned whether traditional understandings of play are valid today. We have said that for the young child, play is an important part of learning, but that free play, initiated by the child, needs to be balanced with purposeful play where the teacher mediates and co-constructs knowledge with the child. According to this view, the concept of play is broadened to include opportunities for both learning and teaching.

BIBLIOGRAPHY

Anning, A. 2006. 'Early years education: Mixed messages and conflicts', in *Educational studies: Issues and critical perspectives,* edited by D Kassem, E Mufti & J Robinson. Berkshire: Open University Press: 5–17.

Anning, A, Cullen, J & Fleer, M. 2009. 'Research context across cultures', in *Early childhood education: Society and culture*. Edited by A Anning, J Cullen & M Fleer. London: SAGE: 1–24.

Bennett, N, Wood, E & Rogers, S. 1997. *Teaching through play: Reception teachers' theories and practice*. Buckingham: Open University Press.

Branscombe, NA, Castle, K, Dorsey, AG, Surbeck, E, & Taylor, JB. 2003. *Early childhood curriculum: A constructivist perspective*. Boston: Houghton Mifflin.

Bruce, T. 2004. *Developing learning in early childhood*. London: Paul Chapman Publishing.

Cannella, S & Viruru, R. 2004. *Childhood and postcolonization: Power, education and contemporary practice*. New York: Routledge.

Chambers, W. & Chambers, R. 1965. *Chambers twentieth century dictionary*. New York: Hawthorne Books.

Christmas, J. 2005. 'Is it OK to play? Perceptions of play in a small rural primary school', in *Perspectives of early childhood education. Contemporary research*, edited by K Hirst & C Nutbrown. Stoke on Trent: Trentham Books: 141–149.

Dahlberg, G, Moss, P & Pence, A. 2007. *Beyond quality in early childhood education and care: A language of evaluation*. London: The Falmer Press.

Dau, E. 2001. *The anti-bias approach in early childhood*. Frenchs Forest NSW: Pearson Education.

Fleer, M, Anning, A & Cullen, J. 2009. 'A framework for conceptualising early childhood education', in *Early childhood education. Society and culture,* edited by A Anning, J Cullen & M Fleer. London: SAGE: 187–204.

Garvey, C. 1977. *Play.* London: Fontana/Open Books.

Gordon, AM & Browne, KW. 2008. *Beginnings and beyond: Foundations in early childhood education.* 8th ed. New York: Thomson Delmar.

Grieshaber, S & Cannella, GS. 2001. *Embracing identities in early childhood education. Diversity and possibilities.* New York: Teachers College Press.

Howard, J. 2017. 'Play and development in early childhood', in *Introduction to early childhood studies,* edited by T Maynard. London: SAGE.

Jensen, H, Pyle, A, Zosh, JM, Ebrahim, HB, Scherman, A, Jyrki Reunamo, J & Hamre, BK. 2019. *Play facilitation: The science behind the art of engaging young children.* Billund: The Lego Foundation.

Johansson, E & Pramling Samuelsson, I. 2006. Play and learning – inseparable dimensions in preschool practice. *Early Child Development and Care* 176(1): 47–65. http://www.ipkl.gu.se/english/contact/staff/Ingrid_Pramling/nsions in preschool practice. (Accessed 12 December 2010).

Jordan. B. 2009. 'Scaffolding learning and co-construction of understanding', in *Early childhood education: Society and culture,* edited by A Anning, J Cullen & M Fleer. London: SAGE.

Karpov, Y. 2005. *The neo-Vygotskian approach to child development.* New York: Cambridge University Press.

Kerry, T. & Tollitt, J. 1987. *Critical perspectives on Early Childhood Education.* Oxford: Prentice Hall.

Liu, C, Solis, L, Jensen, H, Hopkins, E, Neale, D, Zosh, J, Hirsh-Pasek, K & Whitebread, D. 2017. *Neuroscience and learning though play: A review of the evidence.* Billund: The Lego Foundation.

MacNaughton, G. 2003. *Shaping early childhood.* Berkshire: Open University Press.

MacNaughton, G. 2005. *Doing Foucault in early childhood studies.* London: Routledge.

Moyles, J. 1994. *The excellence of play.* Buckinghamshire: Open University Press.

Mji, G, Kalenga, R, Ned, L, Alperstein, M & Banda, D. 2017. 'Indigenous knowledge exclusion in education systems of Africans: Impact of beingness and becoming an African', in *Handbook of research on social, cultural, and educational considerations of indigenous knowledge in developing countries,* edited by P Ngulube. Hershey, PA: 36–59. doi:10.4018/978-1-5225-0838-0.ch003 (Accessed 16 January 2021).

Mutema, F. 2013. 'Shona traditional children's games and sons as a form of indigenous: An endangered genre'. ResearchGate at http://www.researchgate.net/publication/2712262573 (Accessed 18 January 2021).

Nsamenang, B. 2008. '(Mis)understanding ECD in Africa: The force of local and global motives', in *Africa's future, Africa's challenge,* edited by M Garcia, A Pence & J Evans. Washington: The International Bank for Reconstruction and Development/World Bank: 135–150.

Nsamenang, B. 2010. 'Issues in and challenges to professionalism in Africa's cultural settings'. *Contemporary Issues in Early Childhood* 11(1): 20–28.

Nyota, S & Mapara, J. 2008. 'Shona traditional children's games and play: Songs as indigenous ways of knowing'. *Journal of Pan African Studies* 2(4): 189–202.

Podmore, VN. 2009. 'Questioning evaluation quality in early childhood', in *Early childhood education: Society and culture*, edited by A Anning, J Cullen & M Fleer. London: SAGE: 158–168.

Pramling Samuelsson, I. 2005. 'Can play and learning be integrated in a goal-orientated early childhood education?' *Early Childhood Practice: The Journal for Multi-Professional Partnerships* 7(1): 5–22. https://gup.ub.gu.se/gup/record/index.xsql?pubid=32268 (Accessed on 8 June 2008).

Pramling Samuelsson, I & Carlsson, MA. 2008. 'The playing learning child'. *Scandinavian Journal of Educational Research* 52(6): 623–641. https://gup.ub.gu.se/gup/record/index.xsql?pubid=79233 (Accessed 12 December 2010).

Reader's Digest Association South Africa. 1998. *Reader's Digest illustrated Oxford dictionary.* Oxford: Oxford University Press.

Riley, J. 2003. *Learning in the early years.* London: Paul Chapman.

Rinaldi, C. 2005. *In dialogue with Reggio Emilia. Listening, researching and learning.* London: Routledge.

Rogers, CS & Sawyers, JK. 1988. *Play in the lives of children.* Washington, DC: National Association for the Education of Young Children.

Rogers, S. 2011. *Rethinking play and pedagogy in early childhood education.* Oxon: Routledge.

Semali, LM & Maretzki, AN. 2012. The Pennsylvania State University International Consortium For Indigenous Knowledge. 'What is indigenous knowledge?' http://icik.psu.ed/psu/icik/aboutik/html (Accessed 18 January 2021).

Vygotsky, L. 1978. *Mind in society. The development of higher mental processes.* Cambridge, MA: Harvard University Press.

Wadsworth, BJ. 1989. *Piaget's theory of cognitive and affective development.* London: Longman.

Wood, E. 2009. 'Developing a pedagogy of play', in *Early childhood education: Society and culture*, edited by A Anning, J Cullen & M Fleer. London: SAGE: 27–38.

GLOSSARY

Homophobia – an irrational dislike or fear of homosexuality, gay and lesbian people, or their culture

Perspective – a particular view on an issue

Chapter 11

Pathway to literacy

Linda Rutgers, Annemarie Loubser

In this chapter we consider

- literacy from a developmental and ecological perspective
- elements of emergent literacy
- how emergent literacy is integrated in the Grade R programme
- how to facilitate literacy in the Grade R classroom
- language and literacy-related activities and strategies
- the importance and value of story reading, storytelling and drama
- how to promote language in a literacy-rich environment.

WHAT IS LITERACY?
Language- and literacy-related activities and strategies that can be integrated in the Grade R daily programme
Storybook reading, storytelling and drama

Stories, as has been stressed, play an important role in language development. Stories are important for the child's whole development and must therefore be a part of the daily programme. Storytelling stimulates children's imagination and their use of language. Stories allow children to explore and think about love, hate, jealousy, kindness, power, good and evil, and can transport and connect them to the lives of people they have never known, who come from long ago and places faraway. Telling stories about your childhood experiences helps your children to connect with you (Nal'ibali, 2020). The Grade R child is inquisitive and eager to learn, and stories capture their imagination. Stories can be told, read and dramatised. Each of these strategies can develop specific as well as general aspects of emergent literacy. We differentiate between reading and telling a story in the following way. When you tell a story, you maintain eye contact with the children throughout and often use props (teaching aids such as pictures, puppets or felt figures) to enhance understanding and interest. It can be a story you have read and are now retelling (eg *The three little pigs*) or a story from oral traditions in South Africa.

When you read a story, you are reading it directly from a book and perhaps showing the children the written text and corresponding pictures. Pictures from the book on which your story is based can also be used in the telling of a story. Both forms have their place in Grade R practice. The reading and telling of good stories is not only important for a child's language and intellectual development but also builds within them an appreciation for the enjoyment that literature can bring. For a participatory perspective, you could ask parents to share appropriate stories from their culture with the class.

Find out more

What is a good story in Grade R? The following guidelines will help you to choose a good storybook as well as rhyme or song.
- The children must be able to identify with the characters.
- Whatever happens in the book, song or rhyme, the characters must have relevance for children.
- The characters must not be stereotypical. Stereotyping means that all individuals belonging to a particular group are presented as being identical in characteristics such as beliefs and attitudes. For example, all fathers go out to work and mothers stay at home to look after the family.
- The story must have an interesting plot.
- There must be action, and the characters must have exciting experiences.
- The story, rhyme or song can have adventure and excitement, but no excessive violence and fear.
- The characters must be convincing – even if they are fantasy characters. The way they act must suit the character's age and personality.
- The language must be appropriate and creative.
- The writing style should allow the children to experience the atmosphere of the story. A good story has humour and usually makes them feel happy and content.
- The structure must be logical – that is, have a beginning, a middle and an end. It should have a happy ending.

Stories, rhymes and songs dealing with new facts, people and adventures are appropriate. The Grade R child can, in most instances, differentiate between fantasy and reality, therefore fantasy stories are fine provided they are not too frightening. Grade R children enjoy stories covering a wide spectrum of themes, including animals and simple adventures containing factual material. A humorous and exaggerated story, for example by Dr Seuss, is readily accepted.

Different ways of reading a book
Shared reading

This is an interactive reading experience. Children may, if appropriate, join in the reading of a big book or other enlarged text as guided by a teacher or another experienced reader. Shared reading is generally accomplished using an enlarged text that all children can see. During the reading, the teacher or another reader involves the children in 'reading' together by pointing to each word in the text. This provides the children with the opportunity to participate in the event and behave like a reader. Shared reading models the reading process and strategies used by readers. The teacher deliberately draws attention to the print, and models early reading behaviours such as moving from left to right and word-by-word matching. Shared reading creates a risk-free environment, allowing children to focus on the enjoyment of the story.

The picture walk

In a picture walk, the teacher shows the children the book's cover, and browses through the pages. She encourages the children to talk about what they see, what may be happening in an illustration, and what various elements, such as light, colour, perspective and placement of objects, may indicate about the story. Children draw upon background experiences as they interpret the illustrations. At the conclusion of this exercise, the teacher has a better sense of what (if any) experiences the children may have had with various elements of the story. In addition, the children become engaged with the story through their glimpses of the pictures and are eager to find out what really happens. A picture walk before reading aloud encourages children to anticipate and predict through the illustrations what might happen in the story.

Storytelling and story reading

Storytelling and reading aloud to children are both essential in literacy teaching. Not only does reading aloud provide children with a pleasurable experience, a positive emotional response to reading, and a means of getting 'book' language in their 'heads', it also offers distinct opportunities to become more literate. This does not, however, undermine the value of storytelling. For children with little experience in listening to stories being read aloud, storytelling can serve as a bridge to storybook reading. Storytelling can be adapted on the spot in terms of story length, vocabulary and sentence structure. While storytelling, the teacher can maintain eye contact with the children at all times and look for signs of comprehension (understanding) in them. Displaying some of the pictures from the book or using other props such as puppets while telling the story can enhance listening and understanding, especially for those children learning through a first additional language (FAL). Storytelling should be a regular part of the daily programme. Helping children to tell their own stories is another good foundation for both reading and writing activities.

Table 11.1 The difference between reading and telling a story

READING A STORY	TELLING A STORY
The book is prominent. The reader interprets the words of the writer through voice and facial expression.	The storyteller is central. They are not bound to a book, which implies that their whole body can be used to make the experience more exciting and understandable, and to draw and keep the children's attention.
Children realise the value of the written word. The text remains the same when reread.	The story is intense and unique. It can never again be relived in exactly the same way, which means that a close-knit relationship exists between the story and narrator (storyteller).
The children can page through the book afterwards, relive the story and later 'read' the text themselves.	The story is not always the same. The narrator can adapt the story to a specific audience.
Eye contact is broken only when the reader focuses on the text.	Eye contact is maintained throughout. The situation is more intimate.
It motivates children to listen and to 'read' by themselves.	It encourages actively listening as opposed to simply hearing.
Reading a story suggests that answers may be found in a book.	Answering questions after listening to a story is dependent on the children's ability to listen and understand.
Suitable books may be found to deal with problematic situations in the classroom (eg bullying). After reading the story, it can be related to the classroom situation and promote discussion.	The storyteller can improvise a story to defuse a situation (eg the teasing of a classmate who has forgotten his glasses).

How to read and tell a story

Before you start reading a story from a book, ask the children some questions about it:
- Who are the author and illustrator of the book?
- What do you think this story is about?
- Who might be in it?
- What do you think will happen?

When *reading* a story, let the children sit close to you. Use a natural voice. Use direct speech when representing a character. Alter your voice to suit the character you are pretending to be. Make sure your voice is expressive and your facial expressions change with the different characters. Your enthusiasm is important. When reading a story, if possible, hold the book in such way that

all the children can see the pictures. This means you have to be familiar with the storyline. When you turn the pages, you should be sufficiently familiar with the storyline that you can continue with the narrative.

When *telling* a story, sit either on the carpet or on a small chair while the children sit on the carpet. Tell the story while the children listen. Use visual aids, for example pictures or puppets, to illustrate the main ideas you are presenting. Depending on the situation, you may wish to retell the story using appropriate actions. If the story is short, you may even leave parts for the children to complete while telling it.

You may wish to to substitute your retelling of the story by encouraging the children to retell the story, with your help if necessary. Sometimes ask questions which involve higher-order thinking skills, such as: 'What do you think would have been a better ending?'; 'What would happen if?'; 'How else do you think …?'; etc. The children can then dramatise/sing a song associated with the story.

Children telling stories about their own lives provides an opportunity for them to try out new vocabulary as well as use language to organise thinking and extend their imagination. The teacher's role in storytelling is often to build on children's ideas, add new words, and model sentence structure by posing questions and elaborating or extending what children say as well as giving them the opportunity to elaborate on their initial offering.

> **Something to consider**
>
> Research shows that children who 'read' books for just 20 minutes a day perform better in school. Reading stories stimulates their imagination and helps them to learn about the world. For example, reading books can help children learn about and feel respect for other cultures. Reading also develops their social skills and skills for managing emotions.

Dramatising stories

Many children naturally want to act out stories they enjoy and invite their parents, friends, siblings and even toys to play different characters. Events in stories often raise complicated life issues or they introduce children to aspects of the adult world they may not have experienced before. Dramatising stories allows children to explore various issues. Jealousy, for example, as well as loyalty, revenge and family relationships can all be explored through drama. Drama also gives meaning to the language of the story. While familiarisation of the story is supported through reading and language activities, the story is further reinforced through dramatisation, and language is often used in a playful way.

Making the story real

Concrete items such as puppets, other props and costumes support drama activities based on stories. They help to bring the story off the page of the book and into real life. Children find that things they can touch, hold, see and wear help them with the meaning of the story and enrich the experience. Young children are able to identify with puppets, and in some ways they can be more 'real' to them than a classmate acting as a story character. The puppet show may be used to create speaking situations in which a child using a puppet can actively participate. The child manipulates the puppet, while the puppet 'talks'. As with the use of masks, the use of puppets has the advantage of the child not having to be the main character as the puppet character is in the spotlight. The shy child will especially benefit from this. Puppet shows can include a dialogue between two children, or a group situation can be played out using puppets. Children enjoy talking to puppets and making puppets talk, so they are ideal for dramatising stories.

Many of the stories and activities already described are suitable for involving puppets. Children can make their own simple puppets as an art activity. A decorated paper plate affixed to a stick can represent many different characters. Using puppets gives children exposure and practice in the language of learning and teaching (LoLT) and can reinforce the language used to describe the characters of a story. When making puppets in class, you will often need to show the children a model of the puppet to ensure they understand what they have to do. There are several different kinds of puppets you can make. Some have moving mouths or eyes, some work better for animals, some for people. You can, for example, use paper bags, toilet roll puppets and stick puppets. Choose the type of puppet suitable for your story. Making the puppets can be integrated with the subject of art.

Try this out

See ideas and activities for designing and using puppets on these websites:

http://www.youtube.com/watch?v=p-bMu9lyVu4
http://www.youtube.com/watch?v=mfhiA6iyOYc

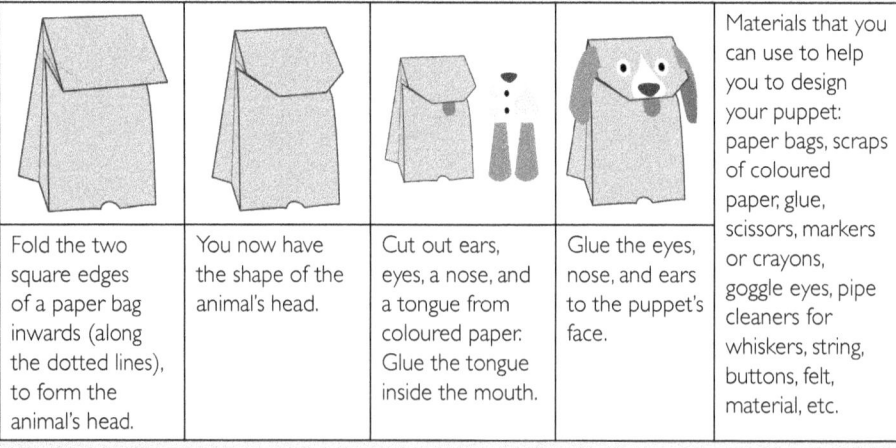

				Materials that you can use to help you to design your puppet: paper bags, scraps of coloured paper, glue, scissors, markers or crayons, goggle eyes, pipe cleaners for whiskers, string, buttons, felt, material, etc.
Fold the two square edges of a paper bag inwards (along the dotted lines), to form the animal's head.	You now have the shape of the animal's head.	Cut out ears, eyes, a nose, and a tongue from coloured paper. Glue the tongue inside the mouth.	Glue the eyes, nose, and ears to the puppet's face.	

> **Story resources for Grade R**
> You may contact Val Morris – also affectionately referred to as Gogo by thousands of little fans of her books – for resources to use in your class. She lives in White River and devotes most of her time promoting literacy among all children of the country. The printing and distribution are supported by the White River Rotary Club of South Africa. Contact Val Morris for more information on Gogo's books and her reading project – *Books in homes*: valmor@telkomsa.net/ Tel: 013 751 1298; cell: 082 466 3363.

Find out more

Find out more about suitable stories for your Grade R class:
- Book awards: *Nestlé Smarties Book Prize*. Available at http://www.librarything.com/bookaward/Nestl%C3%A9%20Smarties%20Book%20Prize
- Book awards: *1001 children's books you must read before you grow up*. Available at http://www.librarything.com/bookaward/1001+Children%27s+Books+You+Must+Read+Before+You+Grow+Up

There are many teacher-guided activities in addition to story time that can promote language. For example, songs, news, calendar and weather discussions, theme discussions, music and movement rings, and other language or literacy activities. Choose activities that work for your class. Each group will be different. Some children love singing songs while others would much rather listen to a story or retell news. Make it a point to recap on concepts that have been taught during the ring time or teacher-guided activities to reinforce learning. Plan one brief activity per concept (eg if the concept is a particular sound (phoneme), you can plan a song, a short story, a short poem or include news that emphasises that particular sound). Do the same for the other concepts that you will teach. Writing the classroom newspaper can be an example of a writing activity where the children see the proper way to form letters and words. This can be the beginning of creative writing. As part of creative art, the children can draw pictures on the newspaper depicting the news of the day. News time can also be moved to the end of the day for a closing time and called: 'What did we do today?'

Listening activities to promote language

The following listening activities can be included to promote language:
- Find poems and rhymes that play with language, like 'Don't put mustard in the custard' by Michael Rosen. Make up guessing games, for example *I'm thinking of an animal. It can gallop. You can ride it. What is it?* Take it in turns. Write and read out a list of rhyming words that have the same sounds, for example 'rain', 'brain', 'main', and another word that is different, such as 'the'. Ask: 'Which is the odd one out?'.

- Play 'Simon says' with slightly more complicated instructions than 'Stand up/sit down'. Perhaps Simon can say: 'Try and jiggle on one leg, flap your arms and hop, rub your tummy and smile!' – not necessarily all at the same time.
- Play yes/no games. A child chooses an object or person and does not tell the other children what or who it is. The other children ask questions to try to find out what the object or who the person is. The child answers 'yes' or 'no' to these questions until someone guesses the right answer.
- Make silly rhyming jokes, for example: 'What do you call a smelly elephant? A smellyphant!'; 'What do you call an elephant watching TV? A tellyphant!'.
- Play 'I spy' games, for example 'I spy something beginning with /a/...' using the sound of the letter.

Writing development: emergent writing

Emergent writing is young children's first attempts at the writing process (Byington, 2020). Most young children begin to write by drawing and scribbling. They write messages, shopping lists, stories and notes, and they 'pretend to read what they have written to anyone who will listen' (Strickland, 2010: 6). Children may name the drawing and say: 'This is my mom, dad, brother or sister or me.' As soon as children can write a few letters, they begin to add these and other letter-like marks to their drawings and scribbles, showing that they know writing takes a specific form and involves certain kinds of special marks (Strickland, 2010).

Strengthening hand and finger muscles

Rather than forcing children to do writing activities before they are ready, focus on other activities that support the development of the hand and finger muscles which enable them to correctly hold and use pencils, crayons, scissors, etc. In order to develop handwriting readiness in Grade R, there are many activities that can be done to improve fine motor control and finger movements. All activities should be done in a fun and playful way. The activities must be positive and encouraging, and developmentally appropriate.

- **Activities that will promote the correct pencil grip:**
    - ✓ Use clothes pegs to help hang up clothes or pictures.
    - ✓ Use water pistols or squeeze trigger containers.
    - ✓ To help the children develop correct finger control, the teacher can break chalk and crayons into small pieces. Let the children pick up and hold a small piece with their fingertips.
    - ✓ Children can imitate finger movements, play with finger puppets, trace designs in the sand or dust/soil, and duplicate forms with play dough.
    - ✓ Roll balls of play dough, clay or therapy putty between the tip of the thumb and the tips of the index and the middle fingers.
    - ✓ Provide art activities that use toothpicks (toothpick art). Do not forget to cut off the top and bottom of the toothpicks to avoid sharp edges. Let the children make their own simple shapes and glue them together.

✓ There are lots of fun things to do with pool noodles or circular strips of foam. Cut the pool noodle/foam into blocks or circles. Put them out with golf tees (see picture below) and let the children create. The children should be encouraged to pick up the tees with the first three fingers (thumb, index and middle finger) and push the tee into the noodle, as shown in the picture.

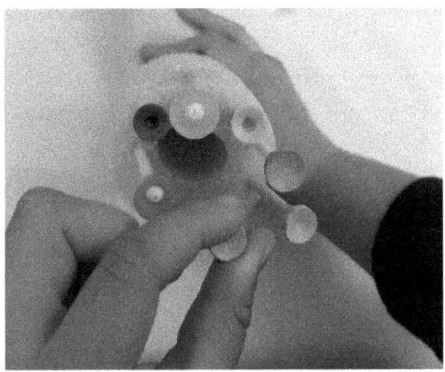 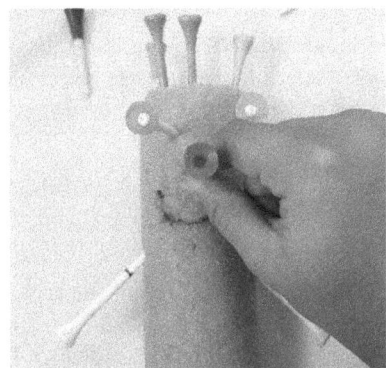

- **Activities involving drawing:**
  ✓ Children can draw in sand with sticks, feathers or straws.
  ✓ They can draw lines and shapes to complete a picture story on chalk boards, as well as draw pictures of people, houses, trees, cars or animals. The teacher can provide clues, if necessary, on how to complete the picture.
  ✓ They can complete simple dot-to-dot pictures and mazes.
  ✓ Remember that Grade R children should not yet be colouring in between the lines. They must not be given too many pictures to colour because of the limited value of this activity. Rather let them use their imagination and draw a picture and then colour it in.
- **Activities involving painting:**
  ✓ Activities could include different things such as playing with fun foam, fingerprinting, and painting with sponges and different sizes of paintbrushes.
  ✓ Many children may need to paint or draw on an easel or vertical surface to help them strengthen the whole arm and shoulder girdle, while others may need light weights to be added to their wrists to promote further strengthening.
- **Activities to develop emergent writing skills:**
  ✓ Picking up objects using oversized tongs and tweezers, and picking up small objects, balls or small macaroni with tweezers or tongs and placing them in a container will strengthen the finger and hand muscles necessary for later writing skills. Once the children can do this, you can gradually reduce the size of the container opening.
  ✓ Other ideas are activating and playing with wind-up toys, pinning small hand-held tops, and popping bubble wrap with the thumb and index finger.
  ✓ Hand out dice for the children to roll on their tables. Show them the proper method of dice rolling and how to cup them tightly in their hand.

Stringing macaroni on wool or yarn and sewing with heavy thread and plastic 'needles' are fun bilateral hand activities.

Linking fine motor development with emergent writing activities

Let the children familiarise themselves with letters and numbers made from sandpaper. The children use their fingers to trace over the sandpaper symbols. Let them trace numbers and letters in the air or in sand. Give children plenty of opportunities to trace lines, shapes and patterns as these activities develop important skills necessary for later handwriting.

You can fill Ziploc bags with colour paint, shampoo or hair gel, seal the bags and let the children draw lines on the plastic with their fingers. A mud mixture could be a cheaper alternative. As they draw lines, the material in the bag will be displaced and they will see the lines they have drawn. The children can also draw lines and patterns with their fingers in sand or flour placed in trays.

Creating an environment that encourages print awareness and language development

When we speak of a print- or literacy-rich Grade R learning environment, we include the Grade R classroom and the other learning spaces provided for Grade R children in the school environment. This also includes the outside play area as well as the sand and water play area. These learning areas are, ideally, equipped with suitable teaching and learning materials that encourage young children from diverse cultural and linguistic backgrounds to listen, speak, 'read' and 'write' during interactions with each other and the resources that surround them.

The Grade R classroom as discussed in Chapter 7 is divided into areas of learning, such as the exploratory/theme table, the literacy/reading corner, the fantasy area, and the educational toy and puzzle area. There should also be a number of charts on display including the weather chart, the seasons chart and the birthday chart, as well as the class rules and the children's names. All resources are purposefully arranged to promote emergent literacy skills in the Grade R classroom. One example of this is the resources that could be placed in the home corner. These resources could include forms, lists, notes, messages, labels, instructions, breakfast and food containers, sweet wrappings, names of places, and names of restaurants and shops.

Another way to create a print-rich environment is through the use of name tags. For young children, the most important letter is the first letter of their first name. Create activities that use children's names, such as having children distribute name tags at the start of the day to the child to whom the name tag belongs. When displaying written words, such as children's names ('Bethany'), furniture labels ('table'), theme and parent posters, and theme table labels use lower- and upper-case letters as appropriate.

Establish a literacy corner and supply it with crayons, pens, pencils, markers, paper, envelopes, old greeting cards, stationery, stamps, a dictionary, telephone books, a list of teachers' and children's names with photos, mailboxes and anything else that you can think of such as texts, emails, pictures and advertisements. Writing tools such as crayons, pencils and blank paper encourage writing development.

Be a good role model – write notes, wear a name tag, keep a calendar and daily planner, post lists of children's responsibilities (helpers' charts), write newsletters to parents sharing with them what their children are doing, and the new ideas and words they are being introduced to (Tang & Gable, 2005). Always remember to use the correct Foundation Phase writing format (font)

The reading corner/area

The reading corner can help children discover that reading is fun. This corner can be seen as a foundation for literacy. As has been said, the corner should be in a quiet part of the classroom (not, for example, next to the art area). Decorate the reading area with posters. The books must not be piled in a heap, but displayed on a shelf and be easily accessible to the children. Have the books facing forward so that children can easily see each book's front cover. An inexpensive way of displaying books is to stretch a rope between two walls and hang the books over it. The shelves or rope must be low enough for the children to see what books are available and to handle them by themselves. The book area should be stocked with a wide assortment of appropriate books for the children to enjoy. Include a variety of book formats, for example class-made books and pop-up books. You could also include magazines, newspapers, comic strips, poems and rhymes. If possible, purchase books on tape, CD or electronically and provide a headset so that children can listen. You can also consider including tablets, videos, DVDs and songs. Include furniture for children to sit on comfortably, for example pillows, cushions, small rocking chairs. Props to support retelling of stories may also be part of the reading corner.

Try this out
Describe the contents of a language-rich Grade R classroom environment. Select a theme and plan vocabulary extension, emergent writing and emergent reading.

SUMMARY

This chapter has explained what is meant by becoming literate in a linguistically diverse society. A developmental and sociocultural approach to language and literacy development offers a broad framework to support children from culturally and linguistically diverse backgrounds. This approach supports emergent literacy and the development of language and literacy skills as a social everyday practice. The key emergent literacy skills were discussed, and examples of emergent reading and writing provided. The importance of a language-rich environment and suitable activities for effective literacy development were given. Grade R teachers have an important role to play in the provision of a literate environment that allows the children to see and experience the ways in which listening, talking, reading and writing are used in everyday life.

BIBLIOGRAPHY

Barone, DMC & Morrow, LM. 2003. *Literacy and young children.* London: The Guilford Press.

Byington, T. 2020. *Promoting preschoolers' emergent writing.* https://www.researchgate.net/publication (Accessed 19 January 2021).

Cazden, CB. 1988. *Classroom discourse: The language of teaching and learning.* Portsmouth, NH: Heinemann (ERIC document No ED383404).

Clay, M. 1998. *By different paths to common outcomes.* Portsmouth, NH: Heinemann.

Davin, R (ed). 2013. *Handbook for Grade R teaching.* Cape Town: Pearson Education South Africa (Pty) Ltd.

Department of Basic Education. 2011. *Home Language. Curriculum and Assessment Policy Statement (CAPS).* Pretoria: Department of Basic Education.

Department of Education and Training. 2020. *Literacy-rich environment.* Victoria: State Government. https://www.education.vic.gov.au (Accessed 18 January 2021).

De Witt, M. 2010. *The young child in context.* Pretoria: Van Schaik.

Fujimoto, C. 2020. *A multimodal analysis of teacher–student interactions in reading.* Georgia: State University.

Joubert, I, Bester, M & Meyer, E. 2008. *Literacy in the Foundation Phase.* Pretoria: Van Schaik.

McBride, S. 2019. *Why are South-African children struggling to read properly?* https://africasacountry.com (Accessed 18 January 2021).

Morrow, LM. 2007. *Developing literacy in pre-school.* London: The Guilford Press.

Neaum, S. 2012. *Language and literacy for the early years.* London: SAGE.

Nomlomo, V & Zilungile, S. 2016. *Indigenous knowledge systems and early literacy development: An analysis of IsiXhosa and IsiZulu traditional children's folktales and songs.* University of Western Cape: South Africa.

O'Carroll, S & Hickman, R. 2012. *Narrowing the literacy gap.* Cape Town: Wordworks.

Pahl, K & Rowsell, J. 2012. *Literacy and education.* London: SAGE.

Palaiologou, I. 2013. *The early years foundation stage. Theory and practice.* London: SAGE.

Pulimeno, M, Piscitelli, P & Colazzo, S. 2020. *Health promotion perspective. Children's literature to promote students' global development and wellbeing.* https://europepmc.org/article/med/32104653 (Accessed 20 January 2021).

Rohde, L. 2015. *The comprehensive emergent literacy model: Early literacy in context.* https://doi.org/10.1177/2158244015577664 (Accessed 18 January 2020).

Strickland, DS. 2010 *Essential readings on early literacy.* Newark, NJ: International Reading Association.
Sutherland, J. 2000. *Primary literacy instruction focus on reading.* Madison Metropolitan School District. http://www.madison.k12.wi.us/tnl/langarts/focusreading (Accessed 13 December 2013).
Tang, L & Gable, S. 2005. *Activities for promoting early literacy (for children ages 3 to 5).* Missouri: University of Missouri.
Whitehead, M. 2010. *Language and literacy in the early years 0–7.* London: SAGE.

GLOSSARY

Developmental approach – an approach that understands and builds on the 'normal' sequence of development

Eco-systemic theory – a theory by Bronfenbrenner that considers that the development of humans occurs as they interact with others and respond to circumstances within the broader society

Emergent literacy – the gradual development of literate skills and behaviour as children are exposed to a stimulating literacy learning environment before they start formal learning in schools

Narrative skills – the practice where children or adults engage in sharing experiences through conversations

Phoneme – the smallest sound units within spoken words

Sociocultural approach – an approach that considers the influence of cultural and social environments on children's development

Chapter 12

Language diversity: teaching a second language in Grade R

Elsabé Wessels, Nkidi Phatudi

In this chapter we consider

- the reasons for teaching a first additional language in Grade R, specifically when the language of learning and teaching of the primary school differs from the child's home language
- the importance of different theories in the teaching–learning of a first additional language in Grade R
- theories in relation to the four language skills: listening, speaking, reading and writing
- developmentally and culturally appropriate teaching–learning activities to enhance the acquisition of a first additional language
- the importance of language ability in the teaching–learning process
- planning and implementing teaching–learning activities to acquire a first additional language
- which teaching–learning activities will be the most effective to enhance the rapid language development of the Grade R child.

INTRODUCTION

The diversity of South Africa's Grade R children requires sensitivity, knowledge and innovation from our Grade R teachers. This chapter aims to help you acquire such attributes. We will clarify the different terms that are used in relation to language, and discuss the contexts in which these terms are applied in South Africa.

In this chapter we use the term 'diversity' primarily in relation to one particular South African reality – children whose home language is not English yet their parents/caregivers have chosen an English-medium Grade R class for them. This situation exists in many of our Grade R classrooms today.

There are, however, many other situations where the language context is similar but the languages in use differ. For example, you could be teaching a child whose home language is isiZulu and yet, due to a number of possible reasons, he/she is learning through Setswana.

In both the examples we have given, the child in question is learning through a first additional language (FAL). The language of instruction in Grade R is, in the first instance, English, and in the second example, Setswana.

To try to capture South Africa's linguistic diversity, we have used specific terms to describe the different language-based contexts found in South Africa today. The terms used are the following:
- Language of learning and teaching (LoLT)
- Home language (HL) and first language (FL)
- First additional language (FAL)
- English first additional language (EFAL) and English second language (ESL).

Different countries use different terminology to describe varying language use, which is why you see different terminology in different literature, for example ESL and FAL. We have tried to use our South African terminology consistently to add clarity. The South African National Curriculum Statement refers to LoLT, HL and FAL, with EFAL also featuring in educational discourse.

Although, as we said at the outset, we have based many of our examples on English, the practices we suggest and examples of activities can just as easily be used in relation to other languages, for example isiZulu as the LoLT and Setswana as the FAL. Except, of course, you will need to bear in mind that English, particularly in the early stages of learning, focuses a lot on rhyme and rhyming words like 'cat' and 'mat'. Rhyming may not be a strong feature in the language you are teaching. However, Setswana and isiZulu may have many words having the same root, thus making it easy for an isiZulu child to learn Setswana. This may not be the case in English as the two languages do not come from the same language family. In general, however, all our suggestions could be adapted for use in other language contexts.

Another important distinction that relates to our contexts is the use of an FAL in our Grade R classrooms in two quite different but interrelated ways. In the examples we have given, the children are learning through an FAL. In other words, their FAL is the medium of instruction (LoLT). The South African curriculum does not suggest the introduction of an FAL as a subject in Grade R – this is left until Grade 1. However, for children who, when they go into Grade 1, will continue to learn through an FAL, it is wise to introduce them to the language in a fun, non-threatening way in the more playful context of Grade R. In Grade 1, if we take English as an example, these children will have English as the LoLT and possibly isiZulu or Afrikaans as the FAL even though their HL is Setswana. It is complex and presents you, as a teacher, with a number of challenges, but they are not insurmountable. A play-based approach towards Grade R can provide the ideal context for a child's early acquisition of EFAL.

SETTING THE SOUTH AFRICAN CONTEXT

The South African context regarding languages is unique. We have 11 official languages, and the education policy provides children with the opportunity to be educated in their home language until Grade 3, after which teaching–learning activities will be presented in English. According to the Pan South African Language Board (PANSALB, 2000), the majority of children in South Africa attend school in a language that is not their HL; therefore, it frequently happens that children are enrolled in English-medium schools where English is being taught as an HL, though the children's HL might be one of the other 10 official languages.

It is generally accepted that learning in one's home language is a key factor in educational success. Internationally, educationalists agree that this is the ideal. However, in the South African context, many parents enrol, for example, their Afrikaans-, Setswana- or isiXhosa-speaking children in English-medium schools expecting better educational results. The reality is that many children whose HL is not English are being taught in English HL classrooms. In some instances, one will find English-, Setswana- and isiXhosa-speaking children in one classroom where the LoLT is English. To complicate the situation even further, the teacher might be speaking Afrikaans as his/her HL! In other words, it is an English (HL) classroom but for the majority, if not all, of the children, the teaching–learning is taking place in an FAL.

Lewis, Jones and Baker (2012) explain that translanguaging refers to using one language to reinforce the other in order to increase understanding and enhance the child's activity in both languages. Thus, a teacher deliberately plans to use both languages and ensure that comprehension of the additional language is supported by the child's HL.

It sometimes happens that the teacher can speak the HL of the child and can use code switching to assist the child in acquiring the FAL. In other cases, the teacher has no knowledge of the child's HL, but can guide the parents/caregivers to use code switching. Sometimes the teacher has no knowledge of the child's HL, and the parents/caregivers have no knowledge of the LoLT and cannot assist the teacher or child in the acquisition of the FAL. Yet another scenario might exist where the teacher has children with a variety of HLs (from foreign countries) and the teacher speaks only English (the child's FAL). For these children to feel competent and confident to enter Grade 1 and continue learning through English, the task is enormous and the challenge to their Grade R teacher multifaceted.

Perhaps the most important aspect of teaching a new language in Grade R is to foster an atmosphere of 'We are all learning' as well as 'All attempts deserve applause'. The teacher should not allow children to be ridiculed by others as they attempt to speak English. Grade R teachers should teach an FAL in such a way that the following occurs:
- Children will value their HL and the role it plays in their cultural identity.
- Tolerance, cooperation and respect for each other's culture is established throughout the school community.

- All children enjoy quality education irrespective of their HL.
- High standards are maintained in speaking both the HL and the FAL.

Creativity, music and arts provide an important context for language growth because of the interaction they provide. Taylor and Leung (2020) emphasise the fact that for young children, literacy is multimodal. In Grade R, visual images, oral language, gestures and art activities should be integrated during language teaching in meaningful classroom contexts. Multimodality creates a platform where the young child, in a multilingual context, can draw on the social, cultural and emotional structures they experience daily in their homes to make meaning of the 'new' language.

What follows will help you address situations similar to the ones we have described. To do this we will provide a brief background in the four language skills of listening, speaking, reading and writing, and then provide *practical* suggestions on how to prepare the Grade R child to achieve competence in the LoLT of the school, even though it is not necessarily their HL. In the Grade R context this means focusing on listening (a receptive language skill) and speaking (an expressive language skill).

WHAT DO WE MEAN BY LINGUISTIC AND CULTURAL DIVERSITY?
Implications and interventions for effective early childhood education

In South Africa, linguistic and cultural diversity implies a variety of different languages and cultures, no one being superior to the other.

As we have stressed, an effective Grade R teacher should provide an accommodating and responsive teaching–learning environment, therefore developmentally appropriate practices and culturally responsive teaching have already been discussed in this book (see Chapter 3).

In the case of teaching a second language, teachers should keep in mind that the Grade R child is emotionally attached to the language and culture of his/her home. This recognition by the teacher is important if he/she is to earn the trust of and strengthen relationships with parents/caregivers. The Grade R teacher should establish a warm, supportive class atmosphere to enable the child to feel emotionally secure and confident enough to explore the new language, but still have the opportunity to use his/her home language. Patience and motivation from all stakeholders are essential, as it takes time to become linguistically skilled in any language. When children make an effort to use the new language, reward them. Rewards need not always be stickers or sweets. Applause from the class or a high five from the teacher can motivate a child.

The importance of maintaining and developing the child's HL is essential. According to the National Association for the Education of Young Children (NAEYC) (1995: 2), care should be taken to ensure that children do not neglect their HL, because the loss thereof might disrupt family communication patterns and damage the child's self-esteem.

It must always be borne in mind that children will make mistakes – this is part of learning, and care should be taken not to correct them in a harsh way. In Grade R we are not seeking flawless, grammatically correct English from children but rather building their confidence and ability to interact in an FAL. Teachers should model understandable correct English, focusing on their pronunciation as well as the speed at which they speak.

Code switching forms an important part of teaching an FAL to young children because it is essential to support the child's comprehension of the new language. Code switching involves switching from one language to another within the course of a single conversation, whether at word or sentence level, to enhance children's understanding. Children learn best when language is contextualised, for example in a theme discussion to which they can relate. In addition, it is argued that the knowledge that children acquire in their first language 'can make second-language input much more comprehensible' (Krashen, 1982: 37).

If the teacher is not able to speak the child's HL, he/she can possibly learn selected relevant words from it, which will demonstrate a teacher's willingness to learn a new language. It could also be seen as affirmation of the child's linguistic and cultural background as well as promoting the idea that 'we are all learning together'. Peer tutoring (a buddy system) can be used, where a child who speaks the same HL but is more competent in the LoLT supports the child who is less able in the LoLT and provides meaning in the HL. Pairing a child whose HL is not the LoLT with one whose home language is the LoLT is another important feature of promoting easy acquisition of the language. According to Wegerif (2011), this interactive approach grounded in conversation creates dialogic spaces in which individual thinking that enhances learning as well as interactions between children is both reinforced and extended.

Another possibility if the teacher cannot speak the child's HL is to make use of demonstrations and/or pictures. For example, if the teacher wants the child to put away his/her schoolbag, he/she could say, 'Put away your schoolbag' while pointing to the schoolbag and walking to the place where it should be put. During the following days, the teacher can simply show the child a picture of a schoolbag, repeat the instruction and reward him/her if the child understands and puts the bag in the correct place. This method, called Total Physical Response, is very effective in contexts where all the children in the class come from a language background other than the LoLT (Mbatha, 2015).

Communication where language is used for simple everyday routines is what Cummins (2000) calls basic interpersonal communication skills (BICS). Cummins, in fact, makes a distinction between communicative language BICS and academic language, which he calls cognitive academic language proficiency (CALP). BICS is a communicative language that depends on a resource-rich environment for its development. An FAL focus in Grade R should be on BICS, and a child learning

BICS needs a warm and nurturing environment that is non-threatening. According to Roseberry-McKibben and Brice (2000: 5), SL learners (in our context, children speaking an FAL) need approximately two years to learn to communicate in English (BICS), which involves fluent conversation and a basic vocabulary in unchallenging situations. Additionally, to be successful in the classroom with English as the LoLT, a child needs CALP, which takes five to seven years to develop. The aim of teaching English FAL in Grade R is to ensure that BICS is successfully developed so that a strong foundation is laid for CALP (Haslan, Kellett & Wilkin, 2005).

> **Something to consider**
>
> You are teaching in a classroom with 30 children, 25 of whom are English HL speakers and five Setswana HL speakers. To affirm the value of the HL, the teacher can arrange opportunities, for example during snack time and free play, where the children can freely communicate in their HL. During free-play activities, allow children to speak the language of their choice.

THE IMPACT OF THEORIES ON THE DEVELOPMENT OF AN FAL

Chapter 2 discussed many theories relevant to Grade R. Applicable theories should be kept in mind when teaching young children a second language or FAL. Young children should be motivated to attempt to use the new language and rewarded when they have success (behaviourism). Furthermore, the social and cultural context in which the language learning occurs should always be taken into account.

According to Piaget (1983), the young child's learning should be supported by real objects and/or pictures, while Vygotsky (1962) reminds us that children should be guided to construct new knowledge through mediation. Vygotsky also guides the teacher to teach in the zone of proximal development (ZPD) so that learning leads to development. The ZPD is the distance between what a child can do unaided and what he/she can with the help of a more knowledgeable other. The guidance from the more knowledgeable other, such as a teacher, is important so that the child can reach a level where he/she can do things unaided. Erikson's theory (1963) of psychosocial development has implications for the emotional aspects of learning an FAL. The young child focuses on his/her ability to gain recognition through performance, therefore the teacher's reactions on all attempts should be positive and encouraging.

Bronfenbrenner's (1979) bioecological systems perspective motivates us to invite all those involved in the child's world to be part of the teaching–learning process. From a maturational perspective, Arnold Gesell (1925) reminds teachers that even though development follows the same pattern for all children, the rate of development might differ – development cannot be rushed. Play and kinaesthetic movements are an integral part of the developmental process.

Furthermore, certain aspects of development happen at sensitive periods when new behaviour (in this case FAL) is acquired more rapidly than others.

Just as children learn and develop at different rates, individual differences exist in how children acquire English as an FAL. For example, some children may experience a silent period (of six or more months) while they acquire English; other children may practise their knowledge by mixing or combining languages.

Keeping this theoretical background in mind, it is also important to distinguish between the skills of language and components/aspects of language that enhance the understanding of the teaching–learning of EFAL in Grade R.

DISTINGUISHING BETWEEN LANGUAGE SKILLS AND LANGUAGE COMPONENTS

The Curriculum and Assessment Policy Statement (CAPS) lists listening, speaking, reading and writing as the four main skills in teaching language. In Grade R, specifically when teaching in an FAL, the focus will be on the receptive language skill – listening – and the expressive language skill – speaking. As active participants in children's learning, Grade R teachers and parents/caregivers should model reading and writing skills in context. For example, when writing shopping lists, invitations and birthday card texts or after a child has drawn a picture, ask the child what the picture is about and write the words that represent this description on the picture. You can have fun games 'reading' different signs such as the neon sign outside a fast-food outlet. Associating names with Disney characters in the pre-reading stage is also useful.

The components of language play a vital role in defining the content and pedagogy of teaching an FAL. The four components of language – phonology, morphology, semantics (including pragmatics) as well as syntax – underpin language instruction at the phoneme, grapheme, syllable, word, sentence and discourse levels.

Phonology and language development

Phonemic awareness is the ability to hear, distinguish and categorise the sounds in speech. Because young children perceive spoken words as wholes, they should be guided through phonological awareness activities to distinguish individual sounds in words. Provide opportunities for children to practise sounds and words to allow them to feel how they are made in the mouth and throat. Be aware that children may have difficulty learning and distinguishing some English sounds that are not present in their HL. It is crucially important to play CDs with rhymes or songs to enable children to hear the correct pronunciation, particularly if the teacher's HL is not English.

As emphasised in Chapter 11, the Grade R child must be able to hear similar and different sounds in a playful context. When young children are involved with various phonological awareness activities, they come to realise that one can actually 'play' with language (Brown, 1998). Yopp (1995) offers the following general recommendations for such activities: keep a sense of playfulness and fun; avoid drill and rote memorisation; use group settings that encourage interaction among children; encourage children's curiosity about language and their desire to experiment with it; allow for and be prepared for individual differences; and make sure the tone of the activity is not evaluative but rather fun and informal.

Manning and Kato (2006) suggest two games:
- **Turtle talk:** Children pretend to be talking like turtles, very slowly, so they can hear each sound.
- **Itty bitty bit:** Children say words bit by bit. Younger children will segment by syllables (pen-cil) and ultimately they will segment by phonemes (/p//e//n//c//i//l/).

Whenever the teacher introduces new vocabulary, he/she can also pretend to be a turtle and divide words into syllables or sounds. Another fun activity is to record what children say or sing, and then play back the recording to allow them to hear their own pronunciation.

Morphology and language development

Morphology involves word construction. Words are made up of smaller parts, called morphemes – for example, the morpheme '-s' changes the meaning of 'dog' to 'dogs'; in other words, singular to plural. Children use morphological awareness to learn new spoken words and how to pronounce them correctly. Knowledge of word structure enhances vocabulary development. For example, 'ski', a single morpheme, can be combined with other morphemes such as '-s', '-er' or '-ing' to change the meaning as well as the word type.

Oral vocabulary refers to words that we use in speaking or recognise in listening. Well-developed oral vocabulary is a prerequisite to communicating effectively. FAL children are not the only ones who may have a limited vocabulary; HL speakers from disadvantaged backgrounds may have had little HL enrichment and may, as a consequence, have a limited vocabulary in relation to their age. Vocabulary can be developed indirectly when children listen to adults reading to them, and directly when they are explicitly taught both individual words and word-learning strategies. By repeatedly exposing readers to rich-content materials and to multiple strategies to learn new words, teachers foster an active, intentional process of building vocabulary (Armbruster, Lehr & Osborn, 2001).

The explicit development of vocabulary is a crucial aspect in learning a new language. Although language should be taught in play-based activities, the careful planning of the sequence and progression of all activities involved is of utmost importance. When teaching vocabulary, be aware of too much too fast. Rather begin at a slower pace and as the children progress and their confidence is built, increase the pace at which new words are introduced.

In Grade R, word-learning strategies involve the labelling of real objects and pictures, starting with the basics like colours, animals and family members. Pictures with the same labels as those on the theme table can be used to build a picture wall, which promotes incidental learning when children start matching the labels to objects or pictures. Playing word games will also help children to memorise words and build vocabulary. Real objects or pictures can be scattered around the classroom, and children asked to bring a particular object or picture to you.

Semantics

Semantics involve the meaning that words convey. Pragmatics includes the social aspects of language, for example taking turns when speaking, how close to stand to other people when speaking, facial expressions and eye contact (ASHA, nd). These important aspects of language are enhanced through socio-dramatic play activities. Reading and telling stories to children and encouraging them to retell them, perhaps using masks and other props, is another useful strategy for encouraging children to use their FAL in a playful context.

Syntax

Syntax involves the grammatical rules of sentence construction that ensure correct word order, which allows a listener to understand what has been said. The ultimate goal of language is effective communication, which can be hindered if a child does not have sufficient syntactical knowledge. Syntactic awareness can be enhanced when children are, for example, invited to join in the repetition of phrases and sentences in children's favourite stories, for example: 'I huff and I puff and I blow your house down'. Commonplace greetings and expressions of thanks can also provide a syntactic focus. The following is an example of a simple greeting dialogue:

'My name is Mary'.
'How are you?'
'Fine, thank you.'
'May I please have some water?' (Substitute 'water' with 'tea', 'cold drink', etc)
'Thank you for the water.' (Substitute 'water' with 'tea', 'cold drink', etc)

The following activities (adapted from Adams, Treinman & Pressley, 1998) are developmentally appropriate and fun. Make sure your choice of resource is contextually relevant as well.
- Describe a picture – the teacher presents a large picture and children take turns to make up a short sentence about what they see in it. These sentences can be written by the teacher into a 'blank' storybook, and individual children can then draw pictures to match the written story. In this way you are building up a class storybook.

- Listen to words in sentences – the teacher reads a sentence with four words, and the children are invited to clap their hands each time they hear a word in the sentence. Alternatively, they could listen to the sentence and then give the number of claps that represent the number of words that they heard. Use monosyllabic words and extend the sentences gradually, for example: *John walks to school* (four claps); *I have a black cat* (five claps); *She eats a pear*; *Please drink your milk*; *Jabu likes his bike.* The teacher can also write the sentence on a strip of paper and cut off each word to indicate to the children how sentences are divided into words and words are used to compile sentences. This should only be done towards the end of the Grade R year.
- Substitute words in sentences – the teacher starts with a short sentence like *I eat bread* and explains that the last word will be substituted (replaced). New sentences like *I eat meat* and *I eat sweets* can be built by the children. Pictures to illustrate bread, meat and sweets will assist understanding.
- Build a sentence – each child adds one word in order to build a sentence.

Exposing children to an FAL in this way will help them to participate in simple conversations. To encourage conversations, the teacher can provide them with a basic dialogue which they can do in pairs and adapt if necessary, for example:

Peter: *Good morning, my name is Peter. What's your name?*
Mary: *Good morning, my name is Mary. How are you?*
Peter: *I'm fine thank you, and how are you?*
Mary: *I'm fine. Will you play with me?*
Peter: *Yes, I will play with you. Let's play with the blocks.* (Substitute blocks with dolls, puzzles, etc.)

When planning teaching activities, the teacher should keep the language skills (listening and speaking) as well as the aspects of language (phonology, morphology, semantics and syntax) in mind to ensure a balanced approach to teaching an FAL.

The teaching–learning activities that follow have been internationally proven to be successful in teaching an FAL to young children.

TEACHING–LEARNING ACTIVITIES

Teachers need to be creative and use continuous assessment to help them make informed decisions about teaching–learning activities, such as how to support individuals, what learning material to use, and the pace and progression of activities. Vocabulary is taught in context and supported by real objects or pictures. Stories should contain repetitive phrases that children can memorise and use to participate, and thus provide a sense of accomplishment. Given the integrated nature of Grade R and the different learning styles and interests of the children, it is suggested that every FAL activity should, where possible, include singing, dancing and creative art.

Usually the following approach works well:

Table 12.1 FAL teaching–learning activities

LESSON/ ACTIVITY PLAN	ACTIVITY STEPS	SKILL/ KNOWLEDGE/ VALUES	ESTIMATED TIME ALLOCATION
Introduction	• Sing a well-known song, tell a well-known story or recite a well-known rhyme	• Speaking • Auditory recall	3 minutes
Content	**Teacher** • Introduces new song, story or rhyme	• Listening	5 minutes
	Children • Sing, dance and/or perform actions depicted in the song, story or rhyme • Say repetitive phrases from story/rhyme • Dramatise story/rhyme with masks and/or props	• Speaking • Learning new vocabulary • Interpreting text through movement • Physical activity	10–15 minutes
Conclusion	• Through drawing or painting, children represent their understanding of the song, story or rhyme	• Thinking and reasoning • Pre-writing – fine motor (strengthening thumb and forefinger grip) • Imagination and creativity	10–15 minutes

Try this out

We have suggested some of the skills and knowledge that can be fostered in these activities. Now add some more of your own.

Themes

Themes and theme tables can promote both HL and FAL. A theme table should display related items and pictures. Some items should be labelled in both the LoLT and, if appropriate, the HL of one of the children in the class. It is better to label concrete objects such as a 'cup' or 'cone' rather than more abstract concepts such as 'rough', 'heavy', etc. Care should be taken that themes (see Chapter 7) suit the children's interest. The theme discussion can be used to teach vocabulary and sentences as well as expand the children's knowledge and understanding of a particular topic.

Throughout the theme discussion, the teacher emphasises the vocabulary that he/she wants them to acquire. Duplicates of the labels are provided, and children have the opportunity to match them with the labels on the theme table. This activity encourages children to pay attention to the printed words, and they might make spontaneous remarks like: '*Red* and *rectangle* both start with /r/'. Individually labelled pictures are better than posters, because they enable children to pay attention to the one word that is being presented. This can also provide an opportunity to assess matching skills.

Introduce a few words at a time rather than too many at once so that children can work with the words, play with them and internalise their meaning. Newly taught words should be repeated frequently in context to try to ensure that children memorise them. Children should also be encouraged to use the newly introduced words within theme teaching or when talking about a book read to them. Songs and rhymes that repeat words frequently provide an opportunity for this.

Songs and rhymes

Songs and rhymes allow a teacher to teach, if necessary, a large number of children even if resources are limited. Young children enjoy songs and rhymes, and, as Murphey (1992) notes, these help children to improve their listening skills, vocabulary, sentence structures, sentence patterns and pronunciation, and ultimately their speaking skills. Action songs and rhymes can be particularly useful because actions help children to understand and internalise the meaning of the words.

Pictures can be used to support the teaching of a song or rhyme. Towards the end of Grade R, word cards can also be used in relation to songs and rhymes, perhaps displayed as incidental print above the picture that relates to the song or rhyme. Word cards can be written in both the LoLT and the children's HL so that a bi- or perhaps multilingual word wall begins to emerge on a wall of your classroom.

An approach in line with this method is the following:
- **Step one:** The teacher models the song or rhyme, pointing to the pictures as he/she sings.
- **Step two:** The individual pictures are discussed in detail.
- **Step three:** The teacher tries to ensure that every child understands the vocabulary in the song and knows how to pronounce the difficult words.
- **Step four:** The teacher and the children sing the song/say the rhyme, pointing to the pictures and/or doing the actions of the song/rhyme.
- **Step five:** The teacher and the children sing the song/say the rhyme and do the actions.
- **Step six:** Individuals take turns to sing the song/say the rhyme, doing the actions or using the pictures.

Find out more

See Appendix 1 for suggestions for a daily programme that specifically acknowledges diversity

See Appendix 2 for songs and rhymes.

O'Sullivan (1991: 3) observed that: 'It is all very well to point out the advantages of teaching literature but the key to success in using literature in the ESL classroom depends primarily on the works selected'. Books should be chosen carefully, taking into consideration the young child's interests and stage of development.

Although every teacher should be led by the unique circumstances of the children and their needs and abilities, the following books are good examples that could be used for teaching EFAL in Grade R:

- *The foot book* by Dr Seuss
- *The little red hen* by Michael Foreman
- *Meerkat in trouble* by Allan Frewin Jones
- *Brown bear, brown bear, what do you see?* by Bill Martin Jr/Eric Carle
- *Tusk tusk* by David McKee
- *The very hungry caterpillar* by Eric Carle
- *Where's Spot?* by Eric Hill
- *The elephant and the bad baby* by Elfrida Vipont & Raymond Briggs
- *No!* by Marita Altes
- *Six dinner Syd* by Inga Moore

Examples of South African-authored storybooks

- *Hi, Zoleka!* by Gcina Mhlophe & Elizabeth Pulles (illustrator.) Shuter & Shooter.
  This is a story many children will relate to. The story is about Sunday school – songs sung and dramas practised – and the performance of these for the congregation. It also considers the apprehension Zoleka experienced when she was called forward to recite a Bible text.
- *Papaniki* by Edna Quail & Ann Berry (illustrator.) Ravan Press.
  The book is about Papaniki, a young rural boy who lives with his grandmother. He likes playing with his friends, but he also has to work, look after the donkeys, fetch water in the wheelbarrow, and help with sowing the crops, etc. The family really wants a donkey cart to make it easier to fetch the water. Papaniki asks his grandmother to make clay pots, which he sells on pension day to make money to buy wood for his uncle to make a cart. While this is happening, the donkeys wander away, and Papaniki finds them down by the river. A crocodile was getting ready to pounce and eat one of them. Papaniki throws stones at the crocodile and saves the donkeys. The family celebrates because he has been so brave and has also managed to get them a donkey cart.

Find out more

Other interesting stories are *The monkey and the crocodile* by Paul Galdone and a series of books by Robert Munsch. Even though the storyline, the content and vocabulary of these books may be too advanced to be used in Grade R for FAL children, this does not mean the books should be discarded. The teacher can tell the story using simplified vocabulary to foster comprehension. Old-time favourites like *The gingerbread man* and *The three little pigs* could also be used.

Something to consider

When reading stories, the teacher should take care to vary the tone and pitch of his/her voice to emphasise the different characters of the story and in so doing enhance understanding. Books can be revisited on a number of occasions. In fact, it is important to repeat well-known storybooks throughout the year. As Peck (2001: 141) advises: 'Many children do not tire of practising a repetitive and rhythmic text several times a day, many days a week'. Additionally, Burns (2006: 22) noted that 'students were almost unanimous in their desire for teachers to read aloud to them'. When teachers read stories, they should try to provide a model of quality English so that the children hear fluent English and correct intonation patterns.

Making the book 'talk'

The following steps are suggested:
- **Step one:** A 'picture walk'. The teacher pages through the book and discusses the pictures with the children by asking open-ended questions. The teacher tries to ensure that all the children understand the vocabulary and encourages the children to predict what they think is going to happen in the story. Discussions could focus on the facial expression of the characters in the book and details in the pictures as well as other aspects. The children's predictions create a purpose for listening because they want to know if their predictions are right.
- **Step two:** The teacher reads the story, perhaps pointing to the words and indicating the direction of the text. After reading the story, the teacher can ask questions to see if the children know the content of the story.
- **Step three:** This involves the rereading of the story on further occasions. While reading takes place, the beginning sounds or rhyming words are emphasised by either saying them more loudly or whispering them. The pictures from the book can be either photocopied or copied to create individual pictures or story cards.
- **Step four:** The children retell the story using picture cards or the book. If picture cards are used, the child who tells the story has to arrange them in the correct sequence and may sit on the teacher's chair to tell the story to his/her peers.

- **Step five:** Many of the children now know the story by heart. They can use fantasy clothes or masks to dramatise it. The children can also construct a simple dialogue to use during dramatisation.
- **Step six:** The children draw a picture of the story and tell the teacher what their picture represents. The teacher then writes simple text on each picture. Children can also be provided with a blank book to draw their own interpretation of the story.

Find out more

Dramatisation is a hands-on experience which provides meaning to language learning. Performing a story can deepen understanding. Once the children have learnt the new vocabulary and can retell the story, they will be able to dramatise it more easily. Encourage children's curiosity about language and allow them to experiment and change the dialogue should they wish to do so. Divide the class into small groups and let each group take turns to dramatise different parts of the story using the newly learnt vocabulary and sentences. Providing all groups with one or more opportunities to dramatise the story allows for meaningful repetition and practice of the newly learnt language. Keep a sense of playfulness and fun. This activity can be repeated, but be aware at all times of the children's interest level and stop the activity if they become bored.

PARENT INVOLVEMENT

Parents/caregivers are the teacher's partners in educating young children and, in particular in this instance, helping them acquire their EFAL. Newsletters and workshops are one way in which to build these partnerships.

As partners, parents/caregivers need to be well informed about the principles of language development, their child's progress in this regard and the role they can play in this process. It may be a good idea to give them some learning material to assist them to engage in the language development process.

In supporting their children in their acquisition of EFAL, parents must be careful not to undermine the value of their HL in any way. We have already emphasised in this book how important it is to maintain and promote the HL while at the same time facilitating the acquisition of EFAL.

Parents should be advised not to pressurise their children in the acquisition of EFAL or expect too much of them at any one time. Children will move at different paces, depending, of course, on a number of factors, as already discussed.

Home literacy experiences in either HL or EFAL could include some of the following events. If a book is used, the language level can be adapted according to whether it is the HL or EFAL of the child concerned. Suggestions to parents/caregivers or possibly older siblings are:

- Read with the child, if possible, every day. Read books, magazines and newspapers, and discuss what you have read together.

- Talk to the child about his/her personal experiences.
- If possible, visit the library regularly together with the child and let him/her select favourite books.
- Read and reread books, ask questions and let the child retell all or parts of the story depending on the language you are using.
- Reread favourite books.
- Sing and play games with the child.
- Write your shopping list with the child.
- Take the child shopping – let him/her help you find the items on your shopping list on the shelves.

Activities that focus specifically on EFAL could include providing the parents/caregivers with an activity bag every two weeks. This bag should contain a printed copy of the rhyme/song/story that is being used in the classroom and pictures of the vocabulary currently being taught. Using this material in relation to EFAL, parents/caregivers could do the following:
- Ask the child to retell (with possible mistakes) the rhyme/story/song.
- Give simple tasks, for example: 'Pick up the picture of the apple', with clear and simple instructions.
- Talk daily (one on one) to the child about events and activities.

In addition, advise parents/caregivers to listen carefully to their children and answer their questions.

Also advise parents/caregivers to focus on their child's ability to make meaning in EFAL rather than using perfectly correct sentences. In other words, the focus should be on fluency rather than accuracy. Encourage parents to be creative and expressive, and to use gestures and other actions to assist understanding. Advise parents to model the correct use of language.

CASE STUDY 1

At the beginning of the year, Tshepo's parents decided to register him in an English-medium Grade R class despite language policies emphasising the importance of HL instruction in the early years. His teacher, Ms Lebelo, also spoke English as her second language, as did all children in the class. The children were in the very early stages of acquiring EFAL and therefore very dependent upon Ms Lebelo for their English acquisition and learning. Most of the children were Setswana HL and could interact easily in this language.

Ms Lebelo decided to label objects in her classroom in both English and Setswana. At the beginning of the year she used, when speaking, English and Setswana interchangeably (code switching). As the children's proficiency in English improved, she gradually withdrew the use of Setswana as the main language, as her final goal was to build the children's ability to converse in English. However, she still used Setswana to facilitate learning. She always introduced new vocabulary through the medium of Setswana followed by English. When the children clearly understood the meaning of the word in English, Ms Lebelo stopped using the Setswana word. Throughout this code-switching process, she made good use of gestures and pictures, and was amazed at the role Setswana played in ensuring that new vocabulary was understood and used meaningfully. Her children are now able to carry out a simple conversation in English and she is hopeful that in time their proficiency will improve.

CASE STUDY 2

Ethan Alabanza entered a bilingual preschool school in Grade R. He was five years old, turning six in November that year. His parents had emigrated from the Philippines and the family could speak English fluently. However, his parents intended to enrol him in an Afrikaans-medium school for Grade 1.

Teaching–learning activities involved the repetition of every single Afrikaans word into English to allow Ethan to understand, to make him feel at home and to build his confidence. During outside play, he would gather English friends and was content with using English as his only language. For the first six months it seemed as if Ethan would not even attempt to speak Afrikaans. However, the teacher remained patient and explained to him the importance of trying to speak Afrikaans and not to worry about making mistakes.

In July that year he attempted his first Afrikaans words. He and his friends were playing in the sandpit and he called the teacher, saying, 'Come have a look. *Ons het iets gebou wat ek geplan het.*' The friends and the teacher made a big fuss of his first attempt at Afrikaans, giving high fives and praising him. The teacher then said, modelling unthreateningly the correct form of the language, '*Dis 'n pragtige tonnel wat jy beplan het.*' Ethan's confidence grew, and after about a week he insisted on taking his learning material home to teach the rest of his family Afrikaans. The next year he went to Grade 1 where he was taught successfully in Afrikaans.

CASE STUDY 3

Jenny, who was recently adopted, entered an Afrikaans preschool in Grade R. She was six, turning seven in October that year. She was Setswana speaking, and her parents were Afrikaans speaking. The teacher could not code switch between Afrikaans and Setswana because she could only speak Afrikaans and English. Jenny's mother was fully committed to helping the teacher in whatever way she could. She would go to the school weekly to be informed of the current language activities Jenny was engaged in, and she would then repeat these activities at home.

Jenny would observe all activities in class and imitate her friends to complete the activities. The teacher wrote vocabulary words in Afrikaans on each picture that she drew, and these became her 'picture dictionary' which stayed in her schoolbag, to be used at home and at school. Jenny was a motivated, confident little girl. She used to greet everybody in the following way: '*Goeiemôre, Meneer, hoe gaan dit met u? My naam is Jenny.*' She had no choice but to play with Afrikaans friends and within three months she could speak Afrikaans. She progressed to Grade 1 the following year and was successfully taught in Afrikaans.

CASE STUDY 4

Xolile has been registered in an English-medium Grade R class. Her teacher, Ms Smith, is an English HL speaker. The class is diverse as it has isiZulu, Sesotho and English HL speakers. However, Ms Smith can only converse in English as she does not have any knowledge of isiZulu or Sesotho. The inclusion of English HL speakers in the class means that English is heard not only in the classroom but also outside in the playground.

To try to meet the needs of the children whose HL was not English, Ms Smith relied on the use of gestures and pictures to convey the meaning of new vocabulary and conversations. Furthermore, Ms Smith had decided to learn some basic isiZulu and Sesotho to try to make the children's transition to English easier. She was also aware that most children learning an FAL will go through a silent period before they start to speak in their new language. After being in the class for two months, the children started to utter their first sentences in English. She overheard two children whose HL was not English speaking to each other in English. One said, 'It's my turn. I'm going to build my house.' Ms Smith had realised the strength of the language acquisition model she chose – immersing children in the LoLT but giving them space to converse in their HL and thereby acknowledging its value.

Questions

Read the case studies above and answer the following questions:
- Describe the contexts in which the four case studies are based.
- How did the teachers facilitate the learning of the target languages, the LoLT, in these instances?
- What is the single most important factor in helping children whose HL is not the LoLT acquire this language? Discuss.

SUMMARY

Given the diverse context of South Africa, learning more than one language can only benefit young children. However, the Grade R teacher should be sensitive to the children's needs, ensuring that language learning in Grade R takes place in a warm, playful atmosphere with developmentally appropriate and culturally responsive practices. In Grade R an important aim is to build confident language users. We do not expect flawless, grammatically correct English from the children. The goal is a sound start to communicative competence. Children are fascinated by stories, songs and rhymes, and using these in Grade R may address any anxieties they might have about acquiring the new language.

BIBLIOGRAPHY

Adams, MJ, Treiman, R & Pressley, M. 1998. 'Reading, writing and literacy', in *Handbook of child psychology*, 5th ed, vol 4, edited by IE Sigel & KA Renninger. *Child psychology in practice.* New York: Wiley: 175–355.

ASHA. American Speech-Language-Hearing Association (nd). http://www.asha.org/public/speech/development/pragmatics.htm (Accessed 11 August 2013).

Armbruster, B, Lehr, F & Osborn, J. 2001. *Put reading first: The research building blocks for teaching children to read.* Washington, DC: National Institute for Literacy. Cambridge, MA: MIT Press.

Bronfenbrenner, U. 1979. *The ecology of human development: Experiments by nature and design.* Cambridge, MA: Harvard University Press.

Brown, A. 1998. *A practical guide to teaching reading in the early years.* London: Paul Chapman.

Brown, CL. 2007. 'Supporting English language learners in content-reading'. *American Psychological Society* 2(2): 31–73.

Burns, B. 2006. *How to teach balanced reading and writing.* New York: SAGE.

Cummins, J. 2000. *Language, power and pedagogy. Bilingual children in the crossfire.* Clevedon: Multilingual Matters.

Erikson, EH. 1963. *Childhood and society.* New York: Norton.

Gesell, A. 1925. *The mental growth of the preschool child.* New York: Macmillan.

Haslan, E, Kellett, E & Wilkin, Y. 2005. *English as an additional language: Meeting the challenge in the classroom.* New York: David Fulton.

Hoover, WA & Gough, PB. 2001. *The reading acquisition framework. (Cognitive framework).* http://www.nap.edu/catalog/6014.html (Accessed 28 August 2012).

Krashen, S. 1982. *Principles and practice in second language acquisition.* http://www.sdkrashen.com/Principles_and_Practice/Principles_and_Practice.pdf (Accessed 12 July 2012).

Lewis, G, Jones, B & Baker, C. 2012. 'Translanguaging: Origins and development from school to street and beyond'. *Educational Research and Evaluation* 18(7): 641–654.

Manning, M & Kato, T. 2006. 'Phonemic awareness: A natural step toward reading and writing'. *Childhood Education* 82: 241–243.

Mbatha, T. 2015. 'EFAL teaching and learning methodologies', in *Introducing English first additional language in the early years*, edited by N Phatudi. Pearson. Cape Town: 68–94.

Murphey, T. 1992. *Music and song.* Oxford, England: Oxford University Press.

National Association for the Education of Young Children (NAEYC). 1995. *Responding to linguistic and cultural diversity recommendations for effective early childhood education. A position statement.* Washington: NAEYC.

O'Sullivan, R. 1991. 'Literature in the language classroom'. *The English teacher.* http://www.melta.org.my/ET/1991/main6.html (Accessed 15 September).

Pan South African Language Board (PANSALB). 2000. *Language use and language interaction in South Africa: A national sociolinguistic survey.* Pretoria: PANSALB.

Peck, S. 2001. 'Developing children's listening and speaking skills in ESL', in *Teaching English as a second or foreign language,* edited by M Celce-Murcia. Boston, MA: Heinle & Heinle: 139–149.

Piaget, J. 1983. 'Piaget's theory', in *Handbook of child psychology,* vol 1, edited by P Mussen. New York: Wiley: 103–128.

Roseberry-McKibben, CA & Brice, A. 2000. 'Acquiring English as a second language'. *ASHA Leader* 5: 4–7.

Southwest Educational Developmental Laboratory (SEDL). 'The cognitive foundation of learning to read: A framework'. http://www.sedl.org (Accessed 15 December 2008).

Taylor, SV & Leung, CB. 2020. 'Multimodal literacy and social interaction: Young children's literacy learning'. *Early Childhood Education Journal* 48(1): 1–10.

Vygotsky, L. 1962. *Thought and language.* Cambridge: The MIT Press. (Original work published 1934.)

Wegerif, R. 2011. 'Towards a dialogic theory of how children learn to think'. *Thinking Skills and Creativity* 6: 179–190.

Yopp, HK. 1995. 'Developing phonemic awareness in young children'. *The Reading Teacher* 4(9): 696–703.

GLOSSARY

Basic interpersonal communication skills (BICS) – day-to-day language needed to interact socially with other people, for example: 'My name is ….' or 'How are you?'

Code switching – switching from one language to another within the course of a single conversation, whether at word or sentence level, to enhance children's understanding

Cognitive academic language proficiency (CALP) – language skills needed for formal academic learning, including the language, for example, of comparison and classification

Culturally responsive teaching – an educational approach that is inclusive of diversity, taking into account the cultural beliefs and practices of children in the class

Developmentally appropriate practice (DAP) – an approach to teaching (grounded in developmental theories) that tries to ensure each child's optimal learning and development

Diversity – in this context, a variety or combination of different language or cultures

English first additional language (EFAL) – English as the first additional language, which is not the home language (HL)

English second language (ESL) – the same as EFAL

First additional language (FAL) – the first language used in addition to the home language

Grapheme – a letter or number of letters that represent a sound (phoneme) in a word; a letter or letters that spell a sound in a word

Home language (HL) and first language (FL) – the language spoken in the child's home

Language components/aspects of language – phonology, morphology, semantics and syntax

Language of learning and teaching (LoLT) – the language the teacher uses when teaching

Monosyllabic words – words with only one syllable (eg cat, bed, pen)

Morpheme – the smallest part of a word that has a meaning

Morphology – the study of how words are formed in language, using morphemes

Peer tutoring (buddy system) – when one child teaches another

Phonemic awareness – the ability to identify and manipulate sounds into syllables or words

Phonological awareness – the understanding that oral language can be broken up into individual words, words into syllables, and syllables into individual sounds or phonemes. Skills include rhyme, syllable awareness, and phonemic awareness

Phonology – the study of speech sounds

Phonological awareness – the ability to focus on the sounds of speech, most importantly on the individual sounds

Play-based approach – contexts for learning through which children make sense of the world, as they actively engage (play) with people and objects

Pragmatics – language in social contexts and ways in which people understand meanings

Receptive language skills – skills used by the child to take in information, for example listening and 'reading'

Responsive/expressive language skills – skills used by children to respond or express themselves, for example writing and speaking

Semantics – the study of meaning in language

Syntactic awareness – children's awareness of how words are put together to form sentences

Syntax – the way in which words are put together to form sentences

APPENDIX 1: SUGGESTIONS FOR A DAILY PROGRAMME THAT SPECIFICALLY ACKNOWLEDGES DIVERSITY

Arrival

Teacher greets every child in the LoLT of the class. Keep it simple and similar every day; the purpose is that children should remember and start using the same phrases, for example: 'Good morning, Tsepho. How are you?' The teacher can role play with another English-speaking child, if necessary, at the start of the year to model the interaction.

First teacher-guided activity

Weather chart – if it is a cold day, emphasise the word *cold* and dramatise shivering, rubbing hands together while saying: 'Today is *cold*'.

Theme discussion – teach vocabulary explicitly; choose four to seven words in the theme (eg hands, feet, eye, nose, ear, mouth, hair). Ensure that you have labelled pictures illustrating the words. It is advisable that the labels of both languages be included – maybe in different colours. The following process can be considered:

- Say the word slowly, showing the picture (eg hands). Let the group repeat the word, pointing to the picture and clapping their hands.
- Let a few individuals say the word.
- The teacher then uses the word in a sentence (if possible with actions, for example: 'I clap my hands').
- Children repeat the sentence with actions.
- If possible, follow up with an action song, such as: 'If you're happy and you know it, clap your hands', etc.

Free play and art activities

Demonstrate in a concrete way what children should do, while at the same time saying what you would like them to do, for example: 'We will cut with scissors'. The children, ideally, will look at one another and even copy from one another in order to be successful.

Second teacher-guided activity

- **Music** – the teacher sings a song first, the children listen and then they copy the teacher. Include appropriate movements such as actions and dance as far as possible.
- **Movement** – demonstrate/model what is expected while explaining in clear, simple language and allow the children to copy your actions. As they 'perform', the teacher can comment on what the children are doing, eg: 'Tsepho is jumping'.
- **Mathematics** – with mathematical activities, one of the best ways to introduce numbers is through singing songs or saying rhymes which feature them, for example: 'One, two, three, four, five, once I caught a fish alive ...'

Routines

Children sing songs while washing their hands and move appropriately, for example: 'This is the way I wash my hands, wash my hands, wash my hands; this is the way I wash my hands early in the morning'.

While children are eating at snack/lunchtime the teacher can move between them and make appropriate remarks about individual children, for example: 'Thandi has an *apple* or *juice*', or 'Sipho is eating *samp* and *beans*'. Remember, children need to hear a word many times before they make it their own, so repetition is therefore important. One instance of repetition could be when the teacher hands out tea, saying, 'This is a *cup of tea*'. The child then answers, 'Thank you for the *cup of tea*'. This simple sentence structure contained in an activity can then be expanded to a range of other activities, for example: 'This is a *ball*. Thank you for the ball'.

Outside play

Try to ensure that all children have someone to play with and talk to. If a child is excluded from play activities because he/she cannot be understood or understand what is being said, ask the child to sit with other children and participate in activities like water play or block construction. As a teacher, try to engage children in one-to-one extended conversations about what they are doing.

Story time

This has been discussed in detail earlier in this chapter.

APPENDIX 2: RHYMES AND SONGS

Some popular rhymes and songs for EFAL children are the following:

One, two three, four, five	The wheels on the bus
One, two, three, four, five	The wheels on the bus go round and round,
Once I caught a fish alive.	round and round, round and round
(Count on the right hand; hold a fish with your hands.)	The wheels on the bus go round and round
	All day long.
Six, seven, eight, nine, ten	*(Add additional verses – they will follow the same*
Then I let it go again.	*pattern as the first verse.)*
(Count the fingers on your left hand; let the fish go.)	The mommies on the bus go talk, talk, talk
Why did you let it go?	The daddies on the bus go read, read, read
'Cause it bit my finger sore.	The grannies of the bus go knit, knit, knit
(Shake finger.)	The babies on the bus go wah, wah, wah
Which finger did it bite?	*(Encourage children to do the corresponding*
This little finger on my right.	*actions.)*
(Hold up the little finger on your right hand.)	

Fun songs are the following:

This is a song about the story *Sleeping Beauty*. There was a princess long ago, long ago, long ago There was a princess long ago, long long ago. She pricked her finger and fell asleep, fell asleep, fell asleep She pricked her finger and fell asleep, long long ago. The princess slept for 100 years, 100 years, 100 years The princess slept for 100 years, long long ago. A great big forest grew around, grew around, grew around	**The farmer's in the dell** The farmer's in the dell, the farmer's in the dell Hi ho, the derry-o, the farmer's in the dell. The farmer takes a wife, the farmer takes a wife Hi ho, the derry-o, the farmer takes a wife. The wife takes a child, the wife takes a child Hi ho, the derry-o, the wife takes a child. The child takes a nurse, the child takes a nurse Hi ho, the derry-o, the child takes a nurse.
A great big forest grew around, long long ago. A gallant prince came galloping by, galloping by, galloping by A gallant prince came galloping by, long long ago. He took his axe and chopped it down, chopped it down, chopped it down He took his axe and chopped it down, long long ago. He took her hand to wake her up, to wake her up, to wake her up He took her hand to wake her up, long long ago. Now everybody's happy now, happy now, happy now Now everybody's happy now, long long ago. *(Children take turns to be the prince and princess; the others spread out their arms to make the forest.)*	The nurse takes a dog, the nurse takes a dog Hi ho, the derry-o, the nurse takes a dog. The dog takes a cat, the dog takes a cat Hi ho, the derry-o, The dog takes a cat. The cat takes a rat, the cat takes a rat Hi ho, the derry-o, the cat takes a rat. The rat takes the cheese, the rat takes the cheese Hi ho, the derry-o, the rat takes the cheese. The cheese stands alone, the cheese stands alone Hi ho, the derry-o, the cheese stands alone.
Basic greetings: girls, boys *(Girls)* Hello, boys Hello, boys How are you? We're fine, thanks We're fine, thanks We hope you are, too. *(Boys)* Hello, girls Hello, girls How are you? We're fine, thanks. We're fine, thanks We hope you are, too.	Touch your nose Touch your finger/foot/arm/leg/face Touch your nose Touch your arm/hand/leg/arm/head Touch your toes

The hokey-pokey	**Head and shoulders**
You put your right hand in	Head and shoulders
You take your right hand out	Knees and toes, knees and toes, knees and toes
You put your right hand in	Head and shoulders
And you shake it all about.	Knees and toes, we all clap hands together.
You do the hokey pokey	
And you turn yourself around	Eyes and ears
That's what it's all about.	And mouth and nose, mouth and nose, mouth and nose *(twice)*
Oh, the hokey pokey	
Oh, the hokey pokey	Eyes and ears, and mouth and nose
Oh, the hokey pokey	We all nod heads together.
And that's what it's all about.	
(Sing additional verses by naming other body parts, for example left hand, right foot, left foot, right hip, left hip, whole self. Sing the tune above for each body part you sing about.)	

Many of these are traditional English songs and rhymes. You can include newer rhymes and songs that you know. *This little puffin* is a useful resource book for teachers as it contains many appropriate rhymes and songs for use in the Grade R classroom. The British Council (https://learnenglishkids.britishcouncil.org/songs]) provides useful LTSM.

A link with South African-authored storybooks is provided below. The link is not comprehensive. You can add the names of additional books to this list.

https://coloursofus.com/23-childrens-books-set-south-africa/

Chapter 13

Early concept development in mathematics/numeracy

Corné Kruger, Elsabé Wessels

In this chapter we consider

- the value of the effective learning of mathematics in Grade R
- the type of mathematics children should be learning and how they learn mathematics
- the teacher's role in the teaching–learning and assessment of mathematics in Grade R
- aspects underlying the successful teaching and learning of mathematics in Grade R, for example the teaching of foundational mathematical skills and the five components of mathematics
- the choice and/or design of appropriate resources
- how to deepen your own understanding of mathematics and enhance your ability to reflect on your own knowledge.

INTRODUCTION: WHY MATHEMATICS IN GRADE R?

Young children are curious and have a natural tendency to explore to try to make sense of their world. Mathematics is an integral part of the young child's world; for example, they have five fingers on each hand, which is 10 in total; their clothes are smaller than their mom's or dad's; and when they eat biscuits or sweets, the number eaten can be counted.

It is important that children start school with a good knowledge of foundational mathematical concepts and an 'I can' attitude to mathematics. Research shows that there is a strong correlation between children's mathematical ability and their sense of self, therefore Grade R children should be encouraged to develop confidence in their ability to understand and use mathematics. According to the National Association of Education for Young Children (NAEYC) (2002), young children's mathematical experiences influence their attitudes towards learning mathematics at a later stage, thus the early learning environment should be engaging and of such a nature that it promotes and encourages children's early encounters with mathematics. Quality teaching and learning opportunities entail developmentally and culturally appropriate activities which are neither too easy nor too difficult for the children to manage.

> **Something to consider**
>
> **What do we know?**
> - Mathematics competence is a critical life skill which plays an important role in all spheres of a person's life.
> - Young children can and should master the basic mathematical concepts and skills which include number concept, matching (including one-to-one correspondence), comparing, classifying (sorting), ordering (seriating) and problem solving – before they start formal learning.
> - First experiences will play a crucial role in Grade R children's perceptions of what mathematics is, the relevance of mathematics in their lives and of their ability to do it.
>
> **What should we do with what we know?**
> - Ensure that all Grade R children master the basic mathematical concepts and skills before they progress to Grade 1.
> - Ensure that all Grade R children experience mathematics as meaningful and useful.
> - Build a strong foundation for mathematical understanding, and ensure that children believe in their own ability to do mathematics in Grade 1.
>
> **What do we need to find out?**
> - How do children in Grade R master mathematics concepts?
> - What is the role of the teacher in Grade R mathematics learning?

HOW CHILDREN LEARN MATHEMATICS

The Grade R teacher should base the learning and teaching of mathematics on the theories of how young children learn (see Chapter 2). The teacher should be aware of what triggers the child's curiosity and be knowledgeable about intentional teaching approaches that successfully mediate mathematical concept formation and problem solving.

The national curriculum implemented in South African schools supports a constructivist view of learning where children are supported to form their own understanding. This curriculum sets out specific content which serves as a benchmark for all teachers countrywide regarding the knowledge and skills that children should master during the various school phases and grades. According to the national curriculum, young children should be at the centre of learning and should be given ample opportunity to 'discover' mathematical ideas hands-on.

Teaching strategies should therefore encourage children to relate to the content, and at the same time promote their inquisitive nature. Because young children learn through their senses as well as through moving and talking, mathematical learning experiences in Grade R should be based on kinaesthetic learning experiences (using and moving the whole body when learning) as well as opportunities for concrete, first-hand exploration of objects. These experiences should form part of the children's lived reality.

As mentioned in previous chapters, children should be immersed in a contextually and culturally appropriate learning environment where issues relating to diversity and the language of teaching and learning underpin mathematical learning.

It is important, especially in the learning of mathematics, to consider the principle of continuity – that is, building new knowledge on existing knowledge. If children have an incorrect understanding of basic concepts, their misunderstandings may prevent them from grasping new mathematical knowledge that draws on the original basic concepts. Mathematical knowledge, of course, is built throughout the daily programme. Mathematical concepts are referred to and reinforced, both intentionally and incidentally, during literacy activities, science, art, music, movement and also free play. For example, in art, children can work with concepts of shape, direction and number. Many of the perceptual-motor skills and concepts referred to in Chapter 4 such as position in space, directionality and visual matching are also an important part of building mathematical knowledge in Grade R.

Something to consider

Mathematics teachers do not always agree on the most effective teaching strategies for mathematics learning in the early years. Lee and Ginsburg (2009) identified nine misconceptions regarding the teaching and learning of mathematics in the early years. These include that young children are not ready for mathematics education; mathematics is only for bright children; only simple numbers and shapes should be taught; teaching language is more important than teachings mathematics; the only responsibility of the teacher is to provide an enriched physical environment and allow children to play; mathematics should not be taught as standalone subject matter; assessment in mathematics is irrelevant when it comes to young children; children learn mathematics only by interacting with concrete objects; and computers are inappropriate for the teaching–learning of mathematics.

Do you agree that these are misconceptions? Give reasons for your choice. Jot down your own philosophy regarding the effective teaching of mathematics in the early years. Read additional literature based on research findings to explore what research has found on the effective learning of mathematics in the early years.

Find out more

Find more information on the teaching of mathematics in the early years at Juta Passmasters.

Before exploring the 'what and when' of mathematics learning, we need to distinguish between conceptual and procedural knowledge, as these two knowledge forms are important in mathematics teaching and learning.
- Conceptual knowledge is based on the relationships children form in their minds. These relationships are all connected in a network of knowledge. Every piece of new incoming information is integrated into the existing network of knowledge, which leads to new understanding (see Piaget, Chapter 2). The environment is the most important component in the formation of conceptual knowledge, which serves as a basis for the next level of mathematical thinking, namely procedural knowledge.
- Procedural knowledge consists of rules, procedures and the rote learning of algorithms. An algorithm is a step-by-step procedure for solving a problem, for example the counting-on algorithm for $5 + 2 = 7$. The child would initially need to rename the first addend (5) and then count on two units 6 and 7 to reach the answer.

Although the Grade R child should not be subjected to the rote learning of rules and procedures, the teacher should understand the link between conceptual and procedural knowledge and be aware of how experiences on a concrete level prepare children for thinking on a more abstract level. Take, for example, the concept of 'equal'. As a teacher, you would try to create informal opportunities for children to share items equally. Sharing equally means that you cut your *whole* sandwich in two exact halves in order to ensure that you and your friend get exactly the same amount. This type of understanding can be seen as a building block for formal mathematics learning where the children will be required to understand how mathematics is presented. For instance, if you divide a packet of 10 sweets into two equal halves, this division is represented by a number sentence, namely $10 \div 2 = 5$, and by $5 + 5 = 10$, where 10 represents all 10 sweets in the packet (the *whole* packet). The concept that a fraction is part of a whole is thus based on a thorough understanding of the concept 'whole' rather than rote learning and remembering a rule. It is difficult for children to remember procedures that have been learnt as isolated pieces of information. It is easier to relate new ways of doing things to knowledge that has been acquired already. Although mathematics teaching in Grade R focuses more on conceptual knowledge, learning should make provision for the development of both conceptual and procedural knowledge. The experience gained in sharing in Grade R helps a child form basic concepts and skills that lay the foundation for later, more advanced mathematical concepts.

> **Something to consider**
>
> **What do we know?**
> - Young children learn by using their senses – touching, seeing and hearing, and also by moving and talking.
> - Mathematics experiences will determine how children learn and if they are able to link new experiences to prior knowledge to form a meaningful knowledge network.
> - Experiential learning includes:
>   - continuity (building new knowledge on existing/prior knowledge)
>   - interaction (between the teacher and child, among children, and when children manipulate and explore real objects)
>   - language (the teacher talking to the children and the children having the opportunity to explain their thoughts and understanding, to ask questions and to use new mathematical terms during play-based learning tasks)
>   - diversity, ie offering a variety of activities at various levels of difficulty to accommodate children's different backgrounds, learning styles and levels of understanding
>   - reflection (thinking about what was learned).
> - Learning from such hands-on experiences supports effective mastering of the fundamental mathematical concepts in Grade R.
>
> **What should we do with what we know?**
> Reflection on the way children master new concepts and the principles of experiential learning should form the background when we explore the role of the teacher in mathematics education in Grade R.
>
> **What do we need to find out?**
> What does the teacher need to do to ensure the effective mastering of fundamental mathematical concepts relevant to Grade R?

WHAT DO WE TEACH IN GRADE R?

Before we can explore how to implement a successful mathematics teaching and learning programme in the Grade R year and the role of the teacher, we need to have a very clear picture of what it is young children should be learning. The language of mathematics is universal and comprises five specific components or content areas:
- Numbers, operations and relationships
- Patterns, functions and algebra
- Shape and space
- Measurement
- Data handling.

However, in order to develop a deep understanding of these content areas, basic concepts and skills need to be in place. Though these foundational concepts and skills are not exclusive to the understanding of mathematics, they are essential to grasp if children are going to develop a good understanding of the five content areas in formal schooling. Hence in Grade R our focus is on assisting children to acquire the basic concepts and skills as well as introducing them to the five content areas. The basic mathematical concepts and skills are *matching (including one-to-one correspondence), comparing, classifying (sorting), ordering (seriating) and problem solving.*

When children are given an opportunity to develop the foundational mathematics concepts and skills, whether through informal play or guided activities, they develop and use specific cognitive processes. A cognitive process is followed when children obtain and store knowledge, thus forming a new knowledge network in the brain. These cognitive processes are essential to ensure that children make sense of mathematical concepts. Only when children are supported in this will they be able to use mathematical skills and knowledge effectively in their lives.

In order to help children in the mastering of the foundational mathematics skills, we have to provide opportunities for specific actions, known as human actions, that support the cognitive processes already mentioned (National Council of Teachers of Mathematics, 2000). These human actions include problem solving, *reasoning and proof, communication, making connections, and representation (presenting ideas in a way that others can understand). All these actions play an important role in effective mathematics teaching and learning. They are not unique to mathematics but are applied by humans in all facets of life to *solve problems and make sense of their world. Together with the foundational concepts and skills, these human actions enable children to make sense of the mathematics content areas. If these concepts, skills and actions are well understood by children, they are more likely to succeed in their construction and understanding of mathematical concepts.

> When we discuss how children acquire the various mathematical components (content, concepts and skills), try to identify the human actions that are also being developed, which are marked with an asterisk (*) – see the discussion that follows.

Figure 13.1 sets out the relationship between the foundational concepts and skills, human actions and mathematical content addressed in Grade R.

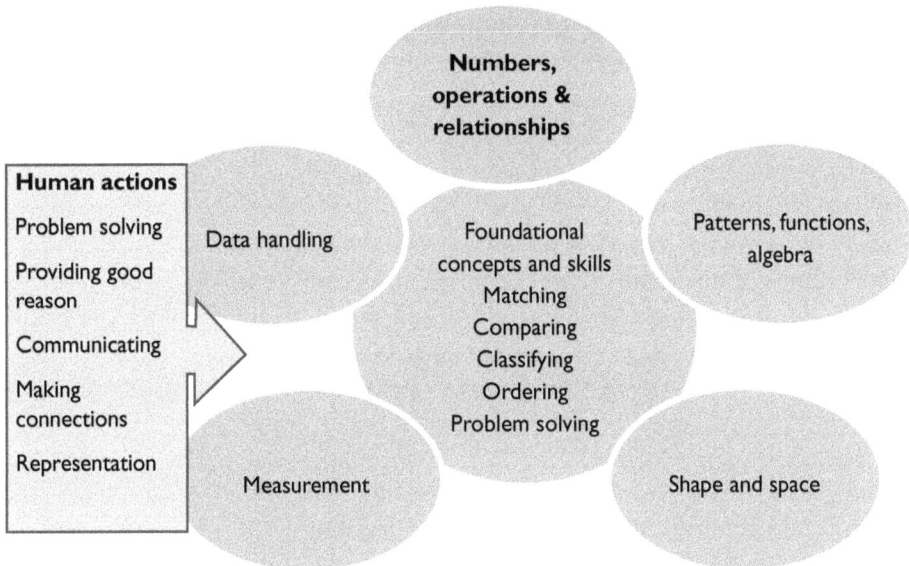

Figure 13.1 The relationship between the foundational concepts and skills, human actions and mathematical content addressed in Grade R

It is important that the teacher distinguishes between: (1) the content areas of numeracy (numbers, operations and relationships; patterns, functions and algebra; shape and space; measurement; data handling); (2) the foundational concepts and skills (matching (including one-to-one correspondence); comparing; classifying (sorting); ordering (seriating); problem solving); and (3) human actions (problem solving; providing good reason; communicating; making connections; representation).

Most mathematics curricula worldwide include these three components. In South Africa, the national school curriculum begins in the Grade R year. The introduction to mathematics should be managed in an informal way and seen as a preparation for formal schooling. We will first explore the foundational concepts and skills before explaining the five content areas.

Exploring the foundational concepts and skills

The following foundational concepts and skills form part of most mathematics learning experiences in Grade R. By supporting the development of these skills, the Grade R teacher lays the foundation for all later mathematics.

Matching

Matching is when one object is paired with another. However, within a mathematical context matching always needs to involve the concept of number. The concept of one-to-one correspondence is probably one of the best examples of matching within a mathematical context, and forms the basis of most mathematical concepts.

The teaching of the concept of one-to-one correspondence can be successfully managed within the Grade R classroom.

During routine periods, like snack time, the teacher hands out, for example, one slice of apple and then one cup of juice to each child, and finally a placemat, etc. The teacher should make children aware that when you share equally there may not be an exact match – that is, after sharing objects equally there may be some extras (or some leftovers) remaining. Matching will therefore make children aware of concepts such as 'more than', 'less than' and 'equal to'. The teacher can ask questions to support this understanding such as: 'There are six children in the red group. Petrus gave each child a lolly but there are four left in the bag. I wonder how many were in the bag before Petrus handed them out?'

As we have repeatedly mentioned throughout this book, all concepts should first be mastered on a kinaesthetic, then three-dimensional or 3D (concrete) level before children progress to a semi-concrete and abstract level (see Chapter 4). Matching each boy in the class with a girl provides conceptual understanding of matching through kinaesthetic experience. Actually making them stand in two opposite rows from each other and linking each boy to a girl with a piece of string provides a meaningful context for *discussion (human action – communication) using terms such as 'more than', 'less than' and 'equal number'. Many more matching tasks on a concrete level should be implemented in a playful way before children can progress to matching objects on two-dimensional (2D) level in a workbook or worksheet (*representation).

When planning and assessing matching tasks, the teacher would work with 'sets' of objects. A set is items grouped together with a certain property in common, for example clothes – the common property is something that can be worn.

When planning and assessing matching tasks, there are various dimensions of difficulty to consider. Below we explain four dimensions:
- The type of sets to be matched (different types of items in the two sets are easier to match)
- The number of items in the two sets to be matched (fewer items in each set are easier to match)
- The difference between the total number of objects in the sets to be matched (same number of objects in each set is easier to match)
- The relationship between the objects in each set to be matched (are the objects in the two sets 'joint or linked'?).

> NB: Keep in mind that all matching activities on a 2D level (worksheets) should first be introduced kinaesthetically and then on a concrete (3D) level.

The following examples serve as explanation of the four dimensions of difficulty:
1. Are the items identical or different? Different items are easier to match.

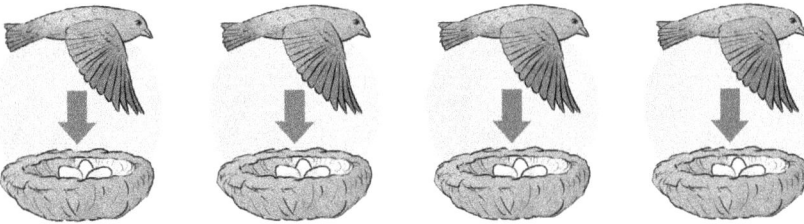

Figure 13.2 One-to-one matching

This matching activity will make sense to the young child, because 'each bird should fly to a nest – only one bird is allowed in a nest, and there are only enough nests so that each bird can have one nest'. Through one-to-one matching, the child discovers that there are four nests and four birds (4 = 4).

2. Are there many items to match or just a few? Five or fewer are easier to match. The number of objects in sets to be matched should correspond with the child's current number concept level. In the beginning of the year, matching four or five items will be a good challenge, while sets may contain up to 20 items by the end of the year as the child's number concept increases.

3. What is the difference between the total number of objects in the two sets to be matched? Even sets are easier to match. The child should therefore start with even sets while the difference between the two sets will gradually increase as the counting range of the child increases. 'There are five clowns and three balloons. If we give each clown a balloon, two clowns will be left without a balloon.' Children discover that 5 is 2 more than 3, which lays the foundation for later operations such as 5 minus 3 equals 2. The difference between sets should never be more than the counting range of the child.

Figure 13.3 Matching the total number of objects in two sets

Vertical and horizontal matching

Remember: Children progress to the more difficult examples only once they have mastered the easier matching activities.

Chapter 13 Early concept development in mathematics/numeracy **295**

The teacher can guide the child to match from top to bottom as in the case of horizontal rows (illustrated previously in the example of clowns and balloons) or left to right in the case of vertical rows illustrated with the example of matching bears to pots of honey. Following these directions also prepares children for writing from left to right, and from top to bottom.

Figure 13.4 Vertical and horizontal matching

Try this out
Do an internet search using the key words 'matching activities' and 'early childhood education' to find new fun activities on kinaesthetic and 3D level for the development of the above concepts.

When children understand the concept of one-to-one matching, it also makes it easier to compare numbers that play a central role in computation or calculations such as addition and subtraction.

Classifying

Even before children enter Grade R they have learnt to organise their world by *connecting information and classifying objects according to common attributes (characteristics). At a young age they are already able to sort objects in their environment into certain groups or categories with the help of the parent/caregiver. The Grade R teacher needs to build onto this prior knowledge by guiding children to identify the 'sameness' that defines the items that belong to a specific group. For example, four-legged animals that are pets and bark are classified as 'dogs' while four-legged animals that are pets and meow are classified as 'cats'.

Where pets are classified in groups of dogs and cats, children form the concept of a set where a set is defined as objects grouped according to a common attribute. Children are thus guided to establish the characteristics of a set through reasoning and proof. Criteria for membership of a set should be specific and well defined to enable children to decide whether the object or idea belongs to a particular set or not.

> **Try this out**
> Identify criteria that could guide sorting activities by Grade R children for the following topics:
> - Pets
> - Trees
> - Shopping
> - Where people live
> - Insects.

Comparing

Comparison is the basis of many mathematical concepts, and children have a natural tendency to compare, for example: 'You have more than me'. Comparison is one way to enable children to solve problems. To do this, children need to compare the total number of objects in one group with the total number of objects in another, they compare sizes and shapes of objects, and compare different lengths and time (eg before snack time or after story time), etc.

Classification has to do with sameness, comparing has to do with difference. Children in Grade R are able to compare differences relating to concepts such as opposites, quantity, size, length, etc. When two children are playing with Lego blocks, the teacher might ask, 'Who has the most blocks?'; 'Who has the least?'; 'Do you have an equal number of blocks?'; 'What do you need to do to ensure that you have an equal number of blocks?' Children will use visual cues, counting and matching as well as reasoning skills to solve these problems. They should also be asked to explain how they reached their answer and to provide proof of their solution, which will indicate their thought processes. The teacher can then assess if they have grasped this foundational concept and skill.

The Grade R teacher should provide ample opportunity for children to compare by focusing their attention on differences in attributes of objects such as shape, length, weight, colour, etc, as well as differences in the number of objects or people, for example comparing the number of boys and girls. Posing informal questions such as: 'How many children have brown bread in their lunchboxes and how many have white bread?' will promote children's acquisition of the skill of comparison. Comparison can also be applied to more abstract situations such as children's preferences: 'Who prefers apples and who prefers oranges?' The results of such a comparison can provide further opportunities for mathematical concept development when children *communicate their findings: 'Twelve children prefer apples while only six prefer oranges. In other words, six more children prefer apples to oranges.' Such conversations assist children to *make the connection with subtraction where they compute (work out) the difference between the larger and smaller groups.

Children can also be asked to line up according to their preference and then paired; a child from one group pairs with a child from the other group. Six children who prefer apples will not be able to pair with a friend in the 'orange' group. This is a good example of how children are supported in the formation of initial mathematical concepts through kinaesthetic learning. This activity allows children to find the answer to: 'How many more children prefer apples to oranges?' The answer, which is the solution to the problem, can be *represented orally (an oral representation), set out using blocks (concrete representation) or through drawings.

Comparison can be included in many activities, which can provide ideal opportunities for integration with other subjects such as Life Skills and Language. Where children have to express their preference regarding a specific song or poem, they are not only guided in making own choices but also learn to respect the preferences of other children in the group and use language to express their views. At the same time, they are counting the total number of children in a specific preference group and informally doing subtraction to *solve a problem. They are also finding the answer to a question and *representing their solutions either orally or concretely, or through drawings. Comparison is the basis for understanding the handling of data (mathematics content area). Comparing is also an essential skill to enable children to order and seriate objects as it allows children to *make the connection between the attributes of an object and its relationship to other objects because of a specific attribute. For example, by comparing the length of crayons, they will be able to arrange them from the shortest to the longest.

Ordering/seriation

Children can order (seriate) when they are able to arrange more than two objects of a set into a specific sequence. Grade R children order objects according to clearly identifiable attributes, for example size (small to big), length (short to long), height (short to tall) or width (thin to thick). More challenging ordering activities include ordering according to colour (from light to dark) or capacity (empty to full).

Figure 13.5 Ordering

Where comparing requires matching two sets of objects or two groups according to an attribute, ordering involves making several decisions based on the *reasoning skills needed to arrange more than two objects. A Grade R child can develop this more advanced skill when provided with ample opportunities for trial-and-error learning. Ordering two sets of objects is called double seriation. A good example might be the story of Goldilocks and the three bears. Papa Bear gets the big bowl, Mama Bear gets the medium bowl and Baby Bear gets the little bowl.

> **Something to consider**
>
> Identify how the activities mentioned in Table 13.1 will provide for the development of the following important human actions:
> - Problem solving
> - Reasoning and proof
> - Communication
> - Making connections
> - Representation.

Table 13.1 Variety of mathematical skills with corresponding topics

MATCHING	CLASSIFYING	ORDERING
Topic: Sport Which ball goes with the tennis racquet, cricket bat, baseball bat, golf iron, etc? Children place the different balls with the different sports equipment. Children can complete a worksheet based on the same topic after mastering the concrete matching task. *Topic: Me* Matching shoes in pairs; matching each finger with a toe, etc.	Classification of objects is always done according to set criteria or specific attributes. Initially the teacher will set the criteria for classification, but children should also get the opportunity to choose their own criteria according to which objects are classified or grouped together. In this case, children should be asked to motivate and explain their criteria for grouping. *Topic: Shoes* The teacher decides on criteria for classifying children's shoes – sandals, closed shoes, colour of shoes, boys' shoes and girls' shoes, etc. Children group the shoes according to the set criteria, and count and compare the number of objects in each group. *Topic: Animals* The teacher explains the eating habits of animals, and the difference between tame and wild animals, pets and farm animals, etc. Children group plastic animals or pictures of animals according to the set criteria, and count and compare the number of objects in each group.	• Order children from tall to short (concrete); from youngest to oldest (abstract) (or let children organise themselves into a specific order). • Children order the blocks from largest to smallest. • Children order vegetables from heaviest to lightest, etc. • Children order measuring spoons, pots and pans, etc from biggest to smallest. • Children order glasses from empty to full, etc. »

MATCHING	CLASSIFYING	ORDERING
Topic: Eating Matching each knife with a fork; placing a spoon in each soup bowl, etc	*Topic: Toys* The teacher explains the different materials toys are made of, the difference between toys for babies and toys for older children, the different toys traditionally for boys and girls, and toys both genders can play with. Children sort toys according to set criteria, for example toys traditionally for boys (cars, boats, aeroplanes, etc), toys traditionally for girls (dolls, tea-sets, jewellery), toys for both genders (bats, balls, roller skates, etc). Children may differ in their views regarding such a grouping, which is welcomed as long as they can motivate their grouping and provide reasons for classification. (Discussions on gender sensitivity could emanate from such activities.)	

BASIC MATHEMATICAL CONCEPTS AND MATHEMATICAL CONTENT AREAS

We have briefly explored the mathematical foundational concepts and skills as well as how they promote specific human actions. We will now explain the mathematical content areas. You will have already noticed that aspects of the content areas such as number form part of the foundational skills. Even though the components are presented separately in the curriculum, Mathematics, like all subjects, is taught in an integrated manner, for example, sorting and classifying as a mathematical activity requires counting skills. Children count when they measure or organise data, while knowledge of the attributes of shapes includes counting as well as measuring: *How many* corners does a triangle have? We know a rectangle is a rectangle when a shape has two opposite *long* sides that are equal in length and two opposite *short* sides that are equal in length. When all four sides are the same length we call it a square.

Content area: Numbers, operations and relationships

This content area has the most time allocated to it in Grade R as it forms a basis for the acquisition of all other mathematical concepts. Children need to develop a number system in order to understand mathematics. They need to share their understanding with others and use mathematics in a meaningful way in everyday experiences. A number system is a language used to describe quantities and the relationships between them. Numbers are the tools we use to interpret information, make decisions and solve problems. In Grade R, children will count objects; count forwards and backwards; recognise, identify and read numbers (not write); describe, match, compare and order numbers; add and subtract (using mental mathematics and stories); group and share; and develop an awareness of South African money.

Number concept is the awareness of the 'how many-ness' of a group of objects. When children can recite a range of numbers in order, this does not mean that they can count. They may have merely memorised these number names in the correct order. Counting should always start with a kinaesthetic approach (eg use the children in the class to count the number of boys and girls in the group). To help children form an understanding that each object in a group can be matched with a number name when counting, give each object its own number. For example, place four blocks in a row and label them 1, 2, 3 and 4 from the left. When children count a set of objects, they should be encouraged to touch each one as it is counted or move each object counted from one container to the other. This will ensure that one-to-one correspondence is applied when they match each number name in an ordered sequence with every element in the set. Children will soon discover that the last number assigned is the cardinal number that represents the total number of objects in the set.

As discussed above, initial matching games require children to match objects one-to-one, for example a knife with a fork. Matching objects one-to-one lays the foundation for later knowledge that groups of objects are matched to a specific number to indicate the number of objects in the group. Young children should rather count a small number of objects in a meaningful way than recite number names up to 100 in a meaningless way. Finger rhymes or counting songs are a fun way to master this concept in Grade R.

Try this out
- Ask children to group themselves in groups of two, three, etc. This should ideally be implemented in a fun way, for example while marching to the song 'The ants go marching' (see various videos on YouTube; https://www.youtube.com/watch?v=2S__fbCGwOM)
- Ask children to show two (three, four, etc) fingers with one hand as well as with two hands. When they use two hands, the different ways in which a number can be made up become clear.
- Identify a matching, comparing, classifying and ordering activity that will promote the development of numbers, operations and relationships as set out in the curriculum.
- Make a list of finger rhymes and songs that you can use to help children master counting skills. Order them from a simple to a more challenging level. Ask your colleagues which number rhymes their children enjoy most and also use the internet to add to your list.
- Search the internet for free resources for the song: 'Five little speckled frogs'. Print a copy of the five frogs for each child and help them to make their own set to use for 'counting back' while singing the song. When they colour and cut out their own set of five frogs, they are at the same time strengthening their concept of five while talking about the number of frogs they have already cut out or coloured in and how many they still need to colour in or cut out.

»

- Draw large numbers or dot cards in a straight line on the ground or carpet with chalk and let the children jump from one number (or dot card) to the next in sequence while saying the number out loud as they land on it. Let them also jump in reverse order (counting back). Jumping on every second number, first starting on 1 (3, 5... etc) and starting on 2 (4, 6 ... etc) will provide an opportunity to form the concept of unequal and equal numbers. A more advanced version is where the numbers are drawn randomly (not in a straight line) but still close enough to each other to jump from the one to the next. Children have to search for the next number before jumping. The matching of the number name and the jump is also one-to-one matching, and provides an ideal opportunity for the teacher to assess this competence.

Content area: Patterns and functions

A pattern is something that happens in a regular and repeated way (eg when singing the action song 'Head and shoulders, knees and toes'). When a collection or array of objects or numbers such as △ □ ○ or 5 4 6 2 are repeated in a specific sequence, this forms a repeating pattern that can be identified and described as generalised rules or functions. For example, what will the function or rule of the following pattern be?

△ □ ○; △ □ ○......

The rule of this pattern: The repetition of three geometric shapes in the same order where the first shape is always a triangle, the second always a square and the last is always a circle.

Now could you formulate the function or rule for the following pattern?

5 4 6 2; 5 4 6 2......

Patterns and functions build a foundation for the learning of algebra in the higher grades.

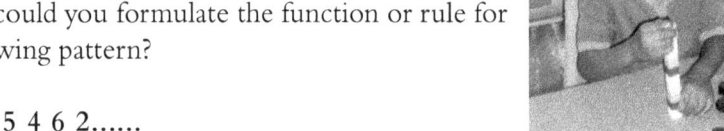

Figure 13.6 Horizontal and vertical patterns

In Grade R, children will copy and extend patterns using real objects (threading beads in a specific sequence); using colours and shapes (to make a frame for a picture). Only when children have developed a sound understanding of patterns and have had numerous opportunities to copy them and create their own on a kinaesthetic as well as concrete level, may they progress to completing patterns on a worksheet, in a workbook, or as part of a software programme for learning. No number patterns are to be taught in Grade R.

Try this out
- Let groups of children arrange themselves in patterns – they may choose the patterns themselves, for example:
  - one tall/one short/one tall/one short, etc
  - one boy/one girl/one boy/one girl, etc.
- The teacher can also arrange children in a certain order, and ask them to identify the pattern, for example two boys, one girl, two boys, one girl, etc.

Using their bodies in the three ways suggested above is an example of patterning kinaesthetically.

Then invite children to make patterns using concrete apparatus.
- Ask children to form a repeating pattern with coloured building blocks, geostacks or beads, and ask them to explain their patterns (*communication).
- Create repeating patterns with vegetable prints or by pasting geometrical shapes cut from coloured glued paper, etc.

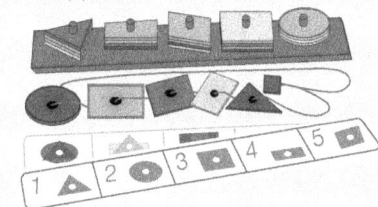

Figure 13.7 Geostacks

Content area: Space and shape (geometry)

Shape and space form an integral part of the child's world. Through manipulating concrete objects, they discover the different attributes of shapes, which lays the foundation for the later and more complex learning of geometry. Toddlers soon realise that their bottle can roll but a wooden block will only slide across the floor. Grade R children have therefore already had experience of space and shape, which the teacher should utilise when introducing new geometrical concepts.

The understanding that every object is positioned in relation to other objects happens through play and guided activities. People are also positioned in relation to objects as well as in relation to each other. For example, John is standing behind the chair, next to Thandi. This awareness, called spatial awareness (see Chapter 4), is an important life skill that plays a role in activities such as writing, reading, sport, performing arts (ballet, dance) and even self-defence.

The concepts of space and shape are closely related. All objects are shaped and all objects are positioned in relation to other objects around them. Space and shape should therefore be presented in such a way that children realise the relationship between the shape of objects, the relationship between them and the possible use of an object because of its shape and sometimes because of its position in space (eg a lift). The following questions will motivate children to reflect on the attributes of geometrical shapes, the relationship between objects in space as well as the possible benefits of shape and space for man:
- Why are apples packed in moulded cartons when they are transported? (Apples are round and they can roll.)

- Why are bricks flat and not round? (The flat sides can be stuck together with cement and fitted onto each other to build strong houses.)
- Why are bricks not round? (Round shapes roll and also have no flat surfaces to stick together.)

The example of the bricks is a good way to help children discover the attributes of shapes as well as knowledge of space between shapes. Through building their own walls with building blocks, they discover the attributes of a brick (rectangular block), as well as the relationship between the bricks. They can be stacked on top of each other to build a wall:

'When I build the first layer of bricks, I put the bricks next to each other, and the next layer of bricks will be put on top of the first layer. The first layer will then be under the second layer. I place my bricks flat on their long sides – this way the wall won't fall over easily. My bricks need to be the same size, otherwise their long sides won't fit on top of each other, and my wall will tumble over.'

The specific attributes of the brick (rectangular block) make it possible to layer the bricks. The spacing of the bricks in relation to each other (next to, on top and under) allows us to build a strong wall. This type of discovery through *reasoning starts to build the children's beginning knowledge of science and geometry.

Let us look more closely at the way children learn about shapes and space.

Shape

In Grade R, children are expected to identify and name 2D (circle and square) and 3D (ball and box) shapes.

Children discover the attributes of shapes (both 2D and 3D) through the hands-on manipulation of objects of various shapes and sizes in various contexts. First experiences with shape should be on a kinaesthetic level where children use their bodies to form shapes – individually or as a group. For example, six children use their bodies to make a rectangle. Then they make use of concrete objects (3D learning). Construction with big blocks and/or empty boxes is an activity that will enhance learning about shapes. Objects that are shaped like a block have a specific function, such as boxes containing food or dice that can be used in number games, etc. Asking a Grade R child why a box is, for example, rectangular and not shaped like a ball, or why a wheel is round and not square, will guide thinking regarding the attributes and purposes of shapes in real-life contexts.

Spatial relationships and games to enhance this understanding

In Grade R, children, as we have said, are expected to describe the position of objects in relation to other objects as well as the position of their own body in relation to an object. Developmentally appropriate activities involve games in which children will experience their position in relation to an object, for example 'I crawl under the table'; 'I stand on the chair'; 'I sit next to the ball'; etc. Knowledge of the position of an object in relation to the body can be developed by using beanbags or wooden building blocks. 'Put the beanbag on your head, next to you, in front of you.' Concept of position in space also involves the children's ability to follow directions and, as a result, move around in the classroom and/or in the outdoor play area. Games such as blindfolding a child and giving him/her instructions to be followed to find a specific object can be a fun way to learn about the importance of direction and position in space, eg 'Take four steps forward, make a left turn, take another four steps forward and make a right turn, stop! What do you feel in front of you?' (eg a square wooden block placed on top of a chair).

Symmetry

An object is symmetrical when one half of it is exactly the same as the other half. Exploring and discovering symmetry in the world around them prepares children for more abstract geometry as well as for understanding various scientific concepts; for example, a doctor needs a good knowledge of the symmetry of the body – external as well as internal. Symmetry plays an important role in designing in various fields, for example graphic designing, transport, technology and clothing. We differentiate between line symmetry and rotational symmetry. If a figure has a line of symmetry, it can be folded along a line so that the two halves match, whereas with rotational symmetry, the shape or image can be rotated and it still looks the same.

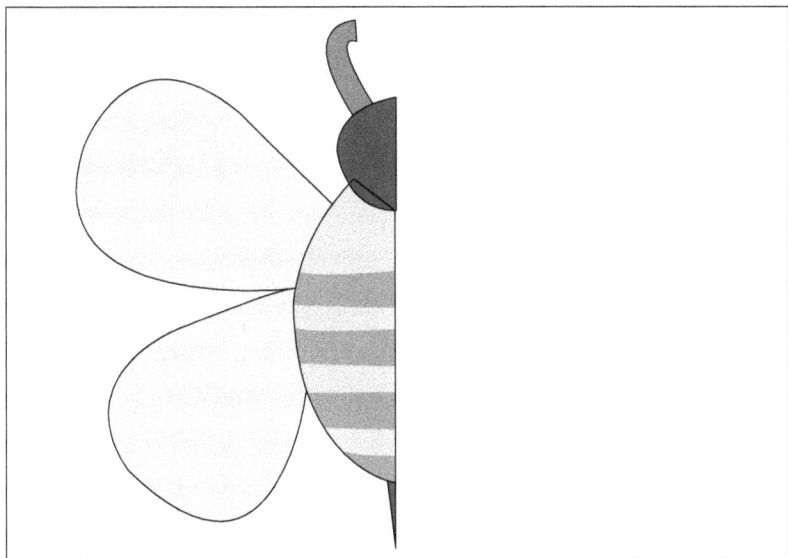

Figure 13.8   Line symmetry

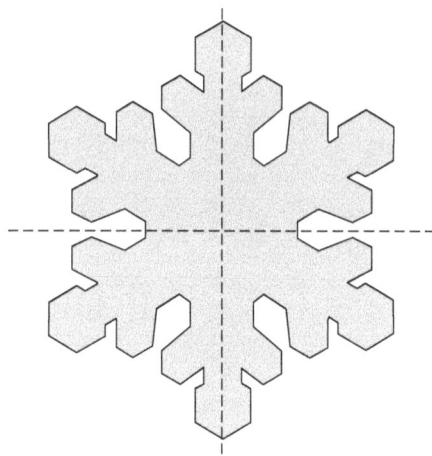

Figure 13.9 Rotational symmetry

Children in Grade R should recognise symmetry in their own bodies as well as in real-life objects and in nature. Art activities can be used to clarify this concept, for example through blob paintings. Children fold a piece of paper to cut out a butterfly with symmetrical wings. Then they open the paper, drip paint on one side only and fold the unpainted wing over the painted one. A gentle rub on the outside of the wings will print the same pattern onto both wings – that is, the end product will show a symmetrical pattern when opened.

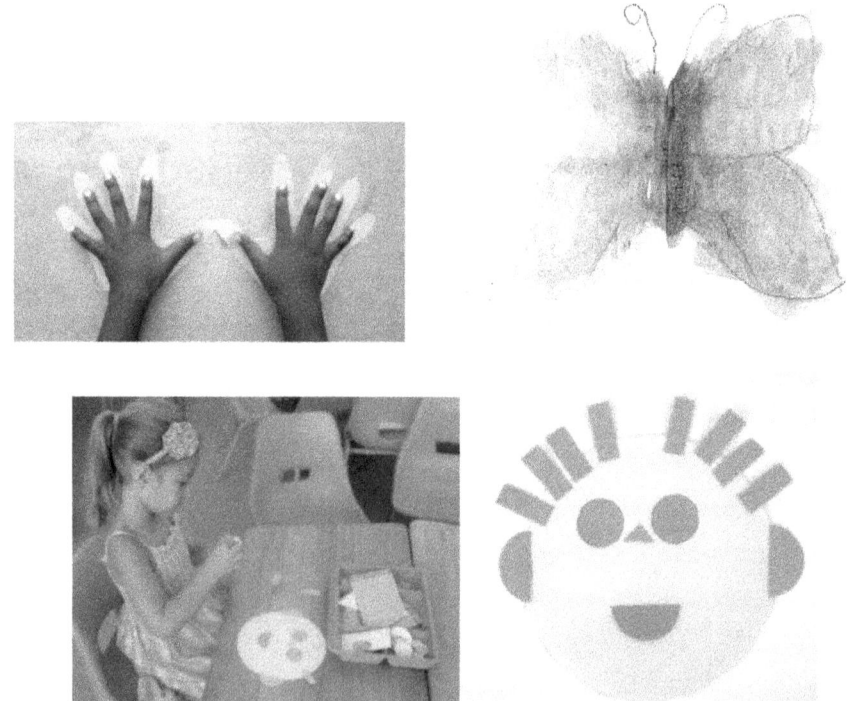

Figure 13.10 Examples of symmetry in art activities

Find out more
Find more information on ways to improve children's spatial skills at Juta Passmasters.

Knowledge of shapes, space and symmetry gained informally through play prepares Grade R children for later learning of geometry, which is often viewed as one of the problem areas of mathematics in higher grades.

Try this out
Tippy-tippy touches – this is a game where children run or walk to touch a shape called out by the teacher or another child. The teacher places different shapes in the play area. These could be 3D (colourful geometric shapes cut from cardboard) or 2D (shapes drawn on the classroom floor or in the playground using chalk). The teacher or the identified child tries to touch the other children before they reach the specific shape called out. Children like to play this game when they know the different shapes that have been laid out. The teacher can start with two shapes and increase the number as children are gradually introduced to more shapes. This game can be played inside or outdoors.

Game: Miss Mouse went into the barn one day ...
This game is played after the children have been introduced to the basic geometric shapes and when they know the basic attributes of at least two different shapes. The game can start off with a few shapes and the teacher can progressively add more as children become more familiar with them. The attributes of the shapes can also increase, such as colour, thickness and size.

The teacher places various familiar shapes in the middle of the carpet. The number and variety will depend on the age and developmental level of the children. The teacher focuses their attention on the different attributes of the shapes by asking questions: 'How many blue shapes, red shapes, etc?'; 'How many circles, squares, triangles, etc?'; 'How many small, large, thick, thin triangles/circles/squares, etc, do you see?' When children know the shapes well, the teacher covers all of them with a large cloth. Children close their eyes. Teacher says the following rhyme while secretly removing a shape from under the cloth:

'Miss Mouse went into the barn one day,
When no one was looking, took something away!'

The cloth is then removed, and the children are given time to identify the missing shape. (Make sure you explain the rules of the game as excited children tend to shout out the answers!) Children should put up their hands to allow the teacher to give more children an opportunity to answer. The children are required to describe all attributes of the missing shape, for example 'Miss Mouse took the red, large, thick triangle'. The game is repeated several times. Children enjoy taking turns to act as Miss Mouse. The 'Miss Mouse-child' has the opportunity to identify if the other children

»

have given all the correct attributes of the shape in his/her hand. This gives the teacher ample opportunity to assess individual children's understandings of a number of concepts such as shape and colour as well as visual memory and visual discrimination.

Although it is not necessary to use expensive resources for this game, using attribute blocks – which are sets of geometrical shapes with different attributes such as thick and thin, small and big, and in different colours – works well for this game. Attribute blocks are extremely versatile and durable, and can be used for many different activities.

Figure 13.11 Attribute blocks

Find out more

Find more information at Juta Passmasters.

Content area: Measurement

To measure is to attach a number to a quantity using a specific chosen unit such as metres (to measure length), grams (to measure weight) or litres (to measure capacity). The development of measuring concepts progresses through three levels:

1. *Direct comparison experiences*
    - *Direct comparison* includes the development of appropriate vocabulary such as comparison of size, length or mass between objects, for example: 'The doll *weighs less than* the car but the truck *weighs more* than the car'; 'You are taller than me but shorter than Martha'; 'It is further to the jungle gym than to the swings'.
    - Estimating before measuring, for example: 'In the story we read that Rex the dinosaur is 12 metres high. How many children do you think will have to stand on each other's heads to be just as tall as Rex?' After guessing, the teacher organises a number of children to lie down head to toe until they measure 12 metres. Such activities will help children to form relationships between the sizes and length of objects.
2. *Using arbitrary units for measurement*
    This level consists of two kinds of measuring units:
    - *Non-uniform, non-standard units.* Children use their body parts as measuring units: one child lies on the carpet and a friend measures his length using his feet heel to toe. These units are not the same size (non-uniform) as the children soon discover that their hands/feet differ in

length, and they get different measurements when measuring the length of the same object. They discover that a body part is not a standard size or unit (same for all people) and therefore cannot be used for accurate measurement. Children will then be guided to realise the need for a measuring unit that can be used by all children and will give the same measurement when an object is measured. Such a unit will also make it possible to compare the relationship between different objects: 'I want to make a tablecloth for my table. I need to find out how long the cloth should be'. Tracy's hand is used to measure the table and just to make sure of the size, the teacher asks big John if he will also measure the table's length. The table measures five of John's hands, but six of Tracy's hands are needed to measure the same length! 'Oh my – now I have a problem, children. Whose hand can I take to the shop to show the shopkeeper how much material I should buy?'

Children should come to the conclusion that we need to find a uniform unit of measurement such as same-sized building blocks, which prepares them for the next level in the development of measuring concepts.

- *Uniform, non-standard units* (paperclips, string, building blocks, etc). The children can now measure the table with the same-sized wooden block, and the teacher can take the block to the shop to make sure she buys material that measures the same as seven of these blocks in length and five of these blocks in width.

3. *Using metric units of measurement*

This is the last level of coming to understand measurement. Although many children come to Grade R with knowledge of metric units, the teacher should make sure that they have a good understanding of arbitrary units before going on to more abstract metric units. Metric units are introduced in an informal way, and children are not yet assessed on this knowledge. However, when a recipe is followed to bake cookies, the teacher will focus children's attention on the numbers used for measurement: a cup of flour is the same as 250 ml. Children observe the numbers on the measuring cup as incidental reading and mathematics.

Comparison forms the basis of problem-solving activities in measuring. The Grade R teacher should ask questions to guide children in their comparison of measurements, for example: 'Which string is the longest?'; 'Which pumpkin is the heaviest?'; 'Which side of the carpet is the longest?'; 'How many times did you need to place your feet heel to toe to measure the long side of the carpet?'; 'How many times did you need to place your feet heel to toe to measure the short side of the carpet?'. To solve these problems, children will use comparison, counting and matching skills. When children understand the concept of measuring, they can also be asked to estimate the measurement before they actually measure.

Time

In Grade R, children can be expected to distinguish between activities that occur during daytime and night-time. Furthermore, they can sequence activities in, for example, the daily programme. Later in the year, pictures of a clock showing the different time slots can be added to the pictures portraying the daily programme to enable children to make the connection between the time on the clock and the time at which an activity takes place.

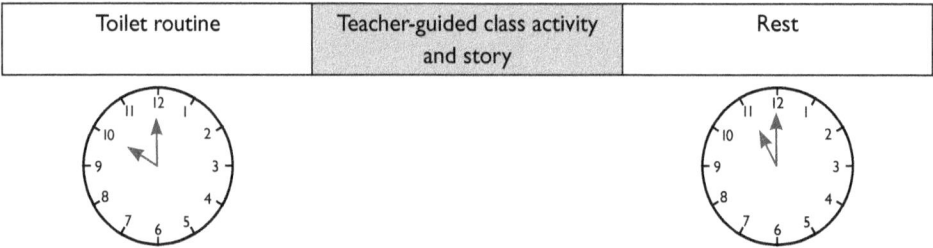

Figure 13.12 Sequencing recurring events in daily life (DBE, 2011: 60)

Referring regularly to the time at which an activity will take place helps children to form a concept of time. For example, refreshment time is when the short arm points to number 10 and the long arm points to number 3; and story time is when both the short and the long arm point to number 12. Keeping to this routine also helps children to feel safe, knowing what to expect and that their parents will pick them up at the arranged time. Building puzzles that depict the sequence of happenings, for example getting ready for school, seasons of the year, the life cycle of a butterfly, etc, further supports the concept of time.

Length

Children can compare their own length to the length of their friend(s) by standing next to each other; the lengths of objects can be compared by placing them next to each other. The teacher should model the appropriate use of vocabulary, for example 'longer', 'shorter', 'taller' and 'wider'. Focusing children's attention on length whenever the opportunity arises further supports understanding of this attribute of objects such as the difference in lengths of characters in a story (which animal in the story is the tallest? How do you know this?) Finger rhymes can also help children to compare the length of their fingers. A good concept of length and accurate measuring of this attribute plays a crucial role in later geometry.

Mass

Children should first have the opportunity to compare the mass of two objects by holding them in different hands. Ordering objects from heavy to light by 'feeling' the mass (weight) will help to develop an understanding of mass.

A balancing scale can then be used to compare the weight of different objects. There are various scales on the market that children can use to explore mass as an attribute of objects. An economical way to make a scale is to use a wire hanger. Activities should both introduce and reinforce 'mass' vocabulary, for example 'light', 'lighter', 'heavy' and 'heavier', etc.

Try this out

Coat-hanger balance

What you need
- A coat hanger
- String
- Two identical plastic or cardboard/paper cups
- Scissors
- Masking tape.

Instructions
1. Cut four lengths of string, each one metre long.
2. Poke four holes in each cup with the nail. The holes should be evenly spaced near the rim.
3. Thread a string through two of the holes.
4. Tie a cup to each end of the hanger and secure it to the hanger with a piece of masking tape.
5. Hang the hanger somewhere where it can hang freely.
6. Put objects in each cup to find out which is the heavier one.

If the hanger tilts to the right, the object in the cup on the right is heavier than the one in the cup on the left.

Volume and capacity

Volume is how much space an object takes up and includes solids, fluids and gases while capacity is the amount of liquid a container can hold; for example, a litre bottle can hold a litre of milk. Playing with water or sand provides real-life opportunities to learn about volume and capacity. Children can be guided to compare the amount of water or sand in two containers (the space that the sand or water takes up in the container) or count how many cups of water fill a litre bottle. Use words like 'more than', 'less than', 'full' and 'empty' to build children's mathematical vocabulary.

Following a simple recipe in a baking activity provides a fun way to learn about the important role of volume and capacity in real life. Outdoor or indoor free play with sand, water or substances such as flour or rice provides opportunity for the exploration of these measurable attributes and to use related vocabulary.

Content area: Data handling and analysis of data

Data refers to information which can be represented in a number of different ways, in statements, graphs and tables. Graphs are used to show a comparison of information visually. Rainfall, sports results and election polls are all represented in a graphical or summarised form as statistics. By representing data in this way, we can make sense of trends and patterns. At Grade R level, the focus should be on children sorting and classifying objects according to their attributes, organising data about the objects, and describing the data and what they show. Children can collect sets of data from their real-life experiences and show the results of their data collection in simple graphs. In Grade R, children can collect everyday objects like leaves, buttons and blocks, and sort objects according to shape, colour or size. These objects can be represented by pictures as well as simple graphs.

Figure 13.13 Data represented in a simple graph

Figures 13.13 and 13.14 are examples of how children's objects from the class can be used to make a simple graph. To analyse the data, the teacher can ask children to count how many scissors, crayons or dough cutters they see.

In Figure 13.15, children are sorting sweets according to colour. To analyse the data, the teacher can ask questions like: 'How many red sweets are there?'; 'Which colour sweets are the most?'; 'Which colour sweets are the least?'; 'Are there any two colours of sweets that are equal in amount?'

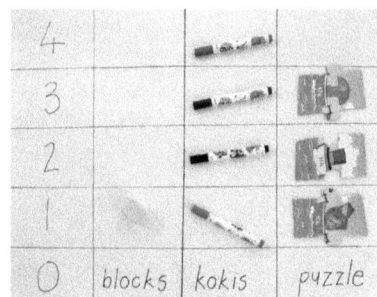

Figure 13.14 Example of a data graph

Figure 13.15 Sorting and organising sweets

Collecting data daily on the weather during the early morning conversation time (ring time) should be part of the daily routine. School outings, for example visiting the fire station, provide opportunities for learning how to collect data. Motivate the children beforehand to collect as much information on the fire station as they can and to give feedback to the group on their return, for example: 'How many firemen work at the station?'; 'How many firewomen work there?'; 'How many fire trucks are there?'; etc. The teacher can guide the children to illustrate their collected data either through a graph, drawing of pictures or choosing their own methods. Additional resources and manipulatives that will promote understanding of the various content areas of mathematics are discussed later in this chapter.

WHAT IS THE GRADE R TEACHER'S ROLE?

As discussed in Chapter 8, the Grade R teacher should rather facilitate and mediate learning than transfer or teach knowledge to the children. Facilitating learning requires that a balance be kept between teacher-guided and child-initiated activities. During child-initiated activities, the children acquire skills through exploration and interaction with objects and peers. However, mathematics in Grade R can be improved through systematic, intentional teaching–learning activities. Care should be taken that children are actively engaged in all teacher-guided activities and not merely following instructions. Explicit and intentional teaching begins with the teacher's modelling of the skill, followed by opportunities for children to practise it through play-based activities. Intentional teaching refers to the many ways teachers can intentionally plan and structure children's experiences so that they support learning in mathematics. These times could include perceptual and numeracy rings. The intentional teaching of mathematics could also happen during other rings such as music, movement and even creative art. It all depends on the chosen learning goals. Effective intentional teaching requires teachers who know the teaching–learning goals to use formative assessment to determine where the children are in relation to these goals, and then support them to make continuous progress. Remember that each child is unique, therefore the planning and implementation of mathematical learning experiences should provide for the different ways individual children experience new concepts, for example their different learning styles.

Good insight into the influences of past experiences which children bring with them assists the teacher in the provision of quality education that is relevant and meaningful for the children. The teacher should encourage children to engage with each other and explore, share, compare, classify and problem solve mathematical concepts and issues. Such interactions can create a valuable opportunity for children to interact and to show their understanding. Discussions during group work therefore serve as a critical source of information which a Grade R teacher can use to determine the child's prior knowledge and to support the development of new mathematical concepts by linking with their prior knowledge.

Language is central to all learning. In mathematics there is a specific mathematical language that a child needs to acquire and use with confidence so that new knowledge can be co-constructed. The Grade R teacher therefore uses language that the children currently understand, but at the same time introduces new terms and phrases to deepen learning. He/she should not rely on spoken language alone but should also engage children in drawing and other activities where they can acquire and demonstrate their understanding of mathematical concepts. Code switching where the children's home language (HL) is not the language of learning and teaching (LoLT) can be used to enhance understanding.

Continuous reflection promotes effective learning. Let children reflect on what they have learned as this can deepen learning and lead to better understanding of a new concept. Individual and group reflections on mathematical experiences can allow children to organise, represent and communicate their experiences, and thereby enhance learning.

The Grade R teacher should thus ensure that the learning environment provides optimal opportunity for the children to master skills, knowledge and values as set out in the curriculum. While children are involved in play-based mathematical tasks, the teacher continuously interacts with them to guide them towards the planned aim of the learning experience. Monitoring and observing the children's actions, discussions and behaviour while they are involved with the tasks can provide crucial assessment data on children's progress. This data should be recorded (see Chapter 9). Although recording of assessment data will serve to report the children's progress to parents/caregivers, one of the main aims of assessment is to enable the teacher to identify children who have not mastered a particular skill or concept so that support can be given.

Some of these aspects will now be explored in greater depth.

Maximising the physical environment to stimulate effective learning of mathematics

The Grade R teacher must create a contextually appropriate environment that provides challenging learning opportunities. This type of environment will offer ample opportunity for experiences on a concrete level. The Grade R classroom should contain many sets of objects for counting, matching, classifying, ordering and creating spatial relations. The environment should include permanent fixtures such as a seesaw and a jungle gym outdoors, commercial resources such as Unifix cubes, peg boards and geostacks, as well as thematic resources such as leaves, toys, etc, that will change according to the theme you have chosen. These types of resources will support appropriate teacher- as well as child-initiated learning experiences.

Implementing permanent fixtures and resources for mathematics learning

Charts can be seen as permanent fixtures and used on a daily basis to enhance mathematical learning. These charts include number charts (number friezes), the weather and birthday charts, an illustration of the daily programme and a height-measuring chart. Colourful charts are used to help ensure that mathematics form part of the children's daily life. An illustrated daily programme which shows the activities and the time at which they take place supports the development of the concept of time – both the passing of time as well as the time at which activities take place. Although children will initially use pictures to begin to construct a concept of time, incidental reading of the time in figures will assist them to begin associating the numbers with the pictures.

A child's birthday is often the most important day of the year for that child, and children also enjoy celebrating the birthdays of their peers. This makes the birthday chart one of the most relevant resources for the teaching of the months of the year or days of the weeks. The integration of *counting* happens in an incidental way, for example: 'How many days before your birthday?'; 'How many children have their birthdays in November?' The birthday chart also provides ample opportunity for the development of *calculation and problem-solving skills,* for example: 'Which month has the most/least birthdays?'; 'How many more children were born in January than in February?'; 'John is how many days older than Sipho?'; 'Let's draw up a graph to demonstrate the number of birthdays per month'.

The weather chart also offers a valuable opportunity to integrate science by collecting data on the weather, and representing the data by means of a picture graph. This chart can also be combined with the birthday chart as both focus on the measuring of time, namely daytime and night-time, the days of the week and months of the year, as well as the seasons of the year. Teachers use different methods to record the weather, such as a chart where children draw a symbol like a sun or a raindrop on a large calendar to present the weather on a specific day. Symbols are then counted every Friday and the weather patterns for the week are discussed and displayed on a graph. Once children have familiarised themselves with the weekly graph and have a good number sense up to the number seven, they can progress to a monthly graph. Some weather charts are reusable, and symbols are mounted on the chart with sticky putty (Prestik) or Velcro.

Teachers who design their own weather chart should consider having it laminated for greater durability as this is a resource used nearly every day of the school year. It should be attractive and colourful, and provide an interesting activity in which children want to participate. Taking turns to keep a record of the weather and change the weather symbols on a daily basis also provides an opportunity to develop important life skills such as taking responsibility. What other areas of the curriculum do you think could be addressed through the use of a weather chart?

The height chart is also a focal point in a Grade R class. The teacher should capitalise on the desire of many young children to be the *tallest* or the one who is growing the fastest in the class, etc. Opportunities for exploring concepts such as 'the same as', 'equal to' and comparisons form the basis of many mathematical concepts which they will build on in later years. The teacher could ask questions such as: 'How many children are taller than one metre?' Although teachers also measure the children's weight (mass) once a term for reporting on their health and wellness, some children might find it humiliating to be the 'heaviest' or even the shortest in the class, and therefore teachers should handle these matters with sensitivity.

Other wall charts can display geometric shapes (circles, squares, triangles, etc), opposites that include mathematical concepts such as length (long and short); capacity (empty and full); mass (light and heavy); and low and high, as well as colours which could be used in classification. While colourful and durable wall charts can be purchased, teachers often prefer to design their own to fit the specific learning needs of the children and the curriculum. Where charts are not available in the children's home language, it is strongly recommended that teachers develop, if necessary, similar charts that are developmentally and culturally appropriate. The internet is a useful source for finding pictures to make posters and charts if you are not very artistic. Keep in mind that young children are drawn to colour and pictures to which they can relate. Wall charts also provide a valuable opportunity for incidental reading. Make sure that resources, like birthday charts, are labelled and that labels model correct language, font and spelling.

The role of outdoor apparatus in mathematics learning should not be underestimated. Focus the children's attention on the colour, shape, size and height of climbing apparatus: 'Which jungle gym is the highest?'; 'What is the shape of the tyres?'; 'Why are tyres round?'; 'What is the shortest way to the classroom?' The relationship between the speed of a seesaw and the mass of each child as well as the time allowed for a child on a swing before the next child gets a turn are all valuable opportunities for planned as well as incidental learning of mathematical concepts.

Outdoor equipment such as the sandpit and water play area also provide valuable opportunities for the measuring of volume, capacity and weight, as well as relationships between objects, for example: 'How many small cups of sand will fit into the bucket?' Problems such as these will also develop comparison skills and allow for an informal integration of counting and computation, for example: 'How many cups of water are needed to fill the bucket compared with those needed to fill the empty cool drink bottle?'; 'If we need five small cups to fill the bucket, how many small cups will we need to fill two buckets?' While children explore and discover many of these concepts on their own in informal play activities, it is also crucial that the teacher includes structured learning activities where children can be guided through questions to construct a range of concepts. These activities also provide an opportunity for informal mathematical assessment.

Implementing thematic-focused and planned resources for mathematics learning

Teachers' weekly and daily planning need to include the resources that will be used to promote learning. The choice of resources is determined by the theme or focus of learning, the mathematics content area as well as the knowledge, skills and/or attitudes and values that you want the children to acquire.

If, for example, your theme is trees, children can also explore length by estimating and comparing the length (height) of trees in the school grounds and ordering (seriating) the trees from short to tall. In addition, children can measure and compare the circumference of tree trunks and engage in data handling as they draw up a graph to show the number of evergreen and deciduous trees, etc, in the grounds.

Try this out

There are many other opportunities for integrating mathematical concepts into the daily programme and to relate these appropriately to the theme. For example, art activities can include 'symmetry' painting to depict a tree or leaf. Put a blob of paint on the one side of the page and fold the page in half with the paint inside. Rub your hand over the outside of the one half of the paper to form a symmetric tree or leaf. Natural sciences as part of Life Skills may include a field trip where children explore symmetry in nature.

Furthermore, to extend learning opportunities in relation to the theme 'Trees', the concept of symmetry could also be explored in a mathematics corner using a variety of leaves.

The following case study depicts a typical discussion during the morning ring to show how this activity prepares the children for exploration in the mathematics corner/mathematics centre which will be part of the indoor free play that is to follow:

CASE STUDY 1

Teacher: *Can someone tell me again what we say when two sides of a shape are exactly the same?*

Mpho: *Symmetry – my body is symmetric – last week we drew our bodies, and both sides are the same.*

Teacher: *That's right, Mpho – and can someone tell me how we know when a shape is symmetrical?*

Siswe: *When we fold it down the middle and the one side fits exactly on the other.*

Teacher: *You remember well, Siswe. Today I placed leaves in our Mathematics corner. Two children are allowed to work there together to find out how many of the leaves are symmetrical. Try to answer the question: 'Are all leaves symmetrical?' To do this, group the leaves that are symmetrical together and place them in one basket, and put the other leaves in the other basket. Count the symmetrical leaves and the ones that are not, and find out which group has the most leaves. Keep your answer a secret as you are only allowed to give your answers when we all sit quietly on the carpet after tidy-up time.*

Try this out

Draw your own flowchart (mindmap) to illustrate how the topic 'Trees' can provide for the learning of the various content areas of Mathematics as set out in the Grade R curriculum.

Also apply this brainstorming technique for the topic 'Water' (see Chapter 8).

Something to consider

Trees as an example of how to provide learning in the Mathematics content area

Here is one possible way of drawing a flowchart.

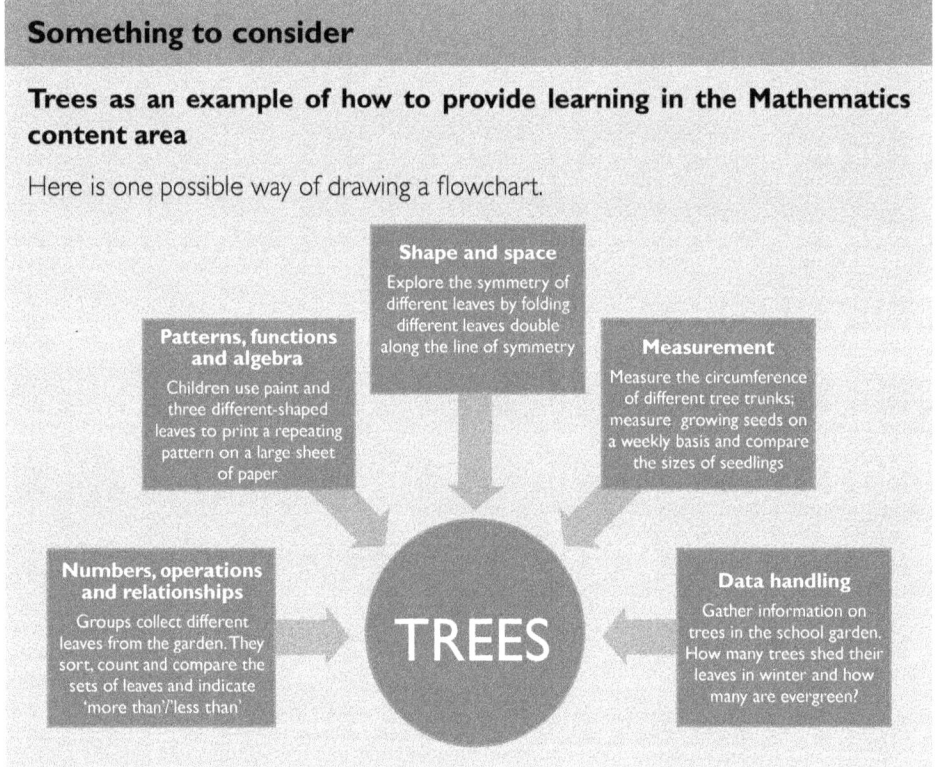

Setting up a Mathematics corner

A Mathematics corner (some schools prefer to use the term Mathematics 'centre' or 'area') is a place in the room where children explore mathematics through manipulating objects. Make sure this area is a safe and exciting space that children are drawn to explore and discover mathematical concepts. The mathematics area should also be separate from the other play areas to allow children to focus on mathematics without interruptions such as other children passing through with their wet paintings, etc. The corner provides a crucial extended opportunity for children to engage with the various concepts to which they have already been introduced. Children could, however, also discover 'new' concepts if the teacher provides a variety of resources which children can freely explore. As with all learning areas/corners, children work independently (see Chapter 7). Your choice of resources is important. Ask yourself the following questions:

- Will these resources contribute to better understanding of the concept?
- Do the resources provide equal opportunities for all the children to learn the specific concept?
- Do all the children have sufficient prior knowledge to benefit from the learning activity or do some children need support?
- Is the activity providing learning opportunities to suit the various developmental levels of all children in the group?
- Are the resources safe?
- Are the resources contextually and culturally appropriate?
- Do they invite participation – for example, is the material suitable for independent learning without supervision?

Independent learning in this sense allows children to collaborate and share thoughts and ideas. This collaborative problem solving not only supports the development of *thought processes (human actions) such as reasoning, but also social and cooperative skills. An example of an appropriate activity for the Mathematics corner could be counting, which would include sorting objects. Let the children choose their own sorting (classification) criteria and explain why they made that choice.

Figure 13.16 Counting activities

> **Try this out**
> Google the keywords *maths, centre, kindergarten* and follow the various links to learn from others in the field of early learning. Ideas for estimation centres, sorting and measuring centres, and novel ideas to support number concept and counting are just some of the few examples other teachers are sharing on the internet.

Presenting developmentally appropriate mathematics experiences

Learning tasks based on games or other activities where children are motivated to interact with their peers provide opportunities to use and practise terminology related to mathematics. 'I have fewer cards than you but Anthony doesn't have as many as I do.' The teacher can then mediate learning with questions such as: 'How do you know you have more cards?'; 'How many more cards do you have than Emily?' These questions are not usually seen by children as interference by the teacher but as a matter of shared interest, which they appreciate. Usually, they will be more than willing to share their thoughts and motivate their statements or solutions. Grouping children around a table where they are all exploring a similar concept, for example constructing a picture by arranging geometric shapes, will encourage children to share their ideas about their designs.

The following case study is based on a discussion between children sitting around a collage table where they received different paper shapes and were asked to construct a house. The shapes included one large square, two triangles, one circle and two rectangles. Children were told that they could fold shapes in half and cut them in half or in quarters to design at least one house with a door and two windows:

CASE STUDY 2

Andy: *I put two triangles together to make the square for the walls of my house.*

Kate: *You should have used the square for that!*

Andy: *It doesn't matter – the two triangles put together also make a block ... a square like yours ... I like it better this way.*

Kate: *Oh ... I see, yes – but now what will you use for the roof then?*

Andy: *What about folding and cutting our shapes – I will cut my square in the middle to make two triangles again. My other triangle will be a tree in the garden.*

This case study clearly illustrates the role of social learning and interaction in mathematical problem solving and learning. Andy's expression of his own knowledge construction is transferred to Kate, who will probably add this knowledge regarding the attributes of a triangle and a square to her existing knowledge network on geometric shapes. The teacher's thorough preparation and clear instructions on ways children can explore the shapes contributed to the successful learning experience and knowledge construction. Instead of being told the attributes and relationship between shapes, these children discover the knowledge themselves, which supports understanding and internalisation more effectively than direct instruction. The teacher can now, by observing and listening, note down on the recording sheet that Andy is starting to understand the attributes of specific geometric shapes and the relationship between them.

Presenting culturally appropriate mathematics experiences

Mathematics learning should include knowledge and understanding of the contribution made by many cultures to the development and application of mathematics and the cultural values that influence mathematical understanding. Young children's lives are intertwined with their cultural background, thus if they are able to link mathematical concepts to their existing cultural knowledge, it becomes more meaningful.

Something to consider

Presenting culturally appropriate mathematics experiences

Consider the following scenario:

Bongani is a six-year-old boy attending Grade R at a rural school. He has never visited the city and his family lives in round huts with thatched roofs. A worksheet asks him to solve the following problem:

How many houses do you see in the picture?

How many houses would Bongani count? Would Bongani be able to recognise all the objects in the picture as houses? If he answers 'four', would his answer be considered wrong? How would such an assessment affect his belief of his own ability to count? What would an experienced teacher ask Bongani to check for true understanding?

This example clearly demonstrates why teachers should be sensitive to children's background and culture. When children experience mathematics as meaningful, they are more motivated to apply the concepts they have learned and in so doing develop their ability to calculate, reason and solve problems. Such motivation will also encourage children to deepen their understanding of relationships and patterns in both number and space in their everyday lives.

Find out more
Find various ideas on multicultural games to be implemented as fun ways to learn mathematics Juta Passmasters.

To summarise
What do we know?

The Grade R teacher's role is to:
- create an effective learning environment for all children in the group
- plan meaningful mathematics learning opportunities that are based on the curriculum and are developmentally and culturally appropriate
- integrate mathematical learning into the daily programme in a meaningful way.

To do this requires a thorough knowledge of how the Grade R child learns, as well as the content of the national school curriculum.

What should we do with what we know?

Continuously reflect on the critical role of the Grade R teacher when planning and implementing mathematical learning experiences.

What do we need to find out?
- What content do we need to teach in Grade R?
- Which resources do we need to implement the curriculum in a developmentally and contextually appropriate and culturally responsive way?
- How do we determine if learning aims were reached?

PROVIDING APPROPRIATE RESOURCES FOR EFFECTIVE TEACHING AND LEARNING OF MATHEMATICS

Throughout this chapter we have continually referred to the importance of using appropriate resources. Many different resources have already been mentioned. Because the use of resources is so important, we are now going to extend and deepen this information.

It is important to remember that resources should be developmentally, culturally and contextually appropriate, and although they should challenge the children to explore mathematics, they should not be so advanced that they are off-putting. As we already know, young children learn through their senses, and resources that include sensory, visual and even auditory learning will promote understanding of mathematical concepts. We also know that young children learn by moving their bodies (kinaesthetic learning).

In short, the Grade R teacher should therefore always try to incorporate the children's bodies when presenting new content (kinaesthetic learning). After kinaesthetic learning, the children should get the opportunity to explore new concepts through the manipulation of concrete material. Only when the child has developed a good understanding of a concept, should he/she engage in more abstract activities such as paper and pencil representations (2D) often found in a workbook or worksheet. These 2D resources should also only be introduced when the child has developed the necessary fine motor and relevant writing skills (see Chapter 4).

Some additional concrete resources

There are numerous durable and colourful commercial materials on the market such as puzzles, geostacks, peg boards, pattern blocks, scales and board games (eg Snakes and Ladders, Spinner board games and Junior Monopoly) based on mathematical concepts that can support the understanding of mathematics by Grade R children. Teacher-made manipulative materials can, however, be used with equal success. Examples include coloured bottle tops or beans to use as counters, for example in games where children keep count of their scores; boxes of odd items that can be sorted and classified; beads on strings in sets from one to 10; geoboards made from strong cardboard and laminated; and so on. Resources need not be expensive. A little initiative can go a long way to making inexpensive but effective resources for the teaching and learning of Mathematics in Grade R.

Although the teacher should collect and prepare resources for each of the five content areas, the most useful resources are those that can be used across content areas. For example, geostacks, a set of colourful stackable geometric shapes, can be used for counting, one-to-one correspondence, shape identification, pattern building, problem solving (eg 'How many more corners does a square have than a triangle?') and many more activities.

Here are a few more ideas for resources and manipulatives that will promote the development of knowledge in the different content areas. See if you have additional ideas which you can add to the list and also reflect on how the resources may be relevant to more than one content area.

Content area: Numbers, operations and relationships

Grade R children have a good knowledge of their own bodies and they know the number of fingers, toes, eyes, etc, that they have. They are also able to match their body parts to specific items; for example, each foot needs a sock and a shoe. This is an example of one-to-one correspondence.

Kinaesthetic learning in numbers and operations does not stop with the counting of body parts, but can be expanded to activities that include the following:
- Addition and subtraction: 'How many eyes do all the boys have together?'; 'How many eyes do all the girls have together?'; 'Which group has the most eyes?'
- The basics of multiplication and division: 'How many eyes do you have?'; 'How many eyes do you and your friend have?'; etc. When children are able to repeatedly add two objects, they will come to understand the concept of repeated addition. It is easy to introduce 5 and 10 as children are able to relate these numbers to the number of fingers on one hand and the number of fingers on two hands. As 5 and 10 will later serve as anchor numbers to develop mental mathematics strategies, it is critical that the Grade R teacher provides ample opportunities for exploration of these numbers.

Figure 13.17 The basics of multiplication and division

Content area: Patterns, functions and relationships

Toys such as building blocks, Lego, dolls and cars can all be used to build patterns. Art activities such as thumbprints or potato prints also develop the concept of patterning. Commercial resources, such as beading sets or pegboards with pattern cards, progressively guide children towards building more complex patterns. They also provide the teacher with a good opportunity for assessing children's concept of patterns and the level at which they can work. Children should, however, also get the opportunity to create their own patterns and describe them to their peers and the teacher.

Content area: Space and shape

Objects such as Lego blocks can be used to develop the concept of position in space. During a game in small groups where each child is handed a few differently coloured building blocks, the teacher gives instructions such as: 'Put the blue block next to the yellow block and the black block behind the yellow block'. This activity will not only develop the children's concept of position in space but also their auditory perception skills such as auditory memory and auditory sequencing (see Chapter 4).

Focus children's attention on the shape of all toys and parts of toys as well as other objects in the school environment, such as furniture, windows, etc. Ask children to paste geometrically shaped cards on objects in and around the classroom to indicate the shape; for example, the clock is round like a circle, etc.

Use play dough to form shapes and construct a picture with them. Art activities also serve as a way to support the children's concept of shape as well as position in space. Commercial resources such as pegboards (see picture), rubber-band pegboards, foam shapes and board games will support concept forming of space and shape.

Figure 13.18 Pegboard and art activities

Content area: Measurement

A length chart, which has been previously mentioned, indicating the children's height (length) is an essential in each Grade R classroom. Other meaningful measurement activities include using Unifix cubes or a ruler to measure the growth of plants in the school yard or seeds that the children planted, which are now growing in pots on the windowsill. Children can also measure rainfall with an empty cool drink bottle planted in the garden. Make sure the bottle top is screwed on properly, cut the bottom off and turn the bottle upside down. Markings (in cm) can then be made on the bottle with a permanent marker, or a ruler can be used to measure the water inside the bottle after rain has fallen.

Figure 13.19 Measuring the size of a book and comparing length

Find out more

View videos on YouTube to find out how teachers use innovative resources to support knowledge development of measurement at Juta Passmasters.

Content area: Data handling

Draw a grid (table) with a thick black marker on a large piece of white cardboard (1m × 1m). Laminate the cardboard or cover it with adhesive plastic. Mount the grid on the wall so that children can access it easily. Use this grid (shown below) whenever you need to draw a graph together with the children. Use erasable markers so that you can wipe it clean afterwards. Concrete objects that are being compared can be pasted on the grid with sticky putty (Prestik) to form a concrete graph. For example, children could paste small plastic animals on the grid when they are comparing wild animals and sort them according to, for example, eating habits (herbivores, carnivores and omnivores).

Organising and pasting geometric shapes on the grid will also integrate the following content areas into one activity:
- Shapes and space (how many different shapes are represented on the graph?)
- Numbers, operations and relationships:
    - Counting – when children count the shapes: 'How many of each shape can you see on the graph?'
    - Operations: 'How many more squares than circles can you see on the graph?'
- Data handling – using the concrete shapes as data, organise them on the graph to show the number of shapes of each kind.

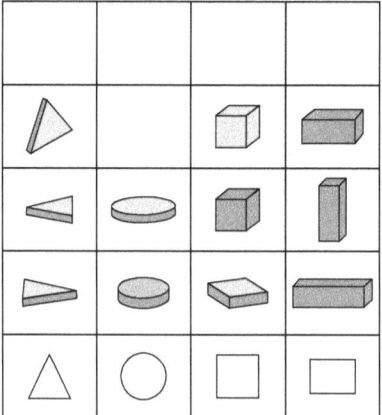

Figure 13.20   Operations

Other objects can also be used for sorting as preparation for collecting and organising data, such as a graph of paper clips sorted according to colour.

SUMMARY

In this chapter we learned that mathematics is part of a young child's everyday life. A teacher should therefore be alert to teachable moments. Children who are guided to realise that mathematics is meaningful in all spheres of life will be more motivated to master new knowledge and skills, and to use them to solve everyday problems.

We have considered the important role of the Grade R teacher in laying the foundations for effective mathematics learning in later years. All mathematics learning builds on a child's number concept and therefore no child should enter Grade 1 without a good concept of the 'how many-ness' of numbers 1–10. The curriculum recognises the importance of this core knowledge by allocating the most notional hours to numbers, operations and relationships between numbers. The informal application of the number concept to other Mathematics content areas through play will pave the way for a smooth transition to more formal Mathematics in all content areas in later years.

In order to support the optimal learning of Mathematics in Grade R, the teacher should know the children and how they learn, and what they need to learn to provide a solid foundation for Grade 1. In addition, the teacher should also have a repertoire of effective teaching strategies and developmentally and contextually appropriate resources to enable him/her to plan and implement appropriate mathematics learning experiences.

BIBLIOGRAPHY

COUNT. 2013. *Guidelines for teaching numeracy in the Foundation Phase.* Revised ed. Johannesburg: Saide.

Department of Basic Education. 2011. *Curriculum Assessment Policy Statement: Grade R Mathematics.* Pretoria: DBE.

Lee, JS & Ginsburg, HP. 2009. 'Early childhood teachers' misconceptions about mathematics education for young children in the United States'. *Australasian Journal of Early Childhood* 34(4): 37–45.

National Association for the Education of Young Children (NAEYC). 2002. *Early childhood mathematics: Promoting good beginnings. A position statement.* Washington. https://www.naeyc.org/files/naeyc/file/positions/psmath.pdf (Accessed 3 March 2012).

National Council of Teachers of Mathematics (NCTM). 2000. *Principles and standards for school mathematics.* Reston, VA: NCT.

GLOSSARY

Algorithm – a step-by-step procedure to solve a problem

Arbitrary (random/haphazard) units for measurement – a non-standard measurement, for example the width of a person's thumb, which differs from person to person (a standard unit is, for example, 1 cm or 1 kg)

Calculation – the use of mathematics or logic to figure out a problem
Capacity – the amount something can hold; for example, a standard cup has a capacity of 250 ml
Carnivore – a meat-eating animal
Circumference – the distance around the outside of a circle
Classify – arranging objects into different classes by unifying characteristics such as size, colour or shape
Compare – to look at two or more objects or people, and note similarities and differences
Computation – to use mathematics or logic to figure out a problem
Conceptual knowledge – knowledge of concepts, for example that a triangle has three sides and three corners, which can only be learned by thoughtful, reflective thinking
Concrete objects – real objects, for example 3D shapes such as real balls, boxes and cones and not only pictures of them
Deciduous trees – trees that lose their leaves at the end of summer
Experiential learning – learning through observation and interaction with real objects, for example when a learner makes meaning from a direct experience
First-hand exploration – exploring real objects and receiving information through the senses
Flowchart – a symbolic representation that describes a process
Foundational (basic) mathematical concepts and skills – basic concepts and skills used in mathematics, for example matching, comparing, classifying, ordering, problem solving
Graph – a chart/picture of values, shown as lines or bars
Herbivore – a plant-eating animal
Human actions – things people do (in mathematics – problem solving, providing good reasons, communicating; making connections; representation)
Kinaesthetic learning – occurs as children engage in physical activity by actively using their bodies to explore, discover and learn through movement
Manipulatives – concrete objects that allow children to explore using a hands-on approach
Meaningful mathematics learning – learning that promotes understanding as opposed to mere memorisation (rote learning), the end result being the realisation of a child's understanding of a concept through his/her ability to apply it
Omnivore – an animal that eats both meat and plants
Pattern and functions – a mathematical pattern that is a repeated sequence of objects or numbers (eg △ □ ○ or 5 4 6 2); a repeated pattern described as a function (eg △ □ ○; △ □ ○ or 5 4 6 2; 5 4 6 2).
Procedural knowledge – knowledge of a procedure to be followed, for example when a packet of 10 sweets is divided equally between two children, it can be represented by a number sentence, namely $10 \div 2 = 5$

Set – a collection of objects

Symmetry – when two sides of an object are identical in appearance (the right side of a pattern or object is exactly the same as the left side)

Three dimensional (3D) – a shape that has three dimensions – width, height and breadth, for example a ball, a cube, a prism, a cone

Two dimensional (2D) – a shape that only has two dimensions (such as width and height) and no thickness, for example a circle, a picture of a square, or a triangle drawn on a piece of paper

Volume – the space occupied by a liquid, solid or gas – that is, the capacity (the unit of measurement is a litre)

Weight – a measurement that indicates how heavy a person or thing is (it relates to mass – the unit of measurement is a gram)

Chapter 14

Life Skills

Susan Greyling

In this chapter we consider

- both the content and value of Life Skills as a subject
- the knowledge, skills and values that teachers require to teach this subject effectively
- how Life Skills can be integrated into every aspect of the daily programme.

LIFE SKILLS IN A SOUTH AFRICAN CONTEXT
What is the subject of Life Skills?

Life Skills is one of the three subjects (the other two being Language and Mathematics) taught in the Foundation Phase. It is both broad and multifaceted, and woven incidentally and intentionally into every facet of the daily programme. For example, when children go to the toilet, we expect them not to push each other and to make hygienic choices such as washing their hands. They are also expected to demonstrate other forms of respect, such as tolerance and an appreciation for diversity. Values such as these inform attitudes and beliefs that should become apparent during teacher-guided activities and child-initiated play. This is only one aspect of Life Skills, which falls under the study area of *Personal and Social Development*. The other areas are *Beginning Knowledge, Creative Arts* and *Physical Education*, all of which will be addressed in this chapter.

Find out more

Curriculum Assessment Policy Statements (CAPS) – Department of Education:
  http://www.education.gov.za/LinkClick.aspx?link=419&tabid=831&mid

Why is Life Skills an important subject?

Life skills enable us to translate knowledge (what we know) and attitudes and values (what we think, feel and believe) into appropriate actions. In the South African context, our democracy calls for active citizenship. This means making informed choices, working with others and dealing, when necessary, with conflict and prejudice. Even at Grade R level, choices are made and the realisation of the consequences that arise from them are important life skills. Life Skills lays the foundations of scientific and historical knowledge, and allows children to explore their creative side and discover the limits and possibilities of their own bodies. In short, children learn about the world they live in, how to interact with that world and why certain decisions are better than others. The multifactorial nature of this subject allows the teacher to consider with the children everything from Science input, for example gravity, to Creative Arts such as dance, and Personal and Social Well-being, which includes teaching respect and managing aggressive behaviour, as well as the origins of man and the possibilities of space. Remember, various skills build on and interact with each other. The acquisition of life skills is a lifelong and continuous process.

> **Something to consider**
>
> Through Life Skills we assist children to acquire the following:
> - Self-belief
> - Independence
> - Coping skills
> - Motivation
> - Confidence
> - Determination
> - The ability to work as part of a group.
>
> In addition, children are encouraged to do the following:
> - Make appropriate choices that promote healthy living.
> - Understand that we as humans are caretakers of our world and play an important role in the preservation of the environment.
> - Be curious and to learn more about their world.
> - Value diversity and exercise tolerance.

The acquisition of life skills should always be collaborative. Children's voices should be heard as you explore with them the 'why' behind, for example, facts of nature and matters of hygiene. If you ask children their opinion, you send out the message that you respect and value what they think and are prepared to listen to them. As we have already discussed in previous chapters, choice of activities and content should be negotiated with children and informed by their specific learning needs and styles. If the children's voices are heard, their learning experiences will be relevant and meaningful for them. Grade R teachers should be familiar with the values embedded in our Constitution (Constitution of the Republic of South Africa Act 108 of 1996).

Find out more

If you are not familiar with this document, you can read about it on the following website:
Constitution of the Republic of South Africa Act 108 of 1996
   http://www.info.gov.za/documents/constitution/1996/a108-96.pdf

You can also find out more about values in education through the following link:
Manifesto on Values, Education and Democracy – Department of Education
   http://www.dhet.gov.za/LinkClick.aspx?fileticket=2vv9jRcRMOQ%3D

Something to consider

What are the aims of the Constitution?
The *Manifesto on Values, Education and Democracy* (Department of Education, 2001) identifies 10 fundamental values of the Constitution. Write them down and use them to answer the following questions:
- What does the Constitution expect of citizens in a democratic South Africa?
- Why is the promotion of values important?
- What does the curriculum aim to develop?
- How can the current CAPS document on Life Skills assist you in this?

The role of the teacher in the mediation of life skills

Grade R teachers create an environment that is conducive to learning. They provide the structure and resources, as well as the appropriate questions and activities that will motivate the Grade R children to explore, experiment, discover and learn. Through these opportunities, Grade R children are encouraged to generate their own knowledge. Grade R teachers need to adopt a child-centred rather than a teacher-centred approach. They provide the structure and stimuli that will encourage children to develop skills and acquire knowledge and appropriate values and attitudes. They enable children to discover how much they know, to generate further learning, to explore their potential and to consider their options. Grade R children become more empowered when they develop the necessary skills to solve some of their problems themselves.

The Grade R teacher should allow opportunities for reflection. As a critical agent, the teacher should be acutely aware that action and reflection are inseparable if learning is to occur. An activity alone is not enough and an experience on its own is not enough; reflection is part of a learning activity. The teacher should ensure that, as far as possible, the power relations among children and between the teacher and the children are equally balanced.

From a subject perspective, a teacher should also know what comprises Life Skills in the curriculum and the time allocated to each aspect.

BEGINNING KNOWLEDGE

The content and concepts of *Beginning Knowledge* have been drawn from *Life Orientation, Social Sciences (History and Geography), Natural Sciences* and *Technology*. The content has been organised into topics that focus mainly on the following:
- The child and his/her relationship with immediate family, extending to the wider community
- The natural environment (flora, fauna, natural resources, etc)
- South Africa (diverse people – cultures, customs, national symbols)
- Environmental awareness events (Water Week, Arbour Day, Youth Day, etc)
- Special celebrations (days) observed in South Africa by diverse cultural groups and the history behind them.

The central focus is on the development of self-in-society. Grade R children should be enabled to make decisions regarding personal, community and environmental health. They should be able to demonstrate an understanding of constitutional rights and responsibilities at an appropriate level, and to show an understanding of diverse cultures and religions.

Beginning Knowledge encourages Grade R children to explore and develop the knowledge, skills and values necessary for successful living and learning, and appreciation for and protection of the environment.

Social sciences concepts

The concepts, skills and processes of history and geography form key elements of the social sciences. Social sciences encourage children to ask and find answers to questions about society and the environment in which they live. Social sciences concepts include conservation, cause and effect, adaptation, relationships, and interdependence and change.

History

Through history, children begin to understand where they come from and the cause and effect of events in South Africa's past. A background in history is developed by the children as they become aware of events in their own lives and begin to recall past experiences. Through history, children become aware of different perspectives on the same event or issue which is crucial to the development of critical thought. Children are introduced to historical inquiry and interpretation by being told stories about the past and asked to draw their interpretation of what happened.

Try this out

Plan suitable activities that you can facilitate in Grade R to make children aware of their social and cultural contexts. Children can do the following:
- Discuss the varying understandings of the concept 'family' in the South African context.
- Count the number of their relatives.
- Draw the family tree and do research to find out about grandparents, great grandparents, etc.
- Relate a story about their family history.
- Discuss how they can show appreciation for the care given to them.
- Talk about their siblings.
- Discuss each person's responsibilities within the family.
- Make a mobile of their family members.
- Draw a picture of a gathering where the whole family is present.
- Identify members of different cultural groups and enquire about the histories of each group.
- Cut out pictures of the different culture groups.
- Be given pictures of different South African contexts and asked to tell a story about that picture.

Something to consider

How will you plan a storytelling activity where children bring objects they value and explain why they value them and the place they play in their life?

Geography

In Grade R children learn about basic concepts and experiences relevant to their local environment. Grade R children should be encouraged to observe and discuss the local population and features of the landscape in which they live, for example water supply, the weather, the seasons and transport networks. They acquire knowledge about rivers, mountains, dams, bridges and buildings, etc, from a variety of different strategies, including theme discussions, creative art and, if appropriate, excursions. Grade R children learn about the weather, temperature, wind and rain through the use of a weather chart, thermometer, rain gauge, wind-sleeve and weathervane.

Our environment is constantly under threat for a variety of reasons, for example pollution from industry. Pollution and destruction of natural resources such as trees lead to the damaging of plant and animal life. Educate children from an early age about respect for the natural environment. Stress, for example, what can happen if littering occurs. Children should grow in the awareness that everyone has a role to play in the conservation of water and the environment.

When children are young their 'world' is restricted to the home, the family, the school and the neighbourhood. As they get older, their horizons widen to include more distant environments like the suburb, the city, the nation and the world. These aspects form the core of geographical inquiry, therefore at Grade R level the focus is on children's personal experiences of the environment. This starts with the self, family and their immediate surroundings such as the home, school, garden and, for example, the park. By investigating their environment, Grade R children learn the following:

- To respect each creature of nature – whether it is an ant or a human being
- To respect the rights and privileges of others in their environment
- That nature belongs to everyone
- To observe the world around them with skill and accuracy
- To become skilful in protecting nature and the environment.

Try this out
Create a story for the Grade R children in your class about a familiar place in the area where they live.

Strategies for developing environmental awareness

Provide opportunities for children to explore and discuss their environment and to identify problems such as excessive refuse in streets (littering) and unsightly dumps. They can discuss personal experiences of familiar places, such as a visit to the park and the people they came across. They can also dramatise problems that arise in the environment, for example cutting down trees and how you could persuade someone that it is not a good thing to do. Stories and creative art are other ways of presenting geographical issues such as the water cycle.

> **Try this out**
>
> Children can collapse discarded cans and cartons, limit the use of paper goods and even control their use of non-destructible plastics. If there is a recycling centre or depot in the community, take the children to visit it. Although the Grade R children may not understand the scientific processes of recycling, they will realise that waste has to be constructively managed. You could even begin a recycling project at school.

Natural sciences

Natural science concepts include life and living, energy and change, matter and materials, and planet earth and beyond. As a Grade R teacher, seek to make connections between the natural world and the manmade world, and between the natural world and the individual. Grade R children and teachers need to be reminded where things come from. The food on our plates did not originate in a can; the clothes we wear were not spontaneously generated in a shop; the books we read did not just come from the store or even the printer. Our lives are intertwined with the natural world.

> **Something to consider**
>
> Grade R children learn about plants, animals and birds, air, water and wind through observation, exploration and experimentation. Science should build on the child's curiosity.

Science in Grade R

Very often a science programme for young children centres on a table that contains plants, rocks, shells or magnets. This approach to the study of science leads to talking about the objects, handling them, describing them, drawing comparisons, performing simple experiments and making charts. Grade R children are always curious, and when a Grade R teacher has enthusiasm, significant learning can result. However, science is much more than a study of natural and physical occurrences and experiments. It also deals with processes through which predictions are made, tested and applied. It is a way of thinking. Scientific process skills are developed during the process of scientific inquiry, which involves observing, comparing, classifying, measuring, experimenting and communicating (DBE, 2011: 8).

From an early age, children make use of scientific processes in every part of their lives as they engage in problem-solving activities. If Grade R children are constantly told what to do and how to do it, without having the opportunity to investigate and discover, this is rote learning and may not lead to further inquiry. Grade R children who have experiences that allow them to investigate and make discoveries develop the skills they will need for independent thinking. Through independent thinking, they can make use of scientific processes for problem solving. Learning how to find answers is considered more important than the answers themselves.

Exploring science

Science in early childhood education encourages children to explore their environments and reflect on their observations and discoveries. Science is part of an ongoing integrated approach in which Grade R children think and construct basic understandings about the world. The basic scientific processes include predicting (making a hypothesis), collecting data and then drawing a conclusion.

The scientific process

As already stated, the scientific process is a cycle of forming hypotheses, collecting data, confirming or rejecting the hypotheses, making generalisations, and then repeating the cycle. The basic skills used in the scientific process include the following:

- **Observing** – children can be encouraged to look carefully for specific actions or information. For example, children can be encouraged to observe the behaviour of a bird on the ground – does it walk or hop? Observation is certainly not limited to visual input; it should involve all the senses – seeing, hearing, smelling, tasting and feeling (touch).
- **Classifying** – this is a basic process skill used in organising information. In order to classify objects or information, children must be able to compare and contrast the properties of objects or information. Very young children begin to classify by function, colour and shape. Children can classify blocks by shape or size, group the materials that are stored in the art area, and sort buttons, leaves, shells or other collections.
- **Comparing** – this is the process of examining objects and events in terms of similarities and differences. It usually involves quantifying, counting, measuring and closely observing. Comparing is important as children observe, for example, the behaviour of a mouse and a guinea pig, and then determine what is similar and what is different about them.
- **Measuring** – this is a basic process skill necessary for collecting data. Measurement does not refer only to using standardised measures. Children can measure the hamster's food by scoop, cut a piece of string the height of their bean plant, compare the sizes of seeds or rocks, or use a beaker to collect ice cubes and observe the amount of water produced when they melt.
- **Communicating** – this is another basic process skill. Children can be encouraged to share their observations and their data collections through a variety of means. They can talk about their findings, make pictorial records, produce charts and graphs, or 'write' narratives in order to share information, data and conclusions. (Often in a Grade R class, the child will draw the narrative and tell the teacher what the picture represents, and the teacher then writes the words on the picture.) The communication process is important, as

children begin to understand how knowledge is created in the field of science.
- **Experimenting** – this is not a new process for young children. They have been experimenting since they first picked up a rattle or threw a cereal bowl off the highchair tray. In the scientific process, experimenting means controlling one or more variables and manipulating conditions. It also means an act or operation for the purpose of discovering something unknown.
- **Relating, inferring and applying** – young children will use the process skills of relating, inferring and applying only in very informal ways. See the explanations and examples below:
  - *Relating* is the process of drawing abstractions from concrete evidence. For example, children who observe water freezing may not be able to relate their observation to the abstract idea that at specific temperatures liquids becomes solids, but their observations still have value for later learning. Relating is developing solutions to unfamiliar problems through reasoning, observation, and experimentation; asking questions such as 'how fast', 'how slow', 'at what rate'; making a logical guess about why something is happening; understanding the relationship between evidence and explanation; designing and conducting simple investigations; asking inquiry-based questions; designing and conducting a scientific investigation to identify and control the things that change (variables); and manipulating simple machines and explaining how they work.
  - *Inferring* is the ability to work out, through reasoning, cause-and-effect relationships or explanations for phenomena when the processes are not directly observable. Examples of such phenomena would be electricity and magnetism.
  - *Applying* is using information from experiences to invent, create, solve new problems, and determine probabilities. Children can be involved in applying scientific knowledge, not in a formal, analytical sense (Brewer, 2007: 388–390), but by using sources of information to help solve problems, using knowledge to solve problems, applying science and mathematics learning, and formulating additional questions.

The cycle of scientific exploration

The steps in the scientific process are not always linear. As children observe some phenomena, they may decide to compare what they see with the observations of others. Grade R children may decide, for example, to experiment and measure the results of adding more water to a solution. They may communicate their findings to others at this point, or may decide to repeat the experiment but to vary it by adding salt water, and so on. Experimenting will require more observations, which may lead to more comparisons or more measurements, and then to more observations. The cycle is usually recursive, not linear (Brewer, 2007: 390).

Find out more

There are three strategies the teacher can use to explore science with the children. These are the following:
1. Formal (teacher-guided) science activities
2. Informal science activities
3. Incidental science activities.

These could be seen respectively as teacher-guided, child-initiated and spontaneous teachable moments that call for mediation.

We will now consider the above-mentioned strategies.

1. Formal (teacher-guided) science activities
Formal science activities that develop the children's observation skills are planned by the teacher. Through these activities, children learn how to be better observers. Not only must Grade R children be able to see, hear, smell, taste and touch, but they must also observe properties, similarities and differences, and changes. They also learn words to help them describe their observations. As children observe, they find their own ways of classification by grouping and ordering materials.

Try this out
Following is an example of how one can develop children's observation skills.
1. Draw a chart, similar to this one, on the chalkboard:

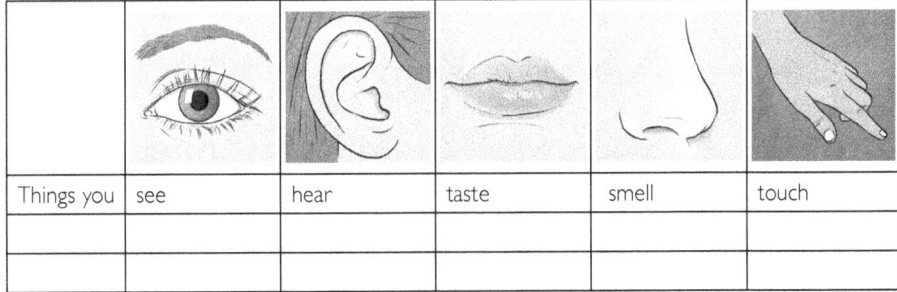

Things you	see	hear	taste	smell	touch

2. Ask a child to choose an item in the room.
3. Let the children describe characteristics under the appropriate headings. If a ball is selected, one child might say: 'I see the ball is red'. Record this observation on the chalkboard; for example, write 'red' under the picture of the eye. Another child might say: 'I touch the ball and it is soft'. Write 'soft' under the picture of the hand, etc.

Children will enjoy seeing their own suggestions written on the board. Do not allow the activity to become a vocabulary lesson. Focus on observing.

The following is one example of a science experiment that would fall into the category of formal science.

Making ice cream

Tell the Grade R children that everything on earth is in liquid, solid or gas form. Today the class is going to focus on liquids and solids. Water, juice and milk are liquids. Liquids are things that cannot hold their shape, such as grape juice. A table, chair and a door are solids. Ask the Grade R children if they can think of their own examples of liquids and solids. Once they have mastered the concepts, ask them if ice cream is a liquid or a solid. The Grade R children might say that ice cream is clearly a solid. Ask the children if something can be both a solid and a liquid. Tell them that today they are going to investigate what happens when the temperature of something changes. Ask the children, 'Do you know what ice cream is made of?' They might say, 'It is made of ice or cream,' or something in between. Tell the children, 'We are going to make ice cream today.'

What you need
- 1 cup milk
- 1 teaspoon sugar
- 1 teaspoon vanilla
- 1 Ziploc bag
- 1 tablespoon salt
- Ice
- Round metal can with a tightly fitting lid (like a coffee can)

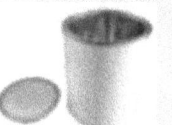

Doing the experiment
Pour the milk (liquid), sugar (solid) and vanilla (liquid) into the Ziploc bag. Make sure the bag is sealed tightly. Next, fill the can halfway with ice and add a tablespoon of salt. Put the bag inside the coffee can and close the lid tightly. Go outside and, with the children, roll the coffee can back and forth for about 15 minutes. Ask the children to predict what might have happened to the milk, sugar and vanilla inside the plastic bag. When you open the tin they can see if their prediction was right. The liquid should have taken on a solid form. Children can then enjoy the ice cream.

Something to consider

Even though baking activities usually form part of creative activities, they can also be seen as the scientific investigations as they provide countless possibilities for scientific discoveries.

> A useful link is the following:
> http://www.youtube.com/watch?v=jLTTb_HFhGs
> CempakaCherasKindergardenBakingClassforMother'sDay.mov

2. Informal science activities

Informal science activities call for little or no teacher involvement. During informal science activities, free investigation by the children takes place.

The following can be used to promote informal scientific learning
- The science learning area/corner
- Plants
- Insects
- The weather.

What is the science learning corner/area? (Refer to Chapter 7)

A science area is a quiet area in the classroom where individuals or small groups of Grade R children can explore materials and make discoveries. The objects in the science area should attract the children's interest. Important points to remember about the science area are the following:
- Never leave objects on the discovery table that could be harmful.
- Children become bored with objects which are left there too long.
- Not all science teaching will take place in the classroom. When the weather is fine, a lot of discoveries can be made outside in the play area. Sometimes you may take the children on nature/discovery walks.

Some considerations in planning a science area are as follows:
- Space (floor, table, display and storage)
- The interests, abilities and needs of the children
- The availability of equipment and materials.

You do not need elaborate equipment. Think rather of everyday items that could be used to develop scientific process skills, for example metric measuring tools such as cups, tapes, rulers, thermometers, magnifying glasses and a scale. You will need boxes in which to store the equipment when it is not being used.

A collection of specimens and natural items is also essential. These could include rocks; minerals; salt; wool; silkworms; cocoons; leaves; seashells; sponges; feathers; insects; corn; seeds; birds' nests; eggs; growing plants; flowers; objects that can float or sink; shapes; things to take apart and put together; objects to smell, taste hear, see, touch; aquarium, terrarium, vivarium; colour paddles; etc.

Discovery aids, some of which have already been mentioned, could include magnifying glasses, magnets, dry-cell batteries, vases, pots and other containers, mirrors, compasses, rubber tubing, stethoscope, etc.

Something to consider

Guidelines for teaching science in Grade R

Encourage each child to observe keenly. Ask questions, for example: 'What do you see?'; 'What is it like?'; 'What do you suppose ...?' A Grade R teacher needs to help children to develop thinking skills by asking them to observe carefully and then ask questions about what they have seen. This could be done in pairs or small groups. Help the children consider different possibilities and explanations.

- Give the Grade R child a variety of experiences relating to, for example, growth (eg seedlings); life (eg insects and reptiles); the elements (eg air, water, sound); energy (eg heat, wind); and the earth and its elements, which include rocks, soil, sand and metals.
- Give each Grade R child opportunities to make discoveries. Provide the necessary equipment and materials that will allow for experimentation and discovery. For example, when you are teaching a theme about plants, you should have a variety of seeds (mealies, beans, peas) and containers with wet cotton wool in your science area.
- Repeat experiences, and relate these to what else the child is doing and learning. For example, after an excursion to the zoo, children could draw pictures of what they have seen, or look at pictures of animals, or try to match, for example, beaks with birds.
- Use a variety of media, such as real specimens, models, pictures, resource persons and trips that allow for direct observation and experimentation. For example, when you are teaching the topic, 'Caring for animals', you could invite people from the SPCA to come to the school; have a dog in your class for one day; display products like dog shampoo, flea powder, tick collar, etc. (Make sure children are aware of safety issues in relation to equipment.)
- Develop in the child a respect for all living things.
- Point out and reinforce safety measures.

3. Incidental science activities

These take place when something happens spontaneously that is of interest to the group. For example, an incidental science session can result from a windstorm when the teacher takes the children outside to see what changes have taken place because of it. Incidental science activities are usually unplanned and often unexpected. Think of some other spontaneous events that have occurred and could have prompted scientific exploration.

Try this out

Example 1	
Floating and sinking	
Purpose	To explain why certain objects float and others sink when put into water.
Materials needed	A collection of suitable objects which can be put into water, for example: corks, wooden sticks, plastic tubing, coins, metal bar or ruler, pebbles, matches, plastic pieces, fabric pieces, etc.
Activity	Let children predict from a collection of objects which are those most likely to float, and give reasons for their thinking. They then test their predictions by putting all the objects one after the other into a container of water. You can give the children the scientific explanation that the water appears to be 'holding up' the floating items, and is in fact exerting pressure or force on them. If the density of the object exceeds the density of water, then the up thrust is not sufficient to hold the object. (Children are unlikely at this age to understand the concept of density. This is knowledge the teacher should have, however, and could plant an idea for further inquiry.)

Plants (natural sciences)

Children are fascinated by anything that grows. Observation skills are sharpened as children look at the variety of plants around them.

Plants in the classroom

- Plants could be grown in bottle gardens.
- Flowers could be planted in a window box.
- Plants can grow in soil, sand, cotton wool and blotting paper.
- Each child could have his/her own container to compare the growth rate of his/her plants.
- Children can watch and record the effect of light, heat, air and water on plants.

Example 2	
Seed growing	
Purpose	To show that plants can only grow under certain conditions.
Materials needed	Seeds, small flowerpots, seed compost, small watering can or jug, coffee tin or any other large tin.
Activity	Help the children predict what they think a plant needs to grow. Then help them test some of these ideas by growing grass, beans or any other seeds under the following conditions: **Pot 1** – soil, no water, light. Plant the seed. Do not water. Place in light. **Pot 2** – soil, water, no light. Plant the seed. Water regularly but keep covered, away from sunlight. **Pot 3** – no soil, water, light. Put seed in empty pot. Water regularly and place in the light. **Pot 4** – soil, water, light. Plant the seed. Water regularly and place in the light.

Pot 2 can be placed in the dark by putting a coffee tin over it to enclose it. Depending on the kind of seed and other environmental conditions, the seeds may all germinate, but the growth should be most vigorous where all the experimental needs are met – that is, pot 4. Grade R children can measure the growth of the different seedlings with a strip of paper or a simple ruler. The results of the experiment can be recorded on a record sheet.

This activity is best carried out in a season where there is rain and it is not too cold. In some areas, during cold dry months the dry indoor air does not allow for good growth.

Outdoor science laboratory

A school garden can provide many learning opportunities. The school garden is your outdoor science laboratory.

What you need
- **Tools** – small hand trowels, small hand forks, hose or watering cans should be provided.
- **Seeds** – a variety is needed. Bean seeds are good to use since they are hardy. They sprout quickly, usually in one day. Grass and sunflower seeds also grow quickly. Pineapple and carrot tops, sweet potatoes and avocado pips root easily. Choose crops that are grown in the local area.
- **The space** – a large area of ground is not necessary for these activities. Even schools in town may be able to find enough space. If they cannot, large baskets or pots can be used. Plants can also be planted indoors in containers.
- Fertiliser.

Suitable activities for Grade R

There are many occasions when you may want children to use the garden for observation. The activities below are just one suggestion. You could modify these according to your own interest, experience and enthusiasm for gardening. In order for children to be creative gardeners, they should be given some choices:
- Where is the best place to plant seeds?
- What seeds should be planted?
- How much water do they need?
- When is the best time of the year to plant seeds?
- How much plant food or fertiliser is needed?

Children could plant locally available seeds and observe their germination and development:
- Do the plants grow at the same rate?
- Are there any small creatures on or around their plants?
- Are any of these creatures eating the leaves of these plants?
- Do any plants have curled leaves?

- Do any plants die?
- Are any two plants exactly the same?

Remember, you can also develop the children's skills in counting. For example:
- Do all these seeds germinate?
- How many germinate?
- How many leaves do the plants have?
- How many seeds did the class plant?
- How many had germinated after a week? After two weeks?
- Point out that one seed produces no more than one plant.

The children should be able to record some of their observations. They can make drawings to show what has happened. They can measure and record the height of plants using strips of paper. Children could plant two different seeds and observe their different development. For example, they could plant a maize seed and a bean seed. Children should be allowed to dig up plants to see what is happening as growth takes place. Observe, discuss and record.

They can compare the growth of their plants with the growth of other children's plants. Is there a difference? Discuss observations. Children can plant vegetables and later make a salad with them.

Try this out
Gardening activities
Discuss with your principal and fellow teachers what local seeds you would choose.

Discuss some of the problems involved in setting up and maintaining a school garden. Some of these problems might be that there is insufficient space for a garden plot or that children or other teaching staff might not be motivated by the idea. There may be seasonal variations so consider when is the best time during the school year for gardening activities, For example, is there a wet season/dry season cycle? Who will look after the plants during weekends and holidays?

Insects and other small animals (natural sciences) can be found in most school grounds. They can also be very useful in teaching science.

Look around the school to discover the best places to find these animals and/or insects.

Where to find small animals/insects
1. In flowering shrubs, bushes and hedges
2. Under big stones, logs and piles of fallen leaves, etc.

Which type of small animals/insects?

Think of flying insects. This group includes butterflies, beetles, most grasshoppers, dragonflies, and many others.

Find a jar. The jar must be as big as possible and quite dry for water will damage the insect's wings. Cover the jar with paper in which small holes have been pierced so that the insect can breathe.

Consider other insects/creatures

If the creature comes from the earth, for example a worm or an ant, a terrarium could be built. A terrarium is a glass-enclosed tank without water. Usually, dirt or sand is placed on the bottom, and plants which the insect likes are added. A terrarium can be made to look like the desert when sand, cactus plants and desert lizards are used. This kind of terrarium is placed in a warm part of the classroom where it gets plenty of sun. A terrarium can also be made to look like a forest or a grassy area. Insects, frogs, small snakes and small lizards can be kept for a while in a terrarium so the children can watch their movements and how they feed. Be careful to ensure that the choice of creature is suitable for young children.

What must be investigated?

Encourage children to discuss questions about the insects and small animals, and to find the answers themselves. What do small animals/insects eat?

The teaching of natural sciences is one of the most enjoyable learning activities in the Grade R class. The children enjoy it because they are actively involved at all times – bringing objects and things for the nature/interest table, doing experiments, etc. If you are positive and open minded, the children will most likely develop an interest in natural sciences.

Find out more

Interest and/or nature table – this table could be formal if used for a theme discussion or science ring, or informal if children initiate exploration. It is a low table on which you can display various items and pictures for the children to observe. If it is a nature table, try to ensure that real things are used, for example a mole cricket in a bottle, or a praying mantis. If you use real things, make sure they are cared for and released into their normal habitat after a few days. This table is an important learning resource, so it should be inviting and encourage participation.

Let us look at the following example of a nature table:
- **Topic:** Autumn
- **Items:** Pods, seeds, leaves, dried grasses collected from your immediate environment
- **Pictures:** Trees with leaves changing colour; children in warm clothing; a windy day; seeds, pods and appropriate food as such as pumpkins

- **Poster:** A theme poster with appropriate words and pictures that provide a visual image for the child.

Value of the nature/interest table

It promotes 'reading', observation, classification and sorting. It should enable children to touch, look at closely, smell and listen to some of the things in our natural environment. It encourages an interest in and respect for the natural world around us. It enriches the children's experience of simple science – that is, of the weather, seasons, plants, growing, measurement, amount, etc. It stimulates and satisfies the children's natural curiosity.

To use the table effectively, the following should apply:
- Allow children to touch, smell, listen to, examine and ask questions about the objects on display.
- Use informal discussions with small groups at the table during the week to promote concept acquisition.
- Be ready to answer and explain any child's questions about the display during the course of the day or week.
- Start with two or three objects, and add something new each day.
- Encourage and accept children's contribution to the table.
- When a child brings a picture or object, add it to the display.
- Extend the topic into the activities of the day – that is, into art, language, physical education (movement), etc.

Technology

Technology has existed throughout history as an activity in which people use a combination of knowledge, skills and available resources to develop solutions to meet their daily needs and wants. The designing process is a series of steps, and should lead from a specific problem to a corresponding solution.

Technology is practical by nature. Children should be actively involved in creative problem solving in this area. Technological process skills include investigation, design, making, evaluating and communicating. This should be borne in mind when planning any activity. Activities could include, for example, building a bridge in the playground using a variety of materials such as balancing beams and wooden boxes; making a home out of old cereal boxes that can protect animals against fierce winds; or making a sunhat. Children would have to investigate a possible design and which materials to choose before making their hat. They would then evaluate its effectiveness, and try to explain why the end product meets the set criteria.

Try this out
Some examples for suitable technology activities

There are numerous visual images of activities available on the Internet. The following website will allow you to access more information:

http://www.kidshealth.org

Search for articles, pictures and video material demonstrating how resources are used and implemented to support a variety of technological process skills. Other websites that might be useful are the following:

http://www.techandyoungchildren.org/children.html
http://www.project2061.org/publications/earlychild/online/.../clements.htm
http://www.educationworld.com/a_tech/archives/tools.shtml
https://www.naeyc.org/yc/files/yc/file/201205/McManis_YC0512.pdf

Find out more

Another important technological process skill that should be introduced to young children for later success in the digital world is coding. Coding (or programming) is a basic language of the digital age – a necessary skill for the 21st century. Coding involves the process of creating step-by-step instructions that a computer needs to follow for its programmes to work. Coding-based systems are everywhere in society and are a part of many children's everyday experiences. Today computers, cell phones and tablets depend on coding to function properly. Cars, robotic devices, washing machines, vacuum cleaners and many other household appliances are also dependent on coding for successful performance (McLennan, 2005; Lee, 2019).

Something to consider

Many early learning skills and concepts that children need to acquire are a foundational part of coding. These skills and concepts have already been referred to in this book. They include many of the perceptual-motor skills and concepts such as spatial understanding and directional language (up, down, backwards, forwards, left, right) as well as number sense, especially understanding the meaning of ordinal numbers (first, second, etc) and one-to-one correspondence (McLennan, 2005). The relevant skills and concepts are developed and reinforced through quality play-based early learning programmes. Young children are already, possibly without teachers or parents even realising it, engaging in many activities related to coding. This is partly because coding is like a game.

»

Precoding skills and concepts can all be practised without a computer and developed during free play (board games that necessitate moving a gaming piece a specific number of spaces across a grid – think of Snakes and Ladders) as well as through teacher-guided activities (movement and music rings; story time, etc). These activities and games provide developmentally appropriate entry points into coding activities. They enable children to explore some of the concepts involved in coding in ways that are meaningful for them.

Because coding involves giving very precise directions to the computer, children need to show competence in various areas such as mathematics, problem solving, communication and literacy and, of course, active listening. Developing and strengthening these competencies improves children's coding abilities, and by offering them opportunities to engage in coding games the competencies are refined. Creating pegboard patterns according to specific instructions could be a fun coding activity.

Coding stories also provide the opportunity to build basic coding competence. In a coding game or story, as one child gives the commands, the other(s) have to listen carefully in order to move themselves or particular items like pegs in the correct direction.

Coding games often tell a story – there is a path the 'programmer' needs to take to move an object or character through different obstacles and settings, eventually arriving at a destination. A story of a child going on a school trip, for instance, would involve a particular sequence of actions. One child – the 'programmer' – would guide the participant(s) in the game through a fixed sequence of set actions that lead to the destination, for example five steps to the left, one step backwards, etc. For the purposes of a coding game at Grade R level, only the movements of the main character should be tracked. Ensure children know and understand the story line and the pathway they are going to code before you start the game. The programmer (the child who gives the instructions) needs to know the sequence of the storyline and how to give precise instructions to enable the gamer (the child who will be moving the gaming piece along the grid) to successfully follow the route, pass each obstacle along the way and reach the end point.

Try this out
Plan a story coding game

Create a grid of squares using masking tape or chalk on the floor or on a tabletop. Make suitable props for the characters and the obstacles they have to negotiate. Choose the story and read it to the children. Make sure it involves a sequence of movements.

The school has planned a trip to the zoo. Sipho, a Grade R child, will get on the bus, travel two kms and disembark at the zoo gate. He will walk around the zoo, moving from the lions to the elephants, and finally to the zebras. To make his way between the animal enclosures, he has to negotiate various obstacles such as a large tree, a fountain, a fallen signpost and a large ice cream cart. This story could be adapted as you wish.

»

How children play

Set up the grid. The teacher or children place the character at the starting point on the grid and put the settings or obstacles on the grid in the order they occur.

Draw up the instructions. As a group, the children determine the instructions for moving the character along the grid. Directional arrows (which can point up, down, left or right when placed on the grid) are visual symbols to represent the instructions. Children can easily make these arrows from cardboard or sticky notes.

Choose a programmer and a gamer. The programmer – or programmers – gives the coding instructions. The gamer is the child – or children – who follows the coding instructions and moves the figure on the grid.

Code the story! The programmer is now responsible for giving instructions – 'Go up 1', 'Go forward 2', 'Go down 3', – to the gamer so that the gamer can move the character along the grid, from start to finish. (The first few times a group codes, an adult might model the roles for the children.) After a new instruction is followed, the programmer places an arrow in each square the character has travelled through, representing the direction of the move on the grid. Code all the moves until the end point is reached (McLelland, 2005).

Encourage and support children so they can complete the entire journey, giving and following correct directions without skipping squares on the grid. Ensure that the directional arrows are left in place during the game to represent the path the character has taken. When the character arrives at the final destination, the journey is complete! Other children can change the story and have a turn.

Children's imaginative stories or favourite retellings can be used as the base for coding games. They can also be encouraged to make up their own 'coding stories' or to change the ending of a favourite story. Some story suggestions include *Goldilocks*, *The three little pigs* and *Not so fast Songololo*.

PERSONAL AND SOCIAL WELL-BEING

Personal and social well-being as a study area is important for young children because they are still learning how to look after themselves and keep themselves healthy (DBE, 2011: 9). This area includes social health, emotional health and relationships with other people and the environment, including values and attitudes. It addresses issues relating to nutrition, disease (including HIV/AIDS), safety, violence, abuse and environmental health.

The notion of health promotion runs throughout the daily programme as teachable moments naturally present themselves during, for example, routines (toilet time, snack time, etc), free play (reinforcing safety issues on the jungle gym) and teacher-guided activities such as a theme discussion on home safety, movement or creative art activities (see Chapter 7).

The content for health promotion will focus on topics such as the following:
- People who help us (clinics, hospitals, ambulance, etc)
- Health-awareness events (Dental, Eye, Organ Week, etc)

- Personal hygiene and cleanliness (eg how to care for our bodies)
- Healthy eating and nutrition
- Posture and fitness, including regular exercise and rest
- Communicable diseases including HIV/AIDS
- Safety in the home and school, and road safety.

Health and wellness: promotion of health

Health education focuses on the promotion of health and the prevention of disease. Through health promotion we encourage health-promoting behaviour and good health habits. We also consider safety in relation to possible risks and injuries. Children's level of wellness is directly influenced by the nature and quality of their living and learning environment.

Personal hygiene/cleanliness

Maintaining standards of personal hygiene is an important life skill. Help Grade R children to understand why cleanliness is important and how to care for their bodies and clothes. Topics such as dental care; hair and nail care; and washing/bathing/showering and toilet routines can be taught both incidentally and through teacher-guided activities.

Environmental hygiene and safety

The school environment should mirror cleanliness. This includes the school toilets and bathrooms, the waste bins, the storerooms and the kitchen/cooking area. Classrooms should be airy and well ventilated, and heaters, if used, should be safely placed.

> **Something to consider**
>
> The advantages and desirability of cleanliness, neatness and healthy habits should be stressed throughout the daily programme.

Healthy eating, nutrition and fitness

A teacher should help Grade R children understand what comprises a healthy diet and how nutritious foods are important in development. Children should have a balanced diet, which means they need a varied diet that includes the following nutrients:
- Protein
- Carbohydrates (starch and sugar)
- Fats and oils
- Minerals
- Vitamins – both fat and water-soluble vitamins.

Remember: Children should also drink sufficient water every day.

Find out more
Consult the following website for some ideas on nutrition for children:
   http://www.eatright.org/kids/article.aspx?id=6442470564

In South Africa today, childhood obesity (ie overweight children) is on the increase. Two importance reasons for this are incorrect diet (eating too much starchy, sugary food) and lack of sufficient exercise. Many children spend too much time watching TV, or playing video and computer games. Children are naturally energetic and enjoy exercise. A teacher can build on this to explain the importance of fitness and suggest ways in which this can be achieved. Encourage children to play outside. They can be encouraged to take part in many different activities, from kicking a ball, playing soccer, riding a tricycle or bicycle, swimming, running, playing catch games and even dancing. Where appropriate and safe, children should be allowed to walk to school.

Find out more
Do an internet search using the following key words to find new fun activities for the development of the above concepts: 'good exercise'; 'examples of lessons/activities that can be used in Grade R'; 'making healthy food choices'; 'the five food groups'; 'get active and eat healthily'; and 'feeding young children'.
   http://www.abbott.com/static/cms.../content/.../gc_infantNutrition_policy3
   http://www.ayso104.org/parents/nutrition.html
   http://www.eatright.org/kids/article.aspx?id=6442470564

Personal safety tips for young children
Children can play a role in ensuring their own safety. Help them to learn their full name and address including city and, if appropriate, phone number with area code and/or their parents'/caregivers' cell phone number. Using a play phone, teach children when and how to dial 10111. Explain to them that they should never accept gifts or rides from people they do not know, or do not know very well, without parental permission. They should also not keep secrets from their parents about gifts they might receive.

School safety for young children
Children spend more time at school than anywhere else other than their own home. To ensure that children have a positive school experience, refer to chapters 6 and 7 on the child-friendly school.

Partner with parents/caregivers to make sure children know how to get to and from school and where safe houses are if they get into difficulty. Teach Grade R children to follow traffic signals and rules of the road when walking or cycling.

Encourage Grade R children to walk to school or to the bus stop or taxi rank with a sibling or friend, and to wait there when necessary with other children.

Using the bus or taxi
- Children should try to arrive at the pickup point at least five minutes before the vehicle is due to depart.
- Teach Grade R children to make sure they can see the driver, and the driver can see them before they cross in front of the vehicle. Tell them to never walk behind the vehicle in question.

Road safety for young children
Remember as a teacher that you are their role model. Set a good example to try to ensure that your Grade R children remain safe, and develop road and traffic awareness. Teach them the meanings of common road signs, how to walk safely on a pavement and how to cross a road. Consider the following:
- What are safe places to cross – for example a pedestrian or zebra crossing, or using, where possible, a light-controlled crossing or a school scholar patrol
- What are unsafe places to cross – for example where they cannot see far along the road or trying to cross a road between parked cars
- How to cross – for example stopping and looking both ways; listening for traffic before crossing; waiting on the pavement until all the traffic coming from both directions has stopped; crossing only when it is safe to cross, then walking straight across the road, and constantly looking and listening out for traffic.

THE CREATIVE ARTS
The Creative Arts consist of four art forms: dance, drama, music and the visual arts. According to CAPS (2011), children in Grade R should be exposed to creative arts that are organised in two parallel and complementary streams – visual arts and performing arts (dance, drama and music).

Early childhood creative art should do the following:
- Allow children to be expressive.
- Subtly balance artistic process and product.
- Be open-ended, allowing children to be creative.
- Allow for discovery and experimentation.
- Allow for active engagement and sustained involvement.
- Be intrinsically motivating.
- Be available to all children.
- Be developmentally and contextually appropriate.

The main aims of creative arts education
The creative arts play an important role in developing children as creative, imaginative individuals with an appreciation of the arts. In addition, basic

knowledge and skills to be able to participate in creative activities are developed by children. According to CAPS (2011), the focus of learning should be on the development of skills through enjoyable, experiential processes. It is the experience not the end product that is important.

The creative arts should aim to promote all areas of the child's development (see Chapter 2). Development in one area will influence development in others. The development of the whole child as an active, social, emotional, intellectual and creative person must be taken into consideration.

Through the creative arts, children have opportunities to refine a number of important skills and concepts that should be in place to enable success in formal schooling, including the skills and concepts that promote emergent literacy and numeracy. These include refinement of gross and fine motor skills, and of many of the perceptual-motor skills including sensory and auditory awareness behaviours (see Chapter 4). The creative arts should thus be promoted in the Grade R classroom. They should not be marginalised and replaced by formal mathematic and literacy teaching. This is a disturbing trend that seems to be creeping into many Grade R classrooms.

Where feasible, these art forms can be **integrated** with literacy, mathematics and other components of Life Skills, for example:
- Physical education and music can include dance.
- Drama and music can include various forms of languages (speech, oral skills, storytelling, role play, voice projection through singing).
- Creative arts, music and dance can include mathematics (eg shape, pattern, time, counting, distance, size, direction, etc).

Some further examples of possible integration could be the following:
Home Language
Drama – speech, sensory perception, oral skills, storytelling, characterisation
Visual arts – visual and spatial perception, patterning, fine motor coordination, shape, colour, contrast, form, texture
Music – listening, voice, aural perception
Dance – vocabulary, spatial orientation behaviours, gross motor and other of important forms coordination, etc

Mathematics
Visual arts – shape, form, pattern
Music – symbols, values, rhythm, time, duration
Dance – shape, counting, numbers, quantities, distance, size, levels, direction

Life Skills
Dance – gross motor coordination, physical control, balance, stamina, strength, imagination, spatial perception, kinaesthetic perception
Drama – fantasy, imagination, role play, concentration, focus, interpersonal and intrapersonal skills

Culture – religion, ceremonies, identity, familiar domestic routines and other cultural practices

Music – gross and fine motor coordination, imagination, rhythm, music skills, aural perception

Visual arts – visual–spatial perception, craft skills, fine motor coordination, expression, imagination

---

Try this out
Integrating visual arts and music
Listen to music and then ask children to draw a picture that illustrates how the music makes them feel. With this activity, Grade R children can, through their natural interest in art and drawing, express how different kinds of music make them feel. This activity could also link with a theme on 'Feelings' or 'Who am I?'

What you need
Drawing paper
Crayons
A mixture of recorded music without lyrics (this can be classical, jazz, New Age, etc)

How to do it
Give drawing paper and crayons to the children. Invite them to listen to different types of music. Let them draw a picture that will illustrate how they feel when listening to a variety of music. Allow the music to guide them in their drawings. Let them share their interpretations.

The implications of multiple intelligences for creative arts education in Grade R

The theory of multiple intelligences recognises that children may be talented in specific areas. Multiple intelligences provide a significant way to identify and work with children's strengths. Visual intelligence involves thinking in pictures – spatial relationships. Intrapersonal intelligences give Grade R children the opportunity to work together on group projects and talk to others about their artwork. We know that children learn in different ways. Some may learn best through art, but for others this may be a new way to construct their understanding of the world.

We will now briefly explore the different components of the creative arts.

The visual arts

Though the visual arts, children are provided opportunities to freely create and explore images of their own world through a wide range of media. Children should be given different visual art experiences that include both paper and pencil representations (2D), such as drawing and painting, as well as 3D work, such as moulding and constructions. Other visual art experiences could include rubbings, printing, cutting and pasting, threading and weaving, as well as collage. Traditionally, baking has been seen as a creative activity, but depending on the process followed, it could also be seen as a technology or science activity.

Following is an example of a baking activity where children can observe how combining different ingredients can become something different. If posed differently, this could be integrated with other subject areas such as Mathematics where the measuring of ingredients is emphasised. In a science activity, jelly can be used to identify solids and liquids and explore how things dissolve. To include a technological emphasis, children could think of other ways to make worm-shaped jelly, for example using containers from the school's anti-waste collection such as thin plastic tubing or narrow cylindrical cannisters.

Try this out

Jelly worms

Ingredients

- Straws
- Packet of jelly
- Water
- Bowl
- Cup
- Rubber band

Method

Pack straws into a cup and secure with a rubber band.
Mix the jelly, following the instructions on the box.
Pour the jelly carefully into the straws.
Put them in the refrigerator.
Once jelly is set, rinse with warm water to release the 'worms' from their straws.

Homemade edible play dough

Ingredients

- 1¼ cups icing sugar
- 1¼ cups powdered milk
- 1 cup corn syrup
- 1 cup peanut butter

Method

Mix all the ingredients together until dough reaches proper consistency for moulding. After moulding, the Grade R learners can eat their artwork or store it for show and tell.

The elements of art

Children should be informally introduced to the elements of art. These include line, form/shape, colour, texture and space.

1. Line

Line can be described as a mark made by a sharpened object. A line is a form that has length and width, but the width is so negligible compared to the length that the impression is created that line is composed of length only. A drawing is made up of lines irrespective of the medium that has been used. It is possible to use line in many different ways. A shape is made up of lines. Line is an element of art that is used to define shapes, contours and outlines as well as to suggest mass and volume.

Some characteristics of line:
- Width – thick, thin, uneven
- Length – long, short, continuous, broken
- Direction – horizontal, vertical, diagonal, curved, parallel, zigzag, etc.

Physical and psychological effects of line

The direction of the line is the strongest of the aspects because it leads the eye and creates focus.

a. Vertical lines are awake, alert, rigid, firm, stable, strong, and defy gravity.
b. Horizontal lines are restful, yield to gravity, and create quiet, repose, passivity, calmness or serenity.
c. Diagonal lines appear undecided, unstable, busy, active, dynamic, restless, dramatic, sporty, lengthening, and reduce horizontal or vertical shapes.
d. A horizontal line combined with a vertical line creates stillness, for example the framework of a building, telephone poles, branches of a tree.

One way to consider line could be as follows:

Horizontal line	Vertical line	Diagonal line	Curved line	Parallel lines
Psychological aspects – rest, peace, calmness	Psychological aspects – strength, power, manliness, discipline	Psychological aspects – movement, speed, unrest, disaster	Psychological aspects – femininity, rhythm, harmony, love, life	Psychological aspects – the over-emphasised feeling of, for example, strength or fear

2. Form/shape

Shape refers to the outside form of an object. It is the edge of an enclosed space. As we have said, it is defined by a line or an outline. It can also be defined by contrasting colour or texture in the surrounding area. Lines can be connected in many different ways to shapes that can be simple or complex as well as circular or angular. A shape can be geometric such as a circle, square, rectangle and triangle, or non-geometric such as an irregular or freeform shape.

Some examples:

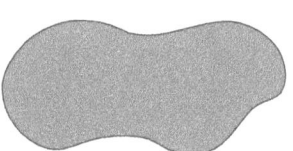

Children can explore shapes in their artwork.

Drawing 1 is an example of a 2D shape that has length and width but no depth, and drawing 2 is 3D with length, width and depth.

3. Colour

We see colour because of the way objects reflect colour rays to our eyes. Colour makes people respond with feeling. We all have favourite colours, and children develop these preferences early in life.

Find out more

http://www.colormatters.com/color-and-vision/how-the-eye-sees-color

---

In Grade R, colours are usually only categorised as follows:
- Primary – red, blue and yellow
- Secondary – mixing two primary colours in equal amounts to get a secondary one (green, orange, violet)

> **Something to consider**
> While mixing colours, always start with the lightest colour and add small amounts of the darker colour until you are happy with the result.

4. Texture

Texture refers to the surface quality of objects or, in other words, how they feel when we touch them. There are two categories of artistic texture: tactile and visual. The tactile sense involves feeling and touch. Layers of paint, dried finger paint and a fabric collage all have texture or a certain feel to them. Encourage Grade R children to work with actual textures and talk about how the object feels when they touch it, for example rough, smooth, etc. Both indoor and outdoor environments are texturally rich.

Encourage Grade R children to go outside with a piece of white paper and a crayon, and explore different surfaces. To do this, place the paper over, for example, the bark of a tree, cement, wood, etc, and rub the side of a crayon over the top of the paper. An impression will appear. Children can also use their visual sense to look at the materials and note similarities and differences between them. Encourage Grade R children to make a texture collage. Let then use language to describe the different textures they include in their collage. Teachers can use open-ended questions to encourage children's exploration: 'How does it feel?'; 'How do you know if the texture is hard or soft?'; 'What words could you use to say if it is rough or smooth?'; etc.

5. Space

Space is determined by the size of the material that is going to be used, for example paper, cardboard, wood, etc. Encourage Grade R children to plan their artwork to fill up the available space. Help them arrange the different elements in the space by asking questions such as: 'How many shapes or symbols will be used?'; 'Where will they be placed?'; 'How much space will be left?'

> **Try this out**
> Design an art activity that explores at least two of the elements that we have described.

Art, children and culture

Families play an important role in Grade R children's creative experiences. In a family where parents, caregivers and other family members value art, children will be motivated to explore their creativity and experiment with new activities. Hopefully their efforts will be complimented and encouraged. We all have the potential to be creative, and teachers should support all children in their exploration of their creativity.

Remember too that culture might influence children's creative experiences. In some cultures, colour plays an important role, as do patterns for decoration, as can be seen in the examples of Ndebele cultural patterns.

Different cultures value different kinds of art. The Grade R teacher should share, where appropriate, different cultural art forms with the children and ask them to bring examples of art forms specific to their culture. Vary activities offered to accommodate all the different cultures in the Grade R class. Creative expression and the arts are influenced by the social contexts in which they occur. The culture not only defines but also determines what 'counts' as creativity and art.

Talking about art

Grade R children enjoy talking about art but are often not given the opportunity because there is too much emphasis on the steps they should follow in order to complete the art activity. Encourage children to talk about their art, read picture books about art, and learn art vocabulary, for example the elements of art. As a teacher you should try to use the correct terminology while doing visual art to expand the children's vocabulary. Building a vocabulary of art is important because it enables Grade R children to participate in the world of art both in and out of the Grade R classroom and throughout their lives.

> **Something to consider**
>
> **Talking to children about their art**
> Encourage children to look closely at an object that they want to reproduce in an art form. Perhaps suggest that they identify simple familiar shapes in the object that could provide a starting point, but be careful not to prescribe how their representation should look.
>
> What follows are common comments made by teachers about children's art. Think about how these remarks could affect children's attitudes to their participation in the visual arts.
> - **Complimentary** – teachers tell children that their art is nice, pretty, lovely, super or beautiful.
> - **Judgemental** – teachers tell children that their art is good or great, or that they could do better.
>
> »

- **Valuing** – teachers tell children that they like or even love their art.
- **Questioning** – a teacher directly and bluntly asks children: 'What is it?' or 'What is that supposed to be?'
- **Probing** – the teacher attempts to draw from children some hint, title or verbal statement about their art.
- **Correcting** – teachers attempt to provide children with specific feedback that will enable them to improve their art or make it 'better' by more closely approximating reality.

The probing type of question is probably the best one to use. You could say to a child, for example, 'Tell me about your picture'. It is important to encourage all children to participate in visual art activities and to counter any 'I can't' or 'I don't want to'. Visual art is an area in which every child has something to offer.

Development stages of visual art and accommodating children's diversity

Children go through various stages in their development of art. We need to appreciate the importance of each one, and acknowledge children's efforts during each and every stage. Even though we might not necessarily be able to recognise what a child has created, we should ask children to explain their creations to us. This will help us to understand the messages children wish to communicate. We can always write the child's explanation on the picture so that the meaning is clear to all.

Following is a summary of some different opinions on the different stages of art development in children and the significance of each one. These stages can be related to aspects of child development as well as emergent literacy and numeracy (see chapters 2, 11, 12 and 13).

KELLOGG'S DEVELOPMENTAL STAGES (1967)	
Stage 1: Scribbles Ages 2–3 – all children, regardless of their culture, make the same markings in the same way at approximately the same age. Ages 2–4 – scribbles take shape and look like circles, ovals, squares, triangles and crosses.	Earliest drawings – enjoying the process of making scribbles on paper 

»

Stage 2: Lines and shapes Ages 3–5 – children begin to make designs from the shapes they have been drawing.	Drawing simple shapes – the beginning of writing 
Stage 3: Semi-representational Ages 4–5 – designs take on the form of people or things. Ages 5–6 – children are at the pictorial stage.	Symbolic representations of real people or things 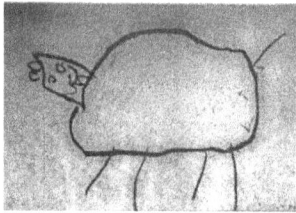

Another model is that of Lowenfeld and Brittain (1987, which is described by Brewer (2007). This model outlines the artistic development of children from the age of one-and-a-half to seven years.

The scribbling stage of child art development
This stage is mostly about the enjoyment of purely making marks.

Whole-hand grip on the marking tool.
The scribbling stage of child art development starts between the ages of 1½ and 4.

Disordered scribbling consists of random marks, varying in style and intensity.

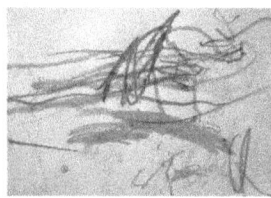  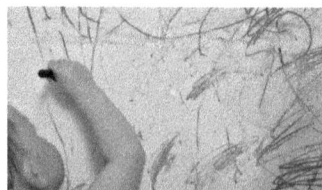

Longitudinal scribbling is a little more controlled, characterised by somewhat parallel marks.

Circular scribbling shows still more control, consisting largely of circles.

The naming scribble stage is when children begin to attach explanations and names to the images they make. Without this information, the pictures remain abstract and mostly unidentifiable. The pictures below are labelled, clockwise from left: A camel, with a 'long long neck'; a train track; a whale 'with water coming out of him'; a crocodile 'with long teeth and dotties – he's got dotties on him'.

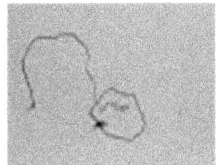
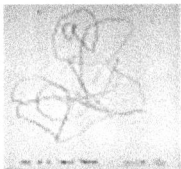
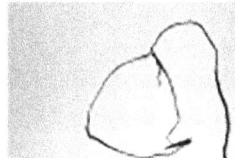
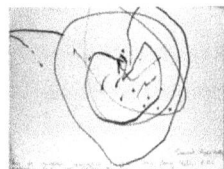

1. The scribbling stage is divided into sub-stages:

Sub-stage 1A – Disordered and random scribbling: 1½–2½ years	**Sub-stage 1B** – Controlled scribbling: 2, 2½–3 years	**Sub-stage 1C** – Named scribbling: 3, 3½–4 years
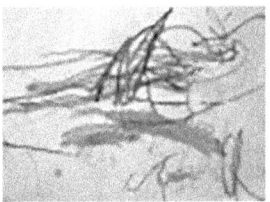		
This involves, for example, the following: • Large muscle, whole-arm movement. • Swing of the arm coming in contact with the paper, resulting in a mark. • Shoulder motions. • Scribbling beyond the confines of the paper. • Exploration – What can I do by moving these tools on paper? • Lines made by simple movements, etc.	This is indicated when: • colours are used unrealistically and children tend to use their favourite colours • children draw simple people with few features • tadpole-figure people are drawn with a large head on tiny body with extended arms • objects are floating in space – not anchored • the figure is normally three heads high, etc.	This is indicated when children do the following: • Give names to their scribbles. • Relate scribbles to things in environment. • Change the name of the scribble during the process. • Hold marking tools with their fingers, showing better fine motor control, etc.

»

2. The symbolising stage of child art development
Pre-schematic: 4–7 years

Children begin to make simple symbols. Their drawings exaggerate the important parts and feature events or objects that stand out in the child's mind. Colour tends to be emotional rather than naturalistic. Children create whimsical images which tend to 'float' – they are not always anchored to the ground and generally do not have a base line. Parts of the drawing, if removed, would probably lose their meaning and not make sense.

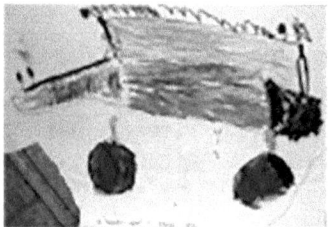

A schema is a generalised symbol that represents a specific concept. For example, a child's stick-figure drawing is used to represent all people. Few examples of the symbolising stage are the following:
- The child's first representational attempts
- Symbolic representation built up from former scribbles
- The appearance of recognisable geometric shapes
- Placement and size random and out of proportion
- Random floating spatial arrangement
- Possible turning or rotating of the paper while drawing
- Distortion and omission of parts in human figure drawing, etc.

A third model of the developmental stages is suggested by Schirrmacher (2008).

EXPLANATION	EXAMPLES
Manipulating the media: Scribbling and mark making: 1–2 years	Sensorimotor experience that results in scribbles
Making shapes, outlines, designs and symbols that have personal meaning: 2–4 years	Carefully drawing shapes; not always concerned about the product
Pictorial art that is becoming recognisable to others: 4–6 years	Making pictures look like something
Realistic art: 5–8 years	Making pictures look real

Find out more

Google the following websites for more information:
    http://journeys-in-art.wikispaces.com/Developmental+Stages
    https://www.google.com/search?tbm=bks&hl=en&q=128522552X
    http://www.learningdesign.com/Portfolio/DrawDev/kiddrawing.html
    https://elenaarenalvilahur.wordpress.com/drawing-developement-children/
    http://www.carolynboriss-krimsky.com/documents/chapter3.pdf
    http://www.d.umn.edu/~jbrutger/Lowenf.html
    http:// www.early-pictures.ch/kellogg/archive/en/
    http://www.scribd.com/doc/81748740/Stages-of-Artistic-Development

Examples of suitable activities for the visual arts

Creative art is not copying the teacher's example. Many teachers like to use photocopied pictures or colouring books as so-called art activities. Although exercises such as 'connect the numbers' to form a picture may be beneficial for mathematics, it has little value as creative art. Workbooks, work charts, colouring books and teacher-drawn pictures are unsuitable for the creative development of young children. Reading stories, showing pictures, looking at and discussing objects as well as living creatures will guide the children when asked to draw a particular picture.

Try this out

Explore the following websites:
  http://www.changingimages.org
  http://www.necicmalaysia.org/view_file.cfm?fileid=53
  http://www.getty.edu/education/teachers/

Something to consider

Can you think of some activities which are used by teachers in the Foundation Phase under the pretext of art? How could you make these activities more creative? How could the following copying activity be made more creative?

The Grade R learners can take glued coloured paper and tear it in small pieces, then paste it on the different fruits, making a fruit bowl collage.

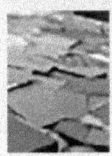     

Music

Music is another important component of the creative arts. Different musical activities include singing, moving in response to different rhythms, playing instruments and listening. A well-organised musical environment provides for a wide range of musical activities and experiences adequate to meet the needs and interests of all children. It also supports and strengthens learning in other subjects, for example mathematics. Listen to number rhymes and songs, for example:

Five little ducks
Five little ducks went swimming one day,
Over the pond and far away.
Mommy Duck said: »

> *Quack, quack, quack!*
> *And four little ducks came swimming back.*
> *Four little ducks went swimming one day,*
> *Over ... etc*
>
> *until ...*
>
> *And no little ducks came swimming back.*
> *Daddy Duck said:*
> *QUACK, QUACK, QUACK!*
> *And five little ducks came swimming back.*

Any variation on this counting rhyme introduces basic subtraction.

Music helps children understand other people and their cultures, and gives increased opportunities for social and emotional development. It is important to know how to include music in the curriculum and optimise its use throughout the daily programme. Music forms an important part of development in the young child's life. According to Le Roux (2005), growing children find pleasure in a music-making, music-loving environment through experiencing musical opportunities for themselves, feeling rhythm in their bodies and making music together.

Grade R children usually follow some skips and steps in a melody (melodic contours and intervals). Melody is the tune of a song. They are able to demonstrate some musical concepts for example fast/slow, high/low, short/long notes of the song, and enjoy longer songs with predictable structures, for example colours, numbers, repetition and rhyme, such as singing the months of the year or days of the week. Grade R children can reproduce the melody in an echo song, for example Father Jacob, and have a vocal range of five to six notes.

> **Father Jacob**
> *Father Jacob*
> *Father Jacob*
> *Are you still sleeping?*
> *Are you still sleeping?*
> *All the bells are ringing*
> *All the bells are ringing*
> *Bim bam bom*
> *Bim bam bom*

Each Grade R child develops musical/rhythmic and bodily/kinaesthetic intelligences through interaction with others and enjoyment of a wide variety of music and movement suited to their developmental level. Grade R teachers fulfil their roles and responsibilities in music education when they select, present and evaluate musical experiences effectively; when they function as motivators, planners, facilitators and observers; and when they integrate music, movement and dance throughout the school day and across all subjects.

Something to consider

Mistakes that teachers sometimes make

The Grade R children are led to sing too low because it is a more comfortable tone for the teacher. The result is that they start droning in a monotonous sing-song.

Sometimes teachers do not select suitable songs. The following aspects are important in selecting songs:
- The song must be simple and suitable for children, for example *Old MacDonald had a farm*.
- It must not be too long. It can consist of repetitive short stanzas (verses), but these must not be too long.
- The voice range must not be too wide. Grade R children start with two-, three- and four-tone songs. Five- to seven-year-olds are comfortable at a range of five to eight tones.
- The song must progress simply, and rhythm complications must be avoided. The song must not be too difficult.

How does one teach a class a song?

Songs are learned through imitation and repetition.
- Before applying the phrase-by-phrase method, the teacher must recite the entire song.
- Background information on the song is also important and can be discussed before teaching the song.
- The meaning of the words can also be highlighted, particularly if the song is not in the children's home language.
- Before singing the song phrase by phrase, children can say the words rhythmically phrase by phrase. However, this is seldom necessary unless the song is in a language the children barely understand or the song has difficult rhythms.
- The imitation and repetition must be presented in such a way that children's listening, concentration and musical memory are stimulated and engaged.
- As soon as the children can 'read', the words must be displayed on the board or a transparency. If you have sufficient music knowledge, graphic notation can then be used to indicate when the pitches go up, down or remain the same. The longer and shorter notes can also be indicated in this way.

»

- Children's listening concentration can be stimulated and improved by asking questions on the form of the song: for example which lines sound the same, almost the same or completely different.
- Children can make their own suggestions on how to improve their rendering of the song. This will encourage them to listen critically.

Try this out
Active Music – Music that will transform your teaching! Free trial for every school… 168 skill-based music lesson plans for 4–11-year-olds with over 500 activities on DVD for easy learning – a must have for all primary teachers!
http://primarymusiclessonplans.com/

Two practical examples of musical games follow. By playing these games, Grade R children can construct mathematical concepts, such as shape and time, as well as exploring rhythm. Play these games with smaller groups of children. They will, for example, not be effective in a class of 35 or more children. You can, however, divide the children into groups and while most children are busy completing a drawing based on their favourite song, the teacher can work with a small group of 10 children.

Find the shape (based on the game *Musical chairs*)
Put out large triangles and squares on the mat. Make sure there is one geometric shape fewer than there are children in the circle. In other words, if there are 10 Grade R children in the circle, put out only nine triangles and nine squares. The teacher will need two rhythm sticks and a triangle, as well as instruments for children who drop out of the game and join her percussion band.

As the game is played, the children who are not standing on a geometric shape or are on the wrong one become part of the percussion band. They follow the teacher and play the rhythm with her, for example four shakes for the square, or three shakes for the triangle. A percussion instrument is a musical instrument that is sounded by being struck or scraped by another object or a hand.

How to play this game
- Explain to the Grade R children that when they hear the **rhythm sticks**, they need to find a **square** and stand on it.
- Now play a march in 4/4 time and play the beat clearly on a wooden block as **1234**. (Beat the stick four times.)

»

- The children must listen attentively and respond quickly. As soon as they identify the sound and that there are four beats of the rhythm sticks, they should stand on a **square**.

- The children who do not have a geometric shape or are standing on the wrong one become part of the percussion band.
- Remove one square, and now play the music in 3/4 time. Play the beat clearly on a triangle as **1 2 3**.
- Again, the children walk in a circle around the geometric shapes.
- Again the children walk in a circle around the geometric shapes.

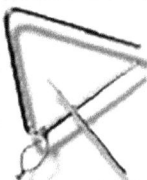

- Children listen attentively and respond quickly as they identify the sound of the triangle playing three beats, and everyone must stand on a **triangle**.

- The children who do not have a triangular geometric shape or are standing on the wrong one become part of the percussion band.
- Remove one triangle.
- Continue with the game until only a few children remain.

Reinforce the rule: Children must **walk around rhythmically in time to the beat** without hurting or pushing one another. It will be similar to playing musical chairs, only now they are specifically listening to the rhythm sticks for four beats or the triangle for three beats.

You could extend this activity by using just the rhythm sticks or the triangles and sounding three or four beats on either instrument. When they hear four beats they go and stand on a square and when they hear three beats they must choose a triangle.

Suggested activities for moving to music

Children skip, hop, march, clap, tiptoe and step to the beat. They make creative movements to music, showing their understanding of rhythm, beat and the feeling of the music. They may make up hand movements to go along with songs. Movements have a more rhythmic quality when listening to music.

The Grade R children can march around in a circle while playing in a rhythm band and participate in a variety of group singing games with simple dance movements to well-known song, such as *Row, row, row your boat*, etc. The rhythm band is one of the primary methods of introducing children to playing music. Children are given maracas, tambourines, bells and rhythm sticks to beat out a simple rhythm. They can do this to accompany a tune being played on a CD or, if possible, a teacher playing the piano.

Try this out

MUSIC, DRAMA, DANCE AND MOVEMENT ACTIVITIES INTEGRATED WITH MATHEMATICS		
DAY	**ACTIVITIES**	**EXAMPLES OF SUITABLE ACTIVITIES FOR A WEEK**
Monday	Movement	**Hopscotch** – Draw a layout for playing hopscotch in the playground. Grade R children jump with one leg in the circle and both legs in the rectangles.
Tuesday	Drama	Children dramatise parts of the story told by the teacher on shapes.
Wednesday	Music	Use music instruments such as triangles, shakers and boxes. The teacher sings a song with a repetitive chorus, for example *Father Jacob* (see previous mention).
Thursday	Dance	Play music with a strong beat, for example *Three blind mice*. The Grade R children make a pattern using their feet, for example a zigzag pattern where some of the children stand in one row, and the other children weave in and out of the row. Put boxes on the floor in a row. Grade R children dance around the boxes.
Friday	Game	**Similarity games** – The children divide up into small groups and brainstorm some common preferences. Based on these preferences, they form small groups, for example those who enjoy dance, drama or movement, and those who prefer music, etc.

Dance, drama and music – a foundation for education: *A study on implementing the performing arts in the early years of education.*
   http://researchbank.rmit.edu.au/eserv/rmit:6350/Crowe.pdf

Dance activities for young children:
   http://www.youtube.com/watch?v=kfdpno3gXtA
   http://www.youtube.com/watch?v=o3huR6KT2pw
   http://www.ehow.com/way_5452925_dance-activities-kids.html

> **Something to consider**
>
> Give an example of an activity that you design for children that will encourage them to move to music.

Drama

Drama is about pretence, and using your imagination to pretend you are someone other than yourself. Most children do this naturally when they engage in dramatic or fantasy play. Drama grows out of dramatic play and has a similar purpose. Drama in the Grade R classroom is defined as experiences in which children play, pretend, role play or create characters or ideas.

The essential characteristic of drama is acting out. In acting out, we are not bound by social norms. We identify rather with our new imagined role and use the environment differently. For example, a desk becomes a dining table laden with food; a crayon box becomes a cell phone, etc.

Drama in Grade R is not the production of plays in which children memorise lines and act given roles. Such productions are more appropriate for older children. Creative drama usually refers to spontaneous productions in which children create or recreate stories, moods or incidents without learning lines or practising their roles. Rather, children can dramatise a song such as *Old MacDonald had a farm*, a simple storybook such as *The three little pigs* or a rhyme such as *Humpty Dumpty*.

Drama in the Grade R classroom can contribute to the general aims of life skills in the curriculum, fostering the development of skills such as the following:
- Critical-thinking and problem-solving skills
- An ability to work cooperatively with others
- An increased ability to understand the perspectives of others
- An ability to communicate more effectively
- An enhanced imagination.

In addition, drama exposes children to everyday situations where they can acquire social skills such as negotiating who does what, developing language through social interaction with other children, and acting out many of their lived experiences, for example buying railway tickets.

Drama also lends itself to the development of speaking skills through dialogues (eg telephone conversations) and role play (eg between a shopkeeper and a customer). Children can also use puppets to dramatise an event.

Find out more

http://www.theatre4youth.co.za/theatre/workshop/56/
http://buzzdrama.com/buzz4schools/
http://www.preschoolthemes.co.za/

Drama focuses on natural expressions of thought, feelings and ideas rather than on polished theatrical performance.

Examples of suitable activities for drama

There are various levels of proficiency when children dramatise a story. Informal drama is the most spontaneous type of enactment. Grade R children spontaneously take on a role or behaviour of someone else. Informal drama and story drama (interpreting a writer's ideas and words rather than creating new ones) are suitable for Grade R children.

Steps to follow when dramatising a story

- **Step one** – the teacher tells the children a story.
- **Step two** – the teacher explains, after they have heard the story, that they are going to act it out. They can use their own words and any movement, sounds and facial expressions they choose.
- **Step three** – the teacher tells the story and then asks children to recall in sequence what happened. The teacher summarises the story for them.
- **Step four** – the children form groups. The number of characters in the story determines the number of Grade R children in the group.
- **Step five** – the children decide on a character for each member of their group, practise their drama and then present it to the class.

Dance

Children communicate through dance, and the focus in Grade R should be on the process of creative movement rather than a polished final product. In dance, children use their bodies to move rhythmically to music. Children should be encouraged to express the message they receive through music in the form of a dance. Dance provides Grade R children with the opportunity to learn non-verbal communication skills and use them effectively.

PHYSICAL EDUCATION

The gross and fine motor skills, balance and posture necessary for all aspects of life, including different sports, games, dance and other learning activities, are specifically developed during physical education and movement. It is important to nurture each child's physical and movement developmental needs in relation to their cognitive, emotional and social well-being. Physical education incorporates a wide variety of activities in addition to sport. It also incorporates a wide range of equipment such as balls, bats, hoops, etc. The Grade R teacher plans opportunities for the children to be active most of the school day. Because children learn kinaesthetically (through their bodies), appropriate movement activities should be included in the teaching of the different subjects (see chapters 4, 7 and 10 for appropriate examples). Children should also be given the opportunity to play games and become involved in lifelong fitness activities (see the section on 'Health and wellness: Promotion of health' in this chapter). Obstacle courses are a fun way of encouraging movement in young children.

Try this out
Designing an obstacle course

Suitable materials to use are chairs or trees, cones, rope, cardboard or plastic boxes, rocks, hula hoops, bricks, and anything else suitable. Give directions after you have created an obstacle course. It could be indoors or outdoors, and as long or short as you like. Include objects the children can climb over or under, stand on top of, walk around or crawl through. Walk the route together, discussing the directions for moving around, over, under, behind, in front of or through each obstacle, for example galloping around the chair/tree, hopping over the rope, crawling through the cardboard tunnel, standing on top of the chair/rock and singing, 'I am happy and I know it, 'cos I'm there'.

An example of an outdoor obstacle course:

Another example of an obstacle course:

Another useful idea for an obstacle course could be using ropes, etc.

»

Ropes, wool, strips cut from waste plastic bags and/or old pantyhose/stockings can be tied together to form a length of rope.
- Thread a rope between the slots or notches in the top of two cones/chairs/trees for jumping over or crawling under.
- Make three circles with three ropes, and jump from one circle to the next.
- Lay a rope in a straight line for children to walk on or to straddle (ie putting a leg on either side of the rope).
- Place two ropes parallel to each other and 30 cm apart. This can be a path for walking, jogging, jumping or hopping along.

Find out more

http://www.education.gov.za/LinkClick.aspx?fileticket=ujnw5lr18MA=
http://www.ibe.unesco.org/curricula/southafrica/sa_al_gu_2003_eng.pdf.

Examples of suitable activities for physical education:
    http://teachers.net/lessonplans/subjects/physical_education/
    http://www.pedagonet.com/PhysEd/physed.htm
    http://www.edu.gov.on.ca/eng/teachers/dpa1-3
    http://www.education.com/activity/physical-science/

Something to consider

Go back to Chapter 4 and revise the key perceptual-motor skills that children should develop. Give your own examples of suitable activities to enhance these skills through physical education, and plan an obstacle course either indoors or outdoors for a Grade R class.

ENHANCING CREATIVITY WITHIN THE CREATIVE ARTS AND PHYSICAL EDUCATION DOMAIN

Creativity in Grade R does not mean all children have to become artists or musicians. Creativity refers to the enhancement of the Grade R child's creative potential in all areas of development. Imaginative planning of activities can ensure that children are encouraged to think and act creatively in all of the three subjects that must be covered in Grade R. For example, a language activity can close with a free drawing of an aspect of a theme, or a mathematics counting lesson could end with children creating a number dance using cut-outs of the numbers to create a dance path. Integrate creative art into different subjects and subject areas so that it receives the attention that it merits.

> **Try this out**
> Jiskha Homework Help – Art: Visual arts: Principles & elements of design
>   http://www.jiskha.com/art/visual_arts/ped.html
>
> Visual arts: Elements and principles of design
>   http://www.princetonol.com/groups/iad/files/elements2.htm

How to recognise creativity

There are some clear indicators that point to creative behaviour. These include openness to the new and unexpected; tolerance for ambiguity; willingness to experiment and take risks; impulsivity; curiosity; preference for complexity; being highly intuitive; sensitivity; flexibility; individualism; nonconformity; daring to be different; independence; playfulness; and a sense of humour. Creative children may be unsocial or very social.

Enabling a quality Grade R environment to promote creative behaviour

An enabling environment, where the Grade R children are encouraged to be active and responsible participants in their own learning, fuels creative behaviours. The environment is one where learning is focused on children's interests, abilities and learning styles. We can teach, but children choose what and how they will learn. In other words, we should promote a child-centred learning and teaching environment.

> **Try this out**
> http://www.aishe.org/readings/...1/oneill-mcmahon-Tues_19th_Oct_SCL.htmll

Providing suitable materials

The Grade R teacher provides materials that allow children to make discoveries. Teachers co-construct meaning with the children and promote sustained shared thinking. Remember that each child's specific background and experience will play a role in how they approach an interactive environment and make sense of their discoveries.

It is also important that teachers are able to select and use existing materials effectively. The teacher can supply a variety of manipulative (concrete) materials (see Chapter 7) to encourage exploration and an active, hands-on approach. Manipulatives can be almost anything – books, posters, real objects, blocks, marbles, grain, pebbles and sticks, paper clips, and even paper that is cut or folded.

When a new concept is being taught, the use of manipulative materials can help the Grade R children to deepen their understanding. They can use these resources during free-play activities, structured activities, when they have finished a teacher-guided task, or simply when they need 'time out'. The following resources can be considered for the selection of learning and teaching support materials (LTSMs) for Life Skills:

- Beanbags, ropes, hoops, balls of different sizes, balancing beams/planks/tyres, outdoor play equipment (tyres, jungle gym, climbing ropes, trees), scarves/strips of cloth, bats, containers (bowls, buckets, tins to be used as targets), skittles/bottles (as targets), hard and flat open surface, sticks, storage containers, swings, bricks, cones, balloons
- Dry media – wax crayons, paper, oil pastels, chalk, 2B pencils, felt-tipped pens, charcoal, sand
- Wet media – paint, ink, dyes, mud
- Brushes of different sizes
- Sheets of paper or scrap paper in various sizes and colours
- Earthenware clay, paper maché, play dough, mud
- Beads (glass, paper, plastic), straws, macaroni, shells, etc, for threading
- Recyclable materials – boxes, toilet roll tubes, polystyrene containers and packing materials, corks, wrapping paper, tinfoil, wool, string, stones, seeds, old newspapers/magazines
- Glue, cardboard strips for glue applicators, scissors, pre-mixed starch
- CD player, CDs, musical instruments
- Old clothes, utensils and containers to be used as 'props' for fantasy and dramatic play
- Puzzles and other manipulative educational toys – bought and homemade
- Plastic lens/magnifying glass
- People – older family members and invited guests
- Print-based sources – workbooks, encyclopaedias, readers, teachers' guides, magazines, brochures, etc
- Electronic equipment – video tapes, audio tapes, multimedia packs, computer software, etc
- Physical/kinaesthetic – specimens, apparatus, models, educational toys, etc
- Information and storybooks (library), books with rhymes and verses
- Picture books, pictures, wall charts and maps, sound cards (frieze), word games

For creative arts specifically, the following are required:
- Open space
- Musical instruments, including found and made
- Audio and audio-visual equipment with a range of suitable music
- Charts and posters
- Variety of props, for example materials, balls, different sized and shaped objects, old clothes

- Visual stimuli for drawing and construction, for example bringing an insect in a container into the classroom and drawing attention to its detail

Some examples of resources that can be used for creative work

 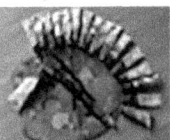    

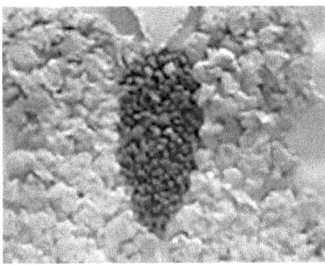

Tissue paper collage

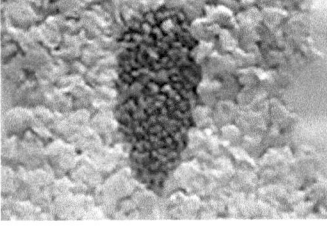

Colouring book page collage
Materials used – crayons, cotton wool balls, tissue paper and confetti

- Natural resources – a natural resource is anything that people can use which comes from nature. People do not make natural resources, but gather them from the earth. Examples of natural resources are air, water, wood, oil, leaves, soil, shells, iron and coal.

A useful resource in the visual art corner is homemade play dough.

Try this out
Homemade play dough

Ingredients
- 1 cup salt
- 1½ cups flour
- ½ cup water
- 2 tablespoons oil
- A few drops of food colouring

Method
Mix all ingredients very well and knead. Store in plastic bags after moulding. If stored properly, play dough will last for up to three weeks and provide much enjoyment for the children.

Find out more

http://artsonline2.tki.org.nz/resources/planning/visualarts.php
http://thewalters.org/teachers/
http://www.ncca.ie/uploadedfiles/Curriculum/VisArt_Gline.pdf
http://www.neatstreets.org/resources/Litter%20and%20Waste.pdf.CachedSimilar
http://www.seomraranga.com/links/visual-arts/
http://www.thutong.doe.gov.za/ResourceDownload.aspx?id=46095

Provide opportunities for self-expression

To enable creativity, provide opportunities for children to hear and be heard by others. Encourage children to talk with each other. At arrival time, some children may have exciting information they wish to share with their friends, so promote informal conversation as they arrive at school. In a small group, Grade R children feel more comfortable talking to each other and more children get the opportunity to talk than in a larger group. It is natural for children to tell stories. Storytellers have played an important role in every culture. When no way of transmitting information in written form existed, societies depended upon storytellers to preserve traditions and maintain culture. Storytelling is still an important part of a child's education. As they tell stories and listen to those told by others, listening and speaking skills are developed. Grade R children enjoy recalling their own experiences. Teacher-made books about news or children's experiences are valuable reading materials. After they have shared their experiences with their friends, they can draw something about their experiences on a piece of paper. Write their names on the paper and staple all of them together to make a 'newspaper', and put it in a prominent place where they can 'read' it daily.

A fun activity for children to express themselves is by allowing them to blow bubbles and then 'tell stories' about them. Children will be encouraged to use their imaginations.

Try this out

Blow the bubble away

Ingredients
- 2 tbsp dishwashing liquid
- ½ cup water
- ½ tsp sugar
- Food colouring

Method
Gently mix the dishwashing liquid and water together. Stir in the sugar and add food colouring last. Use wire coat hangers to blow bubbles.

Provide children with teacher support

The role of the Grade R teacher is to plan opportunities for learning, provide the choices, prepare the environment and guide the experiences. Self-motivation, organisation, creativity and enthusiasm are vital qualities in Grade R teachers. They choose activities that could guide learning, and plan informal assessment to gauge what learning has taken place. Grade R teachers work with the children in groups or on a one-to-one basis. They support children who are having difficulties or need extra assistance. One of the advantages of an informal approach to teaching and learning is that teachers can provide a level of differentiation so that children's differing needs are met.

Find out more

http://www.cie.org.uk/cambridge-for/teachers/curriculum-support/
http://www.nwu.ac.za/webfm_send/61909
https://www.apa.org/education/k12/relationships.aspx
http://scotens.org/2008/10/role-of-the-learning-support-teacher/

DEVELOPMENT AND ASSESSMENT OF CREATIVE ARTS IN GRADE R

Assessment in Life Skills happens mainly through regular and systematic observation of children participating in planned and unplanned activities such as classroom discussions related to topics, physical games and activities, creative arts, oral and practical demonstrations (role play, 'show and tell', etc), dance, musical and drama activities, and indoor and outdoor free play. (See Chapter 9 on assessment for more information.)

> **Something to consider**
>
> Support all children with barriers to learning. Adapt some of the creative art and physical education activities to allow these children to participate and demonstrate competence.
>
> The focus for creative art should be on the development of skills and attitudes rather than a polished end product. It often happens that emotional challenges manifest themselves during creative art. All children should be encouraged to express themselves freely and creatively.

To conclude, the introduction of science, technology, engineering, art and mathematics (STEAM) as an integrated whole into early childhood (and later years) education has afforded new teaching and learning opportunities. In this next section we will reflect on STEAM's welcome inclusion in curricula.

Science, technology, engineering, art and mathematics (STEAM)

Educational demands of the 21st century call on teachers to be innovative and reflective, and to be able to support children to adapt successfully to the rapid changes in all spheres of life. To do this they need a variety of skills that include critical thinking, creative thinking (creativity), cooperation, communication, physical knowledge, logical mathematics and social competencies (Draper & Wood, 2017). These skills therefore need to be new approaches to both subject content knowledge and to teaching methodologies with an increased focus, where relevant, on integration of subject matter and pedagogies.

An innovative approach to this requirement has been the drive to integrate STEAM. The STEAM approach draws on many of the underpinning principles of early childhood education such as it should be child centred, play based and experiential in nature. STEAM supports an integrated approach to both content matter as well as choice of teaching activities.

STEAM is a refinement of STEM (science, technology, engineering, mathematics). STEM was first mooted as an interdisciplinary and applied approach to the teaching of specific disciplines. The importance of integrating the creative arts into the teaching of STEM concepts was soon realised and the new integrated approach became known as STEAM (Sharapan, 2012). To summarise, STEAM is an educational philosophy designed to integrate five key disciplines that support children's natural curiosity and excitement for exploration, while also building a foundation for later academic achievement (Barrett, 2017 cited in Excell & Linington, 2020).

STEAM suggests that learning programmes be designed in such a way that children are provided with a well-thought-out structure that invites them to explore and ask new questions. Thoughtful programme design should lead to the development of skills that can be used across the curriculum in science, mathematics, technology and language. For example, when children learn to compare, sort, count, estimate, classify, measure, graph as well as share their explanations with others participating in their science activities, a transfer of these skills to mathematics, language and technology can be expected (Dejonckheere, De Wit, Van de Keere & Vervaet, 2016 cited in Wahyuningsih et al, 2020).

Learning is strengthened when children acquire the same skills, ideas and concepts in different contexts using different resources. Such occurrences can also enhance positive attitudes and values in relation to STEAM as children are guided, for example, into respecting their environment (Excell & Linington, 2020). STEAM integration helps teachers focus on content (what to learn) and processes (*how* to learn) (Linder & Eckhoff, 2020).

Children are naturally curious. To support this character trait, mathematical and science experiences should be blended using a STEAM approach to make learning interdisciplinary. Curiosity and problem solving should be encouraged by posing thought-provoking questions while asking the young child to identify objects, make comparisons and predict. In this way, young children can learn concepts from different disciplines in different contexts in engaging ways. It is important to remember that a very early exploration of the world sets the stage for later learning and positive attitudes towards STEAM and the environment in general.

Encourage children to communicate about how they solved problems. Lopes, Grando and D'Ambrosio (2017) explain the importance of a classroom rich in opportunities to solve problems. Their study with four- and five-year-old children indicated that those who shared their solutions with each other went on to construct further knowledge. Lopes et al (2017) concluded that experience in problem solving provides children with the opportunity to take informed guesses, to discuss possibilities and to draw conclusions (all previously mentioned important 21st century skills). Young children can represent their reasoning through art or other creative activities (see this chapter).

Find out more

If you would like to pursue research in this field, access the following articles about STEAM:

- 'STEAM learning in early childhood education: A literature review' by S Wahyuningsih et al, in the *International Journal of Pedagogy and Teacher Education (IJPTE)* 4(1): April 2020. https://www.researchgate.net/publication/343363945_STEAM_Learning_in_Early_Childhood_Education_A_Literature_Review
- The National Association for the Education of Young Children (NAEYC) has published a four-part series on STEAM. Use the following website to access these readings: https://www.naeyc.org/resources/pubs/tyc/feb2020/breaking-down-steam

SUMMARY

Life skills provide a framework in which children and teachers can translate knowledge, (what we know) and attitudes and values (what we think, feel and believe) into action. In other words, they help us to know what to do, how to do it and when it is appropriate to do so. Life skills are more than behaviours. They are ways of being – actions and thoughts that are beneficial to both the individual and the broader community. As children acquire life skills, their ability to live and contribute in a meaningful way in the current South African context increases. Children should be able to take what they have learnt in the classroom and apply it to their life outside.

This does not just happen! You as the Grade R teacher need to make sure that the children are given the opportunity to acquire the knowledge, skills, attitudes and values to make this happen, and to know why they make the choices they do. Then, as active citizens, they can contribute meaningfully to society.

BIBLIOGRAPHY

Brewer, JA. 2004. *Introduction to early childhood education. Preschool through primary grades*. 5th ed. Boston: Pearson Education, Inc.

Brewer, JA. 2007. *Introduction to early childhood education. Preschool through primary grades.* 6th ed. Boston: Pearson Education, Inc.

Buchberger, F. 2004. *Active learning in powerful learning environments.* http://www.pa-linz.ac.at/team/homepage/BuchbergerF01%20FBActive.pdf (Accessed 20 April 2013).

Department of Basic Education (DBE). *Curriculum and Assessment Policy Statement (CAPS) 2012. English; Life Skills Foundation Phase Grade R–3*. Pretoria.

Dockendorf, M & Close, S. 1990. *Our primary program: Taking the pulse, Part 1 – A journey through the classrooms*, 125. Reproduced with permission of the British Columbia Ministry of Education, Skills and Training. Educational Innovation (a division of the BC Ministry of Education).

Draper, CL & Wood, S. 2017. 'From stumble to STEM: One school's journey to explore STEM with its youngest students'. *Exchange* (19460406), Epilepsy, kidshealth.org › Teens › Diseases & Conditions (Accessed 26 August 2013).

Excell, LA & Linington, V. 2020. *Playful early childhood care and education*. Cape Town: Juta.

Hendrick, J & Weissman, P. 2007. *Total learning: Developmental curriculum for the young child*. 7th ed. New Jersey: Pearson Education, Inc.

Henig, L. 2002. *Raising emotionally intelligent learners.* South Africa: Smile Education Systems (Pty) Ltd.

Klopper, A. 2005. *Life skills. (FPUN 325 manual)*. Potchefstroom: North-West University.

Kruger, N. 1998. *Facilitating life skills: Self-concept.* Lynnwood Ridge: Amabukhu Publications.

Lee, J. 2019. 'Coding in early childhood'. *Contemporary Issues in Early Childhood* 21(3): 266–269. https://doi.org/10.1177/1463949119846541 (Accessed 3 May 2021).

Le Gragne, L. 2002. 'Towards a language of probability for environmental education'. *SAJHE/SATHO* 22(2): 83.

Lemmer, E & Squelch, J. 1993. *Multicultural education: A teachers' manual*. Pretoria: Sigma Press.

Le Roux, A. 2005. *Music in early childhood development and the Foundation Phase (0–9 years)*. 3rd ed. Pretoria: Le Roux: 286.

Linder, SM & Eckhoff, A. 2020. 'Teaching young children'. *Young Children* 13(3). https://www.naeyc.org/resources/pubs/tyc/feb2020/breaking-down-steam (Accessed 12 May 2021).

Lopes, CE, Grando, RC & D'Ambrosio, BS. 2017. 'Experiences situating mathematical problem solving at the core of early childhood classrooms'. *Early Childhood Education Journal,* 45: 251–259.

Loubser, A. 2009. *School readiness and perceptual skills in the Foundation Phase.* (AGDN 125 manual). Potchefstroom: North-West University.

McKinney, K. 1998. *Engaging students through active learning.* http://www.cat.ilstu.edu/pdf/catjuly98.pdf-50k (Accessed 26 April 2013).

McLennan, DP. 2017. *Creating coding stories and games.* Washington, DC: National Association for the Education of Young Children.

Rooth, E. 1997. *Introduction to lifeskills. Hands on approaches to lifeskills education.* Goodwood: VIA AFRIKA.

Schirrmacher, R. 2008. *Art and creative development for young children.* 6th ed. United States: Thomson Delmar Learning.

Sharapan, H. 2012. 'From STEM to STEAM: How early childhood educators can apply Fred Rogers' approach'. *Young Children* 67(1): 36.

South African Department of Education. 1997. *Policy Document Foundation Phase.* October. Pretoria: Government Printer.

South African Department of Education. 2000. 'Norms and Standards for Educators'. *Government Gazette* no 20844, February.

South African Department of Education. 2002. *Revised National Curriculum Statement Policy Grades R–9 (Schools).* Pretoria: Department of Education.

Van der Merwe, L & Lourens, C. 2009. *Foundation Phase: Music (LSKM 121 Study guide).* Potchefstroom: North-West University.

Van Staden, C. 2005. 'Know the learner', in *The Reception Year. Learning through play*, edited by R Davin & C van Staden. Johannesburg: Heinemann: 39–76.

Wahyuningsih, S, Nurjanah, NE, Rasmani, UEE, Hafidah, R, Pudyaningtyas, AR & Syamsuddin, MM. 2020. 'STEAM learning in early childhood education: A literature review'. *International Journal of Pedagogy and Teacher Education (IJPTE)* April, 4(1): 33-44.

Winkler, G, Modise, M & Dawber, A. 2004. *All children can learn.* Cape Town: Francolin Publishers.

Websites

http://journeys-in-art.wikispaces.com/Developmental+Stages
http://www.early-pictures.ch/kellogg/archive/en/
http://www.education.gov.za/LinkClick.aspx?fileticket
http://www.webmd.com/allergies/allergy-medicine-tips-f

GLOSSARY

Aquarium – a glass or plastic container in which fish and other water animals and plants can live

Child-centred – describes activities that are focused on the needs and interests of the child

Cocoon – (silk) a casing made by moth caterpillars and other insect larvae

Dynamics – how loudly or softly music is played – an expressive musical element

Enactment – adopting actions, feelings, thoughts and/or behaviours of people in specific situations, an ability which typically begins at the age of three

Form – the blueprint of a song; in other words, the structure or the plan of the music

Germination – the process by which a plant grows from a seed

Hands-on material – manipulatives that Grade R children can use to enhance their understanding and learning; promotes learning by doing

Hypothesis – an educated guess about how things work

Minerals – naturally occurring substances that are solid and stable at room temperature

Melody – a musical sequence of pitches

Pulse – beats in a (repeating) series (this is typically what listeners respond to as they tap their foot or dance along with a piece of music)

Obstacle course – a series of appropriately challenging physical obstacles that children must navigate

Rhythm – a term that occurs in all the arts (in music it refers to the combination of short and long sounds and silences)

Seashell – a hard, protective outer layer created by certain animals that live in the sea

Seeds – an embryonic plant enclosed in a protective outer covering called the seed coat

Shape – the form of an object or its external boundary, outline or external surface

Silkworm – the larva or caterpillar of the silk moth

Sponges – are animals (multicellular organisms) that have bodies full of pores and channels allowing water to circulate through them

Tempo – the speed of a song (eg fast, slow)

Terrarium – an area within an enclosed glass container

Timbre – the quality of the sound that makes it unique, determined by the origin of the sound; in other words, which instrument or type of voice produces it

Vivarium – an area, usually enclosed, for keeping and raising animals or plants for observation or research

Waste – an unusable or unwanted substance or material

Index

Please note: Page numbers in *italics* refer to figures or tables.

6Cs, the 4, 5, *5*, 6

A
ability groups 183
action research 12, 16
admission policy, and age 9
affective development 34–35
African
    perspective on development and learning 42
    philosophical thought and child-rearing practices 43
    value systems and play 245
annual planning *192–193*
art *see* creative arts; visual arts
assessment
    aim of 201–202
    of children with barriers to learning 214–215
    comprehensive checklist *223*
    context 210–211
    of creative arts 379–381
    culture and language fairness in 213–214
    cycle 200, *200*, 201
    definition of 188, 198, 217
    holistic checklist *223–226*
    of Life Skills 216–217, *216–217*
    planning of 205–206
    practices 204–205
    process 211–212
    recording and reporting of 212–213
    role players in 212
    sheet (Mathematics) *221, 222*
    strategies 206–209, *208–209*
    and teacher-guided activities 206, 208
    types of 202, 203–204
associative play 232
attitudes towards learning 3, 4, 5, 6
auditory
    blending/closure 86, 91
    discrimination 85, 91
    figure–ground perception 86, 91
    localisation 87, 91
    perception *85*, 85–87, 91
    recall/memory 86, 91
    sequencing 86–87, 91

B
balance 75, 91
basic interpersonal communication skills (BICS) 266, 267, 281
becoming, child 63, 68, 95
BEd Foundation Phase degree 10
Beginning Knowledge 333–350
behaviourism and learning, theory of 29–30
being child 63, 64, 110, 114, 115, 170, *171*
belonging child 63, 64, 114
bioecological systems theory *25*, 25–26
block-play area 133, *133*
body image (activities/exercises) 75, 76, 91
book corner 136–137
brain development 37, 38, 39, 49–50
Bronfenbrenner's bioecological systems perspective 24–26, *25*, 267
buddy system 266, 282

C
CAPS *see* Curriculum and Assessment Policy Statement

child-centred pedagogy 57–58
child-friendly school (CFS) 115, 147
    characteristics of 110–114, 128
    principles of 110
child-initiated
    activities 125, *126*, 127, 206, 313
    play 56, 131, 218, 237, *243–244*
    support 165–166
children
    as active participants 32, 41–42, 50, 203, 231
    and characteristics for participatory learning *163*
    empowering of 166–167
    facts about 19
    listening to and consulting 165–166
    and social and cultural contexts 33, 34
    viewed as becoming, being and belonging 63, 64, 170–171, *171*
    and ways of learning 19–20
chronosystem *25*, 26
circle time *see* ring time; teacher-guided activities
citizenship 5, *5*
class size 9
classifying 296–297, *299–300*
classroom
    characteristics for participatory learning *163*
    location of 7–9
    rules 129
co-constructing (teaching technique) 167–178
code switching 266
coding 348, 349, 350
cognitive
    development 30–32, *31–32*, 69, 91, 189
    domain 50–51
    processes 56, 292
collaboration 4, 5, *5*, 6
communication 4, 5, *5*, 6
    barriers 214
    and language development 55
    process 337
    and schooling preparedness 7
    skills 215, 372
    with parents/caregivers *118*, 119
community
    definition/description of 108
    members 109
    partnerships 109–111
community-based classrooms 8
comparing 297–298
competences 4, 5, *5*, 6
concentration span 182, 189
conceptual knowledge 290, 328
conditioning 29–30
confidence 5, *5*, 6
connectivity 5, *5*
Constitution, the 3, 331, 332
constructive play 235
content 5, *5*, 6
content knowledge 98, 169, 176, *176*, 189
continuity, principle of 289, 291
continuous assessment 156, 186, 199, 200, 203–204, 219
cooperative play 233
counting 300
    activities 300, 301, 302, 319, *319*
    integration of 315, 316, 326, 345
    range 295
Covid-19 pandemic 129, 177
creative arts
    aims of 353–354
    assessment of 379–381
    components of 353
    integration of 354–355
    and theory of multiple intelligences 355
    see also dance; drama; music; visual arts
creativity 4, 5, *5*, 6
    enhancing of 374–375
    environment to promote 150, 375
    idea of 150
    and Reggio Emilia programme/schools 150–152
    suitable materials/resources for 375–377, *377*
    and self-expression 378
    and teacher support 379, *379*
critical
    awareness 177
    thinking 4, 5, *5*, 6
    see also problem solving
cultural
    awareness 58–59
    diversity 59, 265–267
culturally appropriate mathematical experiences 321–322

culturally responsive
   development 3
   pedagogy 58–59
   programme 123–124
Curriculum and Assessment Policy Statement (CAPS)
   aspects of 123–124
   and assessment *220*
   and community-based classes 8
   content of 2, 48, 171, 172
   definition/description of 2, 17, 48, 123
   general aims of 175
   guiding principles of 49–61
   and implementation 176–177, *176*
   interpretation of 10
   purpose of 122–123
   realisation 174–175
   requirements of 9

D
daily assessment 198–199
daily programme
   definition of 125
   example of 125, *126*
   parts of 48
   planning of 124–127
   and teacher-guided activities 48, 124, 125, *126*
dance *370*, 372
data handling 312–313, 326, *326*
decision making, and power relationships 40
decolonisation 44, 227
democracy 17, 110, 119, 120
democratic citizenship, and purpose of Grade R 3
development
   and assessment 206, 210
   and community 108, 109
   and DAP principles 169, *169–170*
   domains of 22, 27
   and environmental factors 24, 25, *25*
   holistic 18, 22, 49–53, 108, 136
   of human personality 34, 35
   meaning of 22
   milestones of 10, 27, 28, 39, 68–71, *69–71*
   and play 228, 229, 230, 239, 241
   stages of 27, 28

developmental
   crisis 35
   domains 28, 68–71, *69–71*
   level, and topics 172
   milestones/norms 10, 27, 28, 39, 68–71, *69–71*
   phases, 27, 28
   principles 27, 28, 63, 169, *169–170*
   theories, critique of 39
developmentally appropriate
   approach to ECE 239
   pedagogy 56
   practice (DAP) 17, 64, 169, 265, 282
   programme 123–124
difficulty, dimensions of 294–295, *295*
disability 105, 110, 111, 113
discovery area 139, *139*
diversity
   and assessment 213, 214
   and daily programme 283–284
   definition of 189, 282
   and language of instruction 262, 263
   and participatory learning 159–160
   and teaching practice 58, 59, 111, 116
   and visual art 361–364
   see also cultural diversity; linguistic diversity
dominance 78, 91
drama *370*, 371–372
dramatising of stories 253–254, *254*, 276

E
early childhood development (ECD) 7, 11, 21, 43, 99
Early Learning Outcome Measures (ELOMs) 28
ecological
   environment 24–26, *25*
   systems perspective 267
educational toy area 134–135
emergent literacy
   and cognitive development 52, 62
   and creative arts 354, 361
   definition of 62, 261
   and learning areas 258, 259
emergent writing, activities 256, 257, 258
emotional
   competence 6
   domain 50

empowering (teaching technique) 166–167
English first additional language (EFAL) 263, 268
    books for teaching 274
    and parent involvement 276–277
    rhymes and songs for *284, 285–286*
English second language (ESL) 263
environmental awareness 333, 335–336
equality 114, 120
equilibration 31
equity issues 30, 58, 114, 120
Erikson's theory of psychosocial development 34–35, 267
ethics
    code of 104, 116, 120
    definition/description of 103, 106
exosystem *25*, 25–26
experiential learning 291, 328
expressive language skill 268
eye movement (activities/exercises) 80, 92
eye–foot coordination (activities/exercises) 80, 92
eye–hand coordination (activities) 79
eye–hand–foot coordination 81, 92

F
facilitating (teaching technique) 167, 177
fantasy play 135, *135–136*, 189, 233, 235, 237
    see also socio-dramatic play
fine motor development 51, 62, 73, 75, 79, *79*, 92, 285
first additional language (FAL)
    teaching of 264–265, 266
    teaching–learning activities *272*
    and themes 272–273
    theories on development of 267–268
first day
    advice to parents 65–66
    general guidelines for teachers 67–68
    ideas for teachers 66–67
fixed equipment (outdoor play area) 141–143
form
    constancy 83–84
    perception 83–84
formal
    assessment tasks 199

schooling, indicators of preparedness for 6–7
formative assessment 199, 203, 204, 219
free play
    role of the teacher 147–149
    safety checklist for *147–148, 148–149*
    see also child-initiated play
functional play 234

G
games with rules 233, 235, *243–244*, 245
gardening activities 345
Gardner's theory of multiple intelligences (MI) 35–36, *35–36*
gender
    differentiation 26
    preferences in play 128, 238, 239
    sensitivity 114
    and toys 300
gender-appropriate behaviour 29, 30
gender-sensitive school 114
geography *334*, 334–336
geometrical shapes 303–304
Gesell's maturational theory 27–28, 267
gifted child 89
Grade 1, failure rate 2
Grade R
    children/learners 8, 9
    classroom (location of) 7–9
    definition/description of 1
    entry into 64, 65
    importance of 2
    invitation to class 65, *65*
    planning for 179–180
    purpose of 3–7
    subjects 171, 172
Grade R teacher
    beliefs and values of 97
    characteristics of 96, *96*
    criteria for qualified 102–103
    definition of 94
    formal qualifications for 2, 10
    personal qualities of 95
    required duties/functions of 10
    roles of 98–100
gross motor development 51, 62, 73, 75, *75*, 92
growth, meaning of 22
gustatory perception 88, 92

H

hand and finger muscles, strengthening of 256–257, *257*
health 7
    education 351
    policy 128–129
    promotion 113, 350, 351–352
    and schooling preparedness 6
    and wellness 351–352
healthy eating 351–352
Higher Education Qualifications Framework 10
history 333–334
holistic
    checklist *223–226*
    development 3, 22, 23–26
    perspective of child development 49–53
    teaching and learning, example of *174*
    view of knowledge, skills, attitudes and values 5
    home environment, and development 2
    home language (HL) 9, 263
    maintaining and developing of 265–266
    see also mother tongue
home/school partnership 118
human
    actions 292, *293*, 293, 328
    needs 23, 24
    personality, development of 34, 35

I

imaging technology 37
inclusive education 105, 111
inclusivity, strategies to encourage 58–59
indigenous knowledge (IK) 44, 107, 108, 245
individual children's needs 58, 59
indoor environment 112
    planning the 130–132, *131*
    play areas 131, *131*, 132–139
    safety checklist for *148*, 149
informal assessment 198–199, tasks 199
information processing model (IPM) *184*, 185–186, *186*, 189
integrated teaching and learning, example of *174*
intellectual
    development (milestones) *69–71*
    functions 49

intelligence
    areas/categories of 35, *35–36*
    definition of 35
intentional teacher 161, *162*
interest table 346–347

K

kinaesthetic
    learning 289, 298, 323, 324, 328
    perception 87–88, 92
knowledge, holistic view of 5

L

language
    activities 254, 255
    components 268
    development 54–55, *69–71*, 258–259, 268–270
    of learning and teaching (LoLT) 9, 263, 266
    and play 245
    and social constructivist theory 33
    and teacher-guided activities 255
language-in-education policy 9
Lansdown's degrees of participation 158, *158*
large-group presentation/work 125, 130
lateral midline (activities) 77, *77*
laterality (activities/exercises) 77–78
learning
    and assessment 206, 210
    and DAP principles 169, *169–170*
    definition/meaning of 22, 29
    difficulties, identification of 28
    dispositions 4, 7
    effective child-centred 57, 58
    holistic 18, 22, 49, 108, 136
    measurement of 39
    and play 56–57, 228, 229, 230, 239, 241
    play-based approach to 10, 282, 291, 313, 314, 348
    styles 36, 57, 58, 62, 160, 183
    teaching strategies to support 199
    and teaching support material (LTSM) 183, 190
learning environment
    enriched 54
    parts of 124
    safe and health-promoting 128

safety checklist for *147–148, 148–149*
teacher's role in design and management of 149
as third teacher 149–150
see also indoor environment; outdoor environment
lesson
   plan formats *195, 196*
   planning 181
   presentation phases 183, *184–185*
life skills
   assessment of 216–217, *216–217*
   definition/description of 330
   and drama 371
   importance of 330–331
   role of teacher in 332
   and teacher-guided activities 330
linguistic diversity 263, 265–267
listening
   activities 255–256
   and consulting (teaching technique) 165–166
long-term memory (LTM) *185*, 186, 190

M

macrosystem *25*, 26
Malaguzzi, Loris 149, 150, 151
manipulative play 235
Maslow's hierarchy of needs 23–24, *23*
mass 311
matching 293–296, *295, 296, 299–300*
mathematical
   language 314
   skills *299–300*
   understanding, and schooling preparedness 7
mathematics
   and appropriate experiences 320–322
   assessment sheet *221, 222*
   basic/foundational concepts of 288, 289, 292, *293*, 293
   components/content areas 291, 292, *293*, 293, 300–313
   corner 318–319
   importance of 287, 288
   and outdoor equipment 316
   resources for 315–318, 319, 322–327
   and teacher's role 313–322

maturational
   perspective 267
   theory 27–28
measurement 308–312, *310*, 325, *325*
mental
   construction 31, 32
   processing 32, 34
mesosystem *25*, 25
microsystem *25*, 25
milestones (of development) 10, 27, 28, 39, 68–71, *69–71*
modelling (teaching technique) 29, 165–166
moral/spiritual domain 50–51
morphology 269–270, 282
mother tongue 9, 214
motor behaviour/response 72
motor development 51, 72
   see also fine motor development; gross motor development; perceptual-motor development
movable equipment 143, *143*
multiple intelligences (MI)
   for creative arts 355
   different areas/categories *35–36*
   theory of 35–36
music
   activities 365–368, 370
   area/corner 139
   concepts 366
   games 368, *368–369*
   moving to 370, *370*
   and songs *366*, 367–368

N

National Association for the Education of Young Children (NAEYC) 116, 265, 287
National Development Plan Vision 2030 2
National Early Learning Development Standards (NELDS) 27
natural sciences 336–347
nature table 346–347
nervous system, development of 27
neurogenesis 37
neurons 37, 38, *38*, 50
neuroscience 27
neuroscience 37–39, *38*, definition of 37
number rhymes and songs 365–366
numbers, operations and relationships 300–302, 323–324, *324*, 326

O

observation 182, 190
   and assessment 198, 199, 202, 206
   sheet 202, 210
   strategies *208–209*
   types of 208
observational learning 29
olfactory perception 88, 92
open day 64
operant conditioning 29
oral
   discussions 206
   language 7, 54, 55, 265
   questions 202, 207
   skills 354
   traditions 249
   vocabulary 269
ordering 298–299, *299–300*
orientation behaviours 73, *74, 75*, 92
outdoor
   environment 112, 140–146, *147, 148*
   equipment 140–145, *141*
   play area 57, *141*

P

parallel play 232
parents
   involvement of 276–277
   advice to 65–66
parent–teacher partnership 115, 117–119, *117–118*
participation, degrees of 158–159, *158, 159*
participatory learning 155, 156–158
   in context of diversity 159–160
   teaching for 160–163, *162, 163*
patterns, functions and algebra 302–303, 324, 328
pedagogical
   documentation 206, 207
   knowledge 98, 115, 169, 176, *176*, 190
   pedagogical content knowledge 176, *176*, 177, 190
pedagogy 56, 57, 58, 62, 88, 240, 241, *241*
peer tutoring 266, 282
'people' factors, influences on development 24, *25*, 25
perception, definition/description of 72
perceptual skills 49
perceptual-motor development 72–81, *74*, 81–88, 92
perceptual-motor
   activities 73, 138, *138–139*
   behaviours 73–75, *74, 75*
   skills 49, 57, 81, 87, 88, *138–139*
perseverance 4
personal and social well-being 350–351
   see also health; safety
phonemic awareness 85, 92, 268, 269
phonology 268–269, 282
physical
   development (milestones) 68–69, *69–71*
   domain 49
   education 372–375, *373–374*
   environment 112–113
   well-being 6, 7
Piaget's theory of cognitive development 30–32, 229, 233, 267
picture walk 251, 275
plants (natural sciences) 343–345, *343*
play areas, setting out indoor 132–139
play
   and African value systems 245
   and age-related stages 232–233
   characteristics of 230–231
   conceptions of 228, 229, 230
   continuum *243–244*, 245
   definitions/meanings of 228
   forms/types of 233, 234–235
   importance of 22, 228–229
   learning through 56–57
   materials and resources 237
   pedagogy of 88, 240, 241, *241*
   teacher's role in 235–238, 240, *243*
   value/benefits of 230–231, 238, *244*
play-based
   activities 127, 168, 210, 230, 269, 313
   curriculum 56, 240
   environment 115
   Grade R programme 10, 13, 348
   mathematical tasks 291, 314
policy documents 3
posture (activities/exercises) 75, 76, 91
power
   notion of 40
   relationships and decision making 40
pragmatics 270, 282
precoding skills 349

print awareness 258–259
problem solving
    and cognitive development 69, 91, 189
    competences *5, 6*
    and drama 371
    and mathematics 288, 292, 309, 315, 319, 320
    and scientific processes 336, 337
    and STEAM 381
    and technology 347
    see also critical thinking
problem-solving skills, and schooling preparedness 7
procedural knowledge 290, 328
professionalism 102, 103, 104, 121, 213
programming *see* coding
psychological tools 47, 98, 106
psychosocial development 34–35, 267
puppets, and stories 254, *254*

R

reading
    corner 258, 259
    and language development 268, 269
    of stories 249–253, *252*, 275–276
reception year 1, 13, 18
receptive language skills 268
recognition (form) 83
recognition through performance 35
reflective planning for and implementation of teaching, learning and assessment 156, *156*
Reggio Emilia programme/schools 149, 150–152, 153
reinforcement (and behaviourism) 29
relational sociology 39, 40
rights-based school 111
ring time 66, 255, 313
    see also teacher-guided activities
road safety 353
role models, imitation of 29
routines 125, *126*, 127
rural schools, and infrastructure 9

S

safety checklist, for learning environment 147, *147–148, 148–149*
safety, for young children 352–353
sand play 144, *145*, 146, *146*

school
    admission policy 9
    and community 109–111, 114
    ensuring an effective 111–112
    garden 344, 345
    and health 113
    leadership (and community involvement) 109
    politics 128–129
    readiness 11, 17
    safety 352–353
schooling, indicators of preparedness for 6–7
science 336
    activities 339–342, *339, 340, 343*
    area/learning corner 341
    and basic skills 337–338
    guidelines for teaching 342
    laboratory 344
    see also natural sciences
science, technology, engineering, art and mathematics (STEAM) 380–381
scientific
    exploration 337, 338–341
    process 337–338
self-assessment 206, *215*, 215–216
self-care, for teachers 101–102
self-confidence 4
self-directed learning 177
self-expression 378
semantics 270, 282
sensory
    awareness behaviours 74, *74*, 92
    perceptual-motor development 81–88
sensory-motor/practice play 233
seriation 298–299
shape 303–304, *307–308*, 326
shared reading 250–251
show and tell 55, 62, *126*
small-group teaching/work 125, 130, 181–182
social
    constructivist theory 32–34
    context, and learning and development 33
    domain 50
    and emotional development (milestones) 69, *69–71*
    environment, and CFS 113
    justice *5*, 10, 30, 111, 120

learning theory 29
sciences 333–335
sociocultural contexts, and development of the whole child 40–41
socio-dramatic play 270
see also **fantasy play**

sociological perspective, and Grade R child 63
sociology 39–40, 41, 42
solitary play 232
songs and rhymes 273–274
South African Council of Educators (SACE) 103, 104, 116
South African Schools Act (1996) 3, 9
space and shape 303–308, 324–325, *325*
spatial
awareness 73, *74*, *75*, 92
orientation (activities/exercises) 76, *76*
relationships 304–305, 326
S–R (stimulus–response) learning 29
stereotypes 56, 57, 160, 239
stories
dramatising of 372
resources for 197
story reading
compared to storytelling 249–250, 251, *252*
different ways of 250–251
guidelines to 252
and teaching a second language 269, 275–276
storybooks
examples of South African 274
guidelines to choosing 250
storytelling
compared to story reading 249–250, 251, *252*
guidelines to 253
subject
annual planning for 180
time allocation per *192*
summative assessment 204, 219
symbolic play 233
symmetry 305–307, *305*, *306*, 329
syntax 270–271, 282

T
tactile perception 87–88, 92
talking, and schooling preparedness 7
see also **oral language**
teachable moment. 22, 147, 149, 154, 239, 327, 350
Teacher Education Plan 10
teacher
basic competences required of 104
and design and management of learning area 147–149
knowledge (role in curriculum implementation) 176–177, *176*
and participatory learning 160–163, *163*
and professionalism (criteria) 102, 103
professional roles of Grade R 98–99
qualifications 2, 10, 102, 104
relationships, and code of ethics 116
required duties/functions of 10
role in play 235–238, 240
role in establishing partnerships 117, *117*, 119
self-care for 101–102
types of 100–101
teacher–child ratio 9, 181, 191
teacher-guided activities
and assessment 206, 208
and daily programme 48, 124, 125, *126*
definition/description of 127, 191
and diversity 283
examples/types of 53, 143, 206
and health promotion 350, 351
and mathematics/numeracy 313
to promote language 255
teacher-guided play 53, 56, 143, 208, 242, *243–244*
teacher–parent/caregiver partnership 115, 117–119, *117–118*
teaching
effective child-centred 57, 58
practice, and children's learning 19, 20, 21
techniques for participatory learning 163, *163*
teaching and learning
approaches to 11–12
reflective planning for and implementation of 156, *156*
strategies 181–183

thematic approach to 53–54
teaching–learning
	activities 271–276, *272*
	planning for 178, 179–183, *178–179*
	and resources 180
technological process skills 347
technology 347–348
telling and instructing (teaching technique) 164–165
temporal awareness 74, *74*, 78–79, *79*
thematic approach, to teaching and learning 53–54
themes (teaching a second language) 272–273
third teacher (environment as) 149–152
time 310, *310*
topics
	distribution of *191*
	for fantasy play *135–136*
	and health promotion 350–351
	and Life Skills 333
	and mathematical skills *299–300*
	presentation and integration of 172, *173*, *174*
transdisciplinary approach, description of 108
translanguaging 264

U
understanding, construction of 31–32
universal child 28, 44

V
value system 19
values
	definition of 106
	holistic view of 5

and SACE 103, 104
of teacher 97–98
visual
	closure 83, 92
	conceptualising 85, 93
	discrimination 82, 93
	memory/recall 82–83, 93
	motor coordination 82, 93
	motor integration 84–85
	perception 81–85, *82*, 93
	sequencing 84, 93
visual arts
	experiences 355–356
	activities 356, *356*, 365
	elements of 357–359, *357*, *358*
	family and culture 359–360
	and vocabulary 360, *360–361*
	development stages of 361–364, *361–364*
vocabulary development 269–270
volume and capacity 311–312
Vygotsky's social constructivist theory 32–34, 40, 229, 267

W
water play 145, *145*, 146, *146*
weekly planning *194*
whole-child development 22–23, *22*, 53
whole-group teaching 181–182
writing development 256, 259

Z
zone of proximal development (ZPD) 33, 267

www.ingramcontent.com/pod-product-compliance
Lightning Source LLC
Chambersburg PA
CBHW041245240426
43670CB00028B/2997